THE FAMILY

Handyman®

BUILD YOUR SKILLS

Build Your Skills
Project Editor Eric Smith
Design and Page Layout Diana Boger, Teresa Marrone
Project Manager Mary Flanagan

Text, photography and illustrations for *Build Your Skills* are based on articles previously published in *The Family Handyman* magazine (2915 Commers Dr., Suite 700, Eagan, MN 55121, familyhandyman.com). For information on advertising in *The Family Handyman* magazine, call (646) 293-6150.

Build Your Skills is published by Trusted Media Brands, Inc. ©2016 Trusted Media Brands, Inc. All rights reserved. This volume may not be reproduced in whole or in part without written permission from the publisher. The Family Handyman is a registered trademark of RD Publications, Inc.

ISBN: 978-1-61765-594-4

A Note to Our Readers

All do-it-yourself activities involve a degree of risk. Skills, materials, tools and site conditions vary widely. Although the editors have made every effort to ensure accuracy, the reader remains responsible for the selection and use of tools, materials and methods. Always obey local codes and laws, follow manufacturer instructions and observe safety precautions.

The Family Handyman
Editor in Chief Gary Wentz
Senior Editor Travis Larson
Associate and Contributing Editors Jeff Gorton, Rick Muscoplat, Mark Petersen, David Radtke, Jason White
Design and Production Vern Johnson, Marcia Roepke, Mary Schwender
Illustrations Ken Clubb, Jeff Gorton, John Hartman, Trevor Johnston, Christopher Mills, Frank Rohrbach III
Photography Tom Fenenga
Senior Copy Editor Donna Bierbach
Administrative Manager Alice Garrett
Lead Carpenter Josh Risberg
Administrative Assistant Peggy McDermott
Production Manager Leslie Kogan
Vice President, Group Publisher Russell S. Ellis

Published by Home Service Publications, Inc.
A subsidiary of Trusted Media Brands, Inc.

Trusted Media Brands, Inc.
President and Chief Executive Officer Bonnie Kintzer

PRINTED IN CHINA

2 3 4 5 6 7 8 9 10

Contents

1 CARPENTRY

2 PLUMBING, ELECTRICAL & HVAC

3 FLOORS, WALLS & CEILINGS

4 TILING

5 WOODWORKING

6 ROOFING, SIDING & GARAGES

7 LAWN CARE

8 CARS & TRUCKS

9 CONCRETE & MASONRY

10 USING TOOLS

Chapter One

CARPENTRY

Frame and roof a shed

Or a garage, or even a small house

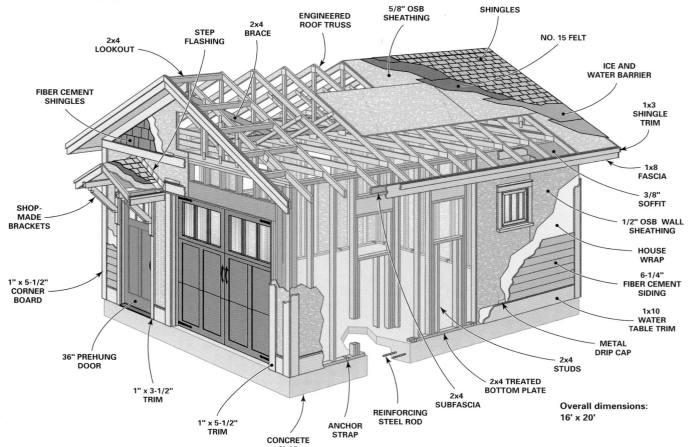

2x4 LOOKOUT

STEP FLASHING

2x4 BRACE

ENGINEERED ROOF TRUSS

5/8" OSB SHEATHING

SHINGLES

NO. 15 FELT

ICE AND WATER BARRIER

FIBER CEMENT SHINGLES

1x3 SHINGLE TRIM

1x8 FASCIA

3/8" SOFFIT

1/2" OSB WALL SHEATHING

HOUSE WRAP

6-1/4" FIBER CEMENT SIDING

SHOP-MADE BRACKETS

1" x 5-1/2" CORNER BOARD

1x10 WATER TABLE TRIM

METAL DRIP CAP

36" PREHUNG DOOR

2x4 STUDS

2x4 TREATED BOTTOM PLATE

1" x 3-1/2" TRIM

2x4 SUBFASCIA

Overall dimensions: 16' x 20'

1" x 5-1/2" TRIM

ANCHOR STRAP

REINFORCING STEEL ROD

CONCRETE SLAB

Framing is one of the most basic and useful carpentry skills you can have. Once you understand framing, you know how to build a house (though, of course, there are a few other trades you'll have to master before the house is complete).

Here we'll walk you through the process of framing walls and installing roof trusses for a simple storage shed. Scale it up a bit and you can build a garage. Add frost footings and more windows and doors and you'll have a house.

Before you get started

A building like this requires considerable upfront planning. In most areas you'll need a building permit. Call your local city hall to find out what's required. In addition to a few sets of building plans, you'll probably need a plot plan of your property so you can mark the new shed location. If you don't have a copy, ask at city hall. Start the permit application process at least a month before you plan to build. After you have the permit in hand, decide if you want to tackle the slab on your own or hire a concrete contractor. If you hire a contractor, get everything in

writing and make sure you're available to answer questions, help locate the anchor straps and bolts and oversee the work. Here are a few more tips for getting started:

■ Call to have underground utilities located 48 hours before you plan to dig. For more information, call 811 or go to call811.com.

■ Order your trusses, windows and doors at least three weeks before you need them.

■ Order your lumber about a week before you plan to start and have it delivered after the slab is poured.

■ Rent scaffolding with wheels to save time and increase safety.

■ Work out a construction schedule and line up friends to help, especially on days when you plan to lift the walls and set the trusses.

■ Cover building materials with plastic tarps to keep them dry.

Build the first wall

There's nothing more rewarding than building walls. In a few hours' time, you'll see a stack of lumber transformed into the skeleton of your new building. The key to success is careful

Set up a cutting station for header parts, cripples and trimmers.

Assemble the window headers so they'll be ready to set in place.

Make sure one person does all of the plate layouts to keep them consistent.

Snap chalk lines to indicate the inside edge of the walls.

Get ready to build   Plan ahead to have jobs for everybody when they arrive. Assign jobs to your helpers according to their skill level.

attention to detail. Any mistakes you make now will haunt you through the entire building process. Start by arranging the plates, studs, headers and trimmers on the slab. Put the treated bottom plate along the edge of the slab. Sight down each stud and place the bowed (crowned) sides facing up. Use straight studs at corners, windows and doors. Build the window openings (Photo 3) and finish by cutting the cripples to fit above the opening.

Stand the wall

Now for the fun part. Gather up your helpers and get ready to stand the walls (Photo 4). Here are a few pointers:

- Place a strip of foam sill sealer over the anchor straps or anchor bolts. You'll set the wall on top of the foam strip.
- Drive stakes into the ground and have 10-ft.-long 2x4s handy for temporary bracing.
- Lift the top of the wall and slide scraps of 2x4 underneath to provide a space for hands to fit under. When the time comes to lift the wall, you'll be able to get a good grip.

- Tilt the top of the wall slightly outward before you attach the braces. This will allow room for standing the end walls.

After standing the wall, make sure it's centered between the chalk lines for the end walls. Then align the bottom plate with the chalk line, wrap the anchor straps around the plate, and nail them to the bottom plate. If you're using anchor bolts instead of straps, predrill the bottom plate for the bolts and lift the wall up and over the bolts.

Plumb and brace the walls

After standing all of the walls and nailing the corners together, it's time to plumb, straighten and brace them. This is one of the most critical steps in the whole building process. If you get it right, everything else will fall into place. If your corners aren't plumb or the top plate is crooked, you'll run into all kinds of trouble as you install the sheathing and build the roof.

Start by plumbing the corners (Photo 5). Push the top of the wall on one end or the other until the corner is perfectly plumb.

continued on p. 10

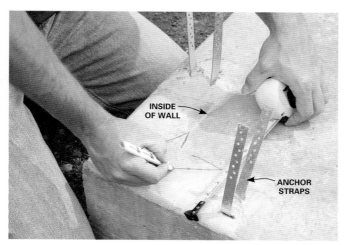

INSIDE OF WALL

ANCHOR STRAPS

CRIPPLE STUD MARK

TRIMMER MARK

KING STUD MARK

1 Mark the wall locations. Measure in 4 in. from the edge of the slab and snap chalk lines. Make sure the lines are parallel and form right angles. Adjust the position of the chalk lines to compensate for a slab that isn't quite square.

2 Lay out the wall plates. Cut the plates to length and tack the top and bottom plates together. Since the sidewalls are identical, we're laying out all four plates at once.

Making the most of your crew

Building is fun and you shouldn't have any trouble lining up some friends to help. We enlisted our office staff to help with this project. But it's best to plan ahead to make sure everybody has something to do when they show up. Here are a few things you can do ahead of time to get ready:

- Restack the lumber so the studs, plate and header materials are accessible.
- Cut the plates to length and make the layout marks on them. It's easier to concentrate when you don't have people breathing down your neck.
- Make a cutting list. This can include header parts, trimmers and windowsills.
- Set up a cutting station with a site-built or store-bought miter saw stand. It's faster and easier to cut 2x4s accurately with a miter saw.
- Check over your tools. Is your saw blade sharp? Do you have enough extension cords?
- Think about the skill level of your helpers and plan to assign them to appropriate tasks.

When your help shows up Saturday morning, you'll be ready to get people started on their jobs.

Arrange the studs, crown up, to prepare for building.

Set up a miter saw station to cut short parts. It's faster than using a circular saw.

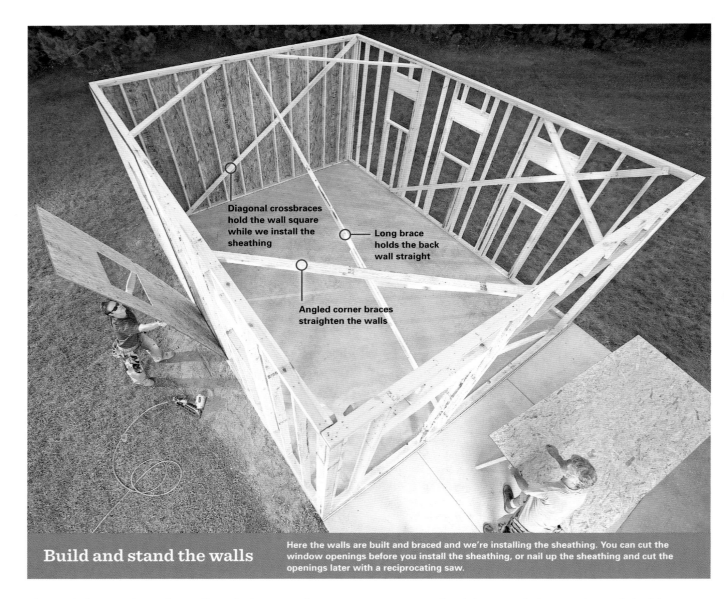

Diagonal crossbraces
hold the wall square
while we install the
sheathing

Long brace
holds the back
wall straight

Angled corner braces
straighten the walls

Build and stand the walls

Here the walls are built and braced and we're installing the sheathing. You can cut the window openings before you install the sheathing, or nail up the sheathing and cut the openings later with a reciprocating saw.

Then nail a long 2x4 brace diagonally to the bottom and top plate, and to one stud in the center. Brace all four walls this way. Then double-check every corner and adjust the braces if needed until all the corners are perfectly plumb.

Next, straighten the top plates. If you have someone with a good "eye," have them sight down the plate while you straighten it with braces (Photo 6). If you don't trust your eye, stretch a mason's line across 1/2-in. blocks attached to each end of the wall. Then adjust the wall until there's 1/2 in. between the stretched line and top plate.

Nail on the sheathing

We ordered 4 x 9-ft. sheets of 1/2-in. OSB (oriented strand board). Here are a few tips for installing the sheathing:

■ If the sheathing doesn't have lines on it, make chalk lines 16 in. in from each edge of the sheet as a guide for nailing into the studs.

■ Drive 16d nails between the bottom plate and the slab. Leave them sticking out slightly so you can support the bottom edge of the sheathing on the nails while you nail it.

■ Use 8d nails as temporary spacers to create a slight gap between sheets. This allows space for the sheathing to expand.

■ Drive nails every 6 in. along the edges and 8 in. apart along intermediate studs.

Get extra help to raise the front wall. It's heavier.

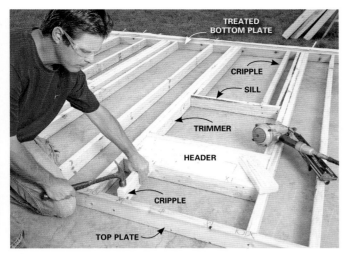

3 **Build the walls.** Follow the layout marks to position studs, king studs, trimmers and cripples. Cut the short cripples above the window openings after the header is in place.

Labels on image: TREATED BOTTOM PLATE, CRIPPLE, SILL, TRIMMER, HEADER, CRIPPLE, TOP PLATE

4 **Stand the walls.** Round up some helpers for standing the walls. Make sure there's someone on the outside to keep the wall from slipping off the slab as you raise it. Have your braces ready to install.

5 **Plumb the corners.** Push or pull the top of the wall to plumb it. Then nail a long 2x4 diagonally to hold the wall plumb until the sheathing is installed. If you don't have a long level, use a short level taped to a straight board.

Label on image: GOOD EYE

6 **Straighten the top plates.** Sight down the top plate and push or pull it until it's perfectly straight. Then brace the top of the wall with long 2x4s. Nail two 2x4s together if necessary.

Sheathing is easier with two people—one to hold the sheet while the other nails.

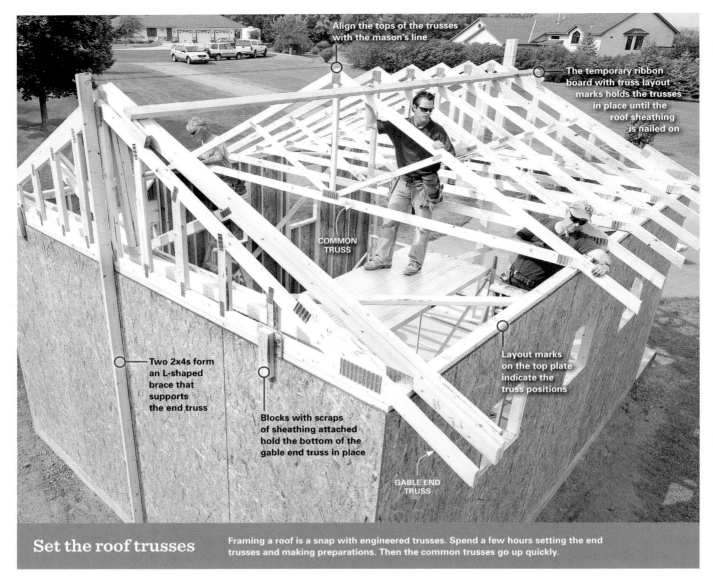

Align the tops of the trusses with the mason's line

The temporary ribbon board with truss layout marks holds the trusses in place until the roof sheathing is nailed on

COMMON TRUSS

Two 2x4s form an L-shaped brace that supports the end truss

Blocks with scraps of sheathing attached hold the bottom of the gable end truss in place

Layout marks on the top plate indicate the truss positions

GABLE END TRUSS

Set the roof trusses

Framing a roof is a snap with engineered trusses. Spend a few hours setting the end trusses and making preparations. Then the common trusses go up quickly.

Set the gable end trusses first

Trusses are a quick way to build a roof—no rafter calculations required. It's almost as easy as standing a row of dominoes. But if you don't take a few precautions, they'll fall like dominoes, too. Start by nailing two long 2x4s together to form an L-shaped brace. The braces should be long enough to extend from the bottom plate to the top of the trusses. Position the braces on both ends of the building, slightly off center and plumb (Photo 7). Attach them securely with screws to the top and bottom plates and to a stud if possible. Next lift up a gable end truss and rest the ends on the top plates. Center the truss so there's an equal overhang on each side and toenail it to the top plate. Put a scrap of sheathing between the top of the brace and the truss and nail the truss to the brace. Repeat these steps on the other end.

Get ready to set the trusses

Setting the remaining trusses will go surprisingly quickly if you take time to get set up first. The goal is to make sure the

trusses are perfectly aligned and properly spaced. Here's how. First stretch a mason's line tightly between nails driven into the braces. Adjust the line so it's centered on the peak of the gable end trusses and about 5 in. above them (Photo 8). You'll use this line to center the common trusses. Next, mark the position of the trusses on the top plate. Draw a line with an "X" to the side the truss goes on. On this building, the center of the first truss is 23-1/2 in. from the outside of the gable end truss and the remaining marks are 24 in. apart. Make the same set of marks on the long 2x4 ribbon board that you'll use to brace the top of the trusses (Photo 9). Finally, set up scaffolding inside the building.

Set the common trusses

You'll need some strong helpers for setting the trusses, so call in a few friends. Start by installing the first truss in the center of the building so you can nail the ribbon board to it (Photo 9). Line up the bottom of the truss with the layout marks and the top with the string line, then toenail the truss to the plates.

7 Brace the gable end trusses. Screw L-shaped braces to each end of the building to support the trusses until the roof frame is completed. Nail smaller blocks to the top plate to keep the truss from slipping off the edge as you set it in place.

8 Stretch a center line. Run a mason's line between nails driven into the braces. Use a level to make sure the line is directly above the center of the gable end trusses. Then align the center of the remaining trusses with the string.

9 Set the common trusses. Mark the ribbon board to match the layout on the top plates and nail it to the end and center truss. Then set the other trusses. Don't remove the ribbon board until the roof is mostly sheathed.

Stack half of the trusses against each gable.

Cantilevered lookouts make a strong overhang

Rented scaffolding makes a great work platform and is a safe way to reach high places

Complete the roof

The next step after setting trusses is to finish the overhang framing and install the roof sheathing. You'll know you've done a good framing job when the sheets of sheathing fit squarely on the roof frame.

Then lift the rest of the trusses onto the top of the walls. Stack half the trusses on each end of the building against the braced gable end trusses. Slide the trusses over the wall from the outside, or carry them inside and lift them up. Use the layout marks on the top plate and ribbon board and the string line to position the remaining trusses before toenailing them to the plates. Connect the trusses to the top plates with hurricane ties.

Finish the overhangs

To make sure the 16-in. overhangs on the front and back of the building don't sag over time, we ordered gable end trusses that are 3-1/2 in. shorter than the common trusses. This allowed us to attach the lookouts to the first common truss and "cantilever" them over the gable end truss (photo above). To make sure the overhangs were straight, we ran the lookouts wild and chalked a line to mark them for cutting.

Rather than add framing for horizontal soffits, we nailed the soffit boards at an angle, directly to the underside of the trusses.

If you finish your soffits this way, remember to rip a bevel on the 2x4 subfascia so it doesn't protrude beneath the plane of the soffit. Sight down the subfascia after you nail it up and drive shims under any dipped-in areas to straighten it. When you're done building the overhangs, nail on the soffits, fascia boards and 1x3 shingle molding. Lay a Speed Square or other straight-edge against the roof sheathing and push the fascia and shingle molding against it to keep them aligned with the plane of the roof (Photo 10).

Install the windows and door

The awning windows used here have a clad exterior with nailing fins. After installing the windows, we added a wood sill, 3-1/2-in.-wide casing, and a beveled drip cap on top to provide a more traditional look. We ordered the door with no brick molding and added the same casing to it.

10 **Nail on the subfascia.** Align the subfascia with the tops of the trusses using a straightedge such as a Speed Square. Have your helper move the subfascia up or down as needed to get the right alignment.

SPEED SQUARE

SUBFASCIA

11 **Sheathe the roof.** Mark the top edge of the sheathing every 2 ft. to indicate the center of the trusses. Then push or pull the trusses to align them with the marks as you nail the sheathing.

LAYOUT MARK

Complete the exterior

The wide corner boards and horizontal water table trim at the bottom of the wall give the shed a classic look that matches the lap siding and shingled gable ends. If you choose to use wide corner boards like ours, you'll have to add an extra 2x4 at every corner and on both sides of every window and door to provide nailing for the ends of the siding. Here are a few tips to ensure the best siding and trim installation:

- Install the soffit and fascia right away so you can get the roof on. The sooner the building is watertight, the better.
- Install the windows, doors and corner boards. Then add the horizontal water table trim along the bottom.
- Install metal drip caps over the water table trim and over the horizontal trim boards on the gable ends.
- Snap chalk lines on the building wrap to indicate stud positions. Then nail the siding to the studs.
- Drill holes for the nails in the ends of the siding boards to prevent breakouts.
- Leave a small gap where siding abuts trim pieces and where siding ends meet. Then fill the gap with caulk.
- Leave a 3/8-in. gap between trim pieces and the concrete slab.

Finishing touches

You can install your own garage door, but the savings aren't great. We spent a little extra to have this door professionally installed. If you use a wooden garage door, brush two coats of paint on the front, back and edges of all the door panels before you install it. For clear finished wood doors like our entry door, brush on four coats of urethane spar varnish. Brush two coats of top-quality 100 percent acrylic paint onto the siding and trim.

By this stage in the project, our volunteer labor was starting to dwindle, but luckily the only remaining tasks were to install the entry door hardware and touch up the paint.

METAL ANGLE BRACE

METAL ANGLE BRACE

Hang the wood brackets with 6-in. metal angle braces lag-bolted to the top of the brackets and to the wall. Build the roof frame and screw it to the wood brackets. Finish up with soffit, fascia and roofing.

There's still plenty to do, even after the framing is complete. It's best to get the roof watertight soon after the soffit and fascia is done. Then you can take your time finishing the rest of the job.

Toenailing

It's all in the angle

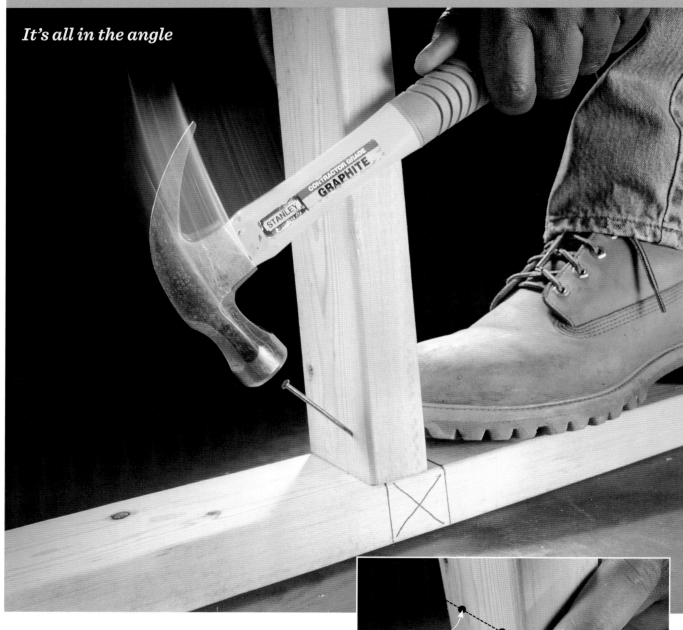

START NAILS HERE

8d NAIL

TIP

If you're not sure where to start the nail, hold it alongside to visualize the path.

AT LEAST 1" PENETRATION

Toenailing—driving a nail at an angle through the end of a board to anchor it—can be frustrating to learn. But it's an essential carpentry skill, and once you master a few tricks for positioning and driving the nails and get some practice under your belt, it'll be as easy as regular nailing. Toenailing not only makes a strong joint but also is a great way to coax stubborn boards into position.

Photos 1 – 3 walk you through the basic steps of toenailing. The key to success is starting the nail in the right spot and angling it a little steeper than 45 degrees. Visualize the path of the nail by holding it against the boards you're joining (photo at right) to determine the right starting spot.

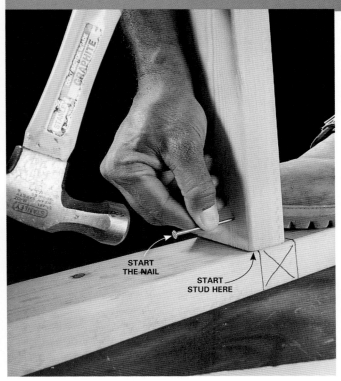

1 **Start the nail.** Position the board in front of the layout line and place your toe against the back. Start the nail by tapping it about 1/4 in. straight in, not at an angle.

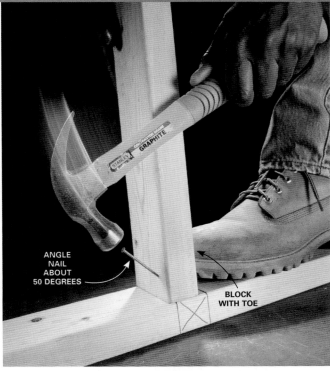

2 **Drive at an angle.** Pull the nail to about a 50-degree angle and set it with a couple of hammer taps. Then let go and drive it in. Brace your toe against the back of the board as you set the nail. It's OK if the board moves slightly past the layout line.

Starting a nail at an angle can be tricky because it'll tend to slide down the board and penetrate too low. It's easier if you begin by tapping the nail point straight in (Photo 1). Then tip the nail at the correct angle and pound it in (Photo 2). As you pound, you'll discover that toenailing pushes the board off position. Reduce this problem by pressing against the board with your toe to hold it in place while you nail (Photos 2 and 3). Also, position the board about 1/4 in. from your mark so the nail will drive it to the right spot.

Driving a toenail requires greater hammer control and precision than regular nailing. Hold the hammer at the end of the handle with a firm but relaxed grip. Swing from your elbow with a little wrist snap at the end of the stroke for extra oomph. Luckily, you don't have to worry about leaving hammer marks when you're rough-framing walls and floors. As the nail gets close to fully driven, adjust your swing ever so slightly away from you so the face of the hammer will contact the nailhead off center. Catching the head of the nail with the edge of the hammer face allows you to drive the toenail completely.

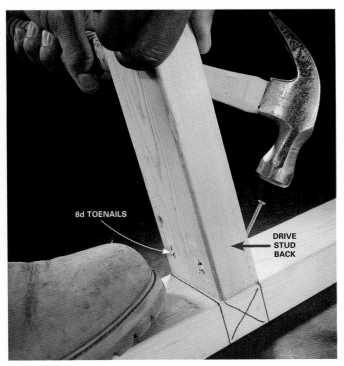

3 **Nail the other side.** Drive toenails into the opposite side to complete the toenailing and at the same time drive the board back to the layout line.

Straighten bowed deck boards

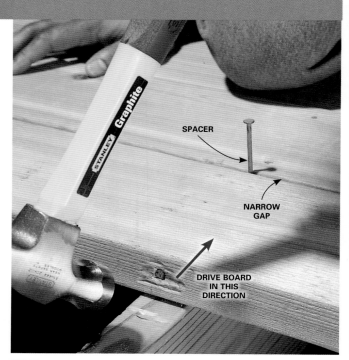

4 Toenail into the edge of a bowed board to move it closer to the adjoining deck board. Start the nail about one-third down from the top of the board and angle it about 45 degrees to catch the underlying joist.

BOWED DECK BOARD

WIDE GAP

16d TOENAIL

SPACER

NARROW GAP

DRIVE BOARD IN THIS DIRECTION

5 Pound the nail with heavy hammer blows to straighten the deck board and close the gap between the two boards. Use a shim or nail to maintain a consistent space between boards.

Here are a few more toenailing tips:
- Drive the nails until the points barely protrude through the end of the first board before you position it, then position the board and drive the nails home.
- Drill pilot holes for the nails with a bit about the size of the nail shank. This works great for toenailing in tight spots.
- Cut a block (14-1/2 in. long for 16-in. on-center studs) to fit between studs when you're toenailing walls. The block acts as a spacer and backer to support the stud while you toenail it.

Put toenailing to work

Toenails have an amazing power to move lumber. This power is especially handy when you're working with framing lumber or decking that's not as straight as you'd like (Photos 4 – 6). Use big nails with big heads like 16d sinkers for these jobs. In fact, if one nail doesn't do the job, drive another alongside to move the board even farther. One carpenter we know pounds in two 16d nails at once for extra holding power.

So remember, the next time your floor joists or studs stray from the line, coax them into place with toenails.

Straighten twisted joists

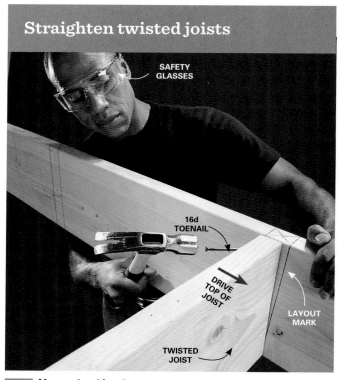

SAFETY GLASSES

16d TOENAIL

DRIVE TOP OF JOIST

LAYOUT MARK

TWISTED JOIST

6 Move twisted framing members into alignment by toenailing in the direction you want the board to go. Continue pounding on the nail until the board is in the desired location. Add a second toenail to move the board farther if necessary.

Ordering doors and casement windows

Ordering the wrong door is an expensive mistake. The terms that describe the hinge position on a door are confusing: **left-handed** and **right-handed**. However, they make sense if you follow the guidelines shown in the photos. Stand with your back to the jamb that has the hinges. If the door is on your right, it's right-handed. If the door is on your left, it's left-handed.

Windows

With casement windows, the swing direction is determined exactly the opposite as it is for doors. To determine the swing on a casement window, picture yourself outside the building looking at the window. If the hinges are on the right, it's a right-hand window; on the left—it's a left-hand window. When you see a casement window drawn on a blueprint or in a catalog, there'll be an arrow drawn on the face of the window to designate swing direction. The arrow points toward the hinge side.

It's best to order doors and windows in person. Then you can draw a picture, as if looking from above, and sketch in the hinge and swing direction. This avoids the terminology confusion and unpleasant confrontations if the order goes in wrong.

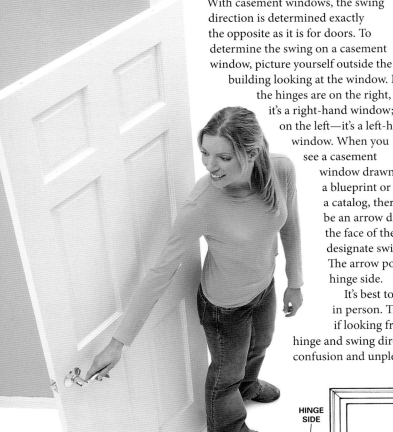

Left-handed

Right-handed

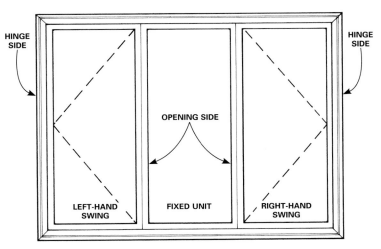

HINGE SIDE · OPENING SIDE · HINGE SIDE

LEFT-HAND SWING · FIXED UNIT · RIGHT-HAND SWING

Rules for notching and boring studs

You get two benefits when you build or remodel with wood studs. The studs provide the strength and framework for the structure, and the empty spaces *between* the studs serve an important function, too: They provide the perfect place—a veritable vertical freeway—to run pipes, vents, drains, wires and ductwork. The drawback? When you have to run pipes, ducts or wires horizontally through the studs, you often have to notch or drill holes—sometimes big ones—to get them to their destination.

But you can't just drill and saw away. There are rules you have to follow for drilling and notching studs. Some rules help ensure the *structural integrity of a wall*. And others are aimed at *protecting pipes and wires* that could be damaged by screws, nails and other fasteners driven into a wall.

You gotta keep the structure strong

There are LOTS of building codes dictating just how large a hole or notch you can cut (Figure A).

The boringly (ha!) technical yet important rules are:

- **Holes in bearing wall studs** (exterior and interior walls that bear the weight of the roof and/or other stories above) may not exceed 40 percent of the width of the stud.
- **Notches in bearing wall studs** may not exceed 25 percent of the stud's width.
- **Holes in non-bearing walls** can't exceed 60 percent of their width.
- **Notches in non-bearing walls** can't exceed 40 percent of their width.
- **The edge of a hole** must be at least 5/8 in. from the edge of a stud.

To appease the plumbing gods, the codes have made at least one notable exception: In bearing walls you can bore 60 percent size holes—as long as you double up the studs and don't drill through more than two successive pairs of these doubled-up studs (Figure A). This allows you to run a short section of "drain, waste, vent" (DWV) pipe through a 2x4 wall without beefing up the whole wall to 2x6 dimensions.

There are other, less specific guidelines: When possible, notch a stud near the top, rather than the bottom. Don't locate holes and notches near large or loose knots, and don't group too many in the same area of the stud. Finally, notch only when necessary; holes weaken it less than notches.

In areas subject to high winds, earthquakes or tornadoes, maintaining wall strength is particularly important. Furthermore, studs with too much "meat" removed tend to bow and warp. Your building inspector will be on the lookout for overzealous notching and boring, so follow the rules.

In reality, few walls ever out-and-out collapse during everyday duty from being riddled with too many holes and notches. But there are LOTS of cases in which unprotected or inadequately protected pipes and wires have been nicked and punctured by screws and nails. Any plumber or electrician will tell you *that's* what you REALLY need to watch out for!

Protect those wires and pipes

The National Electrical Code requires holes containing non-metallic cable (often called Romex) or flexible metal-clad cable (the type you buy with the wires already in it) be set back 1-1/4 in. or more from the edge of a stud (Figure A) to protect the wires from nails and screws. (The 1-1/4 in. screws and nails used to secure 1/2-in. drywall penetrate the studs about 3/4 in.) Most electricians keep their inspector happy by drilling 3/4-in. holes dead center on a 3-1/2-in.-wide stud. This gives them a hole large enough to run two electrical cables and leave 1-3/8 in. of protective wood on each side. If they need to run more wires, they'll drill more holes directly above the others. If a hole comes any closer than 1-1/4 in., your inspector will make you install a 1/16-in.-thick protective metal plate (Figure A). Available in 3-in. and longer lengths, the plates can be found at home centers and hardware stores.

The mechanical codes for plumbing and heating, ventilation and cooling (HVAC) systems also dictate that holes containing

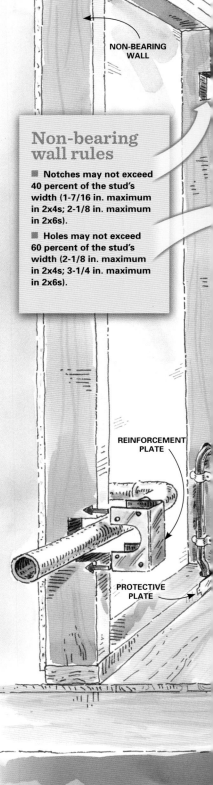

NON-BEARING WALL

Non-bearing wall rules

- Notches may not exceed 40 percent of the stud's width (1-7/16 in. maximum in 2x4s; 2-1/8 in. maximum in 2x6s).
- Holes may not exceed 60 percent of the stud's width (2-1/8 in. maximum in 2x4s; 3-1/4 in. maximum in 2x6s).

REINFORCEMENT PLATE

PROTECTIVE PLATE

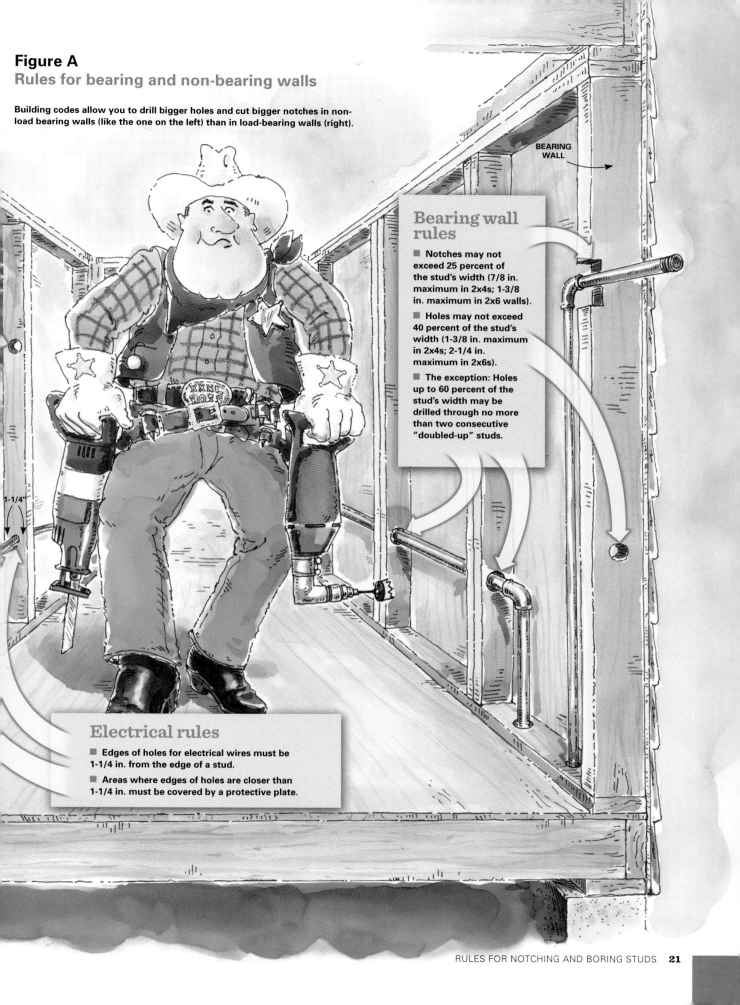

Figure A
Rules for bearing and non-bearing walls

Building codes allow you to drill bigger holes and cut bigger notches in non-load bearing walls (like the one on the left) than in load-bearing walls (right).

BEARING WALL

Bearing wall rules

■ Notches may not exceed 25 percent of the stud's width (7/8 in. maximum in 2x4s; 1-3/8 in. maximum in 2x6 walls).

■ Holes may not exceed 40 percent of the stud's width (1-3/8 in. maximum in 2x4s; 2-1/4 in. maximum in 2x6s).

■ The exception: Holes up to 60 percent of the stud's width may be drilled through no more than two consecutive "doubled-up" studs.

1-1/4"

Electrical rules

■ Edges of holes for electrical wires must be 1-1/4 in. from the edge of a stud.

■ Areas where edges of holes are closer than 1-1/4 in. must be covered by a protective plate.

pipes be set back 1-1/4 in. from the edge of a stud to protect the pipes from fasteners. Those that come closer need to be covered by metal plates; for big pipes, use a long protective plate.

Electricians and plumbers spend lots of time drilling big holes, so they know a few tricks to make the job easier (or avoid it altogether).

Tips for less drilling and notching

1. Before beginning any project, plot out exactly where large pipes and ducts will run and determine how you'll get them there.

2. Wherever possible, run large pipes and ducts vertically into unfinished attics or basements, then install elbows and run the pipe or duct horizontally below the floor joists or above the ceiling joists.

3. Build 2x6 stud walls where DWV pipes and holes exceed the limits shown in Figure A.

4. Rent a right angle drill and use Selfeed or hole saw bits for boring large holes (Figure B). The right angle drill allows you to drill holes square to the stud face. Holes drilled at an angle will wind up oval and therefore larger.

5. Drill holes at least 1/4 in. oversize, especially for hot water pipes. If you don't, they'll make annoying sounds as they expand, contract and rub along studs.

6. Stud shoes—wrap-around, stud reinforcer plates (Figure A)—are sold at home centers and lumberyards. Ask your inspector if they are permissible in special situations.

7. When boring electrical holes, keep them square to the stud for easier wire installation, or *pulling*. This may seem trivial, but angled holes like those shown in Figure C "catch" the wire and keep you from pulling wire through more than two or three studs at a time. Holes in a line (Figure D) let you pull wire through an entire wall length of studs at one time.

Figure B
Keep large holes centered

Use a right angle drill with hole saw bits for boring large holes. Keep the holes centered on the studs and a consistent height off the floor.

Figure C
Angled holes

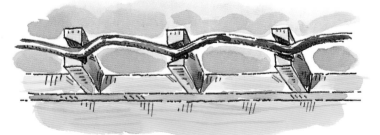

Angled holes are tough to pull wires through because the cable catches on the sharp edges.

Figure D
Straight holes

Holes square to the face of a stud are easy to pull wires through.

Rules for drilling and notching joists

Figure A
How joists work

When weight is applied to a joist, the top edge goes into compression while the bottom edge goes into tension. Improperly sized or placed holes and notches weaken the joist, make it bouncy and saggy, and provide an easy place for it to crack and fail.

You can't simply cut, notch and bore through structural members and expect your house to remain strong and your floors flat and solid. Building "from scratch" with smart planning can limit the need for most notching and boring. It's during remodeling—when you have to run wires, pipes, gas lines and ducts through the joists already in place—that it becomes important to know the rules about tampering with joists.

How joists support floors and ceilings

Joists—the horizontal members that span two walls and/or beams—have to carry the weight of the walls, people, furniture, appliances and other stuff we place on them. When a load is applied to a joist, the wood fibers along the bottom edge go into tension and those along the top go into compression (Figure A). As long as the top fibers and the bottom resist these stresses, the joist will do its job of keeping your floor strong, straight and solid. But when you notch or drill a joist, you cut some of those fibers and reduce the joist's ability to withstand compression or tension. And if you create a hole or notch too big or in the wrong place, you seriously weaken the joist, making it bouncy and saggy, and in a worst-case scenario, give it an easy place to crack and fail. In bathrooms and kitchens, water makes a beeline for these low spots, promoting rot and worsening the situation. And while catastrophic failure is rare, the sag and bounce you experience every time you cross a weakened floor is irritating. Plus, walls crack, doors stick and marbles roll under the dresser. That's the real reason you want to follow the notching and boring guidelines.

Follow the rules to keep your floor solid

You can notch and bore joists without sacrificing critical strength, but you must follow the rules.

If your home is more than 20 years old, your floor joists are most likely **solid wood** 2x8s, 2x10s or 2x12s. The **notching** and **boring** rules of thumb for solid lumber are shown in Figure B. Codes don't directly address how many holes and notches you can cut in a joist. One rule of thumb is to provide twice the distance between holes as the diameter of the largest hole. Also, notching the top of a joist weakens it less than notching the bottom, and you should avoid locating

Figure B
Notching and boring rules

Engineered I-beam rules

- You can never, ever, ever notch or bore through the top or bottom flange or chord.
- You can drill 1-1/2 in. holes anywhere in the web. In fact, most have little perforated knockout holes that can be punched out with the swing of a hammer.
- Drill large holes toward the center of I-beam joists, not toward the ends.
- Leave at least 1/4 in. (or the amount specified by the manufacturer) of web between the edge of the hole and the flange.

Joist boring rules

- Holes must be at least 2 in. from the top and bottom edges of a joist.
- Maximum hole size is one-third of the joist depth.

Joist notching rules

- The maximum depth of a notch at the end of a joist (where it rests on a wall or beam) can't exceed one-quarter of the joist depth.
- Maximum notch depth in the outer third of a joist is one-sixth of the joist depth.
- Limit the length of notches to one-third of the joist depth.
- No notching in the middle third of a joist.

RIM JOIST

2" MINIMUM

ONE-FOURTH OF JOIST DEPTH (MAXIMUM)

JOIST DEPTH

NO NOTCHING IN MIDDLE THIRD OF JOIST

Figure C
Joist clearances for bathtub drains

P-TRAP

Leave at least 6 in. of clearance to one side and 3 in. to the other sides of the drain to provide room for the P-trap.

Figure D
Joist clearance for toilets

3-1/2" MINIMUM FROM CENTER OF TOILET TO NEAREST JOISTS

Leave at least 3-1/2 in. of clearance from the center line of the toilet to the nearest joist to allow room for the waste pipe.

holes (and notches) near loose knots.

Engineered wood I-joists are gradually replacing solid wood joists. If you're remodeling or building with I-joists, your lumber supplier can provide you with a set of hole-drilling standards to follow. The guidelines for these are shown in Figure B.

For those working with the less common **open web** or **floor truss joists** (Figure B), the guidelines are simple: You can't notch or drill them anywhere. Period. The cool thing about these, however, is that the space between cross members is usually big enough to accommodate big pipes, even ductwork.

The **rim joist** (Figure B)—the framing member that runs around the perimeter of your house and that the floor joists butt into—often gets riddled with large holes. This space is the logical exit point for dryer and furnace vents, big electrical service wires and fireplace fresh air intakes. Since the rim joist is continuously supported by the walls or foundation it rests on, the strict notching and hole-boring rules don't apply. Just don't create a large hole or notch directly under a group of studs that support the end of a beam, or a window or door header above.

When in doubt, consult a structural engineer or your local building code official, who will have the final say.

Good planning means less notching and boring

If you're building an addition or a new home, you can avoid most notching and boring by planning ahead to provide adequate pathways and space for pipes and ducts.

For plumbing clearances, follow the guidelines shown in Figures C and D. The place where you'll be most tempted to create oversize holes and notches—under the bathtub—is the part of a floor you can least afford to weaken. A cast iron tub, with water and occupant, can weigh in at more than 800 lbs. If you need to remove part of a joist, double the joists to each side, then add doubled joists between them to carry the load of the severed joist. Use joist hangers for all connections.

To minimize problems with ductwork:
■ Position bathroom vent fans so the ducts can run parallel to the joists—right up to where they exit the house.
■ Make sure not to install joists so they run parallel to, and directly under, walls where you intend to install ductwork.

Finally, if all else fails, drop your pipes and ducts down below the joists and box them in with wood-framed soffits. They're least obtrusive when run along an outside wall or center beam.

Carpentry tricks and advice

Best way to perfect miters

Fine-tuning a miter for a perfect fit is often a trial-and-error process. Practice on smaller test pieces until you get your miter saw set to exactly the right angle, then cut the actual parts.

Forget strings and stakes

You see it in print and on TV everywhere—some stake and board contraption set up to hold strings to help position postholes, or lay out footings or building footprints. But most of the time, there's a much better way. Tack together the construction lumber to outline the structure, square it up and use it as a giant template to do all your marking. Set it aside to do your digging and replace it to set the posts.

Mark, don't measure

Don't use your tape measure unless you *have* to. Holding trim in place and marking it is always more accurate than measuring, often faster and it eliminates mistakes. This is good advice for other types of carpentry work too, like siding, laying shingles and sometimes even framing.

Easy framing formula

You don't need a math degree to estimate framing materials for walls. Here's a formula that works every time, no matter how many doors, windows or corners your walls have:

- One stud per linear foot of wall.
- Five linear feet of plate material (bottoms, tops and ties) per linear foot of wall.

It'll look like too much lumber when it arrives, but you'll need the extra stuff for corners, window and door frames, blocking and braces. Set aside the crooked stuff for short pieces.

Memory (or lack thereof) trick

Stick masking tape to your tape measure for jotting down shapes and numbers. That way you won't forget the length on the way to the saw.

Buy a trim gun

Pros never hand-nail trim anymore. Why? Because air-powered trim guns make the results *so* much faster, better and neater. No splits, no predrilling, no knocking the piece out of place as you hammer, and only itty-bitty holes to fill. Plus, they've gotten cheaper to buy. If you're going to buy just one size, the most versatile choice is one that shoots 5/8- to 2-inch 18-gauge brads.

Throw together a miter saw bench

Whether you're working in your garage, out in the backyard building a shed or up at the in-laws' cabin building a deck, take a few minutes and cobble together a miter saw bench. With a little creativity, you can use just about any materials you have on hand. The only custom work you'll need to do is to rip some spacer boards to make the outfeed support the same height as the saw table. It sure beats kneeling on the grass or perching the miter saw on horses. And the bench does double duty as a super-convenient work surface too.

12 best quick tips

1. Use blue chalk in your chalk lines unless you want permanent marks, then use red.

2. Save a couple of old circular saw blades. They're great for demo work like cutting through shingles, dirty wood or wood that may have hidden nails.

3. Utility knife blades are cheap. Replace them often, especially when cutting drywall.

4. Don't skip the hearing protection. Even the occasional DIYer will lose some hearing from running loud power tools without them.

5. Don't waste all morning on extra lumber runs. Buy more than you need. You can always return the extra.

6. Buy only carbide-tipped saw blades and router bits. They stay sharp for ages.

7. Measure twice, cut once. Oldest one in the book, but still true!

8. Invest in a stout, 1-in.-wide, 20- to 25-ft.-long tape measure. Throw the cheap flimsy one in the junk drawer.

9. Spend $25 to buy a small box of every length of drywall screw there is. You'll use them for everything.

10. Circular saw blades are cheap. Change them at the first hint of dullness.

11. Don't leave cutoffs lying all over the ground. Sooner or later, you'll twist your ankle.

12. Toss that jar of bent, dull and rusty bits. Buy new drill indexes of spade and twist bits and every time you use one, return it to its slot.

Best all-purpose hammer

Whether you're doing rough construction or fine finish work, the best all-around hammer is a smooth-faced 20-ounce with a straight claw. Use the claw to drive the hammer under walls for lifting, to embed it in framing and even to do extremely crude chiseling. But best of all, it's a better shape for pulling nails than the curved claw style.

Nail safety

There is one 'must-do' rule on most pro job sites. Don't ever let a board leave your hand if the sharp end of a nail is sticking out of it. They better be bent over or, better yet, pulled before that board hits the ground. But even with this edict, you may still have to nurse foot punctures occasionally, so get your tetanus shots.

Hire out the big digs

We love any excuse to rent a dirt-moving machine. A day with one of these toys is more fun than a trip to Disneyland and costs less too. But here's the truth: Whether you're moving a pile of gravel or digging a trench, rental machines often cost more than hiring a pro, who can move more dirt before 9 a.m. than a beginner can move all day. So always get a bid from a pro before you head for the rental center.

Marking and cutting curves

Whether you're building a frame for an arched opening, making curved brackets or fashioning arch-top casing, marking and cutting curves is part of the process. Here we'll show you several techniques and tips for marking, cutting and fine-tuning curves. Some methods are best suited for rough curves. Others are refined enough for furniture making. Choose the technique that works best for the project at hand.

Draw large curves with a giant compass

Grab any narrow board or strip of plywood and drill a few holes—voilà, instant compass. Drill a pencil-size hole a few inches from the end of the board. Then drill a screw-size hole at the pivot point. The distance between them should be the radius of the curve, if you know what that measurement is. Otherwise, just use the trial-and-error method, drilling a series of pivot holes until you can swing the trammel and draw the right-size arch. It's easy to draw parallel curves too. Just drill two pencil holes spaced the desired distance apart.

There's no limit to the size of the arch you can draw. If your plan calls for a 10-ft. radius, find a long stick and use the floor as your workbench.

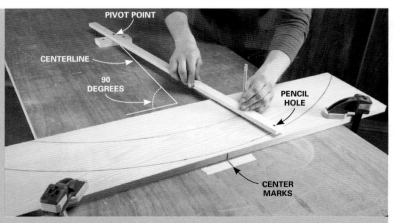

PIVOT POINT
CENTERLINE
90 DEGREES
PENCIL HOLE
CENTER MARKS

Drill two pencil holes for parallel curves

Clamp the board and screw the compass to the workbench. Use a scrap to elevate the compass to the same height as the board you're marking. Make sure the pivot point of the compass is at 90 degrees to the center of the board.

Cut precise curves with a router trammel

This simple router trammel is easy to build and allows you to cut a perfect circle. For circles up to 6 ft. across, use a piece of 1/4-in. plywood, MDF or hardboard that's about 4 ft. long and at least as wide as your router base. Start by removing the base plate from your router and clamping it to one end of the trammel material. If you want your trammel to be stylish, trace around a coffee cup to make a nice-looking rounded end. Then draw tangent lines connecting the circles and cut the sides. If you don't care about looks, simply make a long rectangular trammel.

Trace around the base plate and use the mounting holes as a guide for drilling holes in the trammel (Photo 1). Cut out the trammel and drill a 1-1/2-in. hole in the center of the router end to clear the router bit. Countersink the mounting screw holes so the screw heads won't tear up your workpiece. Attach the router to the trammel with the base plate screws.

Screw the trammel to the workpiece, centering it on the circle you want to cut out. Mount a straight plunge-cutting bit in your router and set the router bit to cut about 3/8 in. deep for the first pass. A plunge router works best, but if you don't have one, hold the router above the wood and start it. Carefully plunge it into the wood and begin moving it counterclockwise around the circle. Complete the circle, then readjust the depth and make another pass until you cut all the way through.

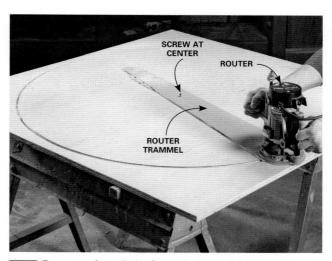

SCREW AT CENTER · **ROUTER** · **ROUTER TRAMMEL**

1 Lay out the trammel. Draw the sides and ends of the trammel. Trace around the base plate and drill holes for the mounting screws.

1/4" MDF · BASE PLATE SCREWS · ROUTER BASE PLATE

2 Rout a perfect circle. Screw the trammel to the center of your workpiece and cut out the circle with your router. Make two or three passes in a counterclockwise direction.

Cut gradual curves with a circular saw

The first tool that comes to mind for cutting curves is a jigsaw, but if the curve is gradual, try a circular saw instead. It's surprisingly quick and easy to cut a smooth curve with a circular saw. This method is for cutting rough curves. Don't try to make furniture with this technique. The trick is to make sure the curve is gradual enough that the blade doesn't bind. If you try this method and the blade binds or starts to heat up and smoke, switch to the jigsaw. The thinner the material you're cutting, the sharper the curve can be. Set the blade depth so it barely projects through the bottom of the wood.

You don't need a jigsaw to cut curves
When you're forming gradual curves, you can speed things up by using a circular saw instead.

BLADE SET SHALLOW

Plastic wood template

Often you can simply "eyeball" the best curve for the job by bending a piece of wood and using it as a template. But variations in wood grain can result in inconsistent curves. Here's a tip to make this technique even better. Use plastic wood or a plastic molding instead. It bends very uniformly and yields near-perfect symmetrical curves. Several brands are available at home centers. Choose a thickness that'll bend to the curve you need. For gradual bends or wide curves, use 3/4-in.-thick material. For tighter bends (those with a smaller radius), use a 1/2-in. x 1-1/4-in. plastic stop molding or something similar. Support the ends of the plastic wood with blocks attached to a strip of wood. Adjust the position of the blocks to change the curve.

Mark an arch with two sticks

Here's a quick way to draw an accurate curve if you know how wide and tall you want the arch to be. Let's say you want to draw an arch that's 3 ft. wide and 9 in. high. Drive two nails at the ends of the 3-ft. baseline. At the center of the baseline, draw a perpendicular line and make a mark 9 in. above the baseline. Drive a nail at the mark. At one end of the baseline, draw another perpendicular line and make another mark 9 in. above the baseline. Drive another nail at this mark. Photo 1 shows how to arrange and connect two sticks that you will use to draw the arch (Photo 2).

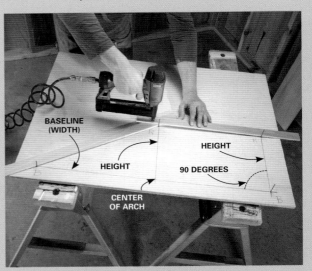

1 Set up for arch drawing with two sticks. Drive nails at the ends of the baseline and at the height of the arch. Lay one stick across two height nails and lay the other from the center height to the end of the baseline. Connect the sticks with short pins or hot-melt glue.

Bent plastic wood makes a perfect curve

Clamp blocks to a 2x2 and spring-fit a length of 1x2 plastic wood between them. Adjust the position of the blocks to change the curve.

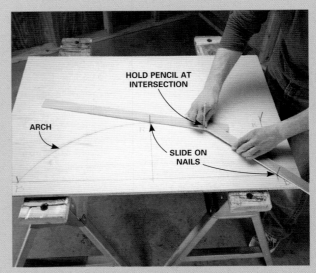

2 Slide the sticks over the nails. Nestle a pencil into the crook of the sticks. With one end of the sticks resting on the baseline end nail and the other on the center height nail, slide the sticks along the nails to draw the arch. Repeat on the opposite side to complete the arch.

Use a pattern and a router for irregular curves

When your plan calls for cutting curved parts and you need to make two or more, first shape and sand a perfect full-size pattern from a piece of 1/2-in. medium-density fiberboard. Then use a router with a top-bearing pattern bit to cut out the parts.

Here are a few tips for routing with a pattern bit. First, use the pattern to mark the shape. Then remove excess material by cutting about 1/4 to 1/8 in. outside the lines with a jigsaw or a band saw. Elevate the workpiece to avoid cutting into your workbench. We used Bench Cookies. But hot-melt glue and scraps of wood are another option. If you're cutting material that's thicker than the pattern bit is deep, cut as deep as you can. Then remove the pattern and use the part as the pattern to complete the cut.

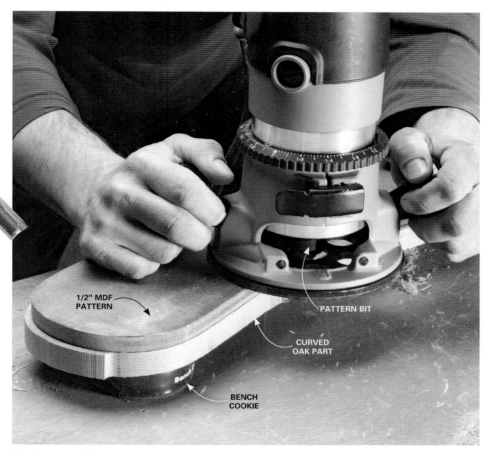

PATTERN BIT

1/2" MDF PATTERN

PATTERN BIT

CURVED OAK PART

BENCH COOKIE

Make matching parts with a pattern

Trace out and rough-cut your part. Attach the pattern with hot-melt glue. Use a top-bearing pattern bit to follow the pattern and shape the part. Move the router counterclockwise around the pattern.

Stack and sand for matching parts

When you have several identical curved parts, the best way to sand them is to stack them and sand them all at once. You'll save time and the parts will all match perfectly. The wider surface keeps you from rounding off edges. If the parts require a lot of sanding, a belt sander is a good choice. If you don't have to remove much wood, try a random orbital sander. The key to success is to keep the sander moving at all times to avoid creating any flat spots. Check your progress by running your hand over the parts. Mark high spots with a pencil so you'll know where more sanding is needed.

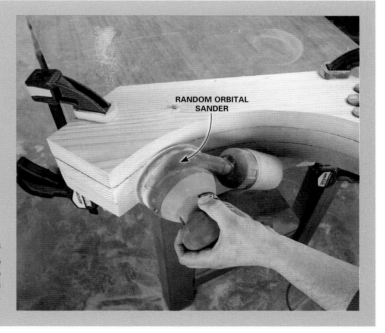

RANDOM ORBITAL SANDER

Use a random orbital sander for tight curves

Line up the parts and clamp them together. If they're small parts like these, clamp them to the workbench to hold them in place. Sand the curves smooth with a belt sander or random orbital sander.

Tick sticking

A simple secret for cutting complex shapes

Every day, boat builders have to cut oddball shapes—ones that would give a typical carpenter fits. But boat builders know an old trick most carpenters don't. This simple technique, called "tick sticking," allows them to mark out even the most complex shapes quickly and accurately.

In a nutshell, tick sticking is a way to plot the key points of an odd shape (usually corners) and transfer them onto a workpiece. Once the key points are marked, you just connect the dots to create a cutting pattern that perfectly matches the desired shape.

At first, tick sticking looks like an exercise for geometry majors. But follow this article and you'll quickly see how this simple technique works.

We used tick sticking here to fit a plywood window seat into a bay, but the same technique can be used to pattern any flat shape onto any material. You need only a few simple tools:

■ **A pencil.** For accurate results, sharpen it and keep it sharp.
■ **A straightedge** such as a framing square or metal yardstick.
■ **A scrap of plywood, drywall or cardboard.** The scrap should be as large as possible but smaller than the shape you want to cut.
■ **A tick stick:** any long, narrow piece of wood cut to a sharp point at one end. We made a fancy, two-piece tick stick by screwing a short, pointed piece of 1x4 to a long 1x4. The short 1x4 piece compensates for the thickness of the 3/4-in. plywood scrap and allows the point to sit flat on the workpiece, making marking easier (Photo 3).

1 Lay the tick stick across the scrap with the pointed end near the line that marks the front edge of the window seat. Trace a line onto the scrap along the side of the stick. Then make two perfectly aligned tick marks, one on the stick and one on the scrap. Label both tick marks "1."

Scribing paper templates

Before you connect the marks you plotted with the tick stick, hold a straightedge against each wall the workpiece will butt into (photo, below). Unless the walls are perfectly flat (few

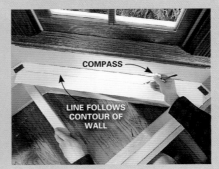

are), you'll see gaps between the walls and the straightedge.

If you connect the tick-stick marks using a straightedge, you'll end up with the same gaps between the walls and the finished workpiece. That's not a problem if you plan to install molding to cover the gaps. But if you need a perfect fit, make paper templates to match the contours of each wall section.

Just tape a strip of heavy paper along the wall and use a compass to "scribe" the contour of the wall onto the paper (photo, left). Then cut along the scribed line with scissors and use the paper template to connect the tick-stick marks on the workpiece (Photo 4).

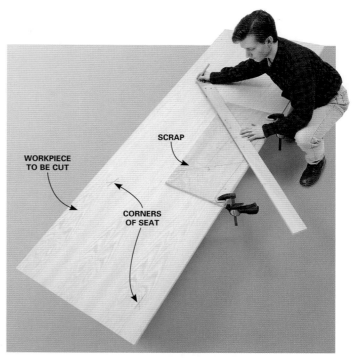

2 Place the point of the tick stick in each corner, and trace lines and number tick marks just as you did for the first line (Photo 1). When you've traced a line for each corner and both front edges of the seat, remove the scrap.

3 Clamp the scrap onto the workpiece flush with the edge of the workpiece. Lay the tick stick along each traced line, aligning the numbered tick marks. Each time you position the stick, make an "X" at the pointed end of the stick. When you're done, you'll have a pattern with each corner of the shape plotted. Then you just have to connect the Xs.

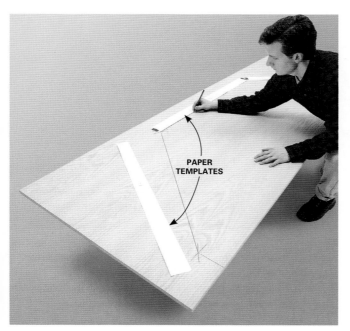

4 Connect the marks using a scribed paper template or a straightedge.

5 Set the workpiece in place and congratulate yourself on a job well done.

Building deck stairs

How to:
- ■ *Estimate step dimensions*
- ■ *Lay out and cut stringers*
- ■ *Assemble the parts*

Whether you're replacing an old, rickety set of deck stairs or building a set for your new deck, deck stairs are among the most challenging projects for the average do-it-yourselfer to tackle. One little mistake in calculations or layout and you'll wind up wasting lots of expensive wood, or worse, you'll build a downright dangerous set of stairs.

But building a strong, safe set of stairs is doable if you meticulously follow the layout and cutting rules outlined here.

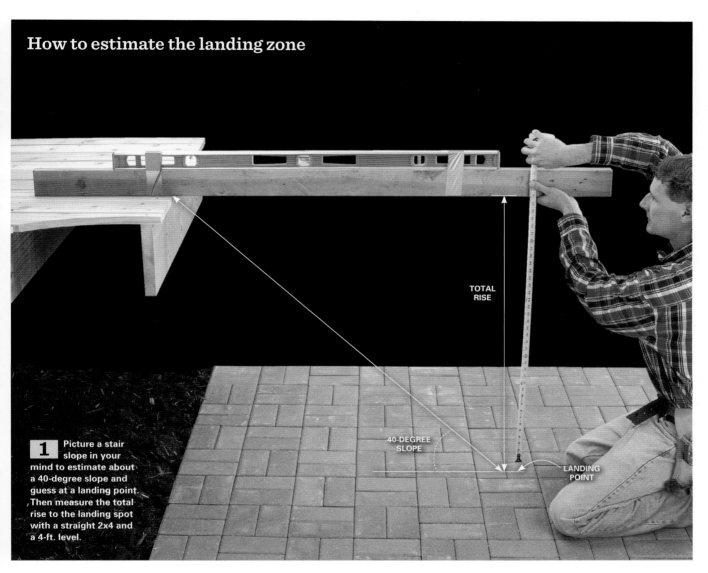

How to estimate the landing zone

1 Picture a stair slope in your mind to estimate about a 40-degree slope and guess at a landing point. Then measure the total rise to the landing spot with a straight 2x4 and a 4-ft. level.

TOTAL RISE

40-DEGREE SLOPE

LANDING POINT

Estimate the landing zone and do the math

You almost always have to design site-built stairs yourself because the number and height of the steps will vary with the landscape. Begin by drawing a side view of your site and adding dimensions (Figure A). That usually means going through the calculations a few times to determine where the stairs will fall and to figure out how long your skirt and stringer material needs to be. This sounds complex, but if you work through it a few times and rely on your sketch, it'll become clear.

Here's what to do:

1. First determine the approximate height "X" (Figure A). Start by estimating where you think the last stair will fall by using a 40-degree slope (Photo 1). Rest a straight board on the deck and

Figure A
Rise and run sketch

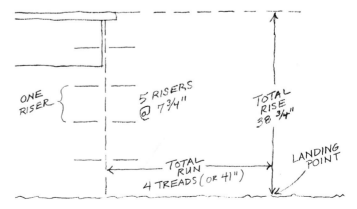

ONE RISER

5 RISERS @ 7¾"

TOTAL RISE 38 ¾"

TOTAL RUN 4 TREADS (OR 41")

LANDING POINT

level over to that spot and measure down to the ground. That'll be the approximate height of the stairs, "X."

2. Now find the approximate number of steps. Divide "X" by 7 in. (an approximate step height) and round off the remainder, up if it's .5 or more, or down if it's less than .5. That'll give you an approximate number of risers (Figure A). The actual recommended riser height is 6-1/2 to 7-3/4 in., but you'll determine that later. If the riser height is too short, redivide "X" by 8 and start again.

On uneven ground, find the number of treads so you can find the exact stair landing point. Simply subtract 1 from the number of risers. (There's always one fewer tread than risers, as you can see in Figure B.) Then, multiply by 10.25 in., the ideal tread width for two 2x6s, to get the total run. Measure out that distance from the deck to find the exact landing point. From this point, you can measure the exact stair height and determine the stringer and skirt length.

3. Measure the exact total rise (Photo 1). Divide the height (X) by your estimated number of risers to find the exact riser height. The figure will usually fall between 6-1/2 and 7-3/4 in., the ideal range. Use this figure for your stringer layout (Figure B). If the riser height isn't in this zone, add or subtract a riser and divide again. This will change the number of treads and shift the landing point, so remeasure the exact height and divide again.

4. Draw a sketch (Figure B) to confirm the plan in your mind and lay out the first stringer (Photos 2 and 3) using the exact riser and tread dimensions and your framing square.

Plan to establish a solid base at the landing point. The base can be a small concrete slab, a small deck or even a treated 2x12 leveled in over a 6-in. gravel base. After you cut the stringers, use them as guides to position your landing.

Cut and mount the stringers by following our photos. In your layout (Figure B), note that:

- The top tread is 3/4 in. shorter than the other treads.
- The bottom riser is 1-1/2 in. shorter than the other risers. Be sure to test-fit the first stringer (Photo 4) before you cut the others. If you made a mistake, you'll at least be able to save the other two 2x10s.

Figure B
Stair layout sketch

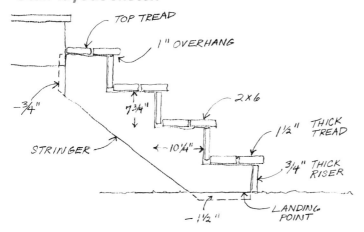

Solid 2x12 skirts for solid stairs and rails

These stairs call for 2x10 treated material for the rot-resistant notched stair stringers (also known as jacks or carriages, Photo 1) that won't be seen. This design also uses 2x12 skirt boards that attach to the sides of the outside stringers. The skirts serve several purposes:

- Cosmetically, they hide the unsightly notched, treated stringers to make your stairs look polished.
- They make it easy to attach the stringers.
- Structurally, they make for rock-solid stairs by reinforcing the stringers, which have been weakened by notching.
- And when it comes time to attach guardrails and handrails to the stairs, you'll have a solid board to fasten pickets or posts to for a wobble-free rail. (If you'd rather not use the 2x12 skirt boards, be sure to use 2x12s for the notched stringers for adequate strength.)

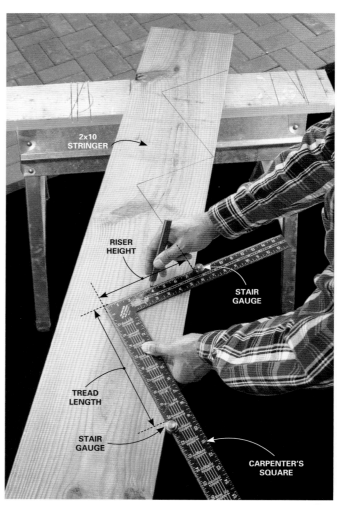

2 Clamp the stair gauges to the carpenter's square. Use the narrow part of the square for clamping the riser gauge and the wider part for the 10-1/4 in. tread. Lay out the stairs by drawing on the outside of the square, sliding the square along until it meets the last mark.

STAIR GAUGES

TOP

SHORTEN RISER 3/4"

3 Mark the top of the stringer to remove 3/4 in. of material to allow for the missing top riser. Mark the bottom of the stringer to remove the tread thickness.

For the parts that show—the skirts, treads and risers (lead photo)—choose material that matches the deck. In our case, that was cedar.

A carpenter's square and a set of stair gauges are crucial

You'll need a 4-ft. level, tape measure, calculator, circular saw and a handsaw. If you don't already have a carpenter's square, now's the time to buy one (Photo 2). To do the job right, pick up a set of stair gauges, too. Stair gauges are little clamps that you tighten onto the square at the proper rise (vertical stair height) and run (horizontal tread depth) for exactly duplicating each step as you draw it onto the stringers (Photo 2). The gauges save time and ensure that all the steps are consistent.

CUT OFF TREAD THICKNESS

BOTTOM

RISER HEIGHT

TIP

Remember, you need one right and one left skirt assembly, not two lefts or rights.

TREAD

RISER HEIGHT

4 Cut only the top and bottom of the stringer with a circular saw. Test-fit the stringer by placing it against the deck, and check the tread level with a small level.

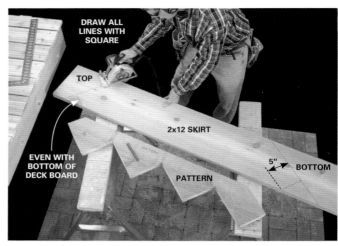

5 Cut the notches with a circular saw. Stop the cuts when you reach the corner of the notch and finish the cuts with a handsaw to prevent weakening the stringers. Use the stringer as a pattern to mark and cut the two other notched stringers.

6 Outline the pattern onto one of the skirt boards. Redraw the top and bottom lines with the carpenter's square and gauges at the original settings. Cut the top off so it will be even with the bottom of overhanging deck boards (see Photo 7) and cut off the end of the bottom so it's about 5 in. high. Fasten stringers to the skirts with 3-in. deck screws spaced about every 8 in., alternating from the front and from the back. Angle the screws so they don't poke through. Nail 2x4 supports to both sides of the middle stringer flush with the bottom for extra support (Photo 7).

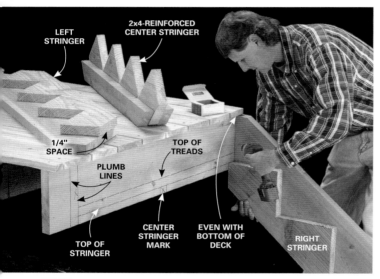

7 Use a level to draw two plumb lines to mark the left and right positions for the skirts, and horizontal lines to mark the top tread location. Tack the skirts to the rim with 3-in. deck screws. Then screw through the back of the deck rim into the skirts with three more deck screws (Photo 8). Center the middle stringer and screw it into the rim with two deck screws.

8 Screw a 2x6 the width of the stringers to the back side of the stringers with two deck screws into each board. Screw two upright treated 2x6s to the back side of the rim and into the horizontal 2x6 with four deck screws into the rim and four more into the 2x6.

Converting decimals to fractions

Not many calculators are set up to give you fractions, and a readout like 7.65 isn't much help for setting the carpenter's square and stair gauges. Use this chart to help you convert the readout to fractions or for converting fractions to decimals for calculator entries. For the decimal equivalent of 1/16 in., simply divide 1 by 16 (.0625).

Choose whichever fraction is closest to the decimal reading for setting your gauges when you lay out your stringers.

.125	=	1/8 in.
.25	=	1/4 in.
.375	=	3/8 in.
.5	=	1/2 in.
.625	=	5/8 in.
.75	=	3/4 in.
.87	=	7/8 in.

BOTTOM
RISER RIPPED
FLUSH TO
STRINGERS

9 Nail on the bottom riser with three 8d galvanized nails into each stringer and square the stairs by "cross-taping" the assembly and shifting it back and forth until the measurements are the same. (The bottom riser will probably need to be ripped to height.)

10 Nail on the second riser board and then screw on the two 2x6 bottom treads, leaving a 1/4-in. gap between the boards. Nail on the next riser, then the next tread and so on to work your way to the top of the stairs.

Designing safe, comfortable stairs

Building codes contain specific requirements for safe stair design. If you follow our directions, your stairs will be legal and safe. In a nutshell, treads should be more than 10 in. deep and risers 6-1/2 to 7-3/4 in. high. Riser heights can vary no more than 3/8 in. (total) within a flight of stairs to reduce trip hazards. Even a 1/4-in. variation can cause tripping.

Decide on the width of the stairs and how many stringers you'll need

If you use 2x6s for tread material, as shown here, you can build stairs up to 48 in. wide with only three stringers because 2x6s can span up to 2 ft. But if you use the common and thinner 5/4-in. bull-nosed decking for your treads, you'll have to keep stringers no more than 16 in. apart and you'll be limited to 32-in. wide stairs with three stringers. For wider stairs, add one or more evenly spaced stringers depending on the width of your stairs and the tread material you choose.

Buying the materials

Measure from the deck rim to the landing spot and add 2 ft. Buy three treated 2x10s, two 2x12 skirts and two 2x4s sized to the next larger length and you'll have plenty of material to work with (the worst mistake is buying material that's too short!). Get a 6-ft. 2x6 for securing the stairs to the deck (Photo 8). You'll also need two 2x6s for each tread and a 1x8 for each riser. Use 3-in. deck screws to fasten the skirts and treads to the stringers and the skirts to the deck. Fasten the risers to the stringers with 8d galvanized nails.

For extra-strong stairs, reinforce the middle 2x10 stringer with 2x4s nailed to both sides (Photo 8).

There are a million ways to fasten the stringers solidly to the deck. Photo 8 shows a simple, foolproof, extra-strong method that works especially well even for open-sided stairs built without skirts.

There you go—a pretty, rock-solid set of stairs ready for balusters and railings.

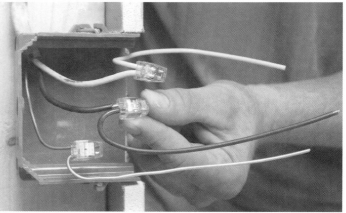

Chapter Two

PLUMBING, ELECTRICAL & HVAC

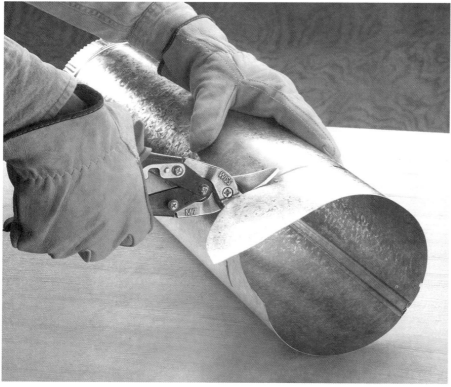

Foolproof faucet installation

Pro tricks to help you avoid those frustrating snags that aren't covered in the directions

A stylish new faucet may promise a quick, refreshing new look to your bathroom, but no one promises a trouble-free installation. In fact, the more expensive and fancy the faucet, the harder the install usually is. The printed directions supply you with the bare basics, but a horde of potential snags makes almost every job a complex one. The following tips will get you through the tough spots and save the big bucks a plumber would charge for a house call like this.

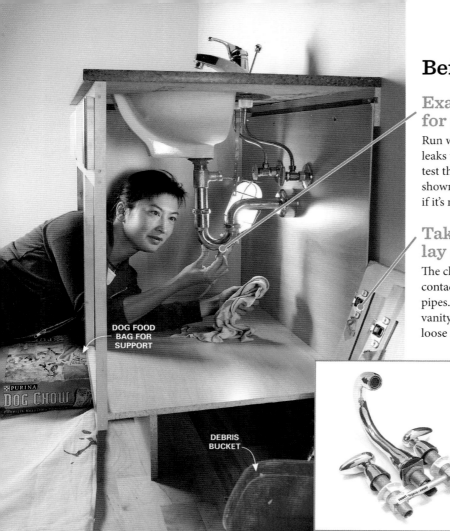

DOG FOOD BAG FOR SUPPORT

DEBRIS BUCKET

Before you dive in

Examine the underside of your sink for unsuspected leaks

Run water through the drain and check for any cracks or leaks that need to be repaired before you start your job. Also test the old P-trap by pushing a thumb on the underside as shown. If it's soft, it's high time to change it out—with plastic if it's not in the public eye or with chrome if it's exposed.

Take off the vanity doors and lay a drop cloth

The cloth will save your flooring from tool scratches and contact with the disgusting debris that comes out of old pipes. It's also worth taking a few minutes to unscrew the vanity doors and remove them for easier access. Tape the loose hinge screws to the doors so you don't lose them.

Pull out your new faucet and check the supply line connector

Supply lines usually won't come with your new faucet. Take your new faucet with you when you buy supply lines to make sure you get the right connector size. Don't trust the labels on the shelf; the supply lines tend to get mixed up. Pros prefer no-burst water supply lines made from flexible, braided stainless steel (photo, p. 46).

Loosen nuts to free stuck shutoffs

Water shutoffs are notorious for seizing up. Instead of bullying them loose, use a wrench to loosen the packing nuts behind the handles about a quarter turn (you'll get a drip of water). That usually frees them. Turn on the sink faucet to be sure the water is completely off. If you still get drips, replace both shutoff valves with quarter-turn ball valves.

Make a complete shopping list before heading to the store

Avoid numerous trips to the hardware store. The plumbing department should not be the place where everybody knows your name! Your shopping list should include two new supply lines (measure the length!), a small tube of 100 percent silicone caulk (clear), Teflon tape, a basin wrench (top photo, p. 45) and a P-trap if needed.

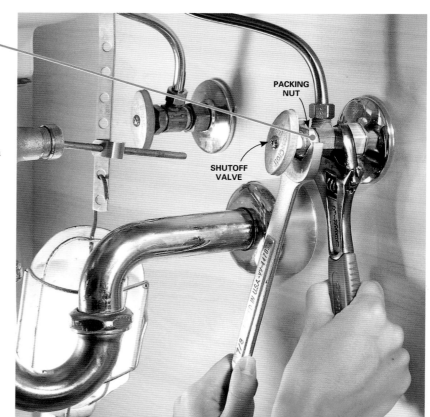

PACKING NUT

SHUTOFF VALVE

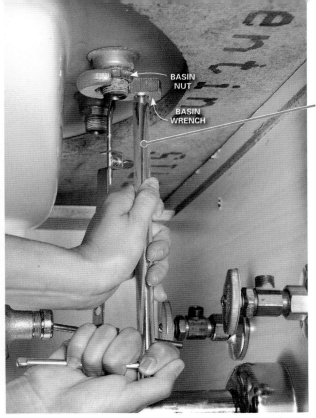

Labels in photo: BASIN NUT, BASIN WRENCH

Out with the old!

Clear the clutter to get at the basin nut

The instructions for your new faucet won't include how to get the old faucet out, so you're on your own with that. Start by removing the supply lines to clear out the clutter.

Your faucet will be held in place under the sink by some sort of nut. If you're lucky, you can reach it with an adjustable wrench. (Remember that you'll be working upside down, so take a moment to make sure you're turning the nut in the correct direction—counterclockwise.) Or if you're really lucky, you can hand-loosen a plastic nut.

Get at inaccessible faucet nuts with a basin wrench

But chances are that you won't have enough space to get the wrench in. Next reach for a basin wrench as shown. A basin wrench has an extension that allows you to reach up into tight spots that you can't get to with a regular wrench. Use your hand to guide the wrench teeth onto the nut while you twist the handle counterclockwise from below. Using this tool can be an awkward and humbling experience, so don't worry if you fumble around a bit. This tool really works!

As a last resort, buy a nut splitter

If the nut seizes up completely, as corroded "pot metal" ones often do, you'll have to use a nut splitter to break it off (photo right). Get one at a plumbing or auto parts store. Buy the size that fits the faucet threads. A length of pipe will help you apply extra torque. Screw the splitter onto the threaded section of faucet with the teeth pointing upward. Using the ratchet, drive the cutting teeth into the nut. This will split the nut in half and it'll pop apart.

NUT SPLITTER

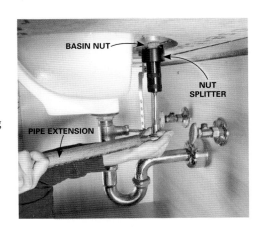

Labels in photo: BASIN NUT, NUT SPLITTER, PIPE EXTENSION

When the pop-up won't pop out

The pop-up assembly consists of a flange (the part you see in the sink) that screws into a body (the part below the sink as shown). If you're lucky, you can simply grab the body (you left the rod on for extra torque) and turn it counterclockwise to unscrew it. Unfortunately, most of the time the flange in the basin also turns, so it won't come apart. At other times it simply won't turn. If you have a helper, have them hold the assembly from the top with pliers.

Cut a stuck pop-up assembly with a hacksaw

If you're alone, the best solution is to cut off the pop-up body from below. Unscrew the locknut, if possible, and cut the stuck pipe above the nut with a hacksaw. This is difficult work, but be persistent. Once the pipe is cut, you can pry out the flange.

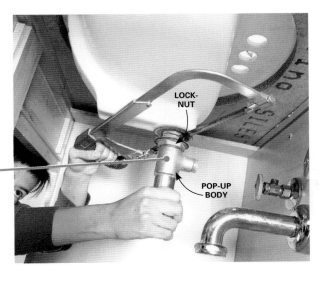

Labels in photo: LOCK-NUT, POP-UP BODY

Installation can be challenging

Dry-fit the new faucet

The new faucet directions are primarily written for new construction, where you install the faucet before the sink goes in and you have plenty of work (wrench) space. In your home, you'll run into tight spots where the instructions, followed to the letter, simply won't work.

Remove the handles and spout and set the faucet body into the sink holes to see if it will go in exactly according to the directions. Check the connection methods and adjustment features, tool access for tightening various nuts, and handle and spout seating on the sink top. They should fit flat without rocking.

BASIN WRENCH

SPOUT NUT

NEW FAUCET BODY

SPOUT ASSEMBLY

Be prepared to improvise

In our case, there was no way to fit the basin wrench, or any other tightening tool, onto the spout nut. The faucet body was in the way (photo, left). We ended up disassembling parts of the faucet body to give us an easy shot with a wrench to tighten up the spout assembly (inset photo, below). Aligning the spout and faucet assembly washer was also critical after tightening the spout. We had to square up the washer by holding a screwdriver on it and tapping with a hammer.

Study the directions and don't hesitate to call the manufacturer for help. Even the pros do it, especially on high-priced (complicated) faucets. Try to find a way around the problem before tossing it all back into the box.

Check your work at the end

NEW SUPPLY LINE

TOILET PAPER

Check for leaks with toilet tissue

When you've finished the entire installation, wipe the valve stem/packing nut zone completely dry and wrap with toilet tissue. Turn on the water and check for obvious leaks at all the connection points. After 10 minutes, check the tissue. If the tissue is damp, tighten the packing nuts or replace the packing or entire valve.

Switch to a plastic P-trap

If your chrome P-trap is in good shape, you can reuse it, but replace the rubber washers. If the trap is out of sight, we recommend switching to a plastic P-trap. They're inexpensive and less likely to leak. Also install new flexible supply lines. Once you've finished the steps shown on p. 47, you're ready to turn the water back on. Remember to retighten the packing nuts behind the oval handles on the shutoff valves if you loosened them earlier.

Getting the new pop-up perfect

"Overflow" the flange with silicone

The flange at the bottom of the sink is a common leak point. During the manufacturing process, the sink drain hole may be overbuffed or cast more in the shape of an egg than of a flat circle. The leak-free solution is to overflow the flange and the area beneath it in the sink with a bead of 100 percent silicone caulk as shown. This will fill in any factory irregularities in the basin. Press the flange into the drain hole and screw the pop-up body on from below. Then tighten the nut (bottom photo). For a white basin, white silicone will look best. Otherwise use clear. Quickly wipe off the excess before it dries and becomes a hassle to clean up.

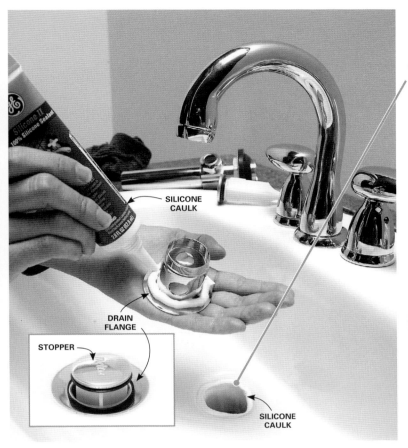

SILICONE CAULK

DRAIN FLANGE

STOPPER

SILICONE CAULK

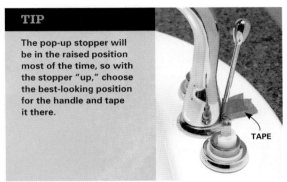

TIP

The pop-up stopper will be in the raised position most of the time, so with the stopper "up," choose the best-looking position for the handle and tape it there.

TAPE

Bend the metal strap so you can clip it farther up the horizontal rod

This will shorten the stroke to raise and lower the stopper.

Tinker with the pivot arm for a smooth operating pop-up

Insert the horizontal arm and stopper into the pop-up body and hand-tighten the packing nut. Slide the metal strap onto the lift rod (handle) and then clip it onto the horizontal rod. Tighten the lift rod setscrew and test the pop-up action. Tighten the packing nut. There's a fine line between a leaky packing nut and a too-stiff pop-up. You'll have to experiment.

SETSCREW

LIFT ROD

METAL STRAP

RUBBER WASHER

METAL WASHER

PACKING NUT

CLIP

HORIZONTAL ROD

Joining plastic pipe

At first glance, plastic plumbing pipe looks easy to cut and join. But don't be fooled. There's more to a top-quality installation than meets the eye. Here you'll learn how to join plastic pipe and guarantee a long-lasting, leak-proof plumbing job.

Make square cuts for the strongest joints

Square pipe ends fit snugly into the fittings, allowing plenty of contact area for the solvent cement to work. They also make a smoother interior surface for better water flow. A power miter saw and other special tube cutters guarantee square cuts, but you don't have to buy them. You can do a good job with just a handsaw and an improvised guide. The photo shows an easy-to-use guide that's made by screwing together scraps of 2x4.

For the best results, use a saw with fine teeth and a blade that's 3 or 4 in. wide. A hacksaw is a poor choice because the narrow blade tends to wander easily. Special saws for cutting plastic pipe are a worthwhile investment if you do much plumbing work. You'll find them in the plumbing tool area or with the handsaws in most home centers and hardware stores. Otherwise, any fine-tooth saw will work.

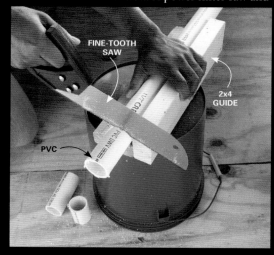

FINE-TOOTH SAW

2x4 GUIDE

PVC

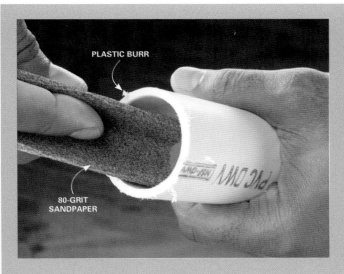

PLASTIC BURR

80-GRIT SANDPAPER

Sand off the saw burrs for a better fit

Plastic burrs left from sawing can cause trouble. Outside the pipe they'll interfere with a good fit. On the inside they can collect debris and slow the water flow. You can remove them with a file or pocketknife, but sandpaper is easier to use and works great. Simply roll a quarter sheet of 80-grit sandpaper into a tube and flatten it slightly to match the curve of the pipe. Then hold the sandpaper at an angle and sand the inside and outside of the plastic pipe until you create slightly beveled edges.

Allow for shrinkage if you dry-fit the pipes

Most novice pipe fitters find it reassuring to cut and assemble a group of pipes and fittings before gluing them together. It's OK to do this as long as you're aware of the pitfalls.

Don't jam the pipe and fitting together too tight. They'll get stuck and can be difficult to get apart. If a fitting does get stuck, just set a block of wood against the lip and pound the fitting loose with a hammer.

Leaving the fittings loose keeps them from getting stuck, but it creates another problem. You can't assume that the final assembly will be the same size as the dry-fit parts. When you apply solvent cement to the pipe and fitting and press them together, you'll lose a little length at each joint. On 1-1/2 in. pipes, this could be as much as 3/8 in. per joint. So keep this in mind if you dry-fit, and allow extra length where fit is crucial.

Another tip is to limit dry fitting to a small group of pipes and fittings. Join this group with solvent cement before moving to the next section.

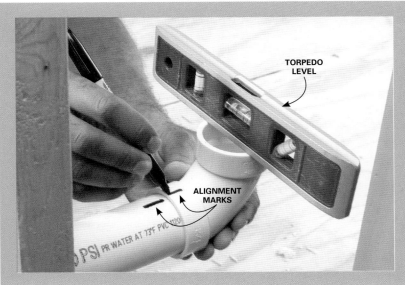

TORPEDO LEVEL

ALIGNMENT MARKS

Mark the pipe and fitting for precise orientation

By the time you spread the solvent cement on both the pipe and the fitting and press them together, you have only several seconds to get the alignment right before the pieces are stuck together. That's why it's a good idea to make alignment marks beforehand on joints where orientation is critical. Dry-fit the pipe and fitting, using a torpedo level if needed to align the fitting, and make a mark across the fitting and pipe. Use these marks to align the fitting and pipe when you join them with solvent cement.

PURPLE PVC/CPVC PRIMER

PUSH AND TWIST FITTING

1 Wipe the inside of the fitting and the outside of the pipe with primer. Spread an even layer of solvent cement on the inside of the fitting and outside of the pipe.

2 Push the pipe into the fitting and twist until the marks are aligned. Press and hold the pipe for about 15 seconds.

Use an even layer of cement and the quarter-turn technique for the strongest joints

Just swiping the pipe with cement and pushing on the fitting won't ensure a strong joint. You want to make sure you have an even layer of cement over all mating surfaces.

If you're using PVC or CPVC pipe, wipe primer around the pipe and into the fitting to prepare it for the solvent cement. Let it dry about 10 seconds. Then spread an even layer of solvent cement on the same surfaces. To keep excess solvent cement from being pushed into water piping, don't apply too much to the inside of the socket on the fitting. At this point you have to work fast to complete the assembly. Align the fitting and pipe about a quarter turn from their final orientation. Then twist the fitting a quarter turn as you press it onto the pipe. Twisting the fitting helps spread the solvent cement

evenly to ensure a solid joint. If you've made alignment marks, make sure they're aligned with each other. Hold the pipe and fitting together for about 15 seconds until the cement grabs. If you let go immediately, the pipe may push out of the fitting, resulting in a weak joint.

CAUTION: The solvent vapors from the primer and cement can make you dizzy and are dangerous to your health. Make sure you have plenty of ventilation or wear an approved organic vapor respirator when working with primer and solvent cement.

Use the proper solvent for each type of plastic

There are three common types of plastic plumbing pipe: PVC, CPVC and ABS. Each requires a different kind of solvent cement. The white or beige pipes (PVC and CPVC) also

require a primer. You don't need a primer with black ABS pipe. Read the label to match the solvent cement to the type of pipe you're using. Avoid universal solvent cements.

Don't sweat it—mistakes are usually easy to fix with a coupling

It's always disappointing to make a mistake. But at least with plastic pipe it's easy to fix. Simply saw out the messed up section, whether it's too long, too short or crooked. Correct the mistake and reassemble the joint with a coupling. In some cases, you can reuse the old section of pipe and fitting. Otherwise, set it aside and cut new parts. You may be able to use the bad section later.

TIP

Buy extra fittings. Having extra on hand will save you a trip to the store. And you can return the extras when you're done.

1 OOPS! The assembled pipes don't reach the predrilled hole because when the pipes were dry-fit they forgot to allow extra length for "shrinkage." See "Allow for shrinkage if you dry-fit the pipes" on p. 49.

2 Saw out the bad section. Fix the goof, using new parts if necessary. Use a coupling to rejoin the parts. Prime (if needed) and cement the parts together.

Use special transition couplings to connect different types of pipes

Transition couplings have a flexible rubber sleeve surrounded by a metal sleeve and band clamps. They're handy for connecting plastic pipe to cast iron, copper or steel, especially if you can't thread on an adapter. Each coupling is labeled with all the different types and sizes of pipes it can join. Home centers and hardware stores keep a few common types on hand. Read the label on the transition coupling to find out which pipe it joins. For less-common connections, contact a local plumbing supplier or ask about ordering a special transition coupling. Rubber couplings without the metal sleeve often aren't code approved. Ask your local inspector if you're not sure.

TIP

Primer—and to a lesser extent the solvent cement—is impossible to remove from most surfaces, including your skin. So if you're working around finished surfaces, cover them with plastic dropcloths and set the primer and solvent cement cans in a dishpan or other plastic container to guard against drips and spills. To prevent spills and contain the fumes, keep the caps on when you're not using the primer and solvent cement.

Slide the pipe ends into the transition fitting. Turn the screws clockwise with a hex head driver to tighten the bands and seal the joint.

Top 10 electrical mistakes

How to recognize and correct wiring blunders that can endanger your home

Mistake | No electrical box

NO JUNCTION BOX

Making connections outside electrical boxes

Never connect wires outside of electrical boxes. Junction boxes protect the connections from accidental damage and contain sparks and heat from a loose connection or short circuit.

Where connections aren't contained in an electrical box, install a box and reconnect the wires inside it. The photo below shows one way to do this for an exterior light mounted on wood siding.

Solution | Add a box

REMODEL BOX

CUT-IN BLOCK

CAUTION: Turn off the power at the main panel when you're doing electrical work.

Cutting wires too short

Wires that are cut too short make wire connections difficult and—since you're more likely to make poor connections—dangerous. Leave the wires long enough to protrude 3 to 6 inches from the face of the box.

If you run into short wires, there's an easy fix. Simply add 6-in. extensions onto the existing wires. The photo below shows a type of wire connector that's easier to install in tight spots. You'll find these in hardware stores and home centers.

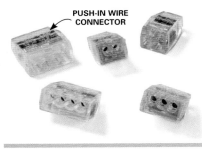

PUSH-IN WIRE CONNECTOR

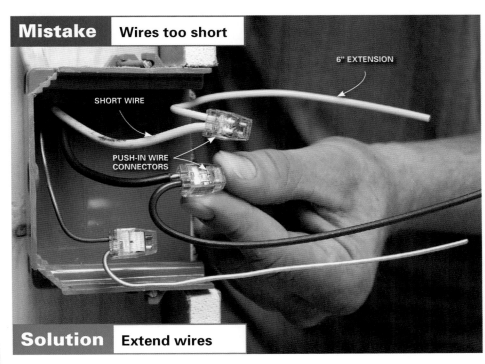

Mistake — **Wires too short**

6" EXTENSION

SHORT WIRE

PUSH-IN WIRE CONNECTORS

Solution — **Extend wires**

Leaving plastic-sheathed cable unprotected

It's easy to damage plastic-sheathed cable that's left exposed between framing members. That's why the electrical code requires cable to be protected in all exposed areas. Cable is especially vulnerable when it's run over or under wall or ceiling framing, as shown here.

Protect, support and secure exposed plastic-sheathed cable by installing wood furring strips or boards alongside or underneath the cable, as shown on the far right. The cable should be stapled to the wood furring strips or boards every 4 feet or more often, for a neater job. In effect, the cable should always closely follow framing members or furring strips or boards in exposed areas in a neat and workmanlike manner.

Mistake — **Unprotected cable**

UNPROTECTED CABLE

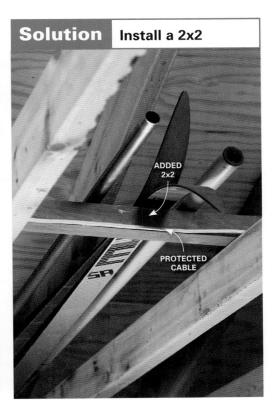

Solution — **Install a 2x2**

ADDED 2x2

PROTECTED CABLE

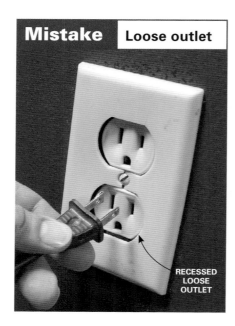

RECESSED
LOOSE
OUTLET

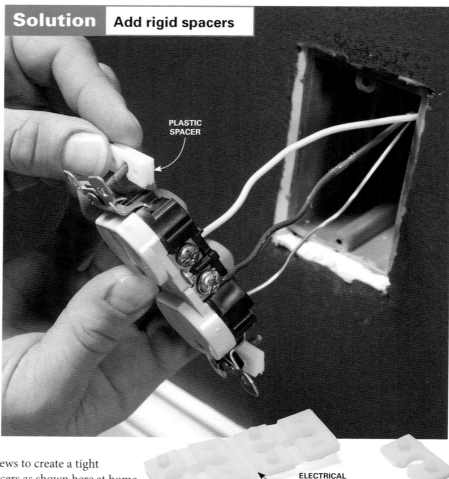

PLASTIC
SPACER

ELECTRICAL
SPACER

Poor support for outlets and switches

Loose switches or outlets can look bad (photo above), but worse yet, they're dangerous. Loosely connected outlets can move around, causing the wires to loosen from the terminals. Loose wires can arc and overheat, creating a potential fire hazard.

Fix loose outlets by shimming under the screws to create a tight connection to the box. You can buy special spacers as shown here at home centers and hardware stores. Other options include small washers or a coil of wire wrapped around the screw.

Installing a three-slot receptacle without a ground wire

If you have two-slot outlets, it's tempting to replace them with three-slot outlets so you can plug in three-prong plugs. But don't do this unless you're sure there's a ground available. Use a tester to see if your outlet is grounded. A series of lights indicates whether the outlet is wired correctly or what fault exists. These testers are readily available at home centers and hardware stores.

If you discover that someone replaced an older two-slot outlet with a three-slot outlet in a ungrounded box, the easiest fix is to simply replace it with a new two-slot outlet as shown (they are still made and available at home centers). However, there are several better options available in the electrical code, such as installing GFCI outlets that provide protection from lethal shock. GFCI outlets will still do their job even if they are not grounded. When replacing outlets also remember that in addition to GFCI protection, AFCI protection and tamper-resistant outlets may be required. Consult with a licensed electrician or your local electrical inspector.

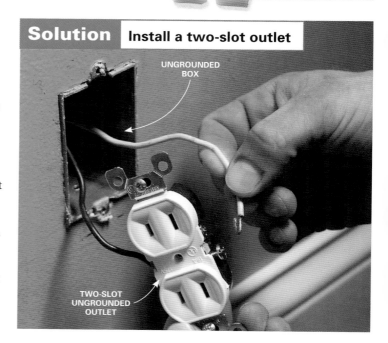

UNGROUNDED
BOX

TWO-SLOT
UNGROUNDED
OUTLET

Recessing boxes behind the wall surface

Mistake · Exposed combustible material

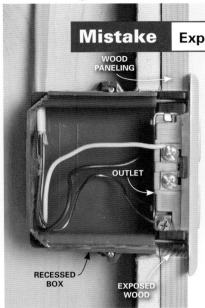

WOOD PANELING

OUTLET

RECESSED BOX

EXPOSED WOOD

Electrical boxes must be flush to the wall surface if the wall surface is a combustible material. Boxes recessed behind combustible materials like wood present a fire hazard because the wood is left exposed to potential heat and sparks.

The fix is simply to install a metal or plastic box extension. If you use a metal box extension on a plastic box, connect the metal extension to the ground wire in the box using a grounding clip and a short piece of wire.

Solution · Add a box extension

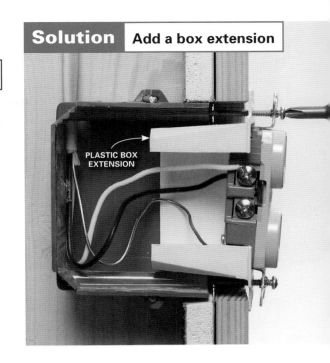

PLASTIC BOX EXTENSION

Mistake · Missing clamp

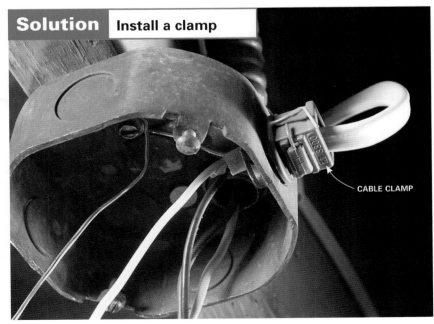

MISSING CABLE CLAMP

Installing cable without a clamp

Cable that's not secured can strain the connections. In metal boxes, the sharp edges can cut the cable sheath and the insulation on the individual wires. Single plastic boxes do not require internal cable clamps, but the cable must be stapled within 8 in. of the box. Larger plastic boxes are required to have built-in cable clamps and the cable must be stapled within 12 in. of the box. Cables must be connected to metal boxes with an approved cable clamp. Make sure the sheathing on the cable is trapped under the clamp, and that about 1/4 in. of sheathing is visible inside the box. Some metal boxes have built-in cable clamps. If the box you're using doesn't include clamps, buy clamps separately and install them when you add the cable to the box (photo below).

Solution · Install a clamp

CABLE CLAMP

Overfilling electrical boxes

Too many wires stuffed into a box can cause all sorts of fire hazards. The National Electrical Code assigns "volume allowances" to determine the minimum size box. Calculate the minimum box size by adding up the "volume allowances" as follows.

1 - for each hot wire and neutral wire entering the box
1 - for all the ground wires combined
1 - for all the cable clamps combined
2 - for each device (switch or outlet—but not light fixtures)

Multiply the total "volume allowances" by a factor of 2.00 for 14-gauge wire and by a factor of 2.25 for 12-gauge wire to get the minimum size box required in cubic inches. Plastic boxes have the volume marked inside the back of the box. Metal box volumes are not marked—they're listed in the electrical code. For metal boxes simply measure the height, width and depth of the box interior to find the approximate volume. Compared to the total cost of your project, boxes are rather inexpensive. Always buy bigger boxes than the bare minimum—you'll be glad you did.

Mistake — Box too small

OVERFILLED BOX

Solution — Install a larger box

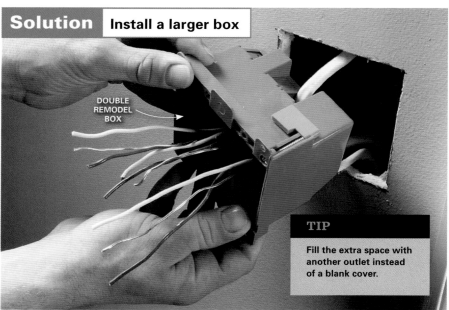

DOUBLE REMODEL BOX

TIP
Fill the extra space with another outlet instead of a blank cover.

Reversing hot and neutral wires

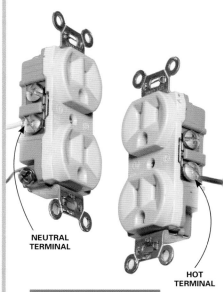

NEUTRAL TERMINAL

HOT TERMINAL

Solution

Identify the neutral terminal

Connecting the black hot wire to the neutral terminal of an outlet creates the potential for a lethal shock. The trouble is that you may not realize the mistake until someone gets shocked, because lights and most other plug-in devices will still work; they just won't work safely.

The neutral terminal is always marked. It's identified by a silver-colored screw. Connect the hot wire to the brass-colored screw. If there's a green or bare copper wire, that's the ground. Connect the ground to the green grounding screw or to a ground wire or grounded box.

Wiring a GFCI backward

GFCI (ground-fault circuit-interrupter) outlets protect you from a lethal shock by shutting off the power when they sense slight differences in current. They have two pairs of terminals. One pair, labeled "line," is for incoming power for the GFCI outlet itself. The other set is labeled "load" and provides protection for downstream outlets. You'll lose the shock protection if you mix up the line and load connections.

Solution | Connect power to the "line" terminals

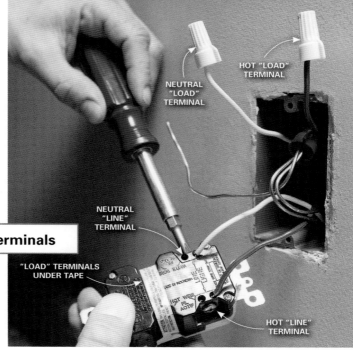

Extension cords for power tools

All UL-listed cords have an electrical current limit that's based on the size of the wire inside and the length of the cord. (**Note:** The bigger the gauge number, the smaller the cord.) A small cord or a long cord that's feeding a power-hungry tool will heat up, especially if it's coiled, because the heat stays contained within the coils rather than dissipating in the air. The smaller the wire and the longer the cord, the bigger the electrical draw and the more heat generated.

Typical cord limits are shown in the chart. Cord sizes are imprinted on the surface of the cord sheathing (see photo). The most common construction cord sizes are 12-3, 14-3 and 16-3. The first digits denote the gauge of the cord while the second number denotes the number of wires it contains.

Two wires carry the current; the third wire is a ground wire. Sixteen-gauge cords are only heavy enough for work lights and small power tools such as drills. If you work with portable table saws, circular saws or other larger tools that draw 10 to 15 amps, get to the hardware store and purchase a 50-ft., 12-3 extension cord. Almost every power tool has a nameplate attached to the motor housing that lists the amperage requirements of the tool.

Just remember: Always fully uncoil extension cords, select a cord that's big enough for the job, and one that is rated for the environment (indoors vs. outdoors). Heavy-duty cords cost a little more but they will take a lot of abuse, last a long time and add years of life to your power tools.

CURRENT LIMITS ON EXTENSION CORDS (AMPS)			
Cord Size	**Cord Length**		
	25 ft.	**50 ft.**	**100 ft.**
18-gauge	7 amps	5 amps	2 amps
16-gauge	12 amps	7 amps	3.4 amps
14-gauge	16 amps	12 amps	5 amps
12-gauge	20 amps	16 amps	7 amps

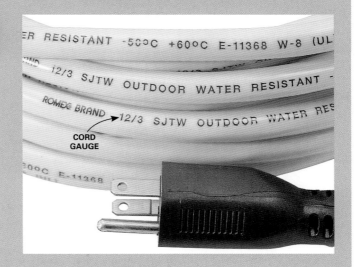

Cutting sheet metal

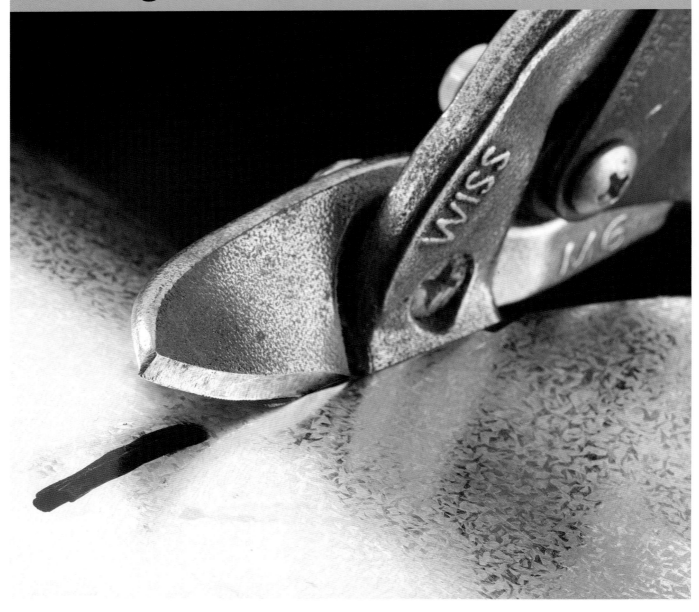

Cutting sheet metal with snips can be tricky and frustrating. The edges are sharp, the cutoffs are stiff and get in the way, the snips bind or you just can't seem to negotiate the curve. These problems are common for those of us who don't work with sheet metal every day. But you don't have to be a tinsmith to cut sheet metal successfully. With the right tool and a few simple techniques, you can make almost any cut with ease.

We'll recommend a pair of tin snips that will get you through 90 percent of the jobs you'll run into. But we'll also indicate the best tin snips to use for each type of cut we show. Then when the time comes you can decide if it's worth investing in another pair of snips to simplify your job.

One snips can do it all...well, almost

There are at least a dozen types of tin snips, and choosing just the right one can be confusing. We'd recommend starting your collection with offset compound snips (Photos 1 and 2). The cutters are offset below the handle so you can keep your cutting hand above the work, and the compound action allows you to cut thicker material with less effort.

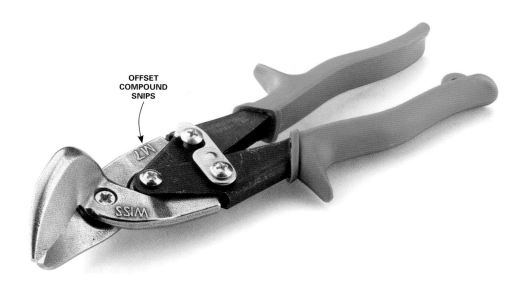

OFFSET COMPOUND SNIPS

Compound snips, also called aviation snips, are color coded. A green snips is designed to cut clockwise curves and a red snips to cut counterclockwise curves. You can use the snips with either hand, but if you're right-handed you'll find it easier to use a green snips for many types of cuts (Photo 1). If you're left-handed, approach the cut from the opposite direction with a red-handled snips (Photo 2). Notice the clockwise and counterclockwise directions of the curved starting cuts. Each snips can do one direction well, but not the other.

There are two ways to cut round ducts

First, if you want to cut a duct near the middle and use both ends, mark and cut the duct before snapping it together. Any tin snips will work for this. But when you come to the thicker locking seam, you'll need the extra leverage of compound snips. Photo 3 shows how to cut through thick metal. If you have to squeeze the handles with excessive force, use a hacksaw instead to avoid damaging the tin snips' blades.

If you only need to trim a few inches from a round duct, it's just as easy to snap it together first. Then use the technique shown in Photos 1 and 2 depending on which color snips you're using. This is an easy cut

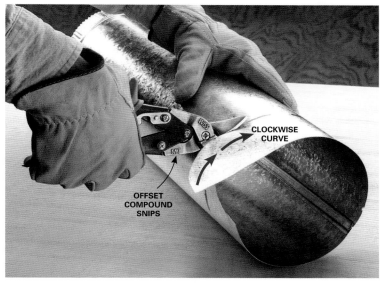

CLOCKWISE CURVE

OFFSET COMPOUND SNIPS

1 Cut a round duct from the right-hand side with green-handled compound snips. Use this technique if you're right-handed or in tight quarters. Keep the top blade aligned parallel to the cutting line to cut a straight line around the duct.

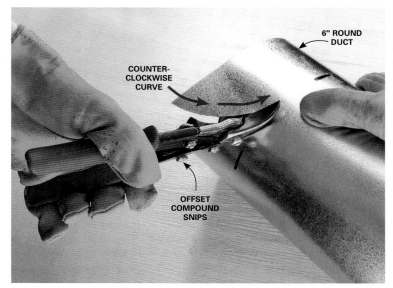

6" ROUND DUCT

COUNTER-CLOCKWISE CURVE

OFFSET COMPOUND SNIPS

2 Cut a round duct from the left side with red-handled compound snips. Use this snips if you're left-handed or in tight quarters. Mark round ducts by measuring in from the end at intervals and drawing a broken line with a permanent marking pen.

STRAIGHT-CUTTING
COMPOUND SNIPS

WISS

M3

3 Nestle thick material deep into the wide open jaws before you squeeze the handles. Straight-cutting compound snips work best for cutting thick or doubled-up sheet metal. They don't cut curves well.

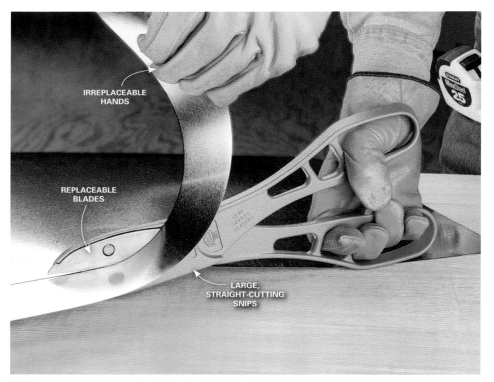

IRREPLACEABLE
HANDS

REPLACEABLE
BLADES

LARGE,
STRAIGHT-CUTTING
SNIPS

4 Long, straight cuts are easier to make with large tin snips. Open the cutters as wide as you can at the start of each stroke, and make long, smooth strokes. Lift the cutoff strip and roll it to the side to prevent it from binding on the tin snips' handle.

to make with the curve-cutting snips shown, but making it with straight-cutting snips would be a challenge. Once again, you may need a hacksaw to cut the thick seam, or use the technique shown in Photo 3.

Make long strokes for long, straight cuts

Compound snips are designed more for leverage and maneuverability than for straight cutting. If you're using compound snips, open and close the jaws fully with each stroke to maximize the length of the cut. Even so, your cut will probably be a little ragged. If you've got a lot of straight cutting to do, buy tin snips like the one shown in Photo 4. It cuts metal almost as easily as scissors cut paper. And the long blades make it easy to cut straight and leave a smooth edge.

As you cut, one side of the sheet metal will ride up and over the lower jaw. Roll this piece back and to the side as you go to keep it from binding on the blade or getting in the way of your hand (Photo 4).

Use curve-cutting snips to cut circles

Making a circular cutout in a duct is simple using the techniques shown in Photos 5 and 6. The key is to use red-handled offset compound snips to cut counterclockwise or green-handled snips to cut clockwise. This is one cut where it really pays to have snips that cut curves. It's difficult to cut a hole like this with straight-cutting snips. Even if you succeed, the resulting hole will probably have a ragged edge.

Combine red and green snips for difficult cuts

If obstructions in a work area prevent you from completing a cut with one set of snips—red-handled snips, for example—switch to green-handled snips and complete the cut by going in the opposite direction. Situations like this, which usually occur when you're modifying heating or air conditioning duct work, are about the only reason to own both red- and green-handled snips.

The next time you tackle a project that involves cutting sheet metal, head to the hardware store or home center and pick up a sharp new pair of snips that's right for the task. You'll be glad you did. The savings in time and frustration will more than make up for the cost of the snips.

CAUTION: Sheet metal edges are razor sharp. Always wear leather or other sturdy gloves when you're working with sheet metal.

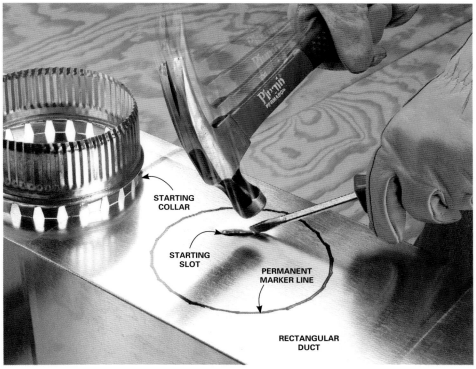

STARTING COLLAR

STARTING SLOT

PERMANENT MARKER LINE

RECTANGULAR DUCT

5 Punch a starter hole for a circular cutout with a straight-blade screwdriver. Pound on the back of the screwdriver with a hammer to puncture the metal and create an opening for the tin snips.

CLOCKWISE CUT

6 Start the curved cut by nibbling at the gash left by the screwdriver with the tip of the offset compound snips until you can slip the lower blade under the metal. Then cut a gradual curve until you reach the curved line. Guide the top blade of the snips along the line to complete the cutout.

Get to know PEX

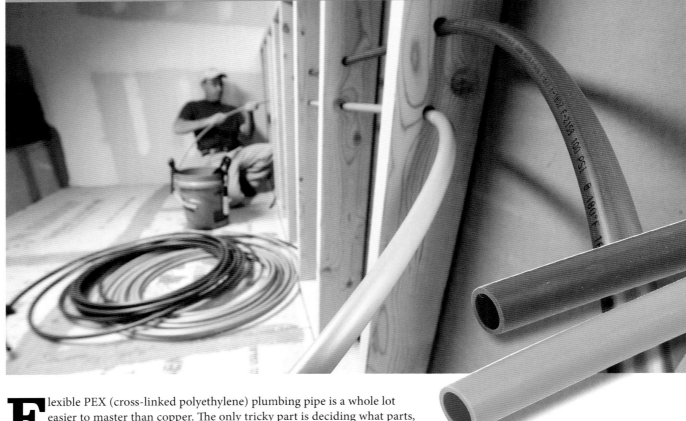

Flexible PEX (cross-linked polyethylene) plumbing pipe is a whole lot easier to master than copper. The only tricky part is deciding what parts, tools and connection system to buy. Here's what you need to know.

Choose a common connection system

Before you choose a system for connecting PEX to fittings, check what's available at the stores where you like to shop. There are a half-dozen systems out there, but most are available only through specialty plumbing suppliers. If you want to shop at home centers and hardware stores, there are two widely available methods to choose from: copper crimp rings and stainless steel cinch rings. You may prefer the cinch system because the tool is smaller and one tool can handle four ring sizes (3/8 to 1 in.). But cinch rings aren't as widely available in some areas, so you may want to choose the crimp system instead. Crimp rings require a different tool for each size or a combination tool, and the bigger tools are awkward in tight spots. Still, you may want to put up with the drawbacks of the crimp system rather than drive across town to get supplies. Whatever system you choose, keep an eye on prices: costs vary a lot from one supplier to another.

Cinch rings

Cinch rings tighten as you pinch the tab with the tool.

Crimp rings

Crimp ring connections are made by compressing a copper ring around the PEX and fitting.

Buy sticks, not coils

PEX has a strong "memory"; it always wants to spring back to its original shape. So working with a coil of PEX is like wrestling with a giant Slinky. For most jobs, you're better off buying 10-ft. "sticks" instead. You may have to pay a few cents more per foot and install a coupler or two, but you'll avoid frustration and kinks. Even plumbers who run miles of PEX every year often buy sticks rather than coils.

Coils are great when you have lots of long runs, but straight "sticks" are a lot easier to work with. The red and blue colors eliminate hot-and-cold confusion.

Stock up on push-ins

Push-in elbows, tees and couplings are the best solution for cramped quarters where there's no space for a crimping or cinching tool. No tool is needed; just push in the PEX and walk away. And since they also work with copper and CPVC, you can carry just a few push-in fittings rather than a huge collection of special transition fittings. Convenience doesn't come cheap, though. Also, check with your local inspector before you use push-in fittings. Some jurisdictions don't allow them in inaccessible locations like inside walls.

Push-in fittings work with copper and CPVC as well as with PEX.

Bend PEX carefully—or not at all

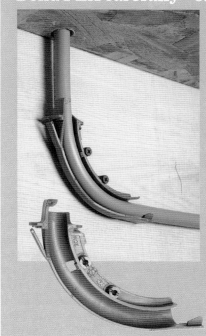

PEX is easy to kink. With one brand, you can restore the tubing by heating it. But with most PEX, you have to cut out the kink and splice in a new section. You can also damage PEX by overbending it. (The minimum bend radius is typically six to eight times the outer diameter, depending on the manufacturer.) One way to avoid kinking and overbending is to use bend sleeves. Keep in mind that— even with a sleeve—a bend requires open working space. In tight situations, save yourself some struggling by using an elbow fitting instead.

A bend sleeve prevents kinking or creating a too-tight bend.

Stub out with copper

You can buy shutoff valves that connect directly to PEX. But don't. PEX can't handle abuse the way copper can. You want to be able to pack more stuff into your vanity and crank that crusty valve closed years from now. So use copper rather than PEX for wall stub-outs. For risers coming out of the floor (or extending down from the ceiling to a laundry tub faucet), use lengths of copper pipe.

Copper stub-outs provide a PEX connection on one end and solid support for shutoff valves on the other.

Get a crimp cutter

PEX fittings cost about three times as much as copper fittings. So you won't want to toss your mistakes in the trash. If you use cinch rings, you can saw or twist off the ring tab, pull off the PEX and reuse the fitting. But sawing through a crimp ring—without damaging the fitting—is a job for a surgeon. Consequently, a crimp cutter is a lifesaver. Just slice off the PEX flush with the fitting and make two cuts in the ring.

A crimp cutter lets you remove crimp rings without damaging the fitting.

Avoid shocks

Non-contact voltage tester
Make sure the power is off

The safest tool to confirm that electrical power is off, even before you touch a wire.

The two most important safety steps to take before opening any electrical box are: (1) Turn off the electrical power to that outlet at the main panel. (2) Double-check the outlet to make sure you turned off the right circuit. A non-contact voltage tester is the best tool for this job. With this tool, you don't even have to touch a bare wire. The tester will flash and/or chirp whenever it comes close to a hot wire. It'll even detect voltage (a hot wire) through the wire's plastic insulation. However, it's not reliable when testing wires covered by metal conduit or metal sheathing.

This tester is powered by small batteries, so make sure it works before using it. Shove the tip into the slots of a receptacle that's live, hold it near a plugged-in lamp cord or hold it against a light bulb that's on. With most testers, you'll see a series of flashes and hear continuous chirps that indicate voltage. Testers may flash and chirp at other times, but without the continuous pattern that indicates a hot wire.

To test whether a receptacle is hot, simply shove the tester nose into or against the plug slots (Photo 1). The hot slot is the smaller of the two. However, you never know if the receptacle was wired correctly, so test the neutral slot too just in case the receptacle was wired wrong. And be sure to check all the slots in the receptacle. Sometimes the lower set in a duplex receptacle will be wired separately from the top. If a wall switch controls the receptacle, make sure the switch is in the "on" position.

Then remove the receptacle cover plate and poke the tester tip close to the screw terminals. If there are no live wires, unscrew the receptacle, then carefully pull it out and test all the wires again (Photo 2). At this point, you can shove the tester deeper into the box to test wires not directly connected to the receptacle. Several circuits may be present in a single box. For your safety you must turn off all circuits to a box before working on it.

To test for power at a switch, you have to remove the cover plate first. Similar to a receptacle, there's usually enough space to poke the tester tip close to the screw terminals (Photo 3, p. 65). If there are no live wires, unscrew the switch, pull it out and test all other wires in the box.

To test a light fixture before removing it, turn off the circuit at the main panel, turn the light switch to "on," remove the bulb and poke the tester all the way down to the center socket button (Photo 4, p. 65). If the fixture is on a three-way switch (two switches), test with one switch first in the up, then in the down position. If no voltage is present, you can safely unscrew the fixture from the electrical box, pull it out and test the other wires in the box as before.

The non-contact tester will also identify hot cables, even if they're covered by plastic insulation (Photo 5, p. 65). This comes in handy when you cut open a wall and find electrical cables and are unsure if they are shut off.

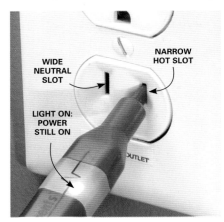

1 Test receptacles to make sure they're off before removing them. Turn power off to the outlet and shove the tester nose into narrow (hot) slot of the receptacle. If you're testing a tamper-resistant outlet, you may need a plug-in tester.

2 Test for hot wires. Pull out the receptacle and push the tester deep into the box to check for other hot wires. If you find them, turn them off at the main panel.

Circuit tester
Test for good grounding

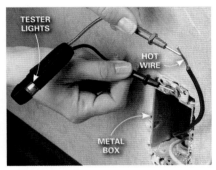

NEON TEST LIGHT

LEADS

The two-lead circuit tester shown here also tests for voltage. When you touch a live hot wire (black or any other color except green and white) with one lead and a neutral (white) or ground (green or bare copper) with the other, the neon test lamp should light. It confirms that power is on and you have a complete (good) circuit. If the light doesn't come on, either the power is off or you have an open (bad) circuit.

This tool is handy in older homes when you want to know if an equipment ground wire (green insulated or bare copper) is connected to ground elsewhere. You often have to check this when you replace older nongrounding-type outlets with grounded ones as now required by the National Electrical Code. You may find an unused bare ground wire folded back into the box, and you have to test it to make sure that it's connected to the rest of the grounding system before using it.

To test a ground wire: (1) Turn power off to switch (confirm with the non-contact voltage tester) and uncap neutral wires (they can remain in a bundle). (2) Disconnect two switch wires and spread bare ends so they don't touch. (3) Turn power back on and identify hot wire with non-contact tester. (4) Confirm that circuit tester is working by carefully touching hot wire with one lead and a neutral wire with the other. Tester will light if it's working. (5) Touch hot wire with one lead and ground wire with the other (Photo 1). If tester lights, ground wire is good.

Follow a similar procedure when working with metal boxes in which no ground wire comes into the box. In this case, you want to find out whether the metal box itself is grounded (through conduit or another method) and will serve as required ground. With wires separated and power on, touch hot wire with one lead and metal box with the other. If lamp lights, you can use metal box as a ground. If lamp doesn't light, in most cases the NEC requires that you upgrade the box to have some means of grounding. Consult a licensed electrician or your local electrical inspector for acceptable grounding methods.

CAUTION: Avoid touching a live hot wire and don't let it touch anything else. Hold the tester leads by the insulated portion while making contact. And turn the circuit off again as soon as you finish the test.

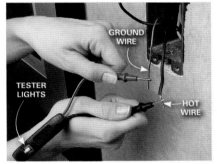

GROUND WIRE

TESTER LIGHTS

HOT WIRE

1 Test the ground by disconnecting and separating wires to a device with circuit off. Turn circuit back on. Touch hot wire with one lead and ground wire with the other lead. The light will come on if ground is good.

TESTER LIGHTS

HOT WIRE

METAL BOX

2 Test whether a metal box is grounded by using the same procedure as in Photo 1, except touch the metal box instead of the ground wire with the second lead. This box is grounded.

WIRE TERMINALS

LIGHT OFF: NO POWER

3 Test switches to make sure power is off. Turn power off at the main panel, remove cover plate and push tester nose close to each of the two switch wire terminals to see if either wire is still hot. Check all switches.

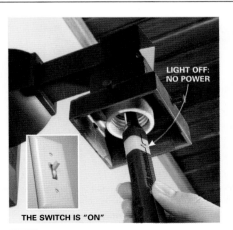

LIGHT OFF: NO POWER

THE SWITCH IS "ON"

4 Turn off circuit to light fixture. Then remove bulb and test contact in the bottom of socket for voltage. Make sure light switch is in the "on" position. Unscrew fixture from wall and test wires before disconnecting them.

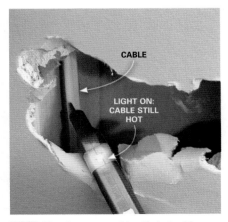

CABLE

LIGHT ON: CABLE STILL HOT

5 Use the tester to identify hot cables (plastic sheathed only) so you can turn those circuits off before sawing or drilling around them.

Continuity tester
Identify wires and test switches

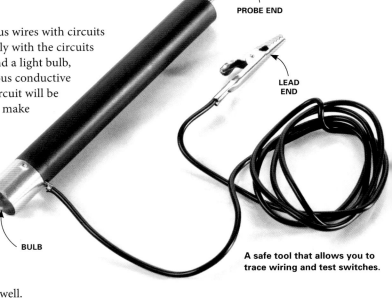

PROBE END

LEAD END

It's difficult and dangerous to trace the routes of various wires with circuits turned on. A continuity tester does it simply and safely with the circuits turned off. It has a probe, which contains a battery and a light bulb, and a wire lead. When you touch the ends to any continuous conductive path, usually a wire, with both the probe and the lead, a circuit will be complete and the bulb will light. In fact, to test the bulb to make sure it's working, simply touch the lead to the probe.

Working with several boxes and can't remember which wire goes where? With the power shut off, simply connect a test wire to a circuit wire in one box (Photo 1), clip the lead to the test wire (Photo 1 inset), and touch the probe to the ends of the circuit wires in the other box. The bulb will light when you find the right wire.

Another great use for the circuit tester is to determine whether a switch is working (Photo 2). Disconnect the switch, connect one lead to one terminal and put the probe on the other while you flick the switch on and off. If the switch is good, the bulb should light up and turn off as well.

BULB

A safe tool that allows you to trace wiring and test switches.

CAUTION: If you have aluminum wiring, don't mess with it. Call in a licensed pro who's certified to work with it. This wiring is dull gray, not the dull orange that's characteristic of copper.

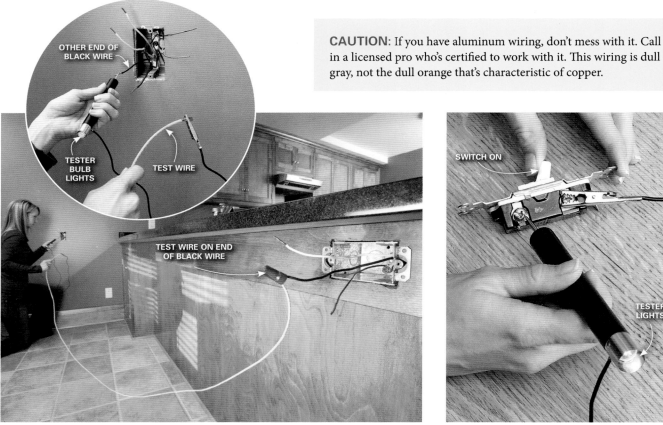

OTHER END OF BLACK WIRE

TESTER BULB LIGHTS

TEST WIRE

TEST WIRE ON END OF BLACK WIRE

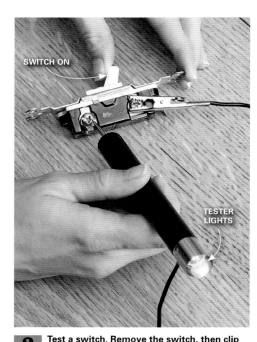

SWITCH ON

TESTER LIGHTS

1 Identify a remote wire by attaching the clip to the wire and probing other wires with the pointed end until the tester lights. The electrical power must always be off.

2 Test a switch. Remove the switch, then clip one lead to one switch terminal. Touch the point to the other terminal and flip switch on and off. The tester light will go on and off if the switch is good.

Tips for safer wiring

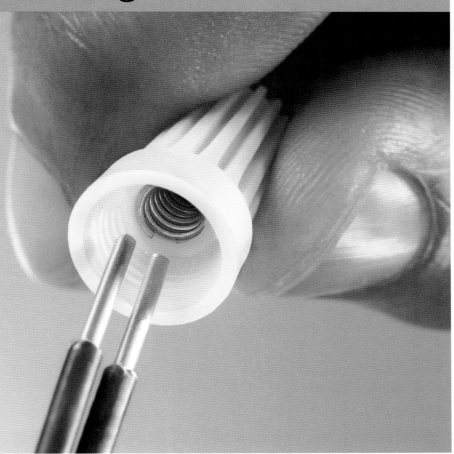

Making tight electrical connections is critical to a safe wiring job. If wires come loose you could get arcing and overheating, which could lead to a fire. However, thanks to reliable connectors and terminals, it's fairly easy to make safe, secure connections. But there are a few things you have to watch out for. We'll show you how to pick the right connector for the job and how to prepare the wires for the best connection. We'll also show you why you should spend a little extra money when it comes time to buy outlets and other electrical devices. With careful attention to detail, you can rest easy knowing your wiring job is as safe as you could possibly make it.

Line up the wire ends, then tighten

With the exception of stranded wire, which we'll talk about on p. 68, it's important to make sure the ends of all wires are lined up before twisting on the connector. Otherwise the connector won't clamp all wires evenly and one or more could slip out.

Start by stripping the ends of the wires. Check the label on the connector package for the length of bare wire to expose. For all but the smallest and largest connectors, this is usually about 1/2 to 5/8 in. Then arrange the wires parallel to each other with their ends aligned. Keep your eye on the wire ends until the connector covers them to make sure none slips out of position. You don't have to twist

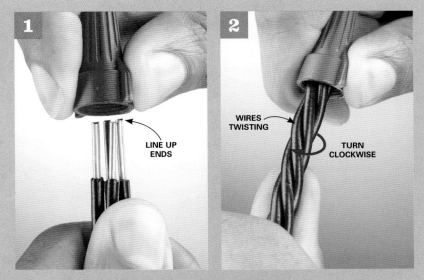

the wires together before you screw on the connector. Simply twist the connector until the insulated wires outside the connector begin to twist. Photos 1 and 2 show how to install the connector. When you're done, tug on each wire to make sure they're all firmly connected.

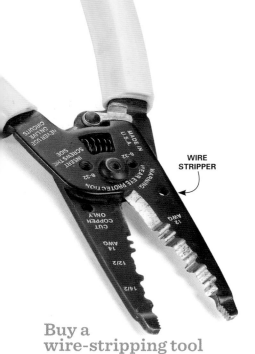

WIRE STRIPPER

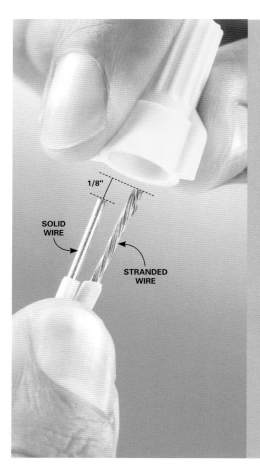

1/8"

SOLID WIRE

STRANDED WIRE

Extend stranded wire 1/8 in. beyond solid wire

If you hold the ends of solid and stranded wire even with each other while you screw on the connector, the stranded wire will often wrap loosely around the solid wires, resulting in a loose connection. This is especially likely when you're joining multiple solid wires to one stranded wire. The problem is easy to prevent by extending the ends of all stranded wires about 1/8 in. beyond the solid wires. Then install the connector as usual.

TIP

Stranded wire is a little larger than the same gauge of solid wire. Use a wire stripper labeled for stranded wire, or use the hole for the next largest gauge of solid wire. Remember to tug on each wire to make sure the connector has a solid grip.

Buy a wire-stripping tool

Wire-stripping tools do a fast, clean job without nicking and damaging the wires. For most standard house wiring requiring 12-gauge and 14-gauge plastic sheathed cable, we like the type shown here. It can cut the plastic sheathing of 12-2 and 14-2 plastic sheathed cable, as well as strip insulation on individual wires.

Choose a connector that fits the wires

Every wire connector is made to join a certain minimum and maximum number of wires. The larger the wire gauge, the fewer it can hold. Always check the approved list on the packaging (photo right) to make sure the connector is listed for the wire combination you want to join. Even though the connectors appear to be color coded, you can't rely on this. For example, one style of yellow connector joins up to four 14-gauge wires, while another connects a maximum of three. You have to check the label on the package or go to the manufacturer's web site to find out. Keep a range of small to large connectors and their packaging on hand so you won't be tempted to make do with the wrong size.

Buy top-quality outlets for the best connections

At most home centers, you can buy economy residential-grade outlets or premium commercial-grade outlets. Spend the extra money. Commercial-grade outlets are made from better materials, take more abuse and last longer. Residential-grade outlets eventually wear out if you use them frequently. If you decide to buy commercial-grade outlets, look for the kind with clamp screw terminals. They resemble the stab-in holes you'll find on economy outlets but actually clamp down firmly when you tighten the screw. If you don't want to spend the extra money to install commercial-grade outlets everywhere, at least put them in heavy-use areas like kitchens, bathrooms, garages, workshops and laundry rooms. Receptacle outlets inside and outside of a home now require one or more of the following types of protection or ratings: AFCI, GFCI, tamper-resistance and weatherproof. Consult with a licensed electrician or your local electrical inspector.

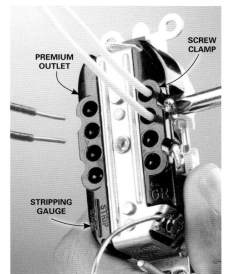

Strip the wires to the length shown on the stripping gauge (photo at left). Loosen the terminal screw by turning it counterclockwise to open the clamp. Then hold the wire or wires, one in each hole, while you tighten the screw. Tug on the wires when you're done to make sure they're securely connected.

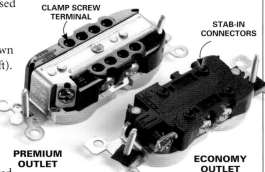

Loop the wire for a secure connection

Since switches and outlets are subject to abuse and possibly some movement when used, it's critical that the connections be secure so they don't work loose. For screw connections, start with a 3/4-in. length of bare stripped wire. Photos 1 and 2 show how to bend the loop and close it around the screw. Wrap the wire clockwise around the screw so that the loop closes as the screw is tightened. Make sure to tighten the screw firmly. Keep in mind that only one wire is allowed under each screw.

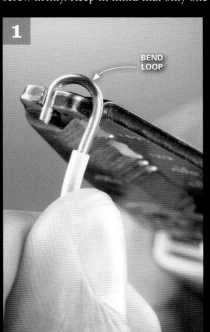

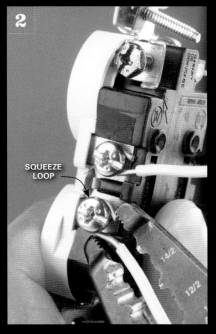

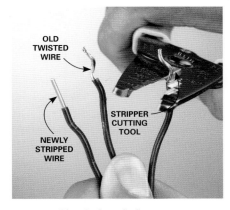

Cut off nicked, bent or twisted ends

Wires that are bent, twisted or nicked are weaker and won't nest together as easily in the connector. Before you reconnect wires to an outlet or switch, or rejoin several wires with a connector, cut off the old bare wire ends and strip the insulation to expose clean, straight wire. It takes a few extra seconds but ensures a better connection.

TIP

If cutting a wire leaves it too short to work with easily, splice on an additional 6-in. length with a wire connector.

Why circuit breakers trip

I t's a dark and stormy night. You flick on the hall light, plug in the coffee maker and crank up the portable electric heater. You're starting to feel comfy, when you hear a faint, yet ominous, click—and everything goes black. It's not a cat burglar or a poltergeist playing tricks with your electrical system. It's an overloaded circuit being protected by a tripped circuit breaker. Kinda spooky and mysterious, eh? Not if you know a few simple things.

What's a circuit? What's an overload?

When electricity enters your home, it goes to a circuit breaker box (or fuse box in older homes), where it's divided into a number of circuits. Each circuit is protected by a breaker or fuse. Bedrooms, living rooms and family rooms where only lights, alarm clocks and other small electrical items are usually used are normally on 15-amp circuits. Kitchens, laundry rooms, bathrooms and dining rooms—places where you're more likely to use toasters, irons, hair dryers and other big-watt items—are usually served by heavier-duty, 20-amp circuits. Major appliances like 5,000-watt electric water heaters and 10,000-watt electric ranges demand so much electricity that they take their own 30- to 50-amp dedicated circuit (Figure D), protected by big, "double pole" breakers.

The circuit breaker, the wire and even the wire insulation are all designed to work as a system—and that system has limits. Try to push more current through a circuit than it's designed for and things start happening (Figure B). Wires heat up under the burden of carrying the excess current. When this happens, the insulation around the wire can degrade or even melt. When insulation melts, current is no longer confined within the wire. That's when fires start. Luckily, the circuit breaker senses the excess current and "trips" to stop the flow of power before damage occurs.

On the night the lights went out at your house, you were fine with only the lights and coffee maker operating. The real trouble began when you plugged in that darn space heater.

Figure A
A properly functioning 15-amp circuit

This circuit has wires and a circuit breaker that can easily carry the amperage and the electrical items being served.

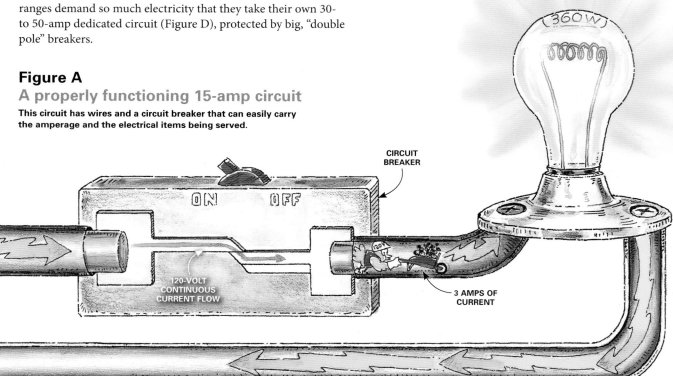

```
120   VOLTS
x 3   AMPS
360   WATTS
```

(360W)

CIRCUIT BREAKER

ON   OFF

120-VOLT CONTINUOUS CURRENT FLOW

3 AMPS OF CURRENT

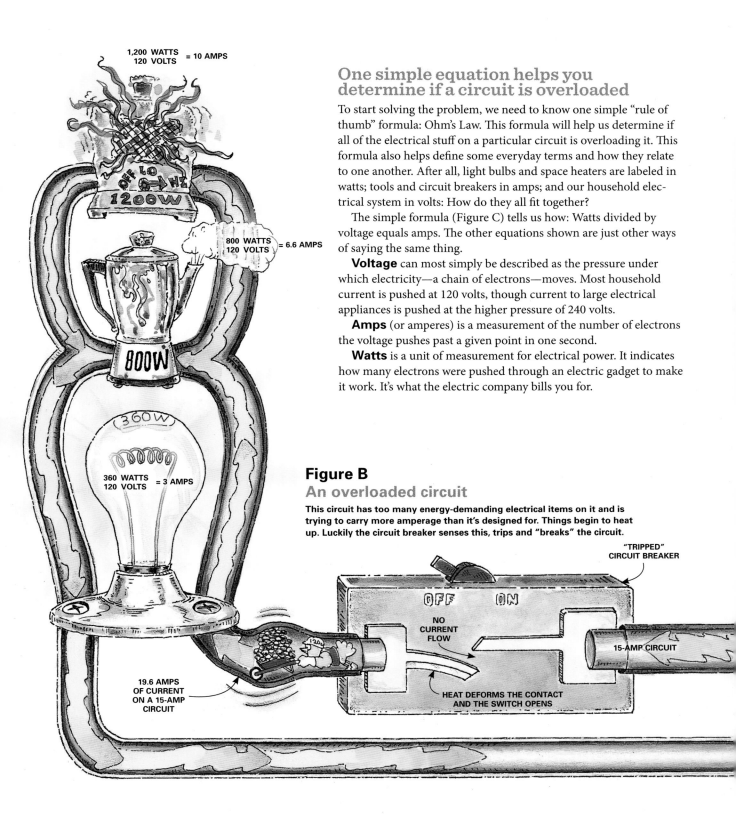

1,200 WATTS / **120 VOLTS** = 10 AMPS

800 WATTS / **120 VOLTS** = 6.6 AMPS

360 WATTS / **120 VOLTS** = 3 AMPS

One simple equation helps you determine if a circuit is overloaded

To start solving the problem, we need to know one simple "rule of thumb" formula: Ohm's Law. This formula will help us determine if all of the electrical stuff on a particular circuit is overloading it. This formula also helps define some everyday terms and how they relate to one another. After all, light bulbs and space heaters are labeled in watts; tools and circuit breakers in amps; and our household electrical system in volts: How do they all fit together?

The simple formula (Figure C) tells us how: Watts divided by voltage equals amps. The other equations shown are just other ways of saying the same thing.

Voltage can most simply be described as the pressure under which electricity—a chain of electrons—moves. Most household current is pushed at 120 volts, though current to large electrical appliances is pushed at the higher pressure of 240 volts.

Amps (or amperes) is a measurement of the number of electrons the voltage pushes past a given point in one second.

Watts is a unit of measurement for electrical power. It indicates how many electrons were pushed through an electric gadget to make it work. It's what the electric company bills you for.

Figure B
An overloaded circuit

This circuit has too many energy-demanding electrical items on it and is trying to carry more amperage than it's designed for. Things begin to heat up. Luckily the circuit breaker senses this, trips and "breaks" the circuit.

"TRIPPED" CIRCUIT BREAKER

OFF   ON

NO CURRENT FLOW

15-AMP CIRCUIT

19.6 AMPS OF CURRENT ON A 15-AMP CIRCUIT

HEAT DEFORMS THE CONTACT AND THE SWITCH OPENS

Calculating why that breaker tripped

The circuit and circuit breaker that you tripped have a capacity of 15 amps, or 1,800 watts (15 amps x 120 volts = 1,800 watts). The lights drew 360 watts, or a measly 3 amps (360 watts divided by 120 volts = 3 amps)—well within the capacity of your 15-amp system. The 800-watt coffee maker (divided by 120 volts) drew 6.6 amps, substantially more power than the lights, but their combined 9.6-amp draw is still within the limits of the 15-amp circuit.

But when you plugged in the 1,200-watt space heater, the 10 amps it required, plus the draw of the other two items, pulled 19.6 amps through a 15-amp system (Figure B). It's like a python swallowing a pig; the system just can't handle the load. The circuit breaker tolerated this for a while. But when the excess current and resultant heat began deforming the two pieces of metal inside the breaker, they started "pulling the trigger." And when the metal pieces bent to a certain point, the trigger snapped two contact

Figure C
The basic formula, Ohm's Law

points apart, interrupting the flow of electricity and shutting down that circuit. If there's a huge, sudden draw on a circuit, or a short circuit or ground-fault, an electromagnetic sensor in the circuit breaker can pull the contact points apart, too. If you have fuses, the excess heat melts a wire inside the fuse, which in turn stops the flow of electricity.

If this had been a 20-amp circuit—one with larger No. 12 wire that could carry 2,400 watts—the breaker wouldn't have tripped. But once the wire is in the wall and the breaker is in the breaker box, there's not much you can do to upgrade an established circuit. But you do have other choices.

Two solutions: The simple and the long-term

The *simple* solution is to plug the space heater into an outlet on a circuit that has excess capacity. You can determine the existing load on a circuit fairly easily: Click off the circuit breaker, then flick on light switches and test outlets to see which ones no longer function. Then add up the total watt load of devices on that circuit. This is often easier said than done. Sometimes a circuit labeled "bedroom" will power outlets in the laundry room. Or the upper and lower outlets of a duplex receptacle will be on different circuits. Once you have a circuit mapped out and the electrical loads added up, you'll be able to tell if you can plug more devices into the circuit without overloading it.

As you add up the electrical loads, keep in mind that a wire rated at 15 amps can carry 15 amps all day long. However, 15-amp breakers and fuses can only carry 12 amps—80 percent of their rating—on a continuous basis.

Figure D
Common dedicated circuits

Appliance	Power Required (watts)
Electric Range	10,000 (240 volts)
Electric Dryer	5,000 (240 volts)
Space Heater	1,000 and up
Clothes Washer	1,150
Furnace (blower)	800
Microwave	700–1,400
Refrigerator (not required)	700
Freezer (not required)	700
Dishwasher	1,400
Central Vacuum	800
Whirlpool/Jacuzzi	1,000 and up
Garbage Disposer	600–1,200
Kitchen Countertop (two circuits)	
Toaster	900
Coffee maker	800
Toaster oven	1,400
Bathroom	
Blow dryer	1,000–2,000

Continuous basis is considered to be a circuit loaded to capacity for three hours or more. This 80 percent rule applies to all breakers and fuses.

The best long-term solution is to install a new dedicated circuit and outlet for the heater. Most electricians will suggest a dedicated circuit for any appliance that will draw more than half the capacity of a circuit. Figure D shows the wattage of appliances that commonly have dedicated circuits. Anytime you install a large electrical appliance—whether it's 120 or 240 volts—install it on its own dedicated circuit with the correct size wire and circuit breaker.

As you can see from Figure E, a 20-amp circuit with larger No. 12 wire can carry more current than a 15-amp circuit with No. 14 wire. When you're wiring or rewiring a kitchen, laundry room, bathroom or dining room, the National Electrical Code will require you to install 20-amp circuits, which can carry more current. If you use a lot of power tools, it makes sense to use 20-amp circuits for your garage, workshop and basement too.

No tampering allowed

Homeowners who put a "penny in the fuse box" to prevent fuses from blowing have *short-circuited brains*. Without a fuse to disrupt the flow of power when too many amps are pushed through a circuit, wires overheat, wire insulation melts and fires break out. And you can't simply replace a 15-amp breaker with a 20-amp breaker; that's the modern-day equivalent of putting a penny in the fuse box. Remember, the circuit breaker, wire and wire insulation are all designed and sized to work together—safely.

240-volt circuits

Larger appliances, like electric water heaters, dryers and stoves, require so much power that electricity is brought to them via 240-volt circuits. That's because the voltage in 240-volt circuits "pushes" twice as hard. For example, a 6,000-watt electric industrial oven on a 120-volt circuit would require a 50-amp circuit (6,000 watts divided by 120 volts = 50 amps). That would require mammoth wires. But that same 6,000-watt oven on a 240-volt circuit requires only a 25-amp circuit (6,000 divided by 240 = 25) and a smaller wire and circuit breaker.

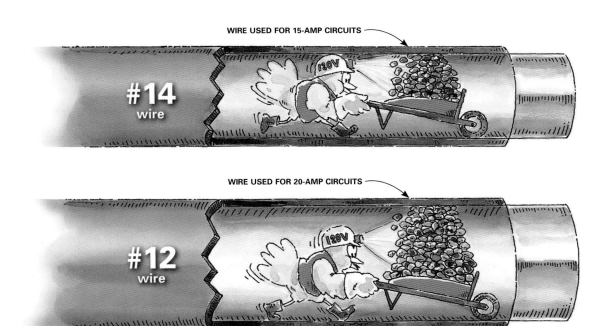

WIRE USED FOR 15-AMP CIRCUITS

#14 wire

WIRE USED FOR 20-AMP CIRCUITS

#12 wire

Figure E
Wire sizes
The larger 12-gauge wire can safely carry more amperage than the smaller 14-gauge wire—without overheating.

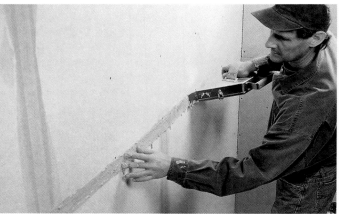

Chapter Three

FLOORS, WALLS & CEILINGS

Working alone with drywall

With special tools and techniques, one person can hang it as easily as two

SUPPORT HOOKS

FINISH SIDE FACES DOWN

Rent a drywall lift for ceiling work

If you have to drywall a ceiling, don't hesitate to rent a lift. It's well worth the daily rental fee and is by far the best way to get a ceiling up without back strain.

Drywall lifts break down into three parts and fit easily into a midsize car. After you reassemble it, release the catch on the wheel and crank it up and down a few times to make sure it's working smoothly. Then lock the lift and hoist one end of the drywall sheet up to the support hook—finish side down. Now lift the other end of the sheet up and slide it onto the second hook as shown. Lift slowly and smoothly—abrupt or jerky handling can pop the front edge of the drywall off the hook.

Tip the sheet so it's horizontal and lock it down. Then wheel the lift into approximate position. Lifts are stable and maneuverable, so you can fine-tune the placement when you raise the drywall (photo above). Then crank it tight. You may need to get up on a ladder to nudge the sheet into place. Put in at least eight screws before lowering the lift.

Make cutouts in place

Cutouts for lights and outlets are much faster and easier to make with the drywall in place, saving the trouble of taking the sheet down and recutting it if a precut hole doesn't quite fit. Use a spiral saw with a drywall bit, available at hardware stores and home centers. First, make sure to push electrical wires at least an inch back into the boxes, out of the way of the cutout bit. Next, measure and mark the approximate center points of the electrical boxes on the drywall, before you put it up. Crank the sheet up, and put in just enough screws to hold it in place, keeping the screws at least 16 in. from the cutout. Then punch the drywall cutout tool through the center mark and run it out to the edge until the bit hits the side of the fixture. Ease the bit up and over the edge to the outside of the can or box and slowly cut counterclockwise around it as shown. Drive nearby screws after the cutout is finished. (See p. 78 for more on using this tool.)

CENTER OF
RECESSED CAN LIGHT

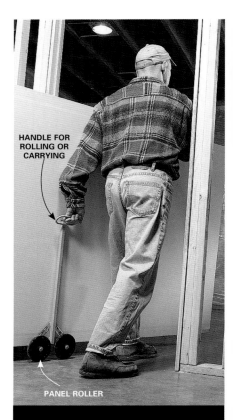

HANDLE FOR
ROLLING OR
CARRYING

PANEL ROLLER

Panel rollers make big jobs small

Have a few dozen sheets to move? Get the next best thing to having somebody carry the drywall for you—a heavy-duty panel roller that carries up to two sheets at a time (or anything else that's flat and heavy). Roll drywall almost effortlessly through the house, as we did in the photo above, using one hand to control the roller and the other to balance the sheet and steer around corners. The wheels tilt and roll over thresholds, and for bigger obstacles, just grasp the handle and lift the drywall as you would with a panel lifter. You can even tuck a sheet under your arm, a very simple and comfortable carrying position. This roller doesn't work on a full flight of stairs. Panel rollers are available at drywall and tool suppliers.

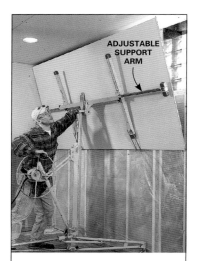

ADJUSTABLE
SUPPORT
ARM

Lifts work for walls, too

A lift works on upper wall sheets just as well as it does on ceilings. After loading the drywall, push the lift to the wall, position the sheet, tip the top edge against the wall and crank it snugly against the ceiling.

Preset nails (and use your head)

When you need to hold a piece up in place without the lift, preset a half-dozen drywall nails around the edges at joist or stud locations before you lift the sheet. Hoist it up, support it tightly against the ceiling joists with a hand and your head (a sponge under the hat helps), then drive in the nails to hold the piece in place. Fasten it off with screws.

HEAD IS
UNDER JOIST

FINISH SIDE

PANEL LIFTER

Ease the strain with a panel lifter

Take the strain off your arms and upper body and make navigating tight spots easier with a plastic panel lifter (shown above), available at home centers. Just hook the panel lifter around the bottom of the sheet at the center point, tip the sheet up and lift, leaving your lifting arm fully extended as if you were carrying a suitcase. Use your other arm to balance the sheet, keeping the drywall close to horizontal. You'll be amazed—you can move drywall with half the effort. But it doesn't work on full flights of stairs. Get a helper for that.

Add nailers instead of recutting

You've wrestled a heavy sheet up, put in half the screws and just noticed that you slightly miscut the sheet. Before you go through the hassle of taking the sheet down and recutting, try these possible fixes:

1. Tack a 2x4 to the side of the joist as a nailer for the next piece (photo right)—or for the piece you've just put up, if it's short.

2. Create a floating seam by screwing the unsupported end to a 1x4 that you slide on top of it. Let the 1x4 overlap the end about 1-1/2 in. Then screw the next piece to the 1x4 as well. Cut the 1x4 longer than the piece you're seaming so that adjoining sheets will help support it.

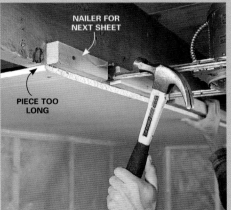

NAILER FOR NEXT SHEET

PIECE TOO LONG

Measure tight but cut loose

Putting drywall up and then taking it down to shave an edge that won't fit is a waste of energy if you're alone. Instead, subtract 1/4 in. from your measurements to make up for rough cuts and wavy walls. It's easier to fill slight gaps with joint compound than to struggle with a tight fit.

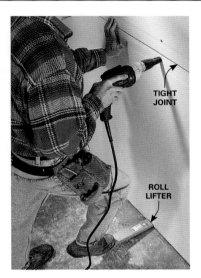

TIGHT JOINT

ROLL LIFTER

ROLL LIFTER

Lever; don't lift

Rather than straining to hold lower sheets up off the floor, lever them up snug against the upper sheet with a pry bar and a block of wood or a roll lifter.

Making cutouts with a spiral saw

This specialized tool is especially worth buying if you have a big drywalling job on the horizon. Here we'll show you how to cut around electrical outlets and lights when you're hanging drywall. You can also make cutouts for windows and doors.

You'll find spiral saws in the tool section of home centers, at drywall suppliers and at online tool sellers. For maximum versatility, consider buying the kit that contains the angle grinder attachment. You'll also need bits. For drywall work, buy a package of guidepoint bits.

Spiral saws are noisy and dusty, so don't forget your safety gear. Safety glasses, hearing protection and a good-quality (two-strap) dust mask are essential.

Setup is simple

After you insert the bit into the collet, pull it out until about 1/8 in. of the smooth part of the shank is showing before tightening the collet. This will help prevent bit breakage. Then adjust the base so that the bit protrudes about 1/4 in. beyond the depth of the material you're cutting.

You'll hang drywall in half the time

When you use a spiral saw to cut outlets, doors and windows, there's no need for precise measuring. Simply mark the approximate center of each electrical box or other opening on the face of the drywall and cut them out after the sheet is loosely attached to the framing.

Before you hang the drywall, turn off the power to the electrical boxes. Then press the wires to the back of the box to avoid damaging them with the bit. A hammer handle works well for this job.

When you hang the sheets, don't place any fasteners within about 16 in. of an electrical box until you've cut it out. Otherwise, the drywall is pressed against the box, and it will break out before you finish the cut, creating extra patching work. Use symbols to mark nonstandard boxes so you'll have a better idea what you're cutting around. For example, draw a square for doublewide boxes or a circle for round light fixture boxes. Make sure you mark and cut every box. Searching for missing electrical boxes buried in finished walls is no fun. Cut counterclockwise when you're going around the outside of a box, window or other protruding object (Photo 3). Move the spiral saw clockwise if you're cutting around the inside of an opening such as a hole in the wall for a recessed medicine cabinet.

Use a spiral saw to get a perfect fit for recessed lights in drywall. You don't need exact measurements.

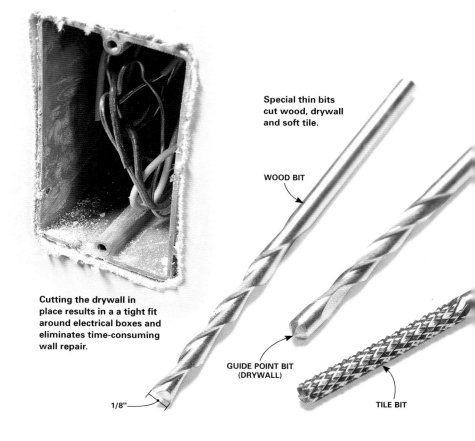

Cutting the drywall in place results in a a a tight fit around electrical boxes and eliminates time-consuming wall repair.

Special thin bits cut wood, drywall and soft tile.

WOOD BIT

GUIDE POINT BIT
(DRYWALL)

TILE BIT

1/8"

It takes practice to get a perfect cut

Cutting around a plastic electrical box isn't quite as easy as it looks. Put too much pressure on the bit and you'll cut right through the side of the soft plastic box. Try to apply just enough pressure to keep the tool moving around the outside edge of the box. Concentrate on feeling the edge of the box. Before you tackle the real thing, mock up a practice board by nailing a spare plastic box to a stud and covering it with a scrap of drywall. Practice routing around the box until you get the hang of it.

1 Mark the approximate center of the box. Hang the sheet with several screws placed at least 16 in. away from the box. Plunge the tip of the spinning bit into the drywall at your mark.

2 Move the tool slowly to the right until you feel the edge of the box, then stop. With the tool still running, move the bit up and over the edge of the box.

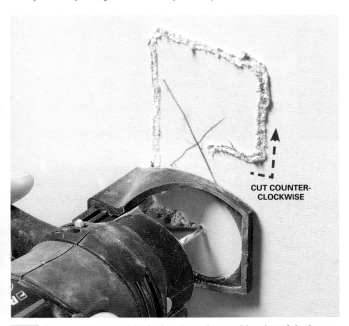

3 Run the bit counterclockwise along the outside edge of the box to complete the cut. Apply just enough pressure to keep the bit in contact with the outside edge of the box.

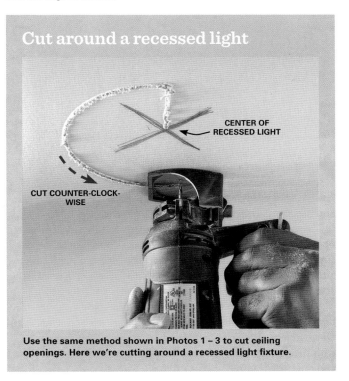

Cut around a recessed light

Use the same method shown in Photos 1 – 3 to cut ceiling openings. Here we're cutting around a recessed light fixture.

Drywall taping

*A color-coded
guide to
flat, smooth,
perfect walls*

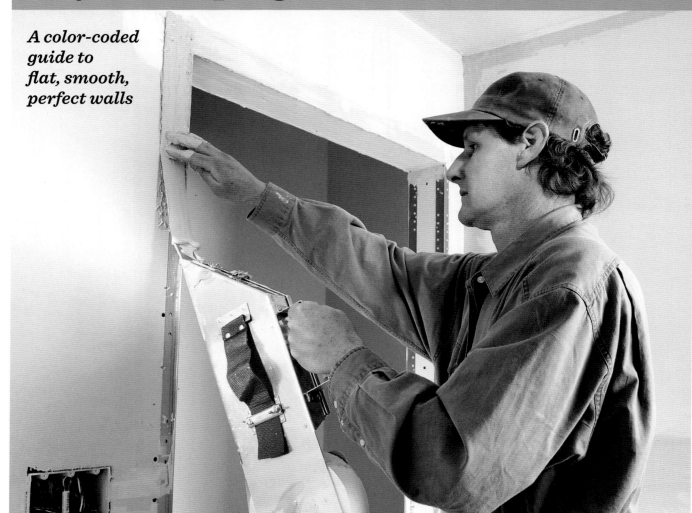

Taping drywall can be a frustrating, gut-wrenching experience. Flaws will show up right after painting and even months later. Nail pops, corner-bead cracks and bad joints will plague your walls forever.

To make your next taping job more successful, we've come up with a novice-friendly guide for getting good results. We've simplified professional techniques so you can learn them easily and recommended the basic tools and materials you'll need to achieve smooth, flat walls ready for paint.

Since 90 percent of the cost of a professional job is labor, taping your walls yourself can save you hundreds of dollars, even on small jobs. The key is a methodical, step-by-step approach with the proper tools and materials. Otherwise, taping will drive you nuts.

We'll show you how to avoid the most common rookie mistake: heaping on mud and then counting on a massive (and filthy) sanding effort at the end to rectify mistakes. We'll also show you how to gradually build up layers, feather edges to avoid ridges and knock off high areas of freshly applied mud.

We've added a color to each coat of mud to make it easier to see the proper order of application. The first coat is orange, the second green and the third yellow.

Although this three-coat taping system is standard, you may find that problem areas require more coats. Even the pros go back over difficult areas a fourth or even fifth time. Carefully examine the walls after each coat to determine areas that need more attention.

Prep work

BROKEN-OUT CORNER

1 Score the paper around broken corners, blisters or other damaged areas in the drywall with a utility knife. Peel the paper away and remove any broken or loose gypsum core. Lightly sand rough paper and scored edges with a sanding sponge.

Buy or rent these taping tools

You'll find a mind-boggling assortment of gimmicky taping tools at home centers. The truth is, most aren't worth having and you can do an excellent job with just the ones we recommend. Banjos (Photos 5 and 6) and clinchers (Photo 3) can speed up and improve the job. They're a must for larger rooms with lots of corners. But for small jobs, skip the banjo, and if you only have a few corner beads to do, nail them on by hand and skip the clincher too.

1. **Four-inch flexible putty knife** (Photo 7) for small filling jobs and applying second- and third-coat mud to angles (inside corners).
2. **Six-inch flexible putty knife** (Photo 2) for larger filling jobs, embedding tape and filling fastener holes.
3. **"Potato masher" mixer** (Photo 5) for hand-mixing a bucket of mud quickly and thoroughly.
4. **Mud pan** (Photo 2) for convenient dispensing of patching, fastener hole and corner mud.
5. A **clincher** (Photo 3) makes quick work of crimping corner beads accurately in place to hold them for nailing.
6. A **12-in. trowel** is less fatiguing and easier to use for applying mud to the joints and corner beads than the standard wide taping knives.
7. A **banjo** is essential for all but the smallest taping jobs for dispensing mud-saturated tape right onto the drywall joints.

Selecting and mixing mud

Mud comes in "setting-type" and "drying-type" varieties.

Buy **setting compounds** only for filling gaps and repairing broken drywall corners (Photo 2). Setting compounds contain plaster of Paris to make them chemically harden. They're available with different setting times, in sandable and non-sandable versions (buy the sandable type). Once mixed with water, setting compounds can harden fast. Mix small batches so you'll have plenty of time to work before the compound sets.

Buy **drying compounds** for actual taping. They come in powder or premixed in 5-gallon pails. We prefer premixed because it's easier to mix and store. Despite its name, premixed compound is not ready for taping when you open the pail. You'll need to add a little water and thoroughly mix the compound to the desired consistency before using it for the first time and before you begin taping each day.

Drying-type compounds come in three forms: taping, topping and our choice, all-purpose. All-purpose is designed to be used for all three coats in the typical three-coat taping system.

A 12 x 12-ft. addition will require about two 5-gallon pails of mud. You won't need more than a few gallons of mud for the first coat, and since it's mixed runnier than succeeding coats, transfer some mud to a clean 5-gallon pail before mixing and thinning it. Don't let our colors throw you off; the mud for the second and third coats is exactly the same.

To keep the mud from drying out as you work, loosely cover the pails. At the end of the day, wipe down the insides of the pails and the bottom of the lid with a sponge to remove any deposits. Otherwise, dried chunks of mud will fall into the mix and you'll discover the little troublemakers when you're spreading mud. Then lock the lids on tightly. Every new day of taping, remix the mud before using, adding water as needed.

Prep work

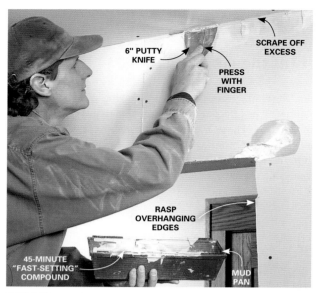

2 Mix 45-minute setting-type taping compound in a mud pan to the consistency of peanut butter. Fill damaged areas and cracks more than 3/8 in. wide with a 6-in. knife. Keep mud flush with surrounding drywall, never raised. Setting compound is hard to sand after it sets.

Buy the old-fashioned, time-tested materials—they're what pros use

Just as with tools, there are many new drywall products on the market purporting to make taping easier. But talk to a pro and you'll find that few of them work any better or are any more durable than the old-fashioned taping supplies like paper tape and 1-1/4 in. solid metal corner beads.

Pick up enough corner beads to cover every corner with a single bead—no splicing!—plus one or two extras to replace mistakes. You'll also need a small box of 1-5/8 in. drywall nails for fastening the corner beads. One roll of paper tape is usually plenty for the average-sized room.

> **TIP**
>
> Drag the knife over all the fastener heads and listen for the metallic "click" of a protruding head. Set the screw- or nailhead slightly below the surface with a screw gun or a hammer.

Spend the time on the prep work; it'll pay off in the end

No matter how accomplished you are as a taper, bad or incomplete prep work will make taping tougher than it has to be.

Photos 1 – 4 show the basic steps so the taping will hold up over the long haul.

3 Cut corner beads to length with tin snips and hold them in place to make sure beads meet perfectly at corners. Clinch corner beads into place with a clincher. Run a 6-in. putty knife along the bead and adjoining drywall (on both sides) to make sure you've left a void to fill with mud. Then anchor the corner beads through the drywall into surrounding framing with 1-5/8 in. drywall nails spaced every 8 in. Drive extra nails into edges that don't lie flat.

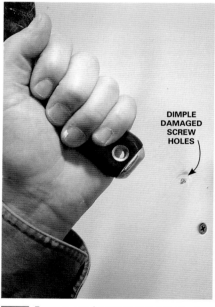

4 Remove any fasteners that have broken through the paper surface or missed the framing, and drive a replacement screw above or below the location into solid wood. Slightly dent the damaged paper left from extracted fasteners by tapping the spot with the butt of the knife handle.

First coat: Embedding the tape

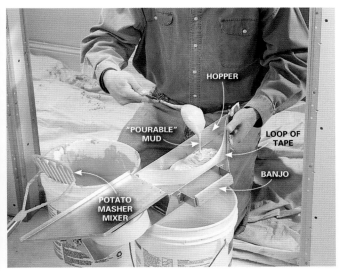

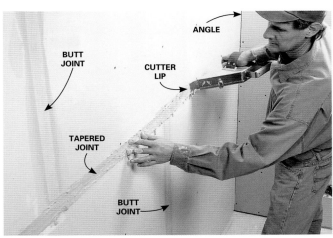

5 Mix the first-coat mud to the consistency of honey with a "potato masher" mixer, adding water as necessary. Load the banjo spool with a roll of tape and ladle mud into the hopper *underneath* a loop of tape.

6 Apply the tape by holding one end of the tape against the joint with your hand while drawing away the banjo to pull out the tape. Press the wet tape into joints by dragging your fingers over the tape. Spread a little mud on the 6-in. knife and embed the tape by dragging the knife over the tape, pressing it tight to the drywall. Mud on the knife lubricates it so it won't pull at the tape. Thoroughly moisten the tape for good adhesion. Cover the butt joints first, then the tapered joints.

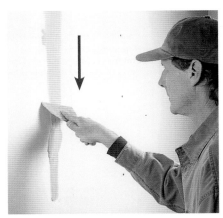

7 Apply the tape to the angles with the banjo and smooth it into the corner with the 4-in. knife, taking care to smoothly crease the tape at the center. Then cover the corner-bead flanges with tape (see opening photo) and scrape off any excess.

8 Fill fastener holes by spreading a narrow band of mud upward over a column of screw- or nailheads with the edge of the 6-in. knife.

9 Drag the end of the knife over the filler swipe to scrape away all of the surface mud. Use this technique at the end of each of the three coats to fill and refill all fastener holes.

The "first coat" consists of applying the mud-saturated tape to all of the joints and corner beads and filling screw or nail holes for the first time. Begin with the butt joints first, then the horizontal tapered joints, then the angles and finally, the corner beads.

The easy way to apply the tape is to use the banjo, which not only dispenses the tape but also evenly saturates it with mud while you pull it off the spool. If you're just working on a small area like a closet, skip the banjo and stick the tape on by hand into a layer of mud, then spread another coat over the top and embed the tape with a knife.

You'll be surprised how quickly you'll learn to play the banjo. The key is to mix the first coat of mud to the consistency of honey (it should be pourable) and spoon it into the hopper

underneath a loop of tape. The right mix will result in even, complete mud coverage on both sides of the tape as you pull the tape out of the banjo and feed it onto the wall (Photo 6). Don't be afraid to get your fingers dirty. As you feed out the tape, press and smooth it onto the centers of drywall joints with your fingers, then use the lip of the banjo to cut the tape to length. While you have the banjo in your hands, stick tape onto several joints at once, and then press the tape flat onto the joints with a 6-in. knife and tool off any excess mud.

After all the joints are covered, apply and flatten the tape over corner-bead edges (opening photo). Although some pros skip this step, a layer of tape is easy, cheap insurance against cracked corner-bead edges later.

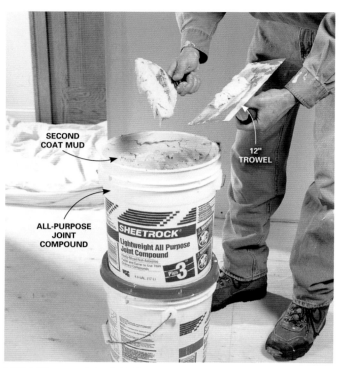

Some pros use special wide taping knives for applying second- and third-coat mud, while others use conventional cement trowels like we did. If you've used knives successfully, great! But if you're a first-timer, you'll probably find a trowel easier to master and less fatiguing. Both take patience and time to get the right touch. When you're first spreading the mud onto the wall to distribute it, hold the trowel at an angle away from the wall and slowly lower the leading edge as you empty the trowel (Photo 11). After the mud is on the wall, go back and hold the trowel flatter to smooth it out.

The second coat is the toughest coat to apply, especially on the butt joints. Don't be shy about spreading this coat over a wide area. It really takes six passes with the trowel to handle a butt joint: three trowel-wide passes to apply the mud and three more to flatten the middle, smooth out the mud and feather the sides. When you're through, the center should barely cover the tape, while the two sides feather out the center mound.

Different joints require different strategies, as we show in the series of photos. Butt joints, which join untapered ends, are by far the toughest because you have to build a wide, gradual "plateau" of mud and feather the edges to make the joint appear flat. In contrast, tapered joints along the long sides of drywall have recessed manufactured edges that are much easier to fill and level. They're handled the same as butt joints, but the second coat doesn't have to be nearly as wide or as built up because of the recess of the tapered edges.

SECOND COAT MUD

12" TROWEL

ALL-PURPOSE JOINT COMPOUND

10 Mix second- (and third) coat mud to the consistency of creamy mashed potatoes, adding water as necessary. Scoop mud out of the bucket and onto the trowel with the 6-in. knife for spreading on the wall.

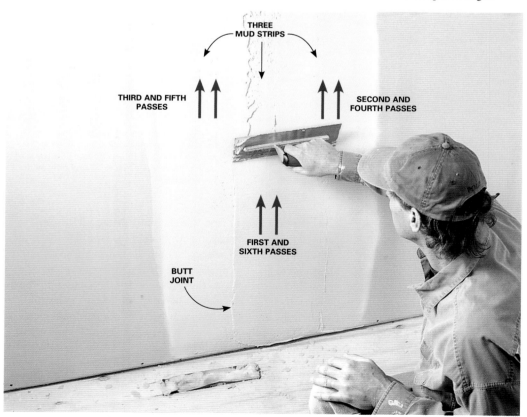

THREE MUD STRIPS

THIRD AND FIFTH PASSES

SECOND AND FOURTH PASSES

FIRST AND SIXTH PASSES

BUTT JOINT

11 Lay on a 1/8-in. thick mound of mud across the centers of butt joints, then two more strips of mud on either side of the center strip. Make three more passes, feather the outer edges flat, then smooth the center.

Filling corner beads is about the simplest of taping tasks because you have the hard, defined surface of the corner bead to guide application (Photo 12). Just make sure to feather the edges flat to the drywall.

Inside angles only get one additional *thin* coat of mud— on one side during the second coat (Photo 14) and on the other during the third-coat layer (Photo 17)—with each side done alternately so one side is always dry when you coat the other side. That way you have a hard surface to drag your knife against. Again, feather all outside mud edges flat, then refill all the fastener holes.

LAY IN MUD

FEATHERED EDGES

LEVELING STROKE

12 Butter the sides of corner beads, then level and smooth out the mud with the trowel. Fill both sides of the corner beads to the brim of the bead, feathering the outer edges flat to the surface of the drywall.

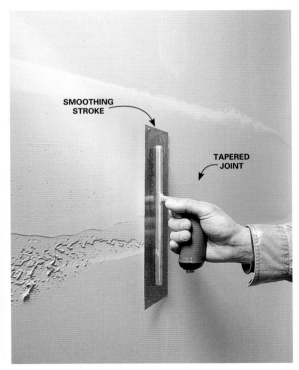

SMOOTHING STROKE

TAPERED JOINT

13 Lay the second coat on tapered joints using the same technique demonstrated in Photo 11, but keep the entire width of this coat only a few inches wider than the length of the trowel.

ALTERNATE SIDES

4" KNIFE

14 Spread a thin layer of mud over one side of vertical and ceiling angles with a 4-in. knife. Apply more pressure to the outside of the knife blade to wipe off excess mud and leave a feathered edge. Refill fastener holes (as in Photos 8 and 9).

Third coat: Fill and smooth low spots and other imperfections

Before getting started on the third coat, scrape down or sand any projecting ridges over seams and any excess mud on the corner-bead edges. If you did a competent job of applying the second coat, the third coat will entail filling in imperfections such as low spots, craters and tool marks. Use a "raking" light to highlight areas that need special attention. Hold the light against the wall so it shines across the surface to make all the problem spots apparent before you start. The second coat shrinks as it dries, so fastener holes and corner beads need to be filled with a third coat of mud.

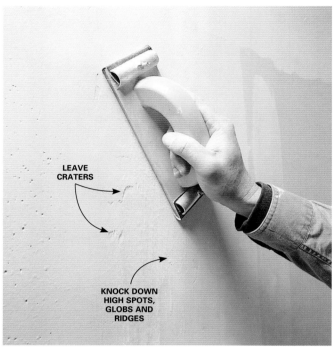

LEAVE CRATERS

KNOCK DOWN HIGH SPOTS, GLOBS AND RIDGES

15 Knock off excess dried mud from the edges of corner beads, tool ridges and high spots before beginning the third coat. Use a drywall sander and 100-grit paper or sanding sponge.

16 Fill low spots and other imperfections and feather the edges on all butt and taper joints. Finish filling corner bead by spreading another coat of mud using the same technique as with the second coat.

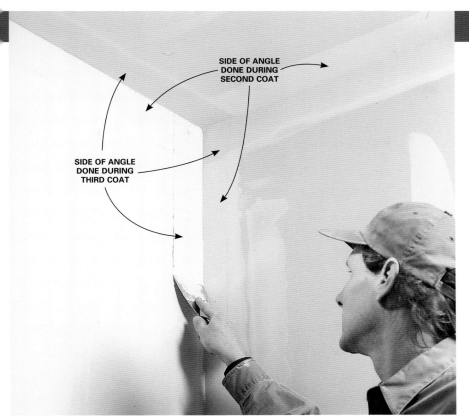

SIDE OF ANGLE DONE DURING SECOND COAT

SIDE OF ANGLE DONE DURING THIRD COAT

17 Spread a layer of mud over the second sides of all angles to finish them. Refill the fastener holes for the third and last time.

Time to sand—yuck!

Sanding is the last step in achieving smooth walls. It's also the least pleasant. Buy yourself a pole sander for the large areas, a hand sander for detail work and 120-grit paper and a medium 3M sanding sponge for cleaning up the angles. The total investment will be money well spent.

Use the raking-light technique to constantly check progress and highlight irregularities that need more work. Be very careful not to oversand, especially in angles and on butt joints where mud layers barely cover the tape. Quit sanding the center of butt joints as soon as inconsistencies disappear. Angles only need light sanding. Try not to sand onto unmudded paper drywall surfaces too much or abraded paper will show through the paint. If you expose tape while sanding, you'll need to add more mud and let it dry before sanding again. Exposed tape will show through multiple layers of paint.

Tips from our expert

Our expert taper gave us this list of important tips for rookies:

- Cut corners off corner beads at roughly 45 degrees because sharp corners tend to curl through the mud (see Photo 3).
- Feather the outside edges of each and every coat wherever you're taping so they're flush with the drywall.
- Never leave up any tape that has a dry bond against the drywall. You'll be able to tell by the light color. Peel back and fill tape that's still wet, or cut out and replace tape that's already dried.
- Don't worry about eliminating small ripples, ridges or craters during the second coat. They'll get filled, scraped or sanded off during the third coat. Just try to get the distribution as even as possible.
- Never return leftover mud to the pail. There are bound to be chunks in it that'll plague you the rest of the job.
- Spray texture won't hide poor taping, so don't get sloppy on ceilings.

Using milk paint

Milk paint delivers rich color, durability and that good old-fashioned charm

A fresh coat of paint on dingy doors and moldings will bring ho-hum rooms to life no matter what type of paint you use. But painting them with milk paint—as shown here—adds yet another dimension. Milk paint's deep, rich, naturally uneven color adds depth and age to whatever you're painting. And if you like, you can stencil on a special design, too. For more details on this unique product, see "Milk Paint Pros and Cons," p. 91.

You won't find milk paint and milk paint bonding agent at most home centers, but some paint stores carry it, and it's readily

1 Sand the door using a fine-grit sanding sponge or sandpaper. Apply putty to any gouges or dents, and then sand smooth. Wash all surfaces with TSP or a TSP substitute, then rinse. The 16d nails at each corner suspend the door and allow you to flip it over to work on the other side without smearing or damaging the wet paint.

FINE-GRIT SANDING SPONGE

16d NAIL

2 Mix the powdered milk paint and water. The blender helps break up and dissolve any dry lumps of paint. Dry lumps will cause streaking and lots of headaches. Add the bonding agent to the first coat to improve adhesion to previously painted surfaces.

WATER

BONDING AGENT

BLENDER

POWDERED MILK PAINT

available online. Just search "milk paint" and "milk paint bonding agent" for suppliers.

Even if you choose to use good old latex paint, read on anyway. The processes shown here for painting, masking and stenciling can still be used. Here's how:

Prep the door and mix the paint

Begin by removing all the door hardware—screws, hinges, latches and knobs. Pound 16d nails, 1 in. deep, in the top and bottom of the door near each corner to use as handles for suspending the door horizontally (Photo 1) and for flipping it over as you work.

Milk paint is typically used over raw wood, but it can be applied over painted surfaces provided you take two precautions: First, lightly roughen the surface (Photo 1) so the paint can "grab." Second, add a milk paint bonding agent to the first coat of paint (Photo 2) to ensure adhesion.

To mix the milk paint, simply combine one part water to one part powder. The key to getting a uniform color is to mix the paint thoroughly in a blender. (Don't fret—it's a safe thing to do, and as long as you wash out the blender immediately, no one will ever know.) This is especially critical if you're combining two colors. Inadequate mixing will result in small dry lumps that hide in the paint mix, only to reveal themselves as dark streaks when

> **CAUTION:** Paint dust and chips from lead paint are hazardous. If your home was built before 1977, the year lead paint was banned, call your local public health department and ask about paint testing details and safe scraping, sanding and cleaning techniques, or visit epa.gov/lead.

you brush on the paint. Strain the paint (Photo 3) to further minimize this problem. If you're going over a painted surface, add one part bonding agent to two parts mixed paint for your first coat of paint.

Practice, patience and painting tips

You can't predict the exact results when you use milk paint; that's part of its charm. Every surface—whether painted or unpainted—absorbs and alters the paint colors differently. Unpainted woods may require only a single coat to reach the color you desire. On the other hand, the white painted door shown here required four coats of the light blue to cover the inner panel but only two coats of the gold to cover the panel molding. Don't worry if you're not happy with the first coat of paint. You can apply additional coats or tint coats until you obtain the density and shade of color you want.

Practice to develop a feel for applying milk paint. If possible, use the back of a closet door or other inconspicuous area to hone your technique. The instructions that come with the paint are excellent. Follow the procedure outlined in Photos 1 – 6 and keep these tips in mind:

- Stir the paint every 10 minutes to keep the pigment from settling. The paint also thickens as it sits out, so once you start working, keep at it.
- For the most natural look, apply your brushstrokes in the direction of the wood grain, even if the wood has been previously painted.
- Apply the paint in long, unbroken strokes, from end to end or side to side.
- Don't go back over the paint once it begins drying. Your brush will leave streaks.

Your first coat may not cover completely. That's OK—just leave

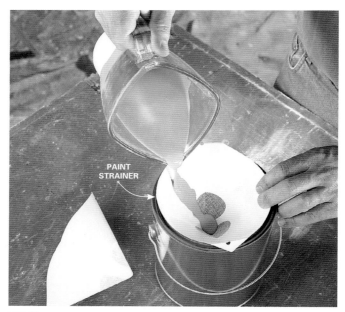

3 Strain the paint using a cone-shaped paint strainer or cheesecloth. The goal is to eliminate dry lumps of powdered milk paint.

PAINT STRAINER

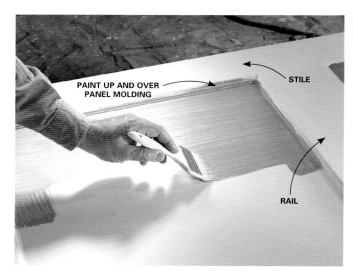

PAINT UP AND OVER PANEL MOLDING

STILE

RAIL

4 Apply paint to the inner panels of the door first, using either a bristle or a sponge brush. Apply paint up, over and onto the panel molding. Start with horizontal strokes along the top and bottom stiles to make sure the moldings, nooks and crannies get a thorough coat of paint, then finish with top-to-bottom strokes. When going over old paint, two or more coats will be required; a single coat may suffice over raw wood.

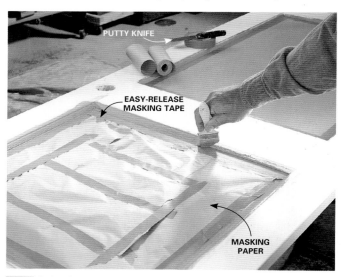

PUTTY KNIFE

EASY-RELEASE MASKING TAPE

MASKING PAPER

5 Paint the panel molding after masking off the completely dry inner panels. Press the masking tape *firmly* in place with the blade of a putty knife so no paint runs under and onto the inner panel. Again, apply paint up, over and onto the rails and stiles to ensure complete coverage.

SPONGE BRUSH OVERHANGS STILES AND RAILS

6 Use a sponge brush to apply paint to the rails and stiles. Paint horizontal rails first, then the vertical stiles. By using a stiff sponge brush and letting it overhang the stiles and rails, you'll get a clean edge without having to use masking tape to protect the molding.

it alone. Subsequent coats will build up layers of color for a more uniform look.

Fancy stenciling with this simple technique

This door was finished by stenciling the top and bottom panels, again using milk paint. Stencils and stencil brushes are sold at hobby stores and online. The stencil we used consisted of four separate stencils, each with a different set of cutouts for applying four different colors. Even though the process is simple, *the single most important thing you can do to ensure success is to practice for 15 minutes on scrap cardboard.*

Tape the first stencil in place, centering the pattern on the

door. Dip the very tip of your special stencil brush in the paint, then dab it repeatedly on a paper towel or other surface (Photo 7) until the brush is almost dry; when it leaves individual bristle marks rather than blobs of paint, the brush is ready. Hold the brush vertically and dab the paint through the cutouts in the stencil. Apply sparingly; you can always add another layer. For a three-dimensional look, darken some cutouts or portions of cutouts more than others.

When you have the right shade and depth of color, carefully remove the stencil. Once the paint is dry (and it dries in as little as five minutes), use the registration marks to position the second stencil, tape it in place, and then apply the second color. Continue until you've applied all colors.

DAB UNTIL
BRUSH IS DRY

STENCIL
BRUSH

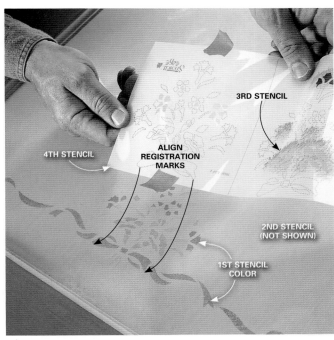

3RD STENCIL

ALIGN
REGISTRATION
MARKS

4TH STENCIL

2ND STENCIL
(NOT SHOWN)

1ST STENCIL
COLOR

7 Practice your stenciling technique. Dip 1/16 in. of the tip of your brush into the paint, then dab the tip on a paper towel or cardboard until it's almost out of paint, or "dry." Then practice dabbing the upright brush through a cutout until you get the depth of color you want.

8 Stencil away! Tape the first stencil in place and apply the first paint color through the first stencil's cutouts, the second color through the second stencil's cutouts and so on. Make certain the previous colors are dry before positioning the next stencil. Apply a clear coat to protect against water marks and dirt. Experiment first; some clear finishes will darken the paint color.

Milk paint pros and cons

Today's milk paints are formulated much like those of old—from milk and other earthy ingredients like lime, clay, ochre and lampblack. Combined, these ingredients produce the rich, slightly uneven coloration often used for country-style furniture and interiors.

Beyond its unique look, milk paint has other special qualities:

■ You can thin it and use it as a stain or wash on raw wood (see photo). You can force-dry it with a hair dryer for a crackled look. You can burnish it with steel wool to give a worn-through, aged look to pieces of furniture.

■ Once applied and dried, the paint is incredibly hard and durable.

■ It doesn't fade.

■ It's nontoxic. It contains no chemical preservatives or petroleum products. It has a slightly "earthy" smell when first applied but once dry is odorless.

■ When stored in a dry, airtight container, the powdered paint will keep indefinitely.

■ It's versatile. As long as the surface is properly primed and prepared, milk paint can be used on bare wood, painted wood, metal, drywall, plaster and even glass.

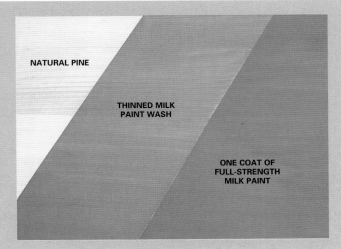

NATURAL PINE

THINNED MILK
PAINT WASH

ONE COAT OF
FULL-STRENGTH
MILK PAINT

On the downside:

■ It's hard to mix two batches that produce the exact same color. Try to mix in one batch all the paint you need for a coat.

■ Milk paint will water-spot easily and its matte finish clings to, and shows, dirt quite readily. Apply a clear topcoat of Danish oil, varnish, polyurethane—virtually any water- or oil-based finish—if the surface is exposed to water or dirt.

■ It will physically lift and pull paint from surfaces with blistered, flaking or poor-adhering finishes. You must scrape, sand, scrub or strip until you're down to a solid base.

Prefinished wood floor

Lay this hardwood floor, start to finish, in one weekend

Installing a new hardwood floor used to be a lot of commotion. You had to schedule an installation and have the installer haul in a pallet of raw hardwood flooring and bang it in with a huge mallet and floor nailer. The next day the work area had to be sealed from the rest of the house as the big sanding machines rolled in and created bags of sawdust. For the next three days, the staining and finishing process made the whole house smell bad, and it took at least a week for the finish to harden before you could bring in the furniture.

However, prefinished flooring has changed all that. Now you can install a new wood floor that's completely finished from A to Z in a single weekend. You'll be amazed at the beauty, practicality and speed of installation of a staple-down prefinished wood floor. You can literally start installing one day and be using the room the next day. And don't confuse this flooring with wood look-alike plastic laminate flooring. The type we show here has a wear layer that can be resanded a couple of times years down the road when the tough factory finish is finally compromised. Most experts agree that this is a 50-year or more floor.

Here we'll show you how to install your own prefinished wood floor. We'll give you tips on buying, cutting and layout and explain how much prep is needed before you start. We'll also give you tips on how to deal with transitions from one room to another.

We chose a special type of prefinished flooring, called "engineered" flooring. It's about 3/8 to 5/8 in. thick and usually made of several layers of wood laminated together, much like plywood. This method of construction creates a floor that's more stable than one made of solid wood, with less seasonal movement and fewer cracks between planks during the dry season. In fact, engineered flooring is so stable that manufacturers allow its use in areas like basements as long as there isn't a moisture problem. Most engineered flooring can be glued down instead when stapling isn't possible, for example, where in-floor heating lies directly below. You can also buy "floating floors" made from wood planks laid on a thin, padded underlayment and simply locked together, with no fasteners. Floating floors can be installed over wood or concrete subfloors. The thin profile of engineered wood flooring makes it a great candidate for remodeling because you can install it over an existing floor without significantly changing floor heights and transitions from one room to another.

For tools, you'll need a flooring stapler (right) and an air compressor. An air-powered finish nailer is handy but not necessary. A jigsaw will cut lengths and intricate cuts around vents and doorways, and a table saw is best for rip cuts near a wall. The other tools are inexpensive. You can get a tap block (Photo 5) and a pull bar where you buy the flooring. Follow the step-by-step photos for the basics and then read the text for tips and special instructions.

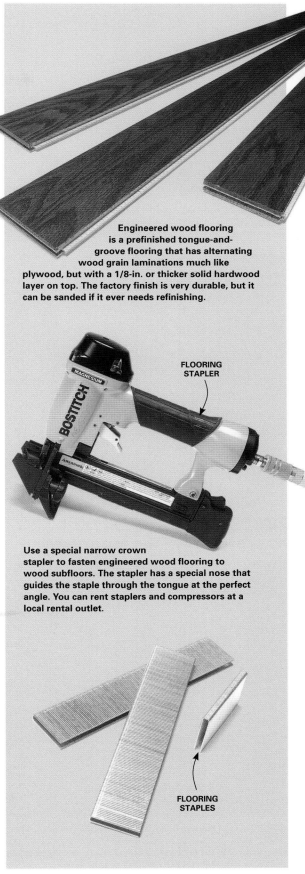

Engineered wood flooring is a prefinished tongue-and-groove flooring that has alternating wood grain laminations much like plywood, but with a 1/8-in. or thicker solid hardwood layer on top. The factory finish is very durable, but it can be sanded if it ever needs refinishing.

FLOORING STAPLER

Use a special narrow crown stapler to fasten engineered wood flooring to wood subfloors. The stapler has a special nose that guides the staple through the tongue at the perfect angle. You can rent staplers and compressors at a local rental outlet.

FLOORING STAPLES

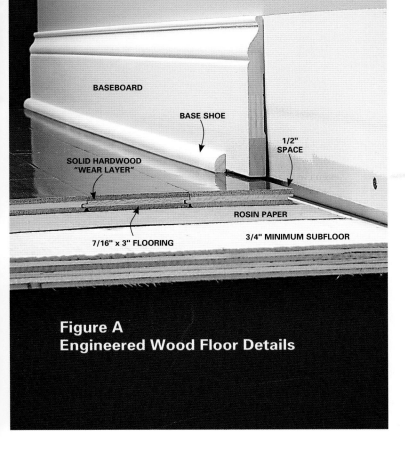

BASEBOARD

BASE SHOE

1/2" SPACE

SOLID HARDWOOD "WEAR LAYER"

ROSIN PAPER

7/16" x 3" FLOORING

3/4" MINIMUM SUBFLOOR

Figure A
Engineered Wood Floor Details

1 Remove the baseboard. Undercut the bottoms of the doorjambs and casing so the flooring can slide under them. Place a piece of flooring under a flexible trim saw and carefully cut the trim.

FLEXIBLE JAPANESE SAW

2 Tape and staple rosin paper to the subfloor. If your manufacturer prefers a different product, use that instead. Snap a line 1/2 in. plus the width of the flooring from the straightest wall in the room.

HAMMER TACKER

ROSIN PAPER

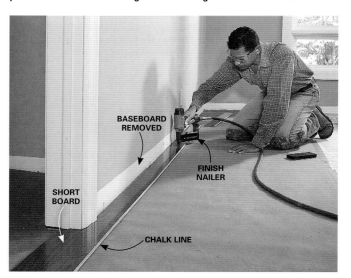

3 Nail the flooring (tongue out) along the line every 16 in. Use long pieces of flooring to establish an absolutely straight start. Slip a short piece into the doorway behind this first strip if a doorway is along the starting wall. It would be difficult to place later.

BASEBOARD REMOVED

FINISH NAILER

SHORT BOARD

CHALK LINE

Picking out the flooring that's best for you

For a wide selection, shop for engineered wood flooring at any retail store that specializes in flooring. Bring a few samples home and live with them for a few days. Then choose the type of wood, the texture (some look hand-planed for a rustic look), the stain color and a satin or gloss finish.

Calculate the area you want to cover and buy an extra 10 percent for waste. Just remember to buy your flooring several days before you start and leave it in the house to acclimate to the ambient temperature and humidity. Also ask the flooring retailer to recommend the appropriate floor stapler and the right length nails. If the store doesn't rent floor staplers, check with your local tool rental outlet. We rented a stapler (Photos 4 and 5) and purchased staples at a home center.

Get your room ready

Engineered wood flooring can be stapled down over a sound plywood or OSB underlayment grade subfloor. You can also staple it over an existing hardwood floor or a vinyl floor (one layer only). Just be sure the existing subfloor or floor is solid underfoot. You may need to add screws to get rid of squeaks or remove carpet or even a layer of floor covering.

If you're laying your new floor over subfloor like we did, make sure the edges of the plywood meet smoothly without ridges between them. If there's a slight raised edge, try adding a few screws and sanding it, or as a last resort, use underlayment filler and trowel it to feather out imperfections. Scrape away any paint globs or drywall chunks and thoroughly vacuum the whole area before starting the project. Also slide a 6-in. scraper along the surface to find any raised nails or screws and drive them down.

Remove the baseboard in the room so you can install the flooring closer to the wall. Most manufacturers want you to leave at least a 3/8-in. and sometimes a 1/2-in. expansion gap between the wall and the flooring.

If you have doors between rooms instead of archways, cut the bottoms of the casing and the jambs with a block of flooring and a flexible, Japanese-style crosscut saw or an oscillating saw. Concentrate on keeping the blade parallel to the floor for a clean, even cut. Vacuum the sawdust.

Cover the subfloor with rosin paper as shown in Photo 2 to create a slip area between the floor surfaces and help quiet any potential squeaks. Some manufacturers prefer a different product instead of rosin paper, so be sure to follow your manufacturer's suggestions. (Floating floors use a padded underlayment.)

Start along the straightest wall

Decide which direction you'd like the flooring to follow. Hallways look best with the planks running in the long direction; other rooms are a matter of taste. Some manufacturers recommend laying the floor perpendicular to the direction of the joists, but if you have a solid 3/4-in.-thick subfloor, either direction is fine.

Measure the width of a plank including the tongue and then add the appropriate wall clearance measurement to that. We needed 1/2-in. clearance. Mark that distance out from the wall at two spots about 1 ft. away from the corner. Measuring from

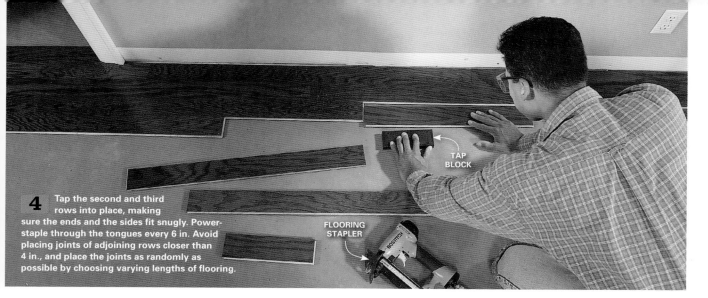

4 Tap the second and third rows into place, making sure the ends and the sides fit snugly. Power-staple through the tongues every 6 in. Avoid placing joints of adjoining rows closer than 4 in., and place the joints as randomly as possible by choosing varying lengths of flooring.

TAP BLOCK

FLOORING STAPLER

the corner isn't always accurate because of a buildup of drywall compound. Tap in a nail at one mark and then pull your chalk line tight through the marks and snap a starting line onto your paper (Photo 2).

If this starting wall has a doorway, be sure to fit a strip of flooring under the casing and jamb because it'll be difficult to slip in later. However, don't nail this piece in until you nail the first row into place. Bring in three boxes of flooring and then select boards from them randomly. Some boxes might contain more light or dark boards, so drawing from several boxes will keep the floor from looking patchy.

Select long strips for the first couple of rows because it's easier to align them with your chalk line (Photo 3). Start 1/2 in. away from the end wall. Face-nail the flooring with pairs of nails every 16 in. Make sure your nail gun sets the nail head just below the surface. Fill these holes later with a matching color putty. The face nailing is necessary because the stapler won't fit that close to the wall at this stage. If you have a piece in the doorway, tap it in and nail it now. Continue with a second row, making sure to alternate end joints by at least 4 in. from the previous row.

By the third row, you'll have enough space to use the flooring stapler. Before you use it, check the pressure at your compressor. Dial it to about 75 psi and test-staple a piece through the tongue somewhere along the floor. If you drive it flush with the wood surface at the tongue, it's perfect. If the staple is too deep or is still protruding above the tongue, adjust the pressure. Drive staples every 8 in. along the rows and get at least two staples in short planks. Tap the ends together and knock the plank sides together with the edge of your tap block (Photo 5).

The flooring is precisely milled, so you should never have to drive the tap block hard with your hammer. If the grooves aren't fitting into the tongues, check for splinters or crushed tongues and remove them or cut them back with your utility knife.

Continue installing the flooring, leaving a 1/2-in. expansion space on each end. Drive hard-to-get-at end pieces into place with a pull bar as shown in Photo 7. If you don't have a pull bar, you can position a pry bar between the wall and the end of the flooring. To avoid crushing the drywall, pry against a drywall knife.

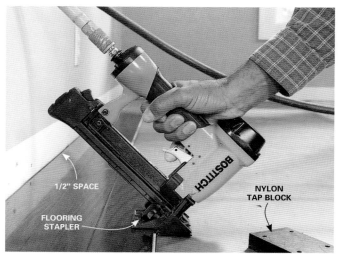

1/2" SPACE

FLOORING STAPLER

NYLON TAP BLOCK

5 Staple through the tongues of the flooring, making sure the boot of the stapler is in full contact with the floor surface. Practice a few shots before you begin, and adjust the pressure from your compressor to 70 to 80 psi, so the driven staple is flush with the wood of the tongue.

BACK SIDE OF FLOORING

6 Cut the flooring from the back side with a fine-tooth blade to avoid splintering. A jigsaw works well, especially for intricate cuts in doorways or around floor vents. Use a small table saw to rip pieces that lie against the end wall. Cut in another room to avoid dust.

Fitting special spots

You may encounter heating vents in the floor and along walls or even radiators in older homes. Floor registers (Photo 11) are easy to cut around. Just be sure to measure the bottom of the register so you get the opening the right size. Wall-mounted registers that meet the floor can often be removed and then repositioned on top of the flooring. Cast-iron radiators are the toughest and will have to be removed before you start and then reinstalled later. You may need a professional to help drain the system, remove the radiator, and then reinstall and refill the system later. Hot water baseboard heat has metal covers along the wall. Lift the covers off (look for clips), then unscrew the metal back plates. You can reinstall them later over the flooring.

After working your way across the room, you'll find that the nailer won't fit for the last two rows. Face-nail instead (Photo 8) and rip the last piece to fit. Use a pull bar to tighten the gaps and then nail the last rows about 1/2 in. back from the tongue edge. There's no need to pair up the nails here because you won't be tapping other pieces into them as you did on the first rows. Rip the last strips using a table saw and make sure to allow for an expansion gap as you did at the start.

7 Tap a special pull bar to tighten the end joints near the ends of rows when there's no room for a tap block.

Transitions to other flooring

Blending one kind of flooring into the next may call for a bit of improvisation and creativity. You can buy several options of prefinished transition pieces from your supplier to solve almost any floor height difference from one room to the next. You may have to modify them slightly with your table saw to make the transition as smooth as possible. For carpeting, it's best to position the last strip of flooring in the center of the doorway or directly under the door. If necessary, pull the carpeting up in the doorway and then restaple it as shown in the photo below.

When you're installing flooring up to an existing vinyl or wood floor, leave an expansion space between the floors and then nail a transition piece over the gap. Be sure to cover the edge of the vinyl to keep it from lifting.

If you can't get a prefinished transition piece to work, make a piece from the same type of wood and then stain it to match your new flooring. The idea is to make the transition as shallow as possible but still sturdy enough to take heavy foot traffic.

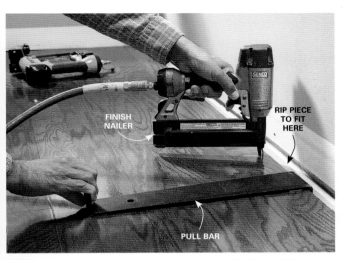

8 Tighten the flooring seams near the end wall with a pull bar, then face-nail the pieces about 1/2 in. back from the tongue. The stapler won't fit into this tight space.

Reversing direction

You can easily continue the flooring through a doorway into another room, but if you want to continue in the opposite direction from your starting point, buy or make your own tongue to glue into a groove as shown in Photo 9. Rip a thin piece from 3/4-in.-thick stock on your table saw and then cut it to width with a straightedge and a utility knife. Check the fit and then glue the tongue into the groove of the plank and tap it into the groove of the existing spot as shown in Photo 10. This is a great way to avoid face-nailing through planks, especially in doorways, where they're most visible.

Finishing touches

Once your flooring is completed, nail your baseboard back into place and cut your base shoe to fit. Fill the nail holes with matching putty. Don't nail the baseboard or the base shoe through the flooring, only into the wall studs. If you need to move heavy appliances like stoves or refrigerators back into the room, roll or scoot them onto thin sheets of Masonite or 1/4-in. plywood and jockey them into position. Use felt pads under tables or heavy chairs to avoid scratches.

Edge options

As you shop for flooring, you'll find three basic edge designs. We chose the square edge design that looks just like traditional wood flooring. This type may have a bit of "over" wood (a slight edge variation from board to board that you can feel with your bare feet). To avoid this, you can choose a micro-beveled edge that is hardly noticeable underfoot (or visible, for that matter). You can also choose a larger, bolder bevel to visually separate the individual planks.

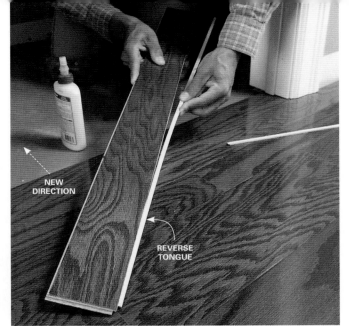

9 Rip a "reverse" tongue from scrap wood and glue it into the groove when you need to switch directions.

10 Tap the reverse tongue into the groove of the existing piece and then reverse direction, nailing into the factory tongues as before.

11 Mix or blend stains to get a match for wood flooring vents or special transition pieces.

Revive a wood floor without sanding

How to renew a floor in half the time—and at half the expense—of sanding

When a wood floor loses its luster, the usual solution is to sand it down to raw wood and completely refinish it. But often, that's the wrong solution.

All wood floors are protected by a clear coating that eventually becomes scratched, scuffed and dull. But as long as the damage is shallow—in the coating and not in the wood itself—you can renew the floor by adding a new coat of polyurethane right over the old finish.

As with any wood-finishing project, 90 percent of this job is preparation. You have to thoroughly clean the floor, touch up any deep scratches and roughen the existing finish so the new finish will adhere well. Expect to spend at least one full day on this prep work. The recoating itself usually takes less than an hour.

Recoating takes a lot less time, skill and money than full-scale sanding and refinishing. And although roughing up the existing finish creates plenty of dust, it's

still much less messy than sanding down to bare wood. There's another advantage: Every time you sand a floor down to bare wood, you remove some of the wood. A solid wood floor can be sanded several times before that's a problem. But laminated floors (glue-down or floating floors) have only a thin layer of good-looking wood veneer over a plywood-like base. The veneer can be sanded once or twice—after that, sanding will expose the plywood core beneath.

SANDING SCREEN

POLYURETHANE

ROUGHENED TEST AREA

MASKING TAPE

1

Test for adhesion

Pick at least two test areas on the floor: one in a high-traffic zone, the other along a wall or in a closet. Clean each area with a wood floor cleaner and roughen a 6 x 6-in. area with sanding screen. Then wipe away the sanding residue, mask around the test area, and give it a coat of polyurethane (Photo 1).

After 24 hours, take a look at the polyurethane. Aside from a few tiny "whiskers" caused by dust particles, it should be smooth. Then scrape the polyurethane with a coin. Press down firmly, but not too hard—even a sound finish might scrape off if you press as hard as you can (Photo 2).

If the polyurethane is smooth and doesn't scrape off with moderate pressure, your test is a success and you can recoat the floor.

But if the polyurethane flakes off as you scrape, or if the surface has a crackled or orange-peel texture (Photo 3), there's something on the old finish preventing the new finish from adhering properly. That "something" could be furniture polish, residue from window cleaner or a hundred other things. But whatever it is, there's only one solution: You have to sand down to bare wood and completely refinish the floor.

SMOOTH SURFACE

2

ORANGE-PEEL TEXTURE

FINISH FLAKES AWAY

3

4 Clean the floor using a wood flooring cleaner. A dull putty knife is handy for scraping up petrified chewing gum and other gunk. For tough marks, use a scouring pad dampened with mineral spirits. If that fails, try sanding screen. As you clean, use pieces of masking tape to mark any deep scratches, ridges or areas where the finish has worn away. You'll have to give these trouble spots special attention later (see "Problem Areas," p. 101).

5 Roughen the existing finish along walls and in corners where the buffer can't reach. The purpose is only to scratch up the finish, not to wear it down—or worse, sand right through it. Three or four passes with the sanding screen are usually enough. Wear gloves to protect your hands from the abrasive screen.

Where recoating won't work

The type of flooring you have doesn't matter. Recoating works on solid wood, laminated wood and parquet floors alike. But a new coat of polyurethane may not stick to your existing finish.

If your floor's finish was applied before the 1970s, it's probably wax, old-fashioned varnish or shellac. No new finish will stick to a wax finish or any other finish that's ever had wax applied to it. Polyurethane might adhere to an old, unwaxed varnish or shellac finish. But these finishes do wear out, and since they're that old, it's best to sand them off and start over.

In fact, if you have an old finish from the days before polyurethane, your only alternative to sanding is wax. If the floor is in fair condition, wax can restore the shine. A wood flooring dealer can recommend a suitable product. Wax is easy to use, but not very durable. You'll probably have to rewax every six months or so.

Even if the existing finish is polyurethane, good adhesion isn't a sure thing. Residue from all kinds of household chemicals, such as furniture polish, glass cleaner, insecticide and wallpaper paste, can interfere with adhesion. Since you can't know for certain all the potions that have landed on your floor, you must test for adhesion before you recoat your floor.

6 Set the buffer on the sanding screen. The screen isn't attached to the buffer at all, but stays put under the weight of the machine. The screen will wear out after 10 to 15 minutes of use. When it does, flip it over or start with a new screen. Check the screen for grit every few minutes and wipe away any large particles that might scratch the floor. Note: Be sure to lock the buffer's adjustable handle in place before you begin buffing.

Problem areas

■ As you're cleaning, you may find deep scratches that go through the finish and into the wood. You usually can't make these scratches disappear completely, but you can make them a lot less noticeable. If your floor is as light or lighter than the floor shown here, first wet the scratch with mineral spirits. A wet coat of mineral spirits produces approximately the same look as a coat of polyurethane. And on a light-colored floor, it might darken the scratch just enough to hide it.

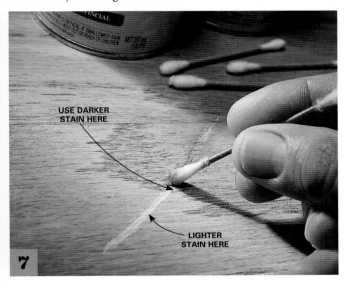

USE DARKER STAIN HERE

LIGHTER STAIN HERE

7

If that doesn't work, apply some wood stain to the scratch using a cotton swab. Because the scratch is rough and porous, it will absorb a lot of stain. So begin experimenting with a stain that's much lighter than the tone of your floor and wipe away the excess stain right after you apply it. For best results, use two stain colors to match the light and dark patterns in the wood grain (Photo 7).

■ If your floor has a high-traffic area where the clear finish is completely worn away, wet the area with mineral spirits to see what it will look like with a coat of polyurethane. If it looks good, clean the area thoroughly, apply a coat of polyurethane and give it at least two days to cure. Then you can buff and recoat the new polyurethane along with the rest of the floor.

■ Look out for ridges. The buffer will eat right through the finish down to bare wood at high spots. And if your floor is colored with wood stain, you'll be left with light-colored strips where the stain has been rubbed off. Photo 8 shows how a solid-wood floor can buckle in high humidity. But smaller ridges, where the wood strips cup slightly or one plank sits a bit higher than the next, can cause just as much trouble.

If you can flatten a ridge by standing on it, fasten it down with a finishing nail or two. If you can't flatten the ridge, you'll have to roughen the area by hand using sanding screen. And remember to avoid that area with the buffer.

■ Stains that have penetrated through the finish as well as the wood can only be removed by sanding. But there's no harm in recoating over them—if you can live with them.

8

RIDGE

SOLID WOOD FLOORING

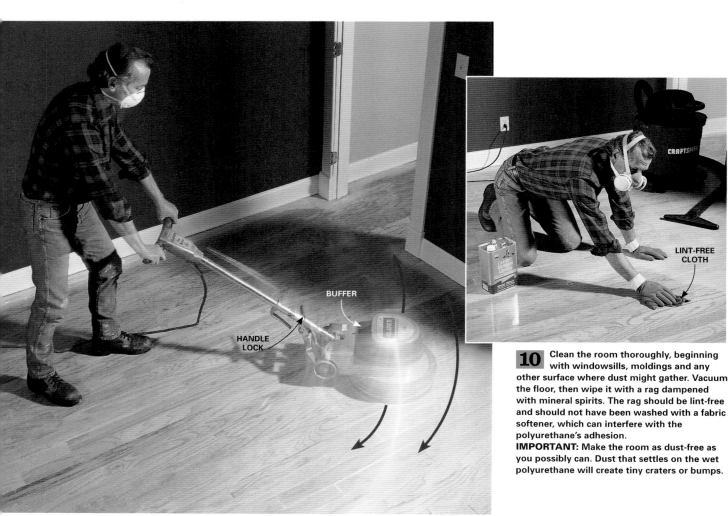

BUFFER

HANDLE LOCK

LINT-FREE CLOTH

10 Clean the room thoroughly, beginning with windowsills, moldings and any other surface where dust might gather. Vacuum the floor, then wipe it with a rag dampened with mineral spirits. The rag should be lint-free and should not have been washed with a fabric softener, which can interfere with the polyurethane's adhesion.
IMPORTANT: Make the room as dust-free as you possibly can. Dust that settles on the wet polyurethane will create tiny craters or bumps.

9 Buff the floor starting at one wall and moving backward across the room. Slowly swing the buffer left and right as you go. Pass over each area only once or twice so you don't cut through the finish. To make the buffer swing to your right, gently lift the handle. To swing left, lower the handle. To control dust, place fans in open windows, close ducts, seal off the work area and wear a dust mask.

Materials

Recoating a typical floor (200 sq. ft. or so) is usually very inexpensive. Most of the money goes for tools and renting the buffer, so recoating floors in two rooms costs only a few bucks more than recoating one room.

All the tools and materials for this project are available at home centers. Wood flooring dealers also carry most of these products. Here's what you'll need:

■ A liquid floor cleaner formulated specifically for wood floors.
■ Scouring pads (a.k.a. "synthetic steel wool") to remove marks on the floor. Regular steel wool will also work, but don't use steel wool if you plan to use a water-based finish; the tiny particles of steel left behind will cause rust stains.
■ A 2- or 3-in. natural bristle brush made specifically for applying varnish and other clear coatings.
■ A finish applicator pad designed to apply floor finishes (Photo 12). You can buy a long handle that screws into the applicator, but any push broom handle will work. Some applicators are made for oil-based finishes; others are made for water-based

products. Check the label.
■ A respirator that has organic vapor cartridges to filter out harmful fumes (Photo 10) while you're using mineral spirits and oil-based polyurethane. These respirators are pricey, but absolutely necessary.
■ A gallon of mineral spirits, 100-grit sanding screen and a dust mask.
■ A buffer (Photo 9), which you rent at a rental center or flooring store. You'll also need a buffing pad (made from synthetic mesh) and sanding screen discs (the same material used to roughen the floor by hand). The screens are available in several grits. Use 150- or 120-grit if available. They're less likely to cut through the finish into the wood than 100-grit. Get at least three screens for a typical room. You can return any you don't use.

TIP

The buffer is a heavy, powerful machine. Learn to control it by practicing on a smooth concrete floor, using only the pad.

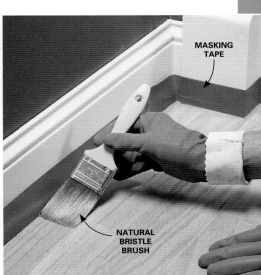

MASKING TAPE

NATURAL BRISTLE BRUSH

11 Brush polyurethane along a wall that runs parallel to the wood strips. Then brush about 3 ft. along adjoining walls. This will give you a 3-ft. wide working area that runs the entire length of the room. Finish that area using the applicator pad (as in Photo 12), then brush along walls to prepare the next 3-ft.-wide section. Even with oil-based polyurethane, you have to move fast so you can begin each section before the previous one starts to dry.

RESPIRATOR

LONG HANDLE

BOX LINED WITH PLASTIC

APPLICATOR PAD

12 Apply polyurethane using an applicator pad attached to a long handle. When spreading the finish, you can dip the applicator into a paint tray filled with polyurethane, but a cardboard box lined with a plastic bag is less likely to tip over. To smooth the finish, first "unload" the pad by pressing it hard against a dry part of the floor. Then drag the applicator lightly across the floor from one end of the room to the other.

Choosing a finish

The best floor finish for a do-it-yourselfer is polyurethane. Other floor finishes are either less durable or much more difficult to work with. You'll find two types of polyurethane at home centers:

The oil-based polyurethanes (or "oil-modified urethanes") are easier to apply because they dry slowly, giving you more time to spread and smooth the finish. They have a yellowish hue and slowly darken with time, which may be good or bad depending on the look you want. The big drawback to oil-based products is the nasty vapor they give off. You must open windows and wear a respirator.

Water-based polyurethanes (or "water-borne urethanes") are generally a bit more durable than oil-based versions. They have a milky color when wet, but they dry crystal clear and remain clear. The milky color makes them easy to see, so you're less likely to miss spots. Still, water-based products are harder to apply because they dry fast.

Note: With either type of polyurethane, be sure it's recommended for wood floors before you buy.

Masking tape tips

Paint cleaner, straighter edges and crisper corners

Masking off baseboard and other trim is a great way to get a professional-looking paint job. You'll get a crisp, clean paint line where the walls meet the trim. And the job will go quicker because you'll avoid the time-consuming "cutting in" with the paintbrush and cleaning up paint spatters from your woodwork. Of course, masking itself requires a little patience and skill. Wavy tape will result in a wavy paint line. Poor adhesion will allow "paint creep." And ragged tape in corners will leave blotches. Here we'll show you techniques that will solve these problems and make your masking job go quickly and smoothly.

Pull from the roll to get the tape perfectly straight

One of the trickiest parts of masking is getting the tape on straight and tight against the wall. There are many techniques, but here's one that works great. Strip 8 to 10 in. of tape from the roll and use the roll itself, held tightly against the wall, to pull the tape straight (Photos 1 and 2). It's a little awkward at first, and may seem slow, but the results are nearly perfect every time. Use this technique wherever you're masking at a right angle to another surface.

TIGHT TO WALL

1 Position the end of the tape precisely and stick it down. Hold it in place while you pull about 8 to 10 in. of tape from the roll.

PRESS DOWN

2 Lay the tape roll flat against the wall and rotate the roll to tighten and straighten it. Slide your finger across the tape to press it down.

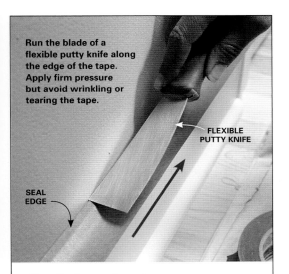

Run the blade of a flexible putty knife along the edge of the tape. Apply firm pressure but avoid wrinkling or tearing the tape.

FLEXIBLE PUTTY KNIFE

SEAL EDGE

Seal the edge to prevent bleeding paint

Seal the tape to the surface by pressing it down firmly with the edge of a flexible putty knife as shown. This is the most important step in good masking and it only takes a few moments. If you skip it, you risk a loose seal that will allow paint to seep underneath. You'll have to scrape off the seeped paint later and touch up the trim.

Keep in mind that you don't have to press down the entire width of the tape. Sealing about 1/32 in. along the edge is all that's needed. Hold the putty knife at an angle as shown. This puts pressure along the critical wall edge of the tape.

1 Press a short section of tape into the corner with the blade of a flexible 2-in. putty knife.

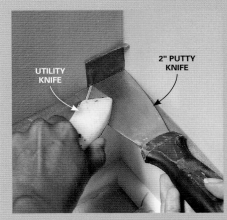

UTILITY KNIFE

2" PUTTY KNIFE

2 Cut the tape using the putty knife as a guide. Peel off the extra tape to create a perfect corner.

Use extra tape to make perfect inside corners

Getting two long pieces of tape to meet exactly in the corner is difficult, so don't try. First of all, don't worry about getting the long pieces of tape to meet in the corner. Start about 3/4 in. from the corner and run them using the method shown above. Then go back and finish the corners with small lengths of tape using the technique shown in Photos 1 and 2.

Use flaps to protect trim from roller spatter

Extending the masking tape with a piece of 3-in. masking paper is all that's needed to protect the woodwork from most roller spatter and drips. Three-inch paper is ideal because it'll stand straight out. Wider paper may seem like a better idea, but it'll sag and won't provide as much protection. And since the 3-in. paper doesn't sag, you'll still be able to close doors without the paper getting in the way.

Apply 3-in. paper along the top trim of windows and doors and along the baseboard. Don't bother to fit the paper tight into corners along the baseboard; you don't need much spatter protection there.

Stick 3-in. masking paper to the underside of the tape to shield trim from paint spatters and drips.

3" MASKING PAPER

3" MASKING PAPER

Tips for removing masking tape

Several things can go wrong when it comes time to remove masking tape. If you wait too long, the adhesive on the tape will harden and remain stuck to the woodwork. Or if the paint sets but isn't completely dry, some of the wall paint may peel off along with the tape. Here are solutions to these problems.

If you're a procrastinator or slow painter, choose tape that's designed to be left on for several days.

To avoid peeling paint, pull the tape off immediately or wait at least overnight for the paint to dry completely. Beware of paint that feels dry to the touch but hasn't hardened and fully bonded to the wall. It may come off along with the masking tape.

Remove tape at about a 45-degree angle to the painted surface as shown to minimize the tendency for paint to peel. And if despite waiting overnight and using a good technique, you notice the paint still peels with the tape, use the edge

of your putty knife or a utility knife to cut the seal between the wall and tape before you remove the tape.

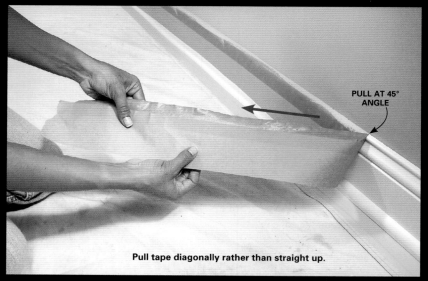

PULL AT 45° ANGLE

Pull tape diagonally rather than straight up.

Install a vinyl tile floor

Durable vinyl tile is easy to install and customize

At first glance, this floor might not look like it's made of the same type of vinyl tile that you may remember from your grandparents' house. But it's still basically the same product. It's inexpensive, virtually indestructible and easier to install than most other flooring materials. The best part is the infinite number of designs you can create once you learn a few special techniques.

Here we'll go beyond basic floor laying to show you how to plan and install a decorative border and how to insert custom shapes into the floor tile. If you're good at measuring and are comfortable using a utility knife, you'll have no problem installing a basic vinyl composition tile (VCT) floor. Our design incorporates circles, but cutting and installing the circles isn't for everybody. It requires patience, attention to detail and a strong, steady hand.

Expect to spend about a day preparing the floor, then a few more days laying the tile, especially if you're installing a floor like ours with borders and custom-cut decorative tiles. You can install a simpler floor without a border or custom tile using the techniques we'll show you and be done in about a day.

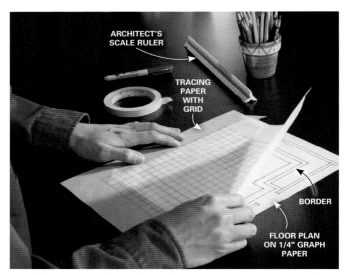

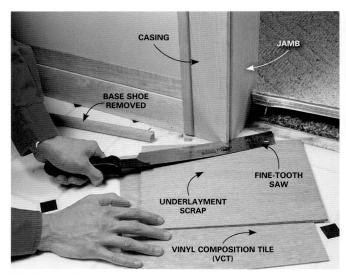

1 Draw a scale plan (1 ft. equals 1/2 in.) of your kitchen on graph paper and add the border. Draw a grid of 1/2-in. squares on tracing paper. Shift the tracing paper around on top of the plan to see how varying the layout affects the width of the partial tiles along the border.

2 Saw off the bottom of door casings and jambs to allow room for the underlayment and tile to slide under. Finish tight cuts with a utility knife and sharp chisel or an oscillating saw.

CAUTION: Many old vinyl floors (pre-1990s) and the adhesive used to install them contain asbestos. Because asbestos can be hazardous when it's disturbed, it's better to cover old vinyl floors with a layer of underlayment than to tear them out.

Don't settle for what's on the shelf— special-order the colors you want

The vinyl composition tile we're using is one of the least expensive flooring options sold at home centers. The most common size is 12 in. square and 1/8 in. thick. Although it's relatively easy to cut with nothing more than a straightedge and sharp utility knife, we'll be using a special VCT cutter for speed and precision. You'll find a few basic colors of VCT in stock and can special-order others. Unlike other modern flooring material, VCT does have to be polished occasionally to maintain a shine.

A scale plan makes custom floor design easy

Before you start shopping for tile, measure the room and draw a scale plan on 1/4-in. graph paper (Photo 1) or use a program like SketchUp. Your goal is to make the cut tiles along the border (or wall if you won't be installing a border) as large as possible. If you get stuck with skinny tiles, place them along an inconspicuous wall. When you find an arrangement you like, transfer the floor plan from the graph paper to a tracing paper grid and make a few photocopies. Now use colored pencils to experiment with different color combinations. After you complete the floor plan, count the number of tiles. Order your tile, adding 15 percent for waste. You'll probably have to order full cartons (about 45 sq. ft. per carton) of each color. Expect to wait a week or two for the tile to arrive.

In addition to tile, you'll need latex adhesive specifically for

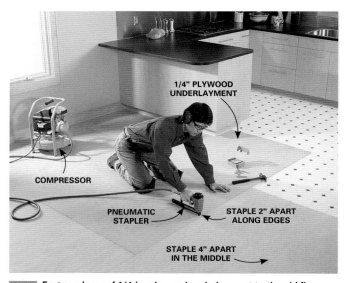

3 Fasten a layer of 1/4-in. plywood underlayment to the old floor with 7/8-in. narrow crown staples using a rented pneumatic stapler. Place staples 4 in. apart in the center of the sheet and 2 in. apart along seams and edges. Stagger the seams, laying full sheets if possible.

VCT; check the label to be sure. This light-colored adhesive spreads easily, has no dangerous solvent fumes and cleans up with water while it's wet. One gallon covers about 200 sq. ft.

You'll also need transition strips at doorways and openings into other rooms and wood base shoe molding to cover the edge of the tile along walls and cabinets.

Careful floor prep is the key to a smooth floor

Even these 1/8-in. thick vinyl tiles won't cover up bumpy floors. Concrete must be structurally sound and dry with no large cracks or uneven sections. Scrape or chip off bumps and fill low spots with floor-leveling compound.

A layer of underlayment (lauan or other special plywood)

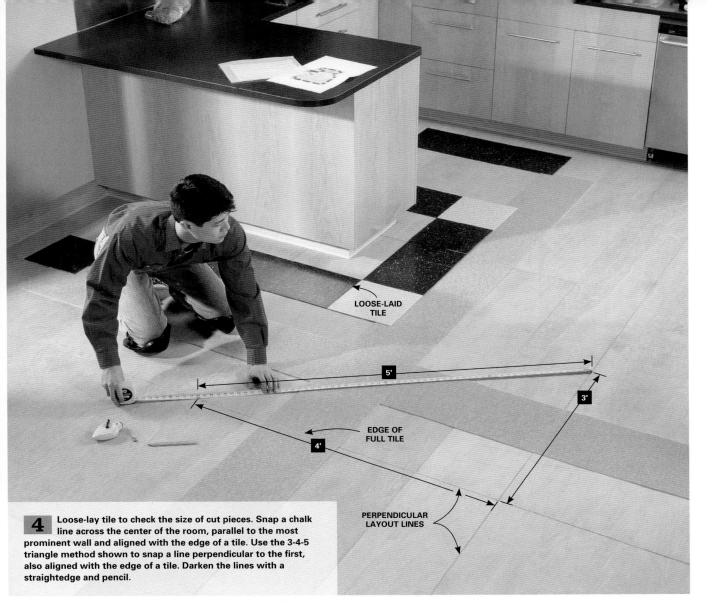

LOOSE-LAID TILE

5'

3'

4'

EDGE OF FULL TILE

PERPENDICULAR LAYOUT LINES

4 Loose-lay tile to check the size of cut pieces. Snap a chalk line across the center of the room, parallel to the most prominent wall and aligned with the edge of a tile. Use the 3-4-5 triangle method shown to snap a line perpendicular to the first, also aligned with the edge of a tile. Darken the lines with a straightedge and pencil.

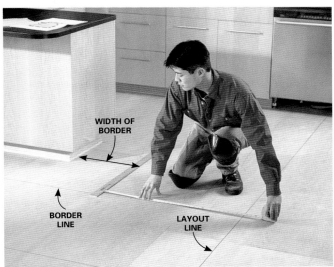

WIDTH OF BORDER

BORDER LINE

LAYOUT LINE

5 Measure from the perpendicular layout lines to mark the exact location of the border. Snap chalk lines for the border and darken them with a pencil.

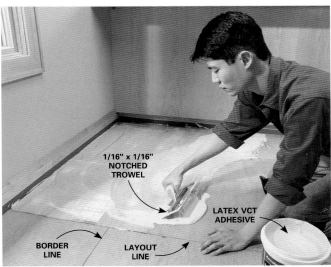

1/16" x 1/16" NOTCHED TROWEL

LATEX VCT ADHESIVE

BORDER LINE

LAYOUT LINE

6 Spread a thin, even layer of VCT adhesive with a 1/16-in. x 1/16-in. notched trowel. Spread glue over half the floor, starting at the wall and working up to the center layout line. Allow the glue to dry until it's clear and tacky.

Press the full tiles into place along the perpendicular layout lines, starting with the first tile at the intersection. Proceed in a stair-step fashion to keep the tiles aligned. See Photos 12 – 14 for instructions on how to make special decorative tiles.

7

Labels in photo: ADHESIVE DRIES CLEAR; STARTER TILE; LAYOUT LINES

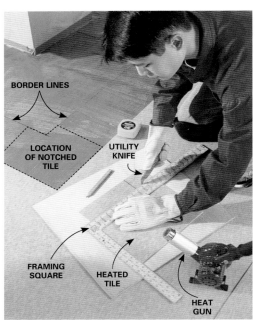

8 Notch tile to fit around border corners. Mark the width of each cut needed to form the notch. Warm the tile about one minute with a heat gun until it's pliable. Then cut the tile using a utility knife and steel straightedge. CAUTION: Keep your hand and fingers out of the path of the utility knife, and wear heavy leather gloves for protection.

Labels in photo: BORDER LINES; LOCATION OF NOTCHED TILE; UTILITY KNIFE; FRAMING SQUARE; HEATED TILE; HEAT GUN

should be installed over wood or old vinyl floors to create a smooth, clean surface for the tile. Underlayment is available at home centers and lumberyards.

Remove base shoe moldings, door thresholds and metal carpet strips, then undercut the door casings (Photo 2).

Allow the underlayment to acclimate to the humidity in your house for a day or two. Then cut it and staple it down (Photo 3). You'll need about 16 staples per square foot, so rent a compressor and a pneumatic stapler that drives narrow crown (1/4- or 3/16-in.) x 7/8-in. long staples for large floors (Photo 3).

Again, a smooth, clean surface is essential. Level uneven seams in the underlayment by filling the low side with floor filler (available at home centers and flooring retailers).

The glue we use allows hours of working time

With the layout lines marked in pencil, you're ready to roll. *Sweep the floor carefully; even a tiny chunk of dirt will eventually show through the tile.* Then pour a mound of adhesive on the floor and spread it (Photo 6), starting at the farthest corner and working up to the lines. Keep a wet rag handy for wiping your hands and cleaning up excess glue. Dried glue can only be removed with mineral spirits or special adhesive remover.

Once the adhesive dries and turns clear, you'll have at least six hours to lay tile—plenty of time to finish tiling the first half of your floor, including the cutting.

The special VCT cutter simplifies the piecework

You'll be able to see the layout lines through the dried adhesive. Place tiles carefully, because after they're pressed into the adhesive, they're very difficult to remove or reposition.

Using the stair-step technique (Photo 7) will help you keep the tile edges precisely aligned and tightly butted together. Refer to your plan for placement of special decorative tiles—in our case,

9 Cut partial tile to butt up against the penciled border line. Attach a stop to your VCT cutter and cut enough tiles to complete the entire row. Press the cut tiles into place.

Labels in photo: CUT TILE DIMENSION; WOOD STOP; SMALL C-CLAMP; RENTED VCT CUTTER

Tools you'll need

- Tape measure
- Hammer
- Fine-tooth saw
- Chalk line
- Square
- Stiff putty knife or scraper
- Utility knife and new blades
- Hacksaw
- 4-ft. straightedge

- Circular saw (for cutting underlayment)
- Heat gun (buy or rent)
- VCT cutter (rent)
- Compressor and narrow crown pneumatic stapler
- 100-lb. floor roller (rent)

SQUARE TILE
FOR CORNER

MARK FOR
PARTIAL
BORDER TILE

FULL-SIZE
BORDER TILE

TIP

If you must reposition or
remove a tile, warm it with a
heat gun until the glue softens
enough to allow the tile to
move. Then slide it into place or
pry it out with a stiff putty knife.

10 Lay the border starting with full tile. Mark and cut partial
tile to complete each section. Continue to measure and
cut tiles to fill the space between the black border and the walls
and cabinets.

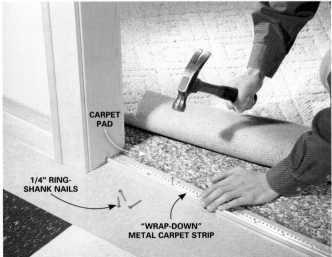

CARPET
PAD

1/4" RING-
SHANK NAILS

"WRAP-DOWN"
METAL CARPET STRIP

11 Nail a wrap-down metal carpet strip over the tile at doorways to
carpeted rooms. Push the carpet to the back of the strip with a
putty knife and trim it flush with a sharp utility knife. Use a hammer and
block of wood to bend the metal down and pinch the carpet.

ELECTRIC
HEAT GUN

BACK SIDE
OF TILE

12 Draw a circle on the face of a tile with a compass. (Use a few
layers of masking tape to protect the tile at the pivot point; see
Photo 13). Heat the tile from the back side with a heat gun set on "high."
Keep the tile moving over the heat source until it's flexible (about 60
seconds). Wear leather gloves to protect your hands from burns.

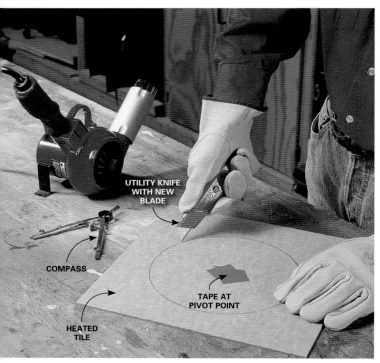

COMPASS

UTILITY KNIFE
WITH NEW
BLADE

TAPE AT
PIVOT POINT

HEATED
TILE

13 Cut a circle from the hot tile by deeply scoring the line with a utility knife. Bend the tile (reheat if necessary) and peel the cutout shape from the surrounding tile. Smooth the rough edge of the circle with 60-grit sandpaper, beveling it slightly to the back side.

circles. You'll notice a "grain" pattern in the tile. Some installers turn every other tile 90 degrees for a checkerboard effect. We chose to keep the grain running in the same direction. To see which look you prefer, experiment by loose-laying some tile on a dry floor.

Lay all of the full tile. Then measure and cut the partial tiles needed to fill out to the border line. You may have to notch a tile for an inside or outside corner or to cut around a cabinet. Photo 8 shows how.

Rent a VCT cutter to ensure precise, clean cuts (Photo 9). If your rental store doesn't have a VCT cutter, you can cut tile on a table saw fitted with a sharp carbide finish blade (wear a dust mask, safety glasses and hearing protection). Another option is to score along a straightedge with a sharp utility knife and break the tile along the scored line. Clean up rough edges with a file or 60-grit sandpaper.

Complete the field tile, then lay the border. Don't worry if the joints between the border tiles don't line up with the joints in the field tile. Start by laying full tiles at the corners. Then cut the last tile in each section to fit (Photo 10). If by bad luck the last tile is going to be less than 1 in. wide, cut an inch off the previous tile to make the last one larger.

Complete the floor by filling in the tiles between the border and the wall (Photo 10). Cut these tiles so the joints align with those of the border tile. You'll end up with a nice-looking square tile at inside corners, but you might have to notch a tile to go around an outside corner.

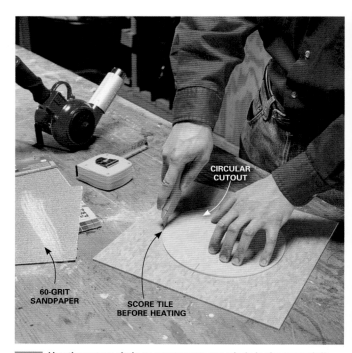

CIRCULAR
CUTOUT

60-GRIT
SANDPAPER

SCORE TILE
BEFORE HEATING

14 Use the cutout circle as a pattern to cut a hole in the second tile. Hold the circle tight to the second tile and accurately score a line around the perimeter with a utility knife. Heat the tile and deepen the scored line with the utility knife. Reheat the tile if necessary and flex it to remove the cutout section. Smooth any ragged edges with a utility knife and press the first circle into the hole.

Create your own custom tiles

Photos 12 – 14 show how to create custom tiles. But don't expect perfect results without a little practice. You don't have to make circles. Use the same procedure to make any shape you can imagine.

Buy special accessories to simplify transitions

There are many ways to make transitions to other types of flooring. But the best way is to use special reducers designed for each situation. Photo 11 shows a professional method for finishing a raw carpet edge. Ask your flooring retailer to recommend transition pieces for your floor.

Routine cleaning and care will help your floor last decades

Clean excess glue from the face of tiles with a damp rag or mineral spirits. Then rent a 100-lb. floor roller and roll the floor to ensure a tight bond between the tile and adhesive. Reinstall your old base shoe moldings or cut and install new ones.

Allow four or five days for the adhesive to fully cure before washing and sealing the floor. To prepare it for sealing, sweep the floor and clean it with a mild neutral detergent. Use a non-abrasive scrub pad to remove stubborn marks. Allow the floor to dry before applying several coats of high-quality acrylic floor polish or sealer.

7 tips for floor prep

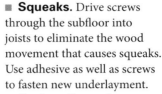

When you're about to lay a new floor, you have the perfect opportunity to upgrade your subfloor to make it solid and squeak-free. While the specifics might vary a bit depending on your new flooring material, consider these issues:

■ **Deflection/stiffness.** If you find soft spots in your floor or areas that "give" as you walk across them, stiffen them by adding framing from below or more underlayment on top. Ceramic tile floors require extra stiffness to keep grout lines from cracking.

■ **Bounce.** If the dinner plates rattle every time you walk across your kitchen floor, you're getting too much vibration or bounce. Corrections must be made from below.

■ **Flatness.** Now's the time to level off high spots and fill low areas so your new floor runs true.

■ **Squeaks.** Drive screws through the subfloor into joists to eliminate the wood movement that causes squeaks. Use adhesive as well as screws to fasten new underlayment.

■ **Surface flaws.** Some flooring, like vinyl, linoleum and carpeting, requires perfectly smooth subfloors or underlayments. Otherwise, every flaw will show through in the surface.

■ **Moisture in concrete.** Always check the moisture level in concrete before laying flooring over it. Trapped moisture will ruin the floor and encourage mold.

■ **Asbestos.** Asbestos, a proven carcinogen, was used in many types of flooring and adhesives. While old flooring isn't hazardous if left undisturbed, don't rip it out unless you know it's asbestos-free. Call your local health department or visit epa.gov/asbestos for instructions about how to collect a sample and have it tested for asbestos.

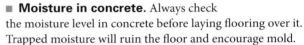

5 tips for adding new floors

The next time you're thinking about adding a new floor, consider these potential problems:

■ Will all the appliances fit? Pay careful attention to the refrigerator if it has a cabinet directly over it with minimum clearance.

■ What about the transition from one room to another? A difference of 1/2 in. to 3/4 in. is usually acceptable, but steeper transitions can look awkward and pose a tripping hazard.

■ If the floor adjoins a staircase, are the stair risers still consistent? Too much buildup on the floor can make the lower or upper step height dangerously different from the rest. Most building codes mandate that no step on a staircase vary in height by more than 3/8 in. from the rest.

■ Door heights can be affected as well. Interior doors can be cut fairly easily, but you usually can't cut off an exterior door at all, much less raise a threshold. And there may be no room for a rug under the door as it swings into the room.

■ Consider the toe-kick space under the cabinets. It should be greater than 3 in. or you could get your work boots caught between the floor and the cabinet.

Chapter Four

TILING

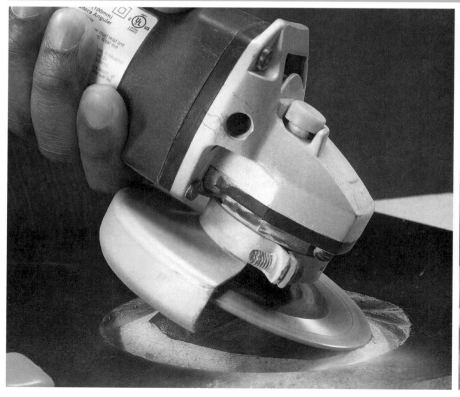

Waterproofing and tiling a shower

howers used to be simple boxes for fear that any special architectural features could lead to a leak—and expensive repairs. But modern tiling materials, especially spreadable waterproof membranes, can put these fears to rest. Now you can build in a bench or other structure with confidence and make showering more convenient and pleasant.

Here you'll learn how to build in three features: a bench, a shelf and an alcove. Included are the key planning steps and the waterproofing and special tiling techniques. This project isn't for a tiling rookie. You should have some hands-on tiling experience before tackling a complex project like this one. But if you have rudimentary framing skills, and have successfully tiled floors, backsplashes or simple shower surrounds, the advanced techniques shown here will enable you to move on to a project like this.

Framing, sheathing and tiling a shower like this one will take you about four full days. The tiling alone will take two days. It pays to rent or buy a "score and snap" tile cutter if you're using 4 x 4-in. tiles like those shown. But if you're using natural stone or larger tiles and your tile layout requires lots of cuts, especially notching, rent a tile saw for a day. You can score and snap glass tile (small mosaic tiles only), but you'll break about every 10th tile—not a big deal if you plan the tile layout well and only have to cut a few.

Plan the layout

First make sure you have enough space in your shower to add a bench. You'll need to leave at least 3 ft. of shower area so you can still move around. This bathroom originally had a 5-ft. tub, which was torn out and replaced with a 4-ft. shower base. This left a 1-ft. space for the bench and the overhead shelf at the end of the shower.

The key to an exceptional tile job is to plan the shower with the actual tile you intend to use. Use the tile to decide on exact dimensions and positions of benches, alcoves and even wall thicknesses so you can use whole tiles as much as possible and minimize cutting.

A foolproof method is to draw a full-scale template of each wall on rosin paper (Figure A and Photo 1). Be sure to draw the walls including the thickness of backer board and any plywood that's needed, like on the bench seat. Then mark existing studs that outline alcove positions. Next, lay the tile on the template to decide on the heights, widths and depths of shower features like benches, alcoves and shelves.

Try to wind up with full tiles outlining or covering those features whenever possible. Notice that this alcove is surrounded by full tiles. Those tiles determined the final position and size of the alcove. (It's easier to deal with cutting the tiles that cover the back of the alcove than the ones that border it.) Notice also that the exact height of the bench allowed for full tiles around it—no cutting needed.

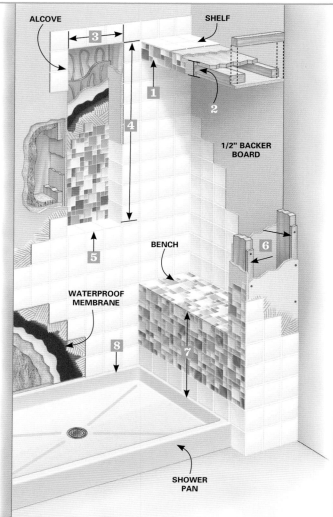

Figure A
Layout objectives

1. Shelf rests on full tile
2. Thickness matches face tile
3. Adjust alcove width for full field tiles
4. Plan height for full field tiles
5. Start alcove at top of tile row
6. Fur out as needed to avoid cutting tiles
7. Full tiles define bench height
8. Start with full tiles at base

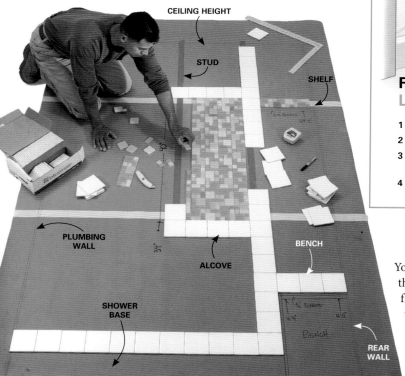

1 Plan the framing and tile layout for each wall on rosin paper cut to match the size of each wall.

Also adjust the thicknesses of walls and ledges for full tiles. You can fur out the 2x4 wall with strips of 1/2-in. plywood so the glass tile will cap the end without any cutting. And choose framing and sheathing thicknesses to achieve the same aim with the shelf edge. If possible, plan the tile for the large wall expanses so that you'll have columns of similar-width tiles at both ends of each wall. Study Figure A to make all of this clear. You won't be able to avoid all tile cutting, of course. The goal is to simplify the tile work as much as possible. The more effort you put into planning the project, the easier it will be to install the tile. And you'll be rewarded with a first-class tile job.

Frame the shower

If you have a space between the shower base and the wall, as shown, start by framing a continuous wall, floor to ceiling, between the base and the wall (Photo 2).

If there's no framing behind the ceiling for anchoring the wall, just screw it to the drywall and then add a bead of construction adhesive around the ceiling plate. Next, frame in the alcove. Use your template to establish the height of the top and bottom and then add blocking there. Fur out the side(s) if needed to accommodate tile sizes within and/or surrounding the opening. If your alcove is on an outside wall, glue 1-in.-thick foam insulation against the outside sheathing using special foam adhesive.

Frame the bench with a 1/4-in. slope so water won't pool. Cap the bench with 3/4-in. plywood, screwing it with 1-5/8-in. screws. Lastly, add 2x6 blocking to anchor any shelves and any missing blocking at any inside corners.

Cement board tile backer is commonly used for shower walls, but shown here is a drywall-type tile backer called DensShield. It's slightly more expensive than cement board but much easier to work with. You score it, snap it and cut it just like drywall.

Whatever material you use, anchor it with 1-1/4-in. cement board screws spaced every 4 in. at seams and every 6 in. everywhere else. If you have a premade shower base, keep the bottom row of backer board just above the lip. The tile will hang down over the lip to direct water into the base.

Next lay a strip of alkali-resistant fiberglass mesh tape over all seams and corners. It has adhesive on one side, but many brands don't stick very well. If you have trouble, use staples to hold it in place. Mix up about a quart of thin-set mortar to the consistency of creamy peanut butter and trowel it over all the seams with a 6-in. putty knife. Try to avoid big buildups, which keep the tile from lying flat.

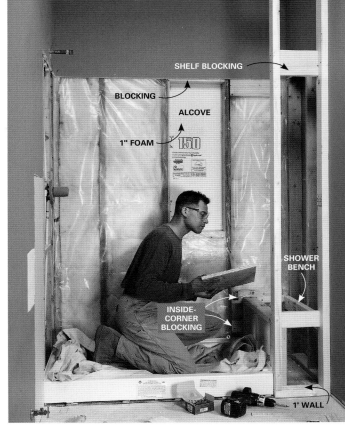

SHELF BLOCKING

BLOCKING

ALCOVE

1" FOAM

150

SHOWER BENCH

INSIDE-CORNER BLOCKING

1' WALL

2 Add blocking to the top and bottom of the alcove, shimming the sides as needed, and fill in the back with foam board. Frame the end wall and then the bench.

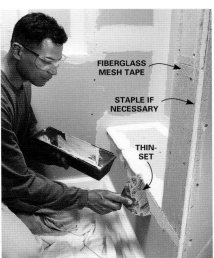

FIBERGLASS MESH TAPE

STAPLE IF NECESSARY

THIN-SET

3 Cover all seams and corners with fiberglass mesh tape. Embed the tape with a thin layer of thin-set.

FIRST COAT OF WATERPROOFING MEMBRANE

4 Coat water-prone areas with two coats of waterproofing membrane.

Apply waterproofing membrane

Any area that will be exposed to lots of water should be coated with two coats of a brush-on waterproofing membrane (available at some home centers and all tile stores). Use disposable brushes and let the first coat dry thoroughly before recoating. The product shown goes on pink and dries to red when it's ready for a second coat (Photos 4 and 5). Focus on areas that will get the lion's share of showerhead water, especially corners and horizontal bench surfaces and recessed alcoves. For extra protection, also coat all of the screw heads in areas that'll get deluged. As with the thin-set, try to avoid big buildups.

WATERPROOFING MEMBRANE

Tile the alcove wall

Use your template as a guide to snap exact tile layout lines. First establish lines for the rows of tiles surrounding the alcove. Then dry-stack and measure tiles to get an exact measurement from the bottom of the alcove to the top of the first row of tile. Draw a level line and screw a 1x2 ledger to the wall (Photo 7). The ledger will ensure a perfectly straight bottom course of tiles and keep them from sliding down the wall before the adhesive sets. (You'll remove the ledger and add the bottom row of tiles later, cutting them to height if needed.)

Mix up about a quart of thin-set at a time (follow the directions on the bag). Comb the thin-set onto the back of the alcove with a 1/4-in. notched trowel (Photo 5). Then press the mosaic tile sections into the thin-set. Lightly tap the tiles with a grout float to embed each small tile evenly with its neighbors (Photo 11). Look carefully for thin-set that works its way out between the tiles and wipe it off with a damp rag; it's tough to scrape off after it sets.

Begin setting the field (wall) tile following your layout lines. After you set each tile, give it a little rap with your fist to better embed it. Dip tiles in water before sticking them to the wall so they form a better bond with the thin-set (Photo 8). Continually check the rows of tile for straightness. When the thin-set is still fresh, you can even out rows just by pushing a level against several tiles at once (Photo 12). Finish tiling the wall, cutting the top row to fit as needed. Leave out the row of tiles where the shelf will rest (Photo 8).

Tile the alcove sill and then the sides and top. Slightly slope the sill tiles toward the shower for drainage by piling on a little extra thin-set on the back side. Match the slope on the bottom tiles at the side by taping the bottom tile even with the row above it and scribing the angle with a full tile (Photo 9).

5 Spread thin-set on the back of the alcove with a 1/4-in. notched trowel and then embed the mosaic tile into the adhesive.

6 Support sagging mosaic tiles with shims and/or nails until the adhesive sets. Tamp all the tiles level with a grout float as shown in Photo 11.

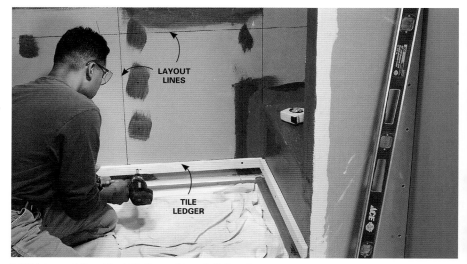

LAYOUT LINES

TILE LEDGER

7 Lay out the critical tile lines with a chalk line. Screw a 1x2 ledger to the studs to support the second row of tiles.

FIELD TILE

DAMPEN TILE

8 Spread thin-set up to the horizontal layout line and around one corner of the alcove. Set those tiles and then continue tiling the wall, leaving out the row of tiles directly behind the shelf.

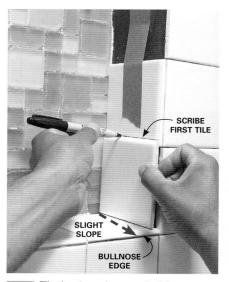

SCRIBE FIRST TILE

SLIGHT SLOPE

BULLNOSE EDGE

9 Tile the alcove bottom shelf first with bullnose-edged tile, sloping it slightly toward the shower. Scribe the bottom side tiles to get the proper angle, and then finish tiling the sides and top.

Tile the bench

Starting at one end, set the tile on the face of the bench. If you're left with a gap at the other end, cut the mosaic into strips and slightly expand the grout lines between rows (Photo 10). Small variations in the width of the lines won't be noticeable. Lay tile on the seat to gauge the final grout line width between the seat and the face tile. Then add the seat tile, working from front to back and aligning the grout lines with the face tile. Make sure the seat tile edges align perfectly with the face tile surface—they shouldn't be backset or overhanging. Finish tiling the rest of the field tile above the bench, stopping at the shelf (Photo 13).

Mount and tile the shelf

Build the shelf 1/8 in. narrower than the opening so you can tip it into place. Leave off the plywood top but add backer board to the underside. Rest the shelf on the field tile and screw it to the blocking behind the backer board with two 3-in. screws at each side. Then screw the 3/4-in. plywood top to the framing with 1-5/8-in. screws (Photo 13) and add the backer board to the top and the front edge.

Tile the edge first, supporting it with a ledger screwed to the shelf underside (Photo 14). Remove the ledger after an hour or so, and then finish tiling the underside and top and the field tile above it. Lastly, remove the 1x2 ledgers and add the bottom row of tiles.

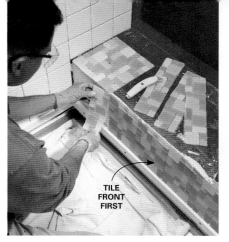

10 Tile the front of the bench first. Cut the mosaic tiles into strips if you need to adjust the spacing to get a better fit with less cutting.

11 Tile the bench and the end of the short wall. Force mosaic tiles evenly into the thin-set with a grout float.

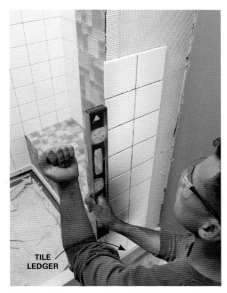

12 Add the rest of the field tile, stopping at the underside of the shelf. Align tile edges at outside corners with a straightedge.

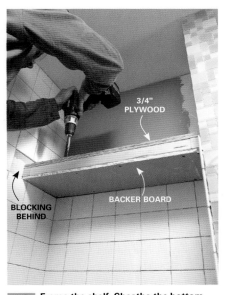

13 Frame the shelf. Sheathe the bottom with backer board, rest it on the tile and screw the sides into the blocking. Add the 3/4-in. plywood and cover the exposed wood with backer board.

14 Screw a support ledger to the shelf underside to support the lip tile. Then tile the underside, top and the rest of the wall tile. The following day, grout the whole works and caulk all inside corners.

Ceramic tile floor

Whether you're replacing an old shabby floor or installing a new one, you can't beat ceramic or stone tile for durability and appearance. When laid properly, it's virtually a forever floor that requires almost no care and maintenance. And you can select materials from a vast array of colors and textures.

What's equally attractive is that you can lay a first-class tile floor yourself, often in one weekend, and save the considerable cost of hiring a pro.

First, install backer board

The backer board is fastened with a combination of screws and thin-set adhesive. Cut and lay out all the pieces before you mix the thin-set (Photos 1 and 2). You can run the sheets in any direction, but be sure to stagger the joints so you never have four corners meeting at one point. Leave a 1/8-in. space between the sheets and along the vanity, tub or shower. The gap along walls must be at least 1/8 in. wide, but a wider gap (about 1/2 in.) makes the panels easier to set in place. After cutting and fitting, label the location of each one and set them all aside.

Vacuum the floor and have your drill and screws ready to go before you mix the thin-set. Read the thin-set's label, then mix according to the instructions. Spread the thin-set with a 1/4-in. notched trowel. Comb in one direction so air can escape when you embed the backer (Photo 3). Drive screws every 6 in. around the perimeter of each piece and every 8 in. "in the field" (across

1 Cover the floor with backer board. Cut inside corners, circles and curves with a drywall saw or jigsaw with a carbide blade. Space pieces 1/8 in. apart and hold each one in place with two temporary screws.

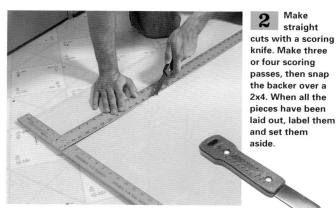

2 Make straight cuts with a scoring knife. Make three or four scoring passes, then snap the backer over a 2x4. When all the pieces have been laid out, label them and set them aside.

3 Comb out a bed of thin-set just large enough for each piece of backer board using a 1/4-in. notched trowel held at a 45-degree angle. Screw the backer down before spreading thin-set for the next piece.

MESH TAPE

4 Press adhesive-backed, alkali-resistant mesh tape over the joints and skim over the tape with thin-set. When the thin-set is firm but not fully hardened, scrape away any ridges with a putty knife.

the face of the panel). If the leftover thin-set is still workable, you can immediately embed mesh tape over the joints (Photo 4). If the thin-set has become too stiff or chunky, mix a new batch. Use "alkali-resistant" tape that's meant for backer board. While the tape coat of thin-set hardens, run a putty knife over all the screw heads to scrape off the "mushroom" bulges around screws. Drive in any protruding screw heads you come across.

Careful layout pays off

Too often, tile novices simply start setting tile in a corner and continue along two walls until the floor is covered. Sometimes they get lucky and the floor looks good. But more often this method leads to trouble: They end up with awkward-looking, thin slivers of tile along a prominent wall or at the doorway. And the tile looks even worse when walls are badly out of square or crooked—a straight grout line running too close to a wall emphasizes the wall's imperfections.

Whether you're laying a simple grid pattern as shown here, or a diagonal pattern with a border, the best tile layout usually calls for centering full tiles between walls so the partial tiles along the edges will end up all the same size. Don't rely on your tape measure and mental arithmetic. Rip open a carton of tile, grab a handful of spacers and experiment with your layout on the floor.

To begin, center rows of tile between walls so you have equal spaces along walls that face each other (Photo 5). Set the two rows parallel to the two most prominent walls. Then make adjustments, trying to achieve these three goals:

- Use full tiles at doorways and along the bathtub or shower. These are usually the only places where the edges of the floor aren't covered by baseboard. If you use full tiles in these exposed spots, you don't have to worry about making smooth, perfect cuts.

- Avoid narrow tiles along walls. Ideally, you'll end up with tiles cut to half size or larger. Avoid cutting tile to widths less than 2 in.
- Minimize cutting and try to avoid difficult cuts. For example: Cutting tile to an L-shape to fit around an outside corner is especially difficult when one arm of the "L" is less than 2 in. wide. The arm tends to break off as you cut.

Chances are, your layout won't meet all these goals. Because the shower stall was the focal point in this bathroom, it was the No. 1 layout priority. Full tiles were used in front of the shower. That left 3-in.-wide tiles along the opposite wall, which was less prominent. Also, to center the tile rows on the shower, cut tiles were used at the doorway.

Once you determine a layout, establish lines to guide your tile positioning. The usual method is to snap chalk lines on the floor. But chalk lines are hard to see after you've spread thin-set, and one row of tile may slip as you set the next row. Here's a more reliable guide: Choose straight boards a foot shorter than the length and width of the room. Tape one edge of each board so thin-set won't stick to them. Then screw the boards to the floor at a right angle to form a guide that eliminates guesswork and shifting (Photo 6).

Set the tile (finally!)

It's usually easiest—and most efficient—to set tile in two phases: First set all the full "field" tiles (Photo 7). Then, when the thin-set has hardened for several hours, cut all the perimeter tiles and set them (Photo 8). Here are some tips for both phases of the job:

- The trowel you use for setting tile may be different from the one you used to embed the backer. The thin-set label tells you which notch size to use relative to tile size.

5 Dry-lay tile to determine the best layout. Start with centered rows, leaving equal spaces at walls. Then reposition rows until you find the optimal layout.

EQUAL SPACES

6 Screw guide boards to the floor following your chosen layout. Position the guides so you can lay all the field tiles without moving the guides. Make sure the guides are at right angles by measuring out a 3-4-5 triangle.

GUIDE BOARD

3'   5'   4'

Two methods for tiling over an existing floor

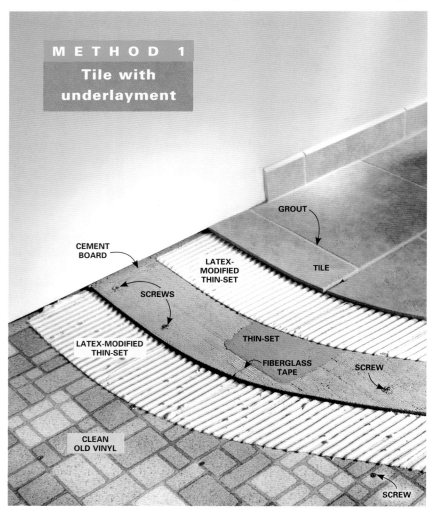

METHOD 1
Tile with underlayment

CEMENT BOARD

SCREWS

LATEX-MODIFIED THIN-SET

GROUT

LATEX-MODIFIED THIN-SET

TILE

THIN-SET

FIBERGLASS TAPE

SCREW

CLEAN OLD VINYL

SCREW

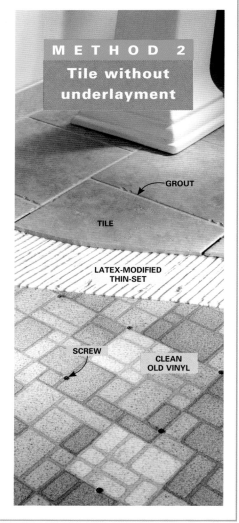

METHOD 2
Tile without underlayment

GROUT

TILE

LATEX-MODIFIED THIN-SET

SCREW

CLEAN OLD VINYL

SPACERS

FIELD TILE

7 Comb out a few square feet of thin-set and set tile against the guides. Continue until all the full tiles are in place. **Tip:** Watch for squeeze-out between tiles and rake it out with tile spacers.

THIN-SET ON PERIMETER TILE

8 Cut and set the perimeter tiles after the thin-set beneath the full tiles has hardened. In spaces too narrow for your trowel, comb thin-set onto the backs of tiles.

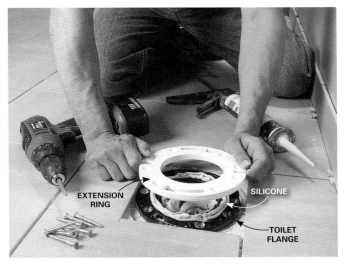

EXTENSION RING

SILICONE

TOILET FLANGE

9 Remove the old screws from the toilet flange and apply a heavy bead of silicone caulk. Fasten the extension ring over the old flange with stainless steel or brass screws.

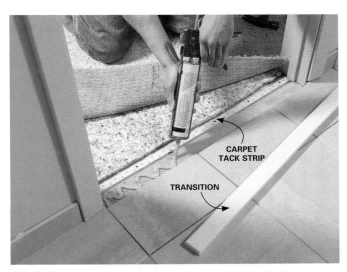

CARPET TACK STRIP

TRANSITION

10 Glue the transition into place with construction adhesive. If carpet meets the transition, you may have to add a new tack strip.

- Dampen the backer with a sponge just before applying thin-set. This keeps the thin-set from drying out too quickly.
- Comb the thin-set in one direction so air pockets won't be trapped under tile.
- Open three or four cartons and mix the tiles as you set them. Pattern and color vary slightly from one carton to the next.
- Don't just set each tile into place; press down on the tile and wiggle it to embed it firmly in the thin-set.

CAUTION: Cement products like thin-set and grout draw moisture from skin and can even cause burns that require medical attention. While most pros work bare-handed, wear gloves if you have any special sensitivity. Also wear eye protection while mixing thin-set and grout.

- Watch for "tipped" corners. When you press a tile in place, it's easy to tilt it slightly so that one corner stands higher or lower than neighboring tiles.
- When you complete a section of tile, inspect it before moving on. Make sure the tiles line up correctly and spacers are in place. Wipe any thin-set off the face of tiles with a damp sponge.
- When the thin-set becomes chunky or too stiff, throw it away and mix more. Never try to extend the life of thin-set or grout by adding water.
- Cut perimeter tile so that caulked joints (at tub) are the same width as grouted joints.

Prepare the floor for grout

When all the tiles are in place and the thin-set has hardened, remove all the spacers. Next, raise the toilet flange by adding an extension ring or two (Photo 9). The extended flange should be flush with or higher than the surrounding tile. When you grout, fill in between the flange and tile. That way, any future leak around the flange will show up on the bathroom floor instead of on the ceiling below.

If you plan to use a glue-down transition as shown here, this is the time to install it. Here's how this transition was handled: First, the old metal strip that covered the carpet's edge was removed. Then a miter saw was used to cut the transition strip to fit between the door jambs. Next, a tack strip was added to hold the carpet in place. Before the transition was glued to the floor (Photo 10), a thin strip of the old vinyl floor was removed.

Grout is too brittle to handle the slight shifting movements that are normal in any room. Keep grout out of joints wherever the floor meets the tub, shower, vanity or walls (Photo 11).

Pack the joints with grout

The thin-set directions will tell you how soon you can grout the floor—usually 24 hours. Grouting isn't complex. Just plop a couple of scoops of grout onto the floor in a corner, work the grout into joints (Photo 12) and scrape off the excess grout before moving to the next section. In addition:

- Mix the grout to a mashed-potatoes consistency. Adding extra liquid makes grout easier to work with but weakens it.
- Don't just spread the grout over the joints; press hard to pack it into the joints. If you're doing it right, your forearm will get a good workout.
- Whether you're filling joints or scraping off excess grout, always push the float diagonally across the tiles.
- Scrape off the excess to leave tile as clean as you can. The less grout you leave on the tiles, the easier cleanup will be.
- When you're done, cover the grout bucket with a plastic bag and set it in a cool place to slow the hardening process. During cleanup, you may find spots that need a little extra.

Grout cleanup

Clean the surface of the tile when the grout is stiff enough to stay put in the joints but still soft enough to wipe off the tile surface. During hot, dry weather, grout can become difficult to wipe away in just 10 minutes, so get ready for cleanup before you even mix the grout. You'll need two buckets of clean water, two sponges, a synthetic scouring pad and a dry rag.

As soon as you're done grouting, go to the first section you grouted and wipe across a joint with a damp sponge. If the sponge pulls grout out of the joint, wait five minutes and try again. In cool, damp weather, the grout may stay too soft for an hour. When the grout is hard enough, gently wipe the tile with a damp sponge. Rinse the sponge frequently as you wipe the entire floor (Photo 13). If you come across tough spots, scrub them with the scouring pad. Be careful where you put your feet and knees—don't mar your perfect grout joints.

Immediately after the first pass, grab the second bucket of clean water and the fresh sponge and make a second, more thorough pass. Then, as the tile surface dries, wipe it with a dry terry cloth. The dry haze should buff off easily. If not, go for fresh water and

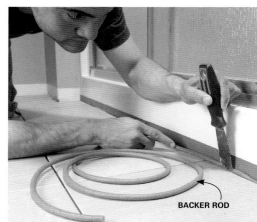

11 Push backer rod into joints that will be caulked later. The foam rod keeps grout out of joints. After grouting, pull out the rod and caulk the joints.

BACKER ROD

12 Work the grout back and forth across the floor, diagonal to the joints and holding the float at a 45-degree angle. Then scrape off the excess grout, holding the float almost upright.

GROUT FLOAT

13 Wipe grout off the tile surface with a damp sponge. Wipe gently on the first pass so you don't pull grout out of the joints. Rinse the sponge often.

sponge the floor again. If you can't get rid of the haze, don't panic. Products that remove haze are available wherever tile is sold.

Finishing up

Let the grout cure overnight before you caulk joints, set the toilet or reinstall baseboard. Grout sealer is a good precaution against staining: Some products can be applied 24 hours after grouting; others require a two- to three-week wait. If you have leftover tile or grout, keep them in case you have to make repairs in the future. Be sure to write down the brand, color and retailer of the tile.

Tiling over tile

Want to change the look of an old tiled floor? As long as there are no cracks in the existing tile (indicating underlying problems in the concrete), you can tile on top of it. In fact, pros do it all the time.

Surface preparation is paramount. Start by making sure all the tiles are solidly bonded to the floor. Tap them lightly with a wood mallet or a chunk of 2x4. A hollow sound is an indication that a tile is loose. Remove and reset any loose ones with thin-set. Next, use a 4-ft. level to find any high spots and grind those down using a right-angle grinder with a masonry wheel. Then sand all the tiles with a belt or orbital sander (80-grit) to scratch any surface glazes. Remove any moldy or loose grout with a rotary tool or carbide scraper. Vacuum the tiles and clean with detergent and water to remove dirt, sealers and wax. Rinse the surface with clear water and let it dry.

Buy a latex-modified thin-set and mix it in small batches to keep it from skinning over. Complete adhesive coverage is critical on large tiles (12 in. or larger) and even more important when you're tiling over tile. Some installers prefer to "flatback" each tile with the flat edge of the trowel before applying the tile to the combed thin-set. Others prefer to use a larger-notched trowel (1/2 x 1/2 in.) to apply the thin-set. Whichever method you use, always comb the adhesive in one direction (no swirls). Then set the tile on the floor and slide it perpendicular to the combed thin-set to knock down the rows and spread the adhesive.

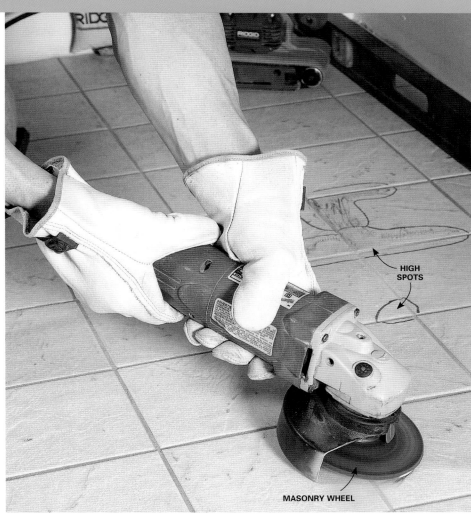

HIGH SPOTS

MASONRY WHEEL

1 Lay a level on the old tile and mark any high spots. Grind them down with a grinder. Roughen the tile with 80-grit sandpaper.

2 Spread a flat layer of thin-set on the back of large tiles for better adhesion. Or, use a larger-notch trowel.

3 Press the tile onto the floor thin-set and slide it perpendicular to the combed lines.

Glass tile vanity top

A dramatic weekend face-lift

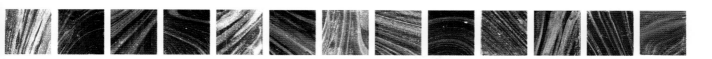

This vanity top would be at home in any luxury bathroom. Even though we chose relatively expensive glass tile, the completed top cost us less than half the cost of custom granite, marble or solid-surface tops. Glass mosaic tile like we used is perfect for a project like this because you can adjust the size of the top to use only full tiles and avoid cutting. Plus, you can choose from hundreds of colors, textures and patterns to create a look that's perfect for your décor.

You'll be able to finish this project in a weekend using standard carpentry tools and a 3/16-in. V-notch trowel, a grout float and a grouting sponge. A microfiber cloth works better than a cotton rag for cleaning off the grout haze. You can buy them at home centers, hardware stores and most discount retailers. You'll also need buckets for mixing thin-set and grout and for rinse water. Don't forget a pair of rubber, vinyl or latex gloves and safety glasses.

Round up the materials

Start by choosing the tile. (This could be the hardest part!) If your local tile shops or home centers don't have tile you like, shop online like we did. To duplicate our project, choose a 3/4-in. square mosaic that's 1/8 in. thick and has a mesh backing. Avoid mosaics that are held together with a removable paper face. They're difficult to install.

Here's a list of other materials you'll need:

■ **Plywood.** We used two layers of 5/8-in. plywood, which, combined with the 1/4-in. backer board, resulted in a 1-1/2-in.-thick top, a perfect thickness for two courses of our 3/4-in. tile. If your tiles are a different size or you want a different top thickness, adjust the plywood and backer board thicknesses accordingly.

■ **Tile backer board.** We purchased a lightweight tile backer board that you can cut with a utility knife. Cement backer board would also work well.

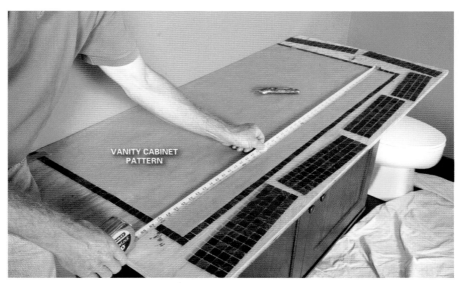

1 Design the top to avoid cutting tile. Cut a paper pattern the size of the vanity cabinet and lay it over the tile. That makes it easy to size the top for full tiles.

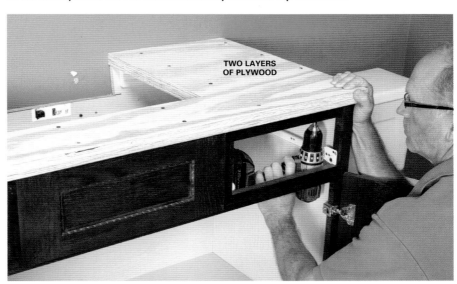

2 Build the plywood base. Two layers of plywood make a stiff, strong base for the tile. Mark and cut the plywood carefully to make sure the top is perfectly square.

■ **Thin-set mortar.** Look for special glass tile mortar. It's white and specially formulated to stick well to glass tile. It's available in a powder that you mix with water. Standard modified white thin-set will also work.

■ **Cement board screws.** Choose screws that are labeled for use with cement board. They have a special corrosion-resistant coating.

■ **Cement board tape.** Check the label—it must be cement board tape so the mesh will hold up to the alkaline cement products.

■ **Grout.** We used nonsanded grout because we wanted smooth grout lines. You can also use sanded grout. Make a sample board by gluing a few glass mosaic tiles to a scrap of wood and grouting them to make sure you like the result.

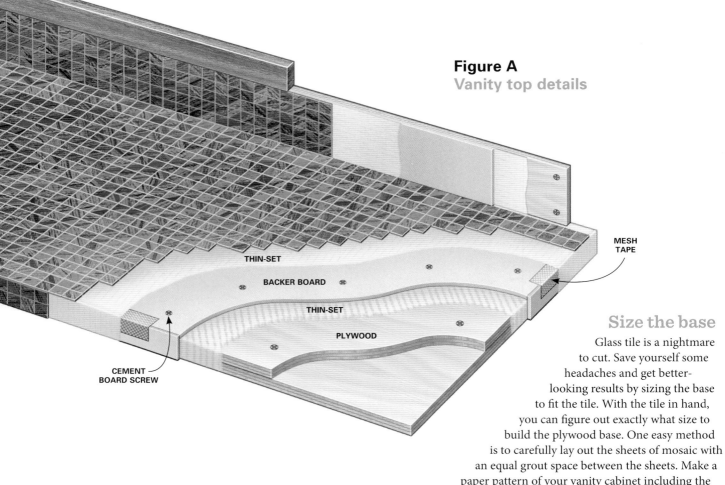

MESH
TAPE

THIN-SET

BACKER BOARD

THIN-SET

PLYWOOD

CEMENT
BOARD SCREW

Size the base

Glass tile is a nightmare to cut. Save yourself some headaches and get better-looking results by sizing the base to fit the tile. With the tile in hand, you can figure out exactly what size to build the plywood base. One easy method is to carefully lay out the sheets of mosaic with an equal grout space between the sheets. Make a paper pattern of your vanity cabinet including the thickness of the door or drawer fronts. Arrange the pattern over the sheets of tile and adjust the position until there's an equal-width tile on each side. Use the pattern to determine the overhangs, based on where full tiles occur. Aim for about a 1/2-in. overhang on the sides and between 1/2-in. and 1-in. past the drawers on the front. Cut the mesh backing so the sheets of tile are the size of the top. Now carefully measure the width and length of the tiles. This will be the finished size of your countertop after it's tiled.

The plywood base has to be smaller than the size of the finished top to accommodate the backer board, tile and thin-set. To figure the size of the plywood, add the thickness of the tile (1/8 in.), the tile backer board (1/4 in.) and the thin-set (1/16 in.) and subtract this amount from the width (front to back). Deduct twice this amount from the length (side to side). It's critical that you cut the plywood to exactly the right size, so double-check all your math (Photo 1).

Build the base

Cut both layers of plywood, being careful to make exact cuts. Then plan the sink location and make the sink cutout. Self-rimming sinks usually include a template that you can use to trace the cutout onto the plywood. Cut the backer board to the same size as the

*Save yourself some headaches
and get better-looking results
by sizing the base to fit the tile.*

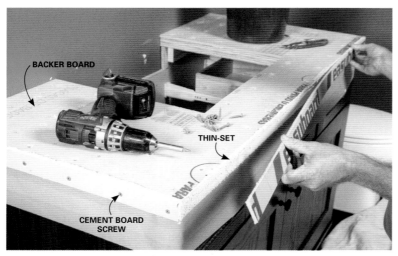

3 **Cover the base with backer board.** Tile backer board forms a waterproof layer for a long-lasting countertop. Quarter-inch-thick backer is all you need over the strong plywood base.

BACKER BOARD

THIN-SET

CEMENT BOARD
SCREW

plywood and make the sink cutout. You'll also need strips of backer board to cover the edges.

Screw the two layers of plywood together. Space screws about 8 in. apart. Then screw the plywood to the vanity cabinet, making sure the overhang is even on both sides and that the front edge is parallel to the vanity cabinet (Photo 2).

Next, cover the plywood with backer board (Photo 3). Cut and test-fit the backer board first. Then mix powdered thin-set mortar with water to about the consistency of peanut butter. Spread it onto the plywood with a 3/16-in. V-notch trowel. Finally, screw the backer board to the plywood, placing screws about 8 in. apart.

The last step before tiling is to wrap the corners of the backer board with cement board tape. Start by vacuuming and then wiping the top and edges with a clean cloth to remove dust. Wrap the adhesive-backed tape around the corners and press it down. Then cover the tape with a thin layer of thin-set mortar. After the thin-set hardens, scrape off any lumps and dust off the top again to prepare it for tiling.

Tile the countertop

Photos 4 – 6 show how to spread the mortar and embed the tile. Before you start, cut the mesh backing to form strips of tile for the edges and make the sink cutout. Trim the mesh tight to the tile so you don't have any mesh whiskers sticking out. Then arrange the tile in the shape of the vanity and within easy reach of the vanity top so you can easily reach it after spreading the thin-set.

Mix and spread the thin-set. Pay close attention to Photo 4; it shows an important tip. Flattening the mortar after you spread it with the notched trowel prevents thin-set from filling the grout spaces when you embed the tile. Any thin-set that gets into the grout spaces has to be cleaned out before you can grout the tile, so this tip will save you a lot of time and effort.

Set the tiles on the top and edges as quickly and accurately as possible (Photo 5). You need to work fast so you can make slight adjustments to the tile before the thin-set starts to set up. When you're satisfied that the tile top and edges are perfectly aligned, embed the tile (Photo 6). Let the thin-set harden overnight before grouting.

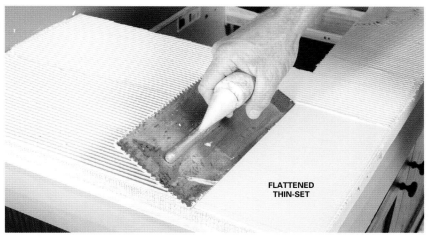

FLATTENED THIN-SET

4 **Comb out, then flatten the thin-set.** Use a 3/16-in. V-notch trowel to spread a layer of thin-set over the backer board. Then flatten it with the straight side of the trowel.

LINE UP GROUT SPACES

5 **Start setting the tile at the corner.** For perfectly aligned grout joints, start by setting a strip of tile on the front and side edges, and a full sheet of tile on top. Adjust the tile until the grout lines on the top line up with the grout lines on the front and sides.

FLAT WOOD BLOCK

6 **Embed the tile with a wood block.** Tap the top of the mosaic tile with a flat block of wood to level the surface and ensure a secure bond with the thin-set.

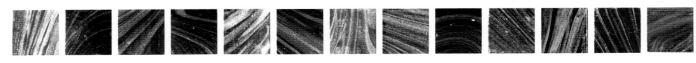

7 **Grout the tile.** Work the grout back and forth in different directions to completely fill the joints and eliminate voids. Well-packed joints are the key to a lasting grout job.

8 **"Tool" the grout with a damp sponge.** Wait until the grout starts to set up before tooling. Wring out the sponge until it's just damp. Then rub it over the tile in a circular motion to smooth and shape the grout and fill tiny voids and pinholes.

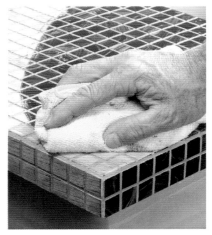

9 **Buff off the grout film.** Wait until the grout is hard before buffing it. Then polish it with a microfiber cloth to remove the haze.

Grout the tile

Photos 7 – 9 show how to grout the tile. Start by mixing the grout according to the directions on the package. Let it rest for about 10 minutes—this is called "slaking." Then mix it again. It'll often thicken a bit after slaking and require a bit more water. The grout should be the consistency of mayonnaise.

Here are some grouting tips:

■ Work the grout from all angles with the float to completely fill the joints (Photo 7).

■ Scrape off the excess before it starts to set.

■ Wait until the grout starts to harden before cleaning it with a sponge. If you can't make a fingerprint, it's hard enough.

■ Keep the rinse water clear and wring all the water out of the sponge when you're cleaning the grout. Use a clean side of the sponge for each cleaning stroke.

■ Use a damp sponge to tool the grout after it sets up (Photo 8). Wait about 15 minutes after cleaning before tooling the tile.

■ Coat the grout with a grout sealer to help prevent staining and make it more water-resistant. Wait two or three days before sealing.

Finishing touches

We added a backsplash before setting the sink. A backsplash could be as simple as tiles attached to the wall with thin-set, or something more elaborate. We screwed 3/8-in. plywood to the wall, covered it with 1/4-in. backer board and surrounded it with 3/4-in.-thick oak trim. Then we tiled over the backer board, grouted the tile and caulked the seam between the countertop and the backsplash with a fine bead of clear silicone caulk.

Glass tile mirror

The mirror frame is made from a 3/4-in. x 4-1/2-in. oak board with a 1-5/8-in.-wide dado on the face to accommodate a band of tile and a 3/8-in. rabbet on the back to hold the mirror. We cut the dado with dado blades mounted on a table saw. A router would also work. We sized the frame so we wouldn't have to cut tiles at the corners. After mitering the parts and staining the frame, we set the tile strips in a thin bead of construction adhesive. Then we finished it off by masking the wood and grouting the tile.

Granite tile countertop

G ranite tile makes an attractive, durable countertop for either a kitchen or bathroom. Tile stores have a large selection of granite tiles. You can also find granite tile with bullnose edges and outside corners. You can order it through tile stores or online.

A few weeks before you tear off your old countertops, pull out a pencil and pad and calculate the number and types of tiles needed (or use a program like SketchUp). Measure, then sketch your countertop on graph paper, including the sink. Label the tiles (bullnose, field, corners) to assess what's needed where.

Make a dry run first

Once you build your base (see Figure A), you're set to start laying tile. But first do a dry run. Dry-fitting gives you time to experiment with the arrangement of the tiles so that the natural color and grain variations flow from one tile to the next. A dry run also lets you cut the tiles all at once. Check the bag of thin-set for the proper-size trowel for the granite tile. Leave a slight gap between tiles so that you can make adjustments for out-of-square corners. Grout and seal the tile, and caulk between the tile and the backsplash.

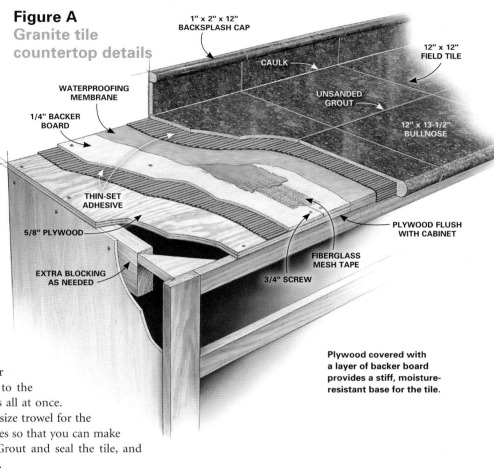

Figure A
Granite tile countertop details

- 1" x 2" x 12" BACKSPLASH CAP
- CAULK
- 12" x 12" FIELD TILE
- WATERPROOFING MEMBRANE
- UNSANDED GROUT
- 1/4" BACKER BOARD
- 12" x 13-1/2" BULLNOSE
- THIN-SET ADHESIVE
- 5/8" PLYWOOD
- PLYWOOD FLUSH WITH CABINET
- FIBERGLASS MESH TAPE
- EXTRA BLOCKING AS NEEDED
- 3/4" SCREW

Plywood covered with a layer of backer board provides a stiff, moisture-resistant base for the tile.

WATERPROOFING MEMBRANE

PLASTIC SHEETING

1 Protect the tile base against water damage with a coat of waterproofing membrane.

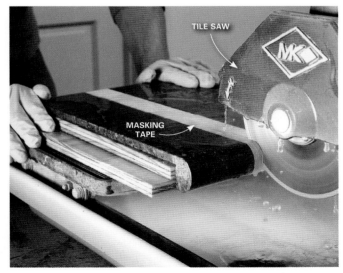

TILE SAW

MASKING TAPE

2 Set bullnose tiles on scraps of plywood to cut them. Granite is difficult to mark clearly, so stick on some masking tape and mark the tape. Soften cut edges by rubbing them with a honing stone.

Precision cuts with a diamond tile saw

There's no substitute for a diamond tile saw when you have to make fine cuts—corners, curves, slivers—or cut stone or other hard tiles. Here you'll learn how a tile pro makes the tricky cuts that result in a first-class job.

Tile-cutting diamond wet saws are available at rental stores, home centers and tile stores that cater to DIYers.

Set the saw up outside or in your garage or workshop. If a finished room is more convenient, cover the floor and wall behind the saw with plastic dropcloths. Then fill the water reservoir with water.

Even though the tile saw looks scary, the blade is abrasive rather than toothed and therefore safer than wood-cutting saws. You'll still want to take precautions, as you would with any other saw.

Basic cuts

The photo below left shows the basic technique for making straight cuts. Wait for a stream of water to cover the blade before you start cutting. Watch the line as you cut and slightly adjust the position of the tile to keep the blade on the line. Move the tile slowly through the blade for the best-quality cut. If you hear the saw slow down, you're cutting too fast. Harder materials require slower feed rates. When you finish the cut, keep both hands on the tile and slide the table back and clear of the blade before you reach to switch off the saw.

Special techniques

The photo below shows how to make a freehand diagonal cut. Use this technique to cut any angle marked on tile. The key is to sight down the cutting line and align the blade with the line. If your tile is too large to fit between the fence and blade, lay the tile on top of the fence.

Saw safety

1. Plug the saw into a GFCI-protected outlet.
2. Don't wear jewelry or loose-fitting clothes. Tie back long hair.
3. Wear safety glasses and hearing protection.
4. Use both hands to guide the tile through the blade.
5. Keep your fingers away from the blade.

Basic square cuts

WATER HOSE

WATER RESERVOIR

SLIDING SAW BED

Mark the tile with a lead or grease pencil. Set the tile against the fence on the sliding saw bed and line up the diamond blade with the cutting mark. Turn on the saw and wait for water to flow over the blade. Hold the tile and slowly feed it into the blade. As the cut nears completion, gently push the two halves of the tile together to prevent the tile from breaking before the cut is complete. When the cut is complete, carefully slide the bed and cut tile back toward you until the tile is clear of the blade.

Diagonal cuts

MASKING TAPE

Sight down the cutting mark and align it with the blade. Hold the tile in this position and guide it through the saw. Wear safety glasses.

TIP

Place a strip of masking tape on shiny, hard-to-mark tiles and mark on it instead.

Notching for corners

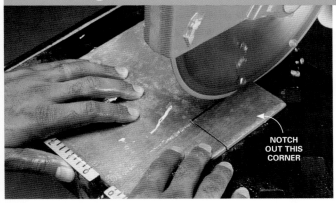

1 Cut along both lines until the cuts intersect in the corner. Break out the waste piece.

NOTCH OUT THIS CORNER

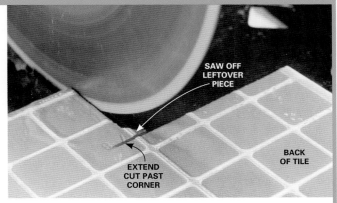

SAW OFF LEFTOVER PIECE

EXTEND CUT PAST CORNER

BACK OF TILE

2 Invert the tile on the sliding bed, then saw from the back of the tile to remove the remaining bit of tile and create a clean corner. You can cut a little past the corner on the back side.

Cut miters on stone as easily as wood

Fancy borders or stripes, called "listellos" in tile lingo, are a popular decorative feature that often requires miter cuts to fit around corners. A diamond wet saw makes these cuts effortlessly with the technique shown in the photo below.

There's a trick to slicing off slivers

Removing a tiny sliver of tile is tough because the blade tends to wander off the edge of the tile. The solution is to trap the blade between the tile you want to trim and a scrap (below, right). You may have to make several passes to shave away enough material.

Cutting curves is no problem

You can even use your saw to cut inside curves (Photos 1–3, p. 134). After breaking out the tile fingers (Photo 2, p. 134), use the abrasive diamond blade to grind away excess tile and smooth the curve. Be careful, though; too much sideways pressure could damage the expensive-blade. Move the tile slowly across the blade, pressing lightly and nibbling off a fraction of an inch with each pass (Photo 3). Grip the tile firmly with both hands and tilt the edge closest to the blade up and off the bed to get a perpendicular cut.

Cut miters with a block

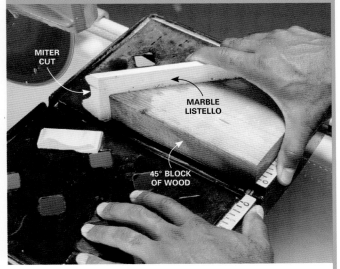

MITER CUT

MARBLE LISTELLO

45° BLOCK OF WOOD

Hold the tile trim against a block of wood cut at a 45-degree angle. Guide the tile through the saw to cut the angle.

Slice a sliver

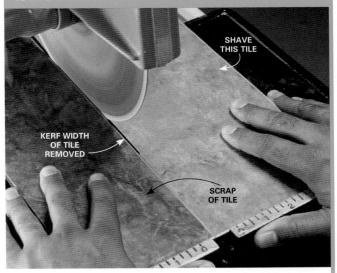

SHAVE THIS TILE

KERF WIDTH OF TILE REMOVED

SCRAP OF TILE

Butt a scrap of tile against the edge of the tile you want to trim. Push both pieces through the blade, using the basic cutting technique (p. 132). Repeat this process until you've trimmed enough. Each pass will remove 1/8 in. or less.

Cut an inside curve

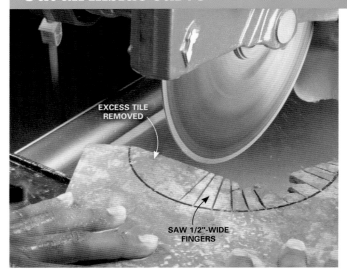

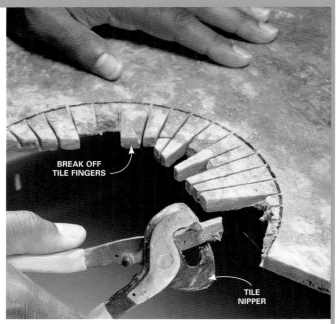

1 Cut away excess material with two angle cuts. Then make a series of cuts to the curved line about every 1/2 in. For the cleanest breaks, try to cut at a right angle to the curve, as if you were cutting the spokes of a wheel.

Tips for common problems

With a little practice, cutting tile on a wet saw is almost trouble free. But there are a few common problems that are easy to avoid or fix with the right techniques.

Some types of tile tend to break when the cut is almost complete. The photo below shows the solution. Straying from the line is another common problem, especially when you're cutting without a fence or guide. You can't force the blade back to the line by twisting the tile. Instead, back up and recut the tile, slicing off a small amount of tile until the blade is back on track.

2 Snap off the sawed sections with a tile nipper or by tapping each with the handle of a screwdriver or trowel.

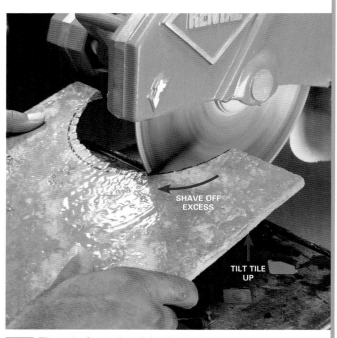

3 Tilt up the front edge of the tile and clean up the cut by shaving away the excess. Remove no more than 1/16 in. at a time.

Prevent chipping

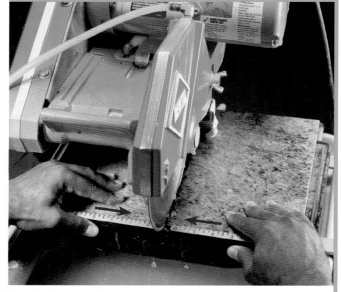

Press both halves of the tile together until the cut is complete to prevent the tile from breaking and chipping at the end of the cut.

TIP

If you have just a few cuts to make, mark your tiles and bring them to a tile store that will cut them for you. The cost is usually minimal.

Tough tile cuts with a grinder

SMOOTH CONTINUOUS RIM

Stone, porcelain and glass tiles offer beautiful options for bath and kitchen tiling projects. But cutting these hard materials presents a unique challenge. Straight cuts are easy to make with a diamond wet saw. But cutting curves and holes requires special techniques.

Here you'll learn how to use an inexpensive angle grinder with a diamond blade to cut perfect circles and squares in even the toughest tile. Diamond blades are sold in home centers and most hardware stores. When you're choosing a diamond blade, look for one with a continuous, rather than segmented rim for the smoothest cut.

Be aware, though, that cutting with a dry-cut diamond blade creates a lot of dust and noise. So make sure you cut in a well-ventilated area (or better yet, outside!) and wear hearing protection, a good-quality two-strap dust mask and safety glasses.

Tilt the blade for circles

Many tile jobs require you to cut one or more large round holes for floor drains or shower valves. Photos 1 – 3 show how to cut a hole for a shower valve. Shown here is how to cut a hole that's entirely within a single tile, one of the most difficult cuts. In the next section (below) you'll see an easier method to use for cutting curves in the edge of a tile.

Even with this method, try to avoid a tile layout that places the edge of the circular cutout less than 1/2 in. from the edge of a tile. It's better to shift the entire layout instead. Otherwise, chances are good that you'll break the tile at the narrow point while cutting.

The method shown for cutting a circle with a grinder and diamond blade requires you to cut around the circle a number of times, making a deeper cut with each revolution. The key is to maintain the same angle and shave off progressive layers, moving the cut closer to the center of the circle (Photo 2).

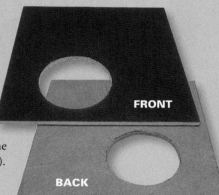

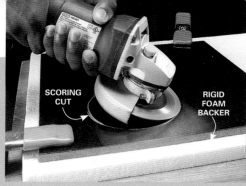

1 Score the front of the tile along the circle guideline with the diamond blade. Tilt the grinder about 30 degrees and cut about 1/16 in. deep.

2 Move the blade 1/8 in. to the inside of the line and make a deeper cut. Continue moving the blade away from the line and cutting deeper until you cut completely through.

3 Grind off rough edges and trim back to the line for a perfect curve.

Rough out semicircular cuts before trimming to the line

1 Score the profile with the saw, then cut in from the edge of the tile to remove as much waste as possible.

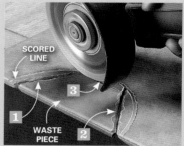

2 Make a series of closely spaced cuts up to the scored line. Break off the waste. Then grind the edges smooth.

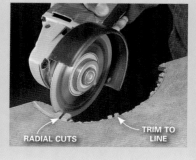

The process for cutting semicircles from the edge of tiles is similar to the technique shown above for full circles. You start by marking the cut and scoring the face of the tile on the line. Then, rather than deepen the scoring cut, simply remove the excess tile with straight cuts (Photo 1).

Before you remove the excess tile (Photo 1), be sure to make short cuts on both sides of the semicircle (1 and 2). Then connect the cuts as shown (3). Rather than make this connecting cut in one pass, make a series of progressively deeper shallow cuts until you're through the tile.

Now complete the semicircle with a series of radial cuts—like the spokes of a wheel (Photo 2). Finish by cleaning up the rough edges with the diamond blade. Or remove the "tabs" with a tile nipper (a pliers-like biting tool). Then grind the edges smooth.

FRONT

BACK

Make a dish-shaped cutout for small, rough holes

Most plumbing pipe holes are covered by a decorative escutcheon or hidden by a fixture base, so a precise round hole isn't necessary. Use the technique shown here to make rough, round holes.

Start by marking the circular cutout on the back of the tile. Then plunge the diamond blade down through the tile, keeping it centered on the hole so that the slot made by the blade extends equally on both sides of the circle marks (Photo 1). Check often to see when the slot through the front of the tile reaches the edges of the desired cutout. Then use the length of that plunge cut to gauge the diameter of a second, larger circle. Draw that larger circle on the back of the tile (Photo 2). Use this circle as a guide for making the rest of the plunge cuts. Rotate the grinder about a blade's width and make another plunge cut, stopping at the outer circle. Continue this process until you finish the hole.

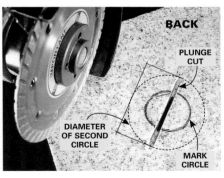

1 Center the cut on the hole and plunge slowly from the back. Stop when the slot through the face of the tile lines up with the edges of the desired cutout.

BACK

PLUNGE CUT

DIAMETER OF SECOND CIRCLE

MARK CIRCLE

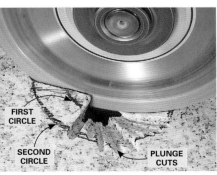

2 Draw another larger circle to guide the depth of the remaining cuts. Make repeated plunge cuts until the circle is complete.

FIRST CIRCLE

SECOND CIRCLE

PLUNGE CUTS

Plunge-cut from the back to make square or rectangular cutouts

Cutting rectangular or square holes for electrical outlets is simple with this method. The key is to avoid cutting beyond the corners of the square where the cut might be visible. Plunge-cut slowly from the back and check often to avoid going too far.

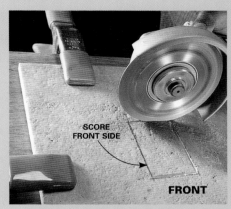

1 Mark the cutout on the front and back of the tile precisely. Then score the front of the tile about 1/8 in. deep along the line.

SCORE FRONT SIDE

FRONT

2 Flip the tile over and plunge the cut from the back. Stop and check often. Stop when the cut lines up with the corners of the marked square on the front. Plunge-cut the remaining three sides.

BACK

PLUNGE CUT ON THE BACK

STOP CUT AT CORNER

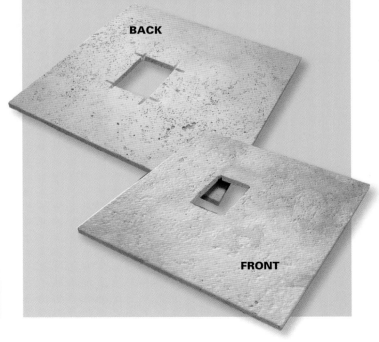

BACK

FRONT

Grouting tips

Grouting can be a rewarding task. It's the last step in a tile job, so you know you're almost done. And filling the joints with grout brings out the beauty of the tile. But if you've ever had grout turn rock hard before getting it off the tile, you know grouting can also be a nightmare. So to help you avoid problems and get the best results with the least effort, we've assembled these grouting tips.

Seal porous tile before grouting

If you don't seal porous tile and stone, grout will stick like glue and be nearly impossible to clean off. There are two different products that can make it easier to clean grout from porous stone and tile. If you're installing a matte finish tile or other tile with a rough or porous surface but don't want the sheen that a sealer would leave, apply a liquid grout release product. Grout release forms a thin film that prevents grout from sticking but washes off as you clean off the grout.

Use a sealer rather than grout release if you want to enhance the color of stone or leave a "wet" looking finish. You may have to apply another coat of sealer after grouting for maximum protection and to enhance the color of the stone.

Apply a thin coat of sealer to porous stone. Follow the application instructions on the label. Wipe up excess sealer with a cloth to avoid puddles. Then let the sealer dry before you grout.

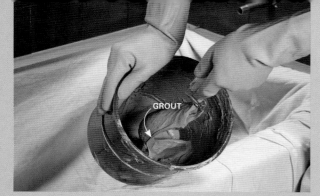

Remix the grout after letting it set for 10 or 15 minutes. Add a little water if the grout is too thick.

Let the grout slake

It's tempting to skip this step, but it's important to let the grout set for 10 minutes after mixing. This step, called slaking, allows the water to completely moisten the dry ingredients. Remix the grout after the slaking period and adjust the mixture by adding a little more powder or water until you reach the viscosity of mayonnaise. Be careful, though—it doesn't take much of either to radically change the consistency.

Fill the joints by pushing the grout at an angle to the joints with a grout float. Start in one corner and work methodically to fill all the joints.

Force grout into the joints

For a long-lasting grout job, make sure all the joints are completely filled with grout. To accomplish this, make several passes over the same area from different directions with the grout float. Hold the float with its face at an angle of about 45 degrees to the tile to force the grout into the joint. When the joints are filled, remove excess grout from the face of the tiles by holding the float at almost 90 degrees to the tile and scraping it off.

Don't spread too much grout at once

Temperature and humidity affect how quickly grout starts to harden after you spread it on the wall. And once it does start to harden, you'll really have to hustle to get it cleaned off the tile and get the joints shaped before the grout turns rock hard. Avoid this problem by grouting small areas at a time. Start by spreading grout onto a 3 x 3-ft. area. Finish grouting, shaping the joints and cleaning each section before proceeding.

Scoop grout from the bucket with your grout float and apply it to the wall with upward strokes. Don't worry about getting it into the joints yet.

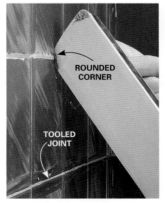

Pull the rounded corner of the grout float over every joint to shape them.

Tool the joints

Shape and compact the grout by dragging a tool across every joint. The tool can be anything from the rounded corner of the grout float to the rounded end of a toothbrush handle. Whatever is handy and has about the right radius to create a slightly concave joint will work. Don't use metal tools. They can damage the tile or leave marks.

Use a clean, damp sponge to remove grout

Start with a clean bucket of water. Wet your grouting sponge and wring it out until it's just damp. Then, starting along one side of the grouted area, position the sponge so that the corner of one long side of the sponge is in contact with the wall and drag the sponge in a continuous stroke up the wall. Now rotate the sponge to expose a clean corner and repeat the process alongside the first stroke. When you've used all four corners of the sponge, rinse it in clean water, wring it out, and continue the process until you've cleaned the entire area once. Clean the tiles two or three more times using the same process until they're free of grout residue. A thin film of grout may appear when the water evaporates. Buff this off with a soft cloth.

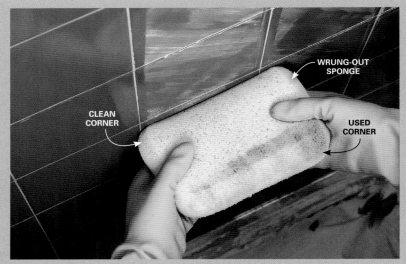

Remove grout from the face of the tile with the corner of a damp sponge. Swipe from bottom to top, using a clean corner of the sponge for each stroke.

Don't scrub the grout or use too much water

Let the grout harden slightly before you clean off the excess. Test the grout by pressing on it with your finger. When it's hard enough to resist denting, you can start cleaning the excess grout from the face of the tile and shaping the joints. Two common mistakes at this point are using too much water, and scrubbing the tile like you're washing a wall. Too much water will weaken the tile and cause the grout color to be uneven when it dries. And scrubbing doesn't remove grout efficiently; it just moves it around.

Don't use a dripping wet sponge to clean grout from the tile. If water runs down, the sponge is too wet.

Remove grout from inside corners and along the tub to make room for caulk. Use a utility knife for narrow spaces or an old screwdriver or putty knife for wider joints.

Remove grout from corners before caulking

Because it's flexible and can handle slight movement, caulk is used at corners instead of grout. For a good tile installation, apply a neat bead of matching caulk at vulnerable areas like along the tub or countertop and at inside corners. But to achieve a good-quality caulk joint, you'll first have to remove the grout from these areas. Most home centers and tile shops will have caulk to match the color of your grout.

Cutting marble

Cutting marble is simple and straightforward with a diamond blade wet saw (Photo 1). But push the tile through slowly. Marble and other soft stones like slate haves flaws and fracture lines where the stone can easily break, especially at the end of a cut. You may have to cut in from each end about an inch before completing cuts (Photo 3). Saw cuts leave slightly rough edges. Smooth these with 200-grit wet/dry sandpaper. (For granite and ceramics, use a special rub stone.)

Cutting the holes for a tub spout, faucet and shower head can be tricky (Photos 2 – 4). Some marble tiles are fragile, so fully support the tile with plywood when cutting or drilling it. Work carefully near brittle edges and corners.

1 Set the fence to width and make straight cuts with a diamond blade wet saw. Cut slowly. Smooth the cut edges of marble with 200-grit wet/dry sandpaper.

2 Cut holes for tub and shower spouts with a 1-1/4-in. carbide- or diamond-grit hole saw. Use light pressure to avoid cracking the tile.

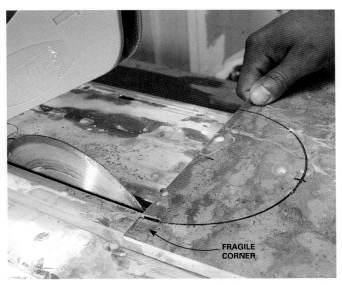

3 Start curved cuts near narrow edges with the wet saw to avoid breaking the tile.

4 Clamp the tile to 1/2-in. plywood to provide full support when you cut curves with a jigsaw. Then slowly cut through both with a carbide-grit blade (diamond-grit for harder tiles). Cover the saw base with painter's tape to avoid scratching the tile.

Chapter Five

WOODWORKING

Iron-on edge banding

With a roll of wood veneer edge banding and a few simple tools, you can cover raw plywood edges so the plywood is nearly indistinguishable from solid wood. Iron-on edge banding is wood veneer with hot-melt adhesive preapplied to the back. You simply hold the edge banding in place, run over it with a household iron to heat the adhesive, let it cool and trim the edges flush.

You'll find edge banding in common species like birch, oak and cherry at home centers and lumberyards. For exotic species and a greater variety of widths, search online or visit a specialty woodworking store. Rolls of edge banding come in lengths of 8 ft. to 250 ft. and widths of 13/16 in. to 2 in. For typical 3/4-in. plywood, buy 13/16- or 7/8-in.-wide edge banding.

7/8" OAK EDGE BANDING

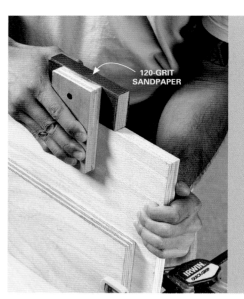

120-GRIT SANDPAPER

Clean up the edges

Saw marks or other roughness will prevent a strong bond between the edge banding and the plywood. To avoid loose edge banding, sand the edges of the plywood smooth before you apply it. To keep from rounding edges while you sand, wrap a quarter sheet of 120-grit sandpaper around a small block of 3/4-in. plywood and screw another scrap to it as a guide. When the sandpaper starts showing signs of wear, remove the screw and reposition the sandpaper. After sanding, vacuum the edge to remove any dust.

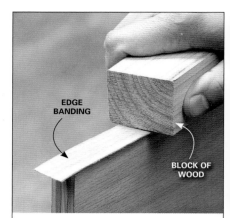

EDGE BANDING

BLOCK OF WOOD

Press it while it's hot

Make sure the edge banding is fully adhered by pressing it down with a block of wood while it's still hot. Go back and forth over the edge a few times while the glue is cooling. Look for any areas that are raised. Heat those spots again and press them again with the block.

"COTTON" SETTING

ROLL OF EDGE BANDING

Iron on the edge banding

Use your regular clothes iron if you wish, but be aware that you may get adhesive on the soleplate. To be safe, buy a cheap iron from a thrift store or discount retailer. Empty the water out to avoid any steam and move the heat setting to "cotton." Use scissors to cut a length of edge banding about 1 in. longer than the edge you're covering. Starting at one end, center the edge banding with equal overhangs on each side and set the preheated iron at that end. Move the iron along the surface, keeping the edge banding centered with your other hand. Move the iron along at a rate of about 2 in. per second. The goal is to melt the adhesive without scorching the wood.

Don't sweat it if you scorch or misalign the banding during application. Just run the iron over it again to soften the glue so you can peel the banding away. Cut yourself a new piece and start over.

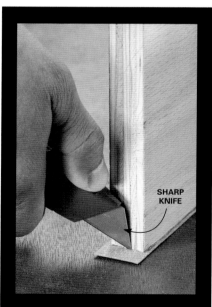

SHARP KNIFE

Slice off the ends

The easiest way to remove the overhanging ends is to simply slice them off with a utility knife. Place the edge banding on a work surface and lightly score it a couple of times. Don't worry about cutting all the way through. Just lift the plywood and bend up the banding to snap it off.

Modify your trimmer

Trimming the overhanging edges flush to the plywood without damaging the edge banding can be tricky. If the trimming blade catches in the wood grain, it can split the thin veneer and you'd have to start over. Prevent that headache by shimming one side of the trimmer with strips of edge banding so that it doesn't cut as deep. Just "tack" the shims on with the iron, making sure to leave a gap where the blades are. Since this trimmer has two cutting sides, you can leave the shims on one side to make the initial pass, and then just flip it over to make the final pass.

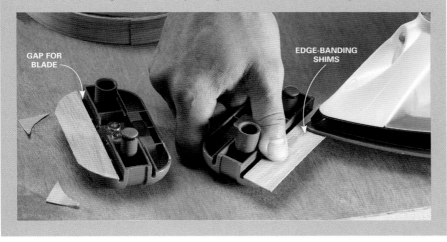

GAP FOR BLADE

EDGE-BANDING SHIMS

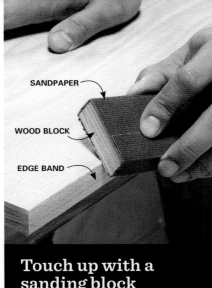

SANDPAPER

WOOD BLOCK

EDGE BAND

Touch up with a sanding block

After you trim them, the edges will be sharp. Ease them with 150-grit sandpaper on a sanding block. Hold the sanding block at a slight angle and smooth out the edge. Sand gently and inspect the edge often to avoid sanding through the thin veneer.

Use a trimmer on edges

The quickest and easiest way to trim the edge banding flush to the plywood is with a special edge banding tool, sold at woodworking stores or online.

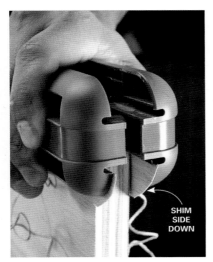

SHIM SIDE DOWN

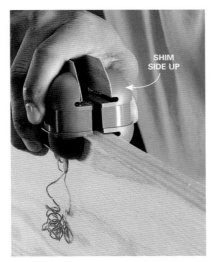

SHIM SIDE UP

Make a shallow pass first

Trim with the shimmed side first. Since less veneer is being removed with this side of the trimmer, the likelihood of runaway splits is greatly reduced. Start at one end and squeeze the trimmer until the shims are against the plywood. Then press down and slide the trimmer along the edge. Thin strips of veneer will peel away from both edges.

Flip the trimmer for the final pass

Flip the trimmer over and use the unshimmed side for a final trimming. When you're through, the edge banding should be almost perfectly flush with the plywood. If you missed any spots, just make another pass or two with the trimmer. The final sanding will remove the sharp edge and any remaining overhang.

SPLICE

Don't

Don't leave a splice where it'll show

Splices can be hard to see on raw edge banding, but they may be highly visible after stain is applied. Inspect the edge banding before you cut it to length so you can cut around splices and avoid surprises later. Avoid waste by using spliced pieces in less visible areas.

Crosscutting on a table saw

Want perfect end cuts every time? Go directly to your table saw and we'll show you how.

Set the miter gauge perfectly square to the blade

The key to accurate right-angle cuts is to square up the miter gauge to the saw blade. Don't trust the angle indicators on the gauge; they're far too sloppy. Instead, go to an art supply or woodworking store and buy a 45-degree drafting triangle. Set one side against the blade and align the gauge to the other side (Photo 1). Be sure the side of the triangle against the blade falls between the teeth tight to the blade "plate." For greater accuracy, have the blade cranked all the way up so you're squaring to the widest part of the blade.

Choose a straight 1x2 or 1x3 board at least 12 in. long for the extension fence (Photo 2). Sometimes you'll need a longer fence, but more on this later. Screw the fence to the miter gauge with the right side projecting a few inches past the saw blade. All miter gauges have a pair of screw holes or slots for this purpose. Choose screws short enough so they don't penetrate all the way through the wood.

Photos 4 and 5 show you how to test the accuracy of and fine-tune your miter gauge setting. You'll find that even tiny adjustments have a big effect.

TIP

Raise the blade all the way and hold a combination square vertically against the blade and the saw table. Adjust the blade tilt as necessary. Don't trust the saw's tilt angle indicator. When checked, the saw shown here was off by two full degrees.

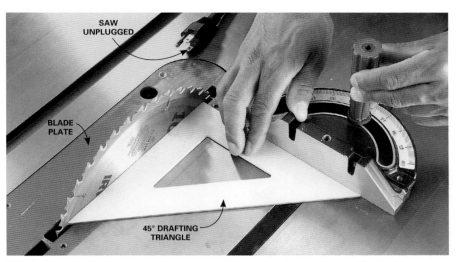

1 Loosen the handle on the miter gauge and square it to the saw blade with a drafting square, then retighten the handle.

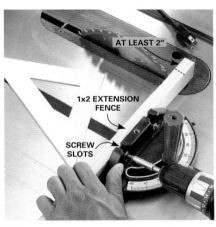

2 Screw an extension fence to the miter gauge from the back side.

3 Start the saw and cut off the end of the extension fence.

4 Hold a 4-in.-wide test piece against the fence, start the saw and push the wood through the blade. Shut off the saw and remove the two halves.

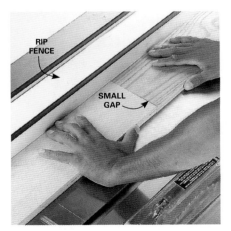

5 Flip one half over and butt the cut edges together against the rip fence. A gap shows that the miter gauge is slightly off. Adjust it and retest.

Make precise square cuts

To make precise square cuts, start by rough-cutting long boards a few inches longer than the final length, with either a circular or a miter saw. (Boards longer than 4 ft. are awkward to cut on a table saw.) Then raise or lower the blade so it's about 1/8 in. higher than the board's thickness. Position the factory end of the board just past the end of the extension fence so the blade will just shave it, and then start the saw.

Always recut factory ends; they're rarely perfectly square. Hold the board snug against the fence and slowly push it through the blade. After each cut, slide the board away from the blade and turn off the saw before you remove cutoff pieces.

Now mark the exact length at the other end and align that mark with the end of the extension fence (Photo 1). Then make the final cut.

PULL AWAY AFTER CUT

1 Mark the board for length and align the mark with the end of the extension fence.

2 Start the saw, hold the board firmly against the fence and push the board completely past the saw blade.

3 Pull the board away from the blade, then shut off the saw and remove the cutoff piece from the other side.

Make accurate 45-degree miter cuts

Perfect miters are almost as easy as crosscuts. Start by setting the miter gauge to 45 degrees (Photo 1) using the techniques we showed on p. 147. Mount an extension fence, moving it toward the blade far enough to cut the end at a 45-degree angle (Photo 2). Then make the fine cuts on your material. Hold your material very tight, or clamp it; the saw blade will try to pull it off line. In general, it's best to make all your miter cuts first, and then any square cuts at the opposite end, where it's easier to be accurate.

For the kind of extreme accuracy needed for complete squares such as picture frames, cut two test boards, push the miters tightly together and check the assembly with a drafting square. If it's not perfect, adjust the miter gauge and repeat. Again, it only takes very small adjustments to make big differences.

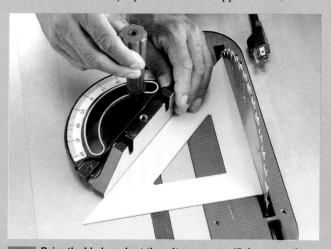 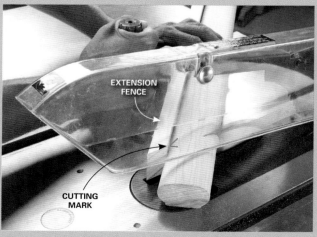

EXTENSION FENCE

CUTTING MARK

1 Raise the blade and set the miter gauge to 45 degrees, using the drafting square. Then mount an extension fence to the miter gauge as shown in Photos 2 and 3 on p. 147.

2 Hold the board *very* firmly against the fence and push the board through the blade to make the cut.

Perfect crosscuts on thick stock

Cutting newel posts, table legs or other thick stock to length has to be done in two steps. Set up your fence exactly as before. A higher fence, at least two-thirds the thickness of the wood, gives better support. Then the trick is to make a first cut halfway through and flip the wood over to finish the cut.

With this technique, the blade guard will block the wood from going all the way through the blade. You'll have to remove it for this task, so cut with caution. Be sure to keep your fingers well away from the blade while you make the cuts.

Raise the blade to cut just over halfway through the post. Make one pass, then flip the post over and align the saw kerf with the end of the fence and complete the cut.

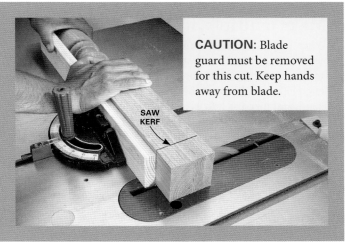

CAUTION: Blade guard must be removed for this cut. Keep hands away from blade.

SAW KERF

MELAMINE CLOSET SHELF

Clamp a straight length of plywood to the side of a sawhorse level with the saw table. Support one end of long boards on the plywood edge while you crosscut them.

Cut long boards with support

Any board much over 4 ft. long is tougher to cut accurately because the table on the saw will no longer support it. As you struggle to keep it flat on the table, it often binds in the blade.

Clamp a piece of plywood or closet shelving (the slippery edge helps the wood slide) to the top of a sawhorse. To adjust the height of the support board, hold a level or a straightedge flat to the table until the board is even with the table top. Resist the temptation to have a buddy support the other end while you push it through the blade. That's dangerous. Avoid that dicey human element.

1-in. crosscutting stop block

When you're crosscutting on a table saw, set the cut length with a block clamped to the fence. Don't ever use the fence directly. That's a good way to get a board kicked back right at you. Ruptured organs and broken ribs—or worse—are a very real possibility.

Instead, clamp a block of wood to the fence before the blade. Then the end of the board will be free of the fence during and after the cut. If you make a block that's exactly 1 in. thick, you can set the fence scale at 1 in. greater than the length you're after. No tricky fractions involved.

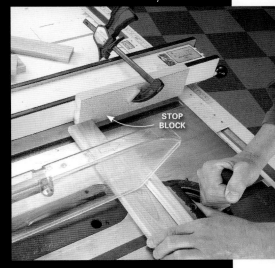

STOP BLOCK

Use a portable table saw

You don't need to use a stationary table saw as shown here to make nice crosscuts. An ordinary portable table saw will do just fine for most cuts. The size of the material you can cut will be limited by the size of the table and the distance from the saw blade to the miter gauge. However, make sure to anchor the saw securely when you're cutting long or heavy material.

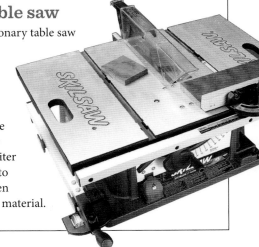

Make multiple, identical cuts

When you're building a bookcase, a piece of furniture or nearly any other project, just about every component will need a matching partner (or several partners) of identical length. The trick is to cut the first board at exactly the right length and then use it to establish a stop block to cut all the others. Here are two techniques for that process, one for short boards and the other for long ones.

Short boards

If boards will be shorter than 18 in. or so, it's best to use a slightly longer extension fence and clamp a stop block to the fence (Photo 1). Cut a slight angle on the stop block. That'll keep sawdust from accumulating between the block and the board. Sawdust buildup will result in boards that are just a wee bit on the short side.

Long boards

It's impractical to have an unwieldy extra-long fence to cut long identical boards. Instead, clamp a secondary fence above the boards and clamp a stop block on the end of that fence as shown in Photo 2. Select extension fence stock that's tall enough to handle both the thickness of the board and the clamp for the secondary fence. A 1-1/2-in. x 3/4-in. board works well for the secondary fence.

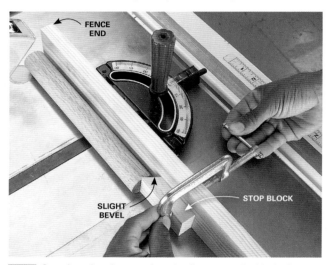

1 Cut a board to the exact length, align one end with the fence end and clamp an angled stop block to the fence. Push each board against the stop block and make the cut.

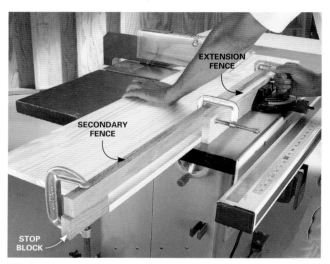

2 Clamp a stop block on the end of a long secondary fence. Adjust the position of the secondary fence and clamp it to the extension fence. Then cut long boards to length.

Safety first

The table saw is arguably the most dangerous power tool in the shop even when you're using it for crosscutting. Here are a few tips to keep you as safe as possible.

- Always unplug the saw when you're squaring up the blade with a drafting square (Photo 1, p. 147).
- Make sure the safety guard support lines up with the blade. There are adjustments on all guards. If it's not lined up, boards can get hung up on the support right in the middle of a cut.
- It's OK to just shave a little from the end of a board. But use caution with cutoffs that are shorter than 2 in. The blade will often catch shorter cutoffs and send them flying.
- **Never use the table saw rip fence as a guide for cutting wood to length. The wood will become trapped between the fence and the saw blade and pose a serious kickback hazard.**

Solid wood nosing for plywood

Plywood is a great material for building cabinets, bookcases and shelves. But exposed edges usually look unfinished unless they're covered with a layer of wood. While wood veneer tape is one way to cover edges, an even better method is to glue or nail on a strip of solid wood nosing. It's good looking and durable, and it protects vulnerable edges from abuse in high-wear areas. It also stiffens the plywood, an important feature for shelving. If you make it even wider than the plywood, as shown here, the extra stiffness will help keep plywood shelves from sagging. And unlike thin veneer edgings, the wood nosing can be routed to create a decorative edge (Photo 8).

Here you'll learn how to glue and clamp wood nosing to plywood and how to sand the top for a perfectly flush surface and nearly invisible joint.

Pipe clamps like the ones shown are available at home centers, hardware stores and lumberyards. They're a good investment. They'll often come in handy for all kinds of gluing projects around the house. Buy a length of black iron pipe (3/4 in. or 1/2 in., depending on your clamps) that's threaded on at least one end to complete each clamp (2-ft. and 4-ft. pipes are the most versatile). You'll also need a belt sander fitted with a 120-grit belt to sand the edges flush, but 100-grit sandpaper wrapped around

a wood or rubber sanding block will also work. It'll just take more elbow grease.

Set up the clamps before you start gluing

Your gluing and clamping operation will go more smoothly if you set up the clamps before you start. That way you can move quickly once you spread the glue. Photo 1 shows the setup we used. Any straight scraps of wood will work for the clamp pads. They protect the nosing and plywood from the metal clamp faces and help spread the force of the clamps over a wider area. Use spacer boards to hold the plywood above the clamps and flush to the top edge of the nosing.

Start with straight-edged plywood and straight nosing boards

You can use any size and thickness of nosing you want. But 3/4-in.-thick strips anywhere from 3/4 to 1-1/2 in. wide are easy to find and look great. If you don't own a table saw, you can cut a clean, accurate edge on plywood by clamping a straightedge to the sheet and using it as a guide for your circular saw. Hardwood boards for nosing are available at home centers and lumberyards. If you want a 3/4-in. x 3/4-in. nosing, you'll have to rip it on a table saw or have it ripped at the lumberyard. Cut the plywood

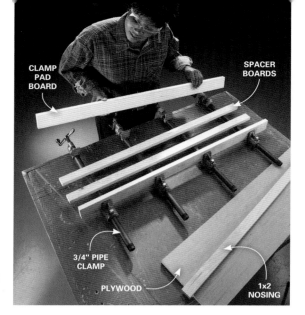

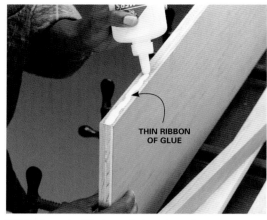

1 Set up the clamps (one every 8 to 10 in.), the clamp pads and the spacers on your workbench. Adjust the clamps to slightly wider than the shelf and nosing.

CLAMP PAD BOARD

SPACER BOARDS

3/4" PIPE CLAMP

PLYWOOD

1x2 NOSING

THIN RIBBON OF GLUE

2 Spread a thin layer of glue, about the thickness and width of a shoelace, along the plywood edge.

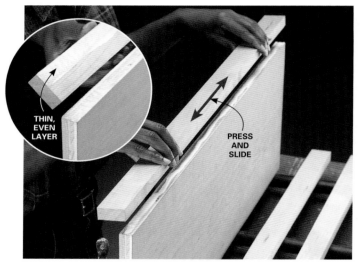

THIN, EVEN LAYER

PRESS AND SLIDE

SLIGHTLY ELEVATED

3 Press the nosing onto the plywood and move it back and forth to spread the glue. A thin layer of glue should completely cover the mating surfaces.

4 Place the shelf and nosing in the clamps. Feel the joint with your fingertip and adjust the nosing until the top is a hair's width above the plywood as you tighten the clamps.

and nosing to length, or if you need more precision, leave it slightly long and cut it off later.

You don't need much glue

A thin layer of yellow wood glue is all it takes to make a virtually indestructible glue joint. Extra glue just makes a bigger cleanup job, and it causes the nosing to slide around, making alignment difficult. To get a feel for the right amount, pull off the nosing after you've slid it back and forth on the glue (Photo 3) and look at the back. You should see a thin, even layer of glue covering both mating surfaces. When you apply the clamps, a small bead of glue should ooze out of the seam.

It's difficult to get the plywood and nosing to line up perfectly flush when you clamp them together. Snug up all of the clamps, but don't tighten them. Then push the nosing up or down to adjust it as you tighten the clamps. Hold the nosing slightly above the plywood, about the thickness of a sheet of paper (Photo 4), and sand it flush after the glue dries (Photo 7).

Don't let the glue harden

Cleaning up glue squeeze-out is easy if you catch it at the right time (Photo 5). At room temperature, the glue will set enough for you to remove the clamps and scrape off the excess in about 20 to 30 minutes. Since the glue hasn't reached full strength, you still have to be careful not to jar the nosing loose. Removing the plywood from the clamps frees them up for the next piece and allows you easy access to scrape glue from both the top and bottom.

Dried glue smears are hard to see and can cause trouble when you apply finish to the plywood. Photo 6 shows how to expose dried glue by wiping it with a damp rag. The wetted glue shows up as a white spot that you can scrape off with a sharp-edged putty knife.

Sand carefully to avoid damaging the veneer

The top layer of plywood is a thin layer of wood, called veneer.

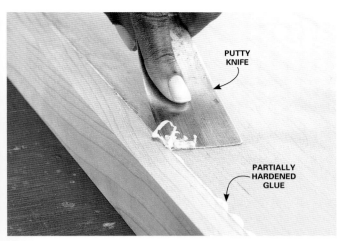

PUTTY KNIFE

PARTIALLY HARDENED GLUE

DAMP RAG

GLUE SPLOTCH

5 Let the glue set for about 30 minutes until it's rubbery and starts to change color. Scrape off the partially hardened glue with a putty knife.

6 Moisten the surface with a damp rag to reveal dried glue smudges. Scrape them off while they're wet. Let the glue set another hour.

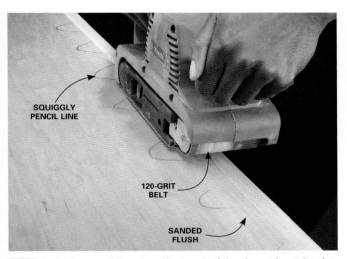

SQUIGGLY PENCIL LINE

120-GRIT BELT

SANDED FLUSH

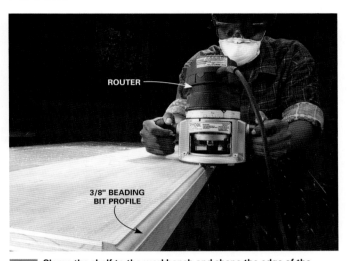

ROUTER

3/8" BEADING BIT PROFILE

7 Scribble a pencil line along the length of the plywood, overlapping it onto the nosing. Carefully sand the nosing with a belt sander and 120-grit belt until the pencil line disappears and the nosing is flush to the plywood.

8 Clamp the shelf to the workbench and shape the edge of the nosing with a router and shaping bit.

It's easy to accidentally sand through this veneer and expose the lower layer of wood, which doesn't match the surface.

Use light pressure and a fine, 120-grit belt on the belt sander. Stop sanding as soon as you see the squiggly pencil line start to disappear over the glue joint (Photo 7). Be careful to hold the belt sander perfectly flat. Tilting it toward the plywood could cause it to sand through the veneer. Tilting it away will bevel the nosing. If the nosing isn't quite flush, finish by hand-sanding.

There are many other methods for getting the nosing perfectly flush to the plywood. Experienced woodworkers use sharp planes and scrapers. A router with a flush-trimming bit also does a nice job. But both these techniques require practice for ideal results.

If you want to dress up the edge of a plywood shelf, simply rout a shape on the solid wood nosing (Photo 8). Make sure to wear safety glasses, hearing protection and a dust mask when routing. Move the router from left to right as you face the shelf.

No-clamp nosing

If you're painting the plywood or you don't mind the look of filled nail holes, you can simply glue and nail the nosing into place rather than messing with clamps. Predrill holes for the 1-1/2-in. finish nails and drive them below the surface with a nail set. Then fill the holes with wood filler or patching compound and sand them smooth before you paint, or fill them with matching putty after you stain and varnish the wood.

Router table techniques

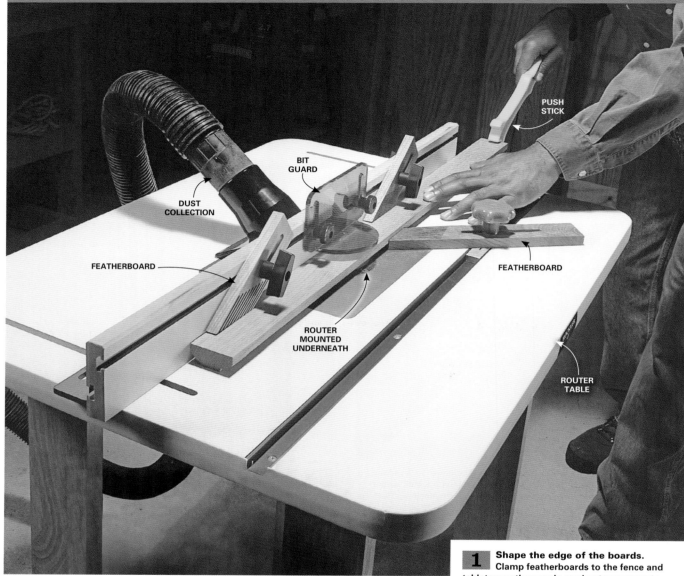

DUST COLLECTION

BIT GUARD

PUSH STICK

FEATHERBOARD

ROUTER MOUNTED UNDERNEATH

FEATHERBOARD

ROUTER TABLE

1 Shape the edge of the boards. Clamp featherboards to the fence and tabletop so they apply moderate pressure to the board. Feed the board through the router at a steady rate. Hook the notch on the push stick over the end of the board and use the stick to push the board past the bit at the end of the cut.

OGEE BIT

Want to double the usefulness of your router? Mount it in a router table and you'll be able to shape long moldings as well as cut decorative edges on small pieces with ease and safety. In this article, we'll show you how to set up and use a router table to cut moldings, rout small pieces freehand, and plane a perfectly straight edge on plywood or other boards.

Make your own moldings

Router tables are great for cutting your own moldings. Using a router table is easier and faster than using a router alone; you don't have to clamp the board. And narrow boards that are hard to shape with a router are a cinch on a router table. Use featherboards and a push stick to protect your fingers (Photo 1).

Start by tightening the bit into the router, mounting the router in the base and adjusting the height of the bit. Don't worry about getting the fence square to the table; it doesn't matter for this type of cut. If your bit has a bearing guide, lay a

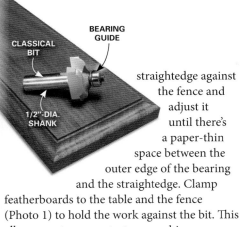

BEARING GUIDE

CLASSICAL BIT

1/2"-DIA. SHANK

straightedge against the fence and adjust it until there's a paper-thin space between the outer edge of the bearing and the straightedge. Clamp featherboards to the table and the fence (Photo 1) to hold the work against the bit. This allows you to concentrate on pushing the board.

To avoid burn marks from the router bit, feed the board at a steady rate without stopping. The rate of feed depends on the bit and type of wood. With experience, you'll learn to judge the best rate by listening to the router and feeling the resistance as you push against the board.

Cuts more than about 3/8 in. deep can strain the router motor, put undue pressure on the bit, and leave a rough or chipped surface on the wood. To avoid this, adjust the fence so the bit removes about two-thirds of the wood with the first pass. Then readjust the fence and make the final pass at a faster feed rate.

Easy end-grain routing

Shaping end grain with a router table and square push block (Photo 2) has three advantages over end-grain routing with a handheld router. First, you're not limited to bearing-guided bits, since the fence is guiding the cut. Second, unlike with handheld routers, it's just as easy to rout narrow pieces as wide ones. And finally, the push block backs up the cut to eliminate the chipping and tear-out commonly associated with end-grain routing. Photo 2 shows how to use a simple square push block to support your work square to the fence as you guide it past the bit.

Plane perfectly straight edges on boards or plywood

It takes a little time and patience to set up your router table for planing the edge of a board, but it's worth the effort, especially for plywood edges. Photo 3 shows you how. The smooth, straight surface left by the router bit makes it easy to create an almost invisible seam when you're gluing wood edging to plywood.

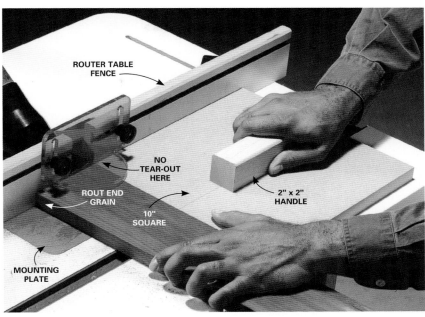

ROUTER TABLE FENCE

NO TEAR-OUT HERE

ROUT END GRAIN

10" SQUARE

2" x 2" HANDLE

MOUNTING PLATE

2 Tear-out–free end-grain routing. Screw a 2x2 handle to a 10-in. square of wood. Hold the workpiece firmly against the wood square and push it past the bit. Maintain slight pressure against the fence to make sure the edge of the square push block stays in contact with the fence throughout the cut.

Buying router tables

With a router table you don't have to hassle with clamping the workpiece. Just guide it over the table and past the bit. You can build your own router table and fence using plans included in many basic router books. You can also choose from dozens of commercially made tables. Buy the biggest tabletop you can afford; you'll get more accurate cuts on long pieces. Fences with two adjustable, replaceable wood or particleboard sections mounted to a solid one-piece metal fence are the best. You can shim out one side (Photo 3) to plane board edges or slide the sections tight to the router bit to eliminate extra space around the bit. Make sure the table has an easily adjustable bit guard and slots in the table to mount featherboards or other accessories. Removable base plates make it easier to mount your router and take it out to change bits and make height adjustments.

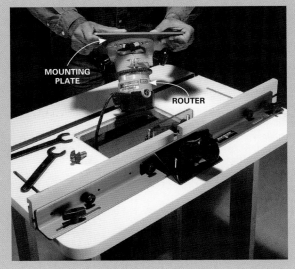

MOUNTING PLATE

ROUTER

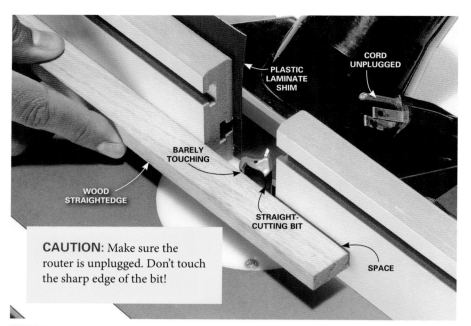

PLASTIC LAMINATE SHIM

CORD UNPLUGGED

BARELY TOUCHING

WOOD STRAIGHTEDGE

STRAIGHT-CUTTING BIT

SPACE

CAUTION: Make sure the router is unplugged. Don't touch the sharp edge of the bit!

3 **Plane straight edges.** Shim out the left half of the fence with a piece of plastic laminate or thin cardboard. Lay a straight board across the shimmed-out fence and against the router bit. Adjust the fence position until the bit just touches the straightedge. Spin the bit by hand to make sure it barely touches at its deepest cut.

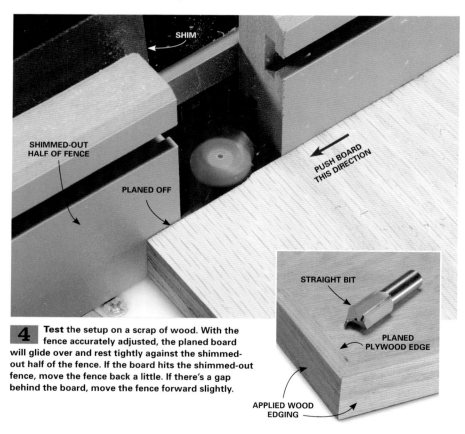

SHIM

SHIMMED-OUT HALF OF FENCE

PLANED OFF

PUSH BOARD THIS DIRECTION

STRAIGHT BIT

PLANED PLYWOOD EDGE

APPLIED WOOD EDGING

4 **Test** the setup on a scrap of wood. With the fence accurately adjusted, the planed board will glide over and rest tightly against the shimmed-out half of the fence. If the board hits the shimmed-out fence, move the fence back a little. If there's a gap behind the board, move the fence forward slightly.

The key to the setup is shimming out the left half of the fence and aligning the bit with it. If your router table fence isn't adjustable, you can attach a piece of plastic laminate to the face of the left half with double-faced tape so it can be removed when you're done.

Here are a few of the tasks you can accomplish with this setup:

- Plane the edges of plywood panels before applying wood edging.
- Remove saw marks from the edges of ripped boards.
- Straighten the edges of boards so they can be glued together.

Router table safety

Router bits spin so fast that they demand your constant attention. Accidents can happen suddenly. Here are a few of the most important safety rules:

- Always unplug the router when changing the bit.
- Push the bit into the collet. Then lift it to expose about one-quarter of the shank before tightening the collet nut. This will keep the bit from coming loose in the collet. At least two-thirds of the bit's shank should be engaged in the router collet.
- Cover the bit with a guard whenever possible (Photo 1).
- Wear safety glasses and hearing protection.
- Use featherboards and push sticks to keep your fingers away from the bit (Photo 1).
- Move workpieces from right to left against the fence.
- Move workpieces counter-clockwise around a piloted bit (Photo 6).
- Never position the fence so the workpiece is pushed between it and the bit.

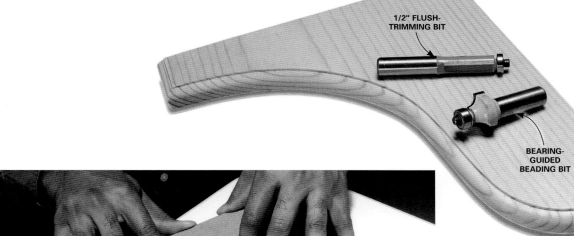

1/2" FLUSH-TRIMMING BIT

BEARING-GUIDED BEADING BIT

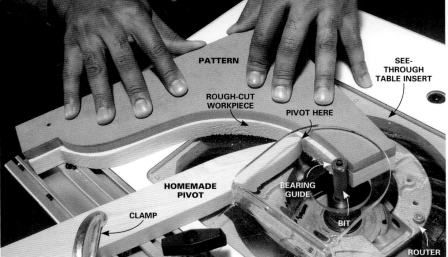

PATTERN

SEE-THROUGH TABLE INSERT

ROUGH-CUT WORKPIECE

PIVOT HERE

HOMEMADE PIVOT

BEARING GUIDE

CLAMP

BIT

ROUTER

5 **Rout freehand with a pattern.** Start freehand routing against piloted bits (bits with bearing guides) by pivoting the board into the bit. The pivot can be a pointed stick as shown or a pin or dowel mounted to the tabletop. Keep pressure against the pivot until the bit is engaged and cutting.

Gain control of freehand routing with a starting pivot

Small pieces that are difficult to hold down while you're shaping them with a handheld router are easy to shape on a router table. Use a bit with a bearing guide that rides against the pattern. Photos 5 and 6 show a 1/2-in. carbide flush-trimming bit being used to duplicate a pattern. You can also shape the edge of small pieces with any bearing-guided router bit using this same technique. Pivot the wood against the starting pivot block for greater control over when it contacts the bit. Some router tables have a hole for a starting pin that serves the same purpose as the pointed stick we're using. It doesn't matter what you use as a pivot as long as it's firmly attached and placed 2 to 3 in. from the bit.

Cut the pattern from MDF (medium-density fiberboard) or tempered Masonite. Sand the edges smooth because the router bit will transfer every imperfection in your pattern to your workpiece. Rough-cut your workpiece with a jigsaw and attach the pattern with small nails, hot-melt glue or double-faced tape.

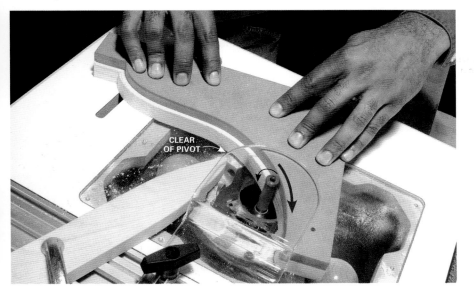

CLEAR OF PIVOT

6 **Move** the workpiece away from the pivot while maintaining moderate pressure against the router bit bearing. Move the workpiece at a steady rate in a right to left, or clockwise, direction.

Working with bent saplings

Learn more about this ancient craft

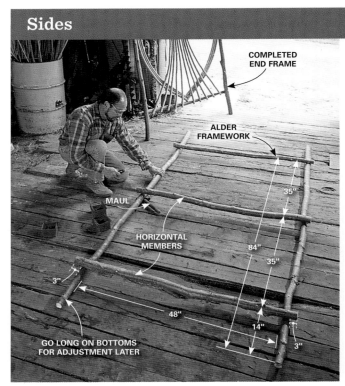

COMPLETED
END FRAME

ALDER
FRAMEWORK

MAUL

HORIZONTAL
MEMBERS

35"

84"

35"

3"

48"

14"

3"

GO LONG ON BOTTOMS
FOR ADJUSTMENT LATER

1 Select four 8-ft. long, 2-1/2-in.-dia. straight saplings for corners, and fasten evenly spaced horizontal members with 3-1/2-in. ring-shank nails. Leave plenty of extra length (at least 14 in.) on the legs for anchoring to the ground and for adjusting to uneven terrain. Overlap the 54-in. horizontal members 3 in. on each end to give a 48-in.-wide end panel.

P eople have been bending, weaving and lashing saplings ever since they figured out what opposable thumbs were for. Shelters, baskets, fish traps—you name it—were made with a bit of leather and a few green saplings or limbs.

The good news is that today you don't have to use dried beaver gut to lash sticks together. Using just about any fastener in your junk drawer and green (live) branches or saplings, you can create all sorts of projects. Best of all, you don't even need much of a plan. Rough out your ideas as you go and wing the actual construction.

We suggest that you proceed in two steps. First, build a simple trellis to get the hang of sapling construction. Then tackle a full-scale project like this arbor.

You only need one power tool

The only power tool we used was a cordless drill to screw the side walls and top section together at the site. Besides that, you'll need a saw to cut large pieces (we used a bow saw; Photo 13), pruning shears for small pieces (Photo 7), and lopping shears for the in-between sizes (Photo 6). A utility knife comes in handy both for easing the sharp edges on end cuts (Photo 3) and for cutting the plastic drain tile used for the footing (Photo 18). The willow bender who helped us preferred a ball peen hammer (Photo 11) to a conventional hammer for nailing because the former is less likely to damage the bark on errant back swings. He'd also

place a hand maul behind the saplings he was hammering together to support the object being nailed. The maul was either hand-held for "up in the air" nailing or set on the floor under the pieces (see Photo 1).

2 Cross-nail from two directions on all larger framing members. Cross-nailing will not only provide a strong anchor but also help prevent splitting at the ends.

RING-SHANK NAIL

CROSS-NAIL 3-1/2" NAILS

3 Soften outer edges by beveling them with a utility knife. Shave off protruding nubs on ends that will be exposed.

4 Gently flex pieces to be used for curved elements. A little initial coaxing will help keep them from splitting during assembly. Bend thicker ends more gradually to lessen the chance of kinking.

NOTE: THE END FRAME IS FLIPPED OVER

5 Flip the end frame over. Tack the center cluster and evenly space the sapling ends for decorative side spray. Position thicker ends at the bottom.

BOTTOM

6 Set the nails and trim ends evenly at the ends with lopping shears after you're satisfied with the placement.

THICK ENDS

45-DEGREE ANGLES

THIN ENDS

7 Cut 45-degree angles on outwardly curving bent saplings, starting with the outside pieces first. Add the other two layers of saplings and fasten them to the horizontal members and to each other by nailing the sides together. Alternate butt ends on each row (thick-thin-thick).

8 Clamp rows together to hold them tightly for nailing.

9 Overlap the second half of each row to sight and match miter angle, then cut with lopping shears and nail into place.

Cut saplings in the fall, winter or early spring

It's best to do your harvesting during the months when the saplings are without leaves. The wood is more pliable and the bark is tougher and harder to damage during assembly. If you're really eager to get started, go ahead and harvest your saplings anytime. But plan on using a bit more patience and care while bending, cutting and assembling.

Before harvesting a lot of stock, test various diameters by bending them. The tighter the bend, the smaller the sapling you'll need to cut. That's why you should have some idea about the design before going into the woods. Plan on assembling your project within a few days of harvesting, when the wood is still fresh and flexible. If your project will stretch over several weeks, cut just enough saplings for that weekend's work.

Although sandbar willow is a great material for bent structures, nearly any green sapling will do. Rustic artisans use dogwood, spirea, cherry, apple, cypress, cedar and bamboo. Weeping willow, with its fragile branches, is a poor choice for larger framing parts, but the delicate branches work well for intricate detailing. Birch is a great, straight sapling for bending but tends to have a shorter garden life than other choices. Experiment to determine the bending qualities of the type of sapling you're considering. If it splinters easily, try another type of wood. A field guidebook is handy to have around to help identify species while you're scavenging.

If your lot doesn't include woods, try these other sources for materials, *but make sure you ask permission first:*

■ Farms are good bets. We found our sandbar willow in a small drainage ditch next to a cornfield.

■ Utility lines are always monitored for invasive tree growth. You can contact utility companies to find out where they'll be cutting to gather downed limbs and saplings.

■ New housing developments are generally cleared prior to construction. It's even better if you can get there before they're cleared because it's easier to select and harvest while the wood is still standing than after it has been damaged by bulldozers or buried in dirt.

■ Nurseries or professional tree trimmers will often let you collect their prunings.

■ Orchards do a lot of pruning and are a great source of fruitwood cuttings.

Use thicker, straight saplings for posts, and mix wood species for the best results

On our arbor we used sandbar willow for all of the curved elements. Small, highly curved decorative details are made of thinner, more flexible members. We chose alder for the framework on the sides and top section (Photos 1 – 3) because it's stiffer than willow and lends the arbor more rigidity. Our alder framework pieces had diameters between 1-3/4 and 2-1/4 in. Selecting straight posts isn't always easy, but we picked the best ones we could find. Try not to get too caught up in the frustration of perfection when building with saplings. When all is said and done, crooked parts will add personality to your sculpture.

10 Cut the arch base out of the same material as the side framework pieces. Add 6 in. to the length so you can hang each side over 3 in. Nail the first arch piece 3 in. from the end, starting with the butt end of the sapling. The height of the arch is arbitrary; we made ours about 2 ft. tall.

11 Add the last two saplings to the side of the main arch, nailing these pieces to the ends and to each other. Use the first arch framework as a template to ensure curve and height symmetry for both arches.

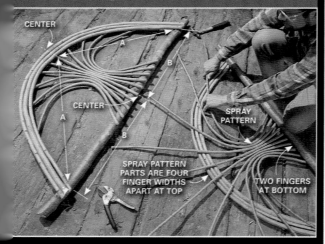

CENTER

A

CENTER

A

B

B

SPRAY PATTERN

SPRAY PATTERN PARTS ARE FOUR FINGER WIDTHS APART AT TOP

TWO FINGERS AT BOTTOM

12 Measure to find the center of the arch's top and bottom. Distances A should be equal. Find B by dividing the length of the bottom by two. Tack the bottom of the two middle pieces and equally space and tack the tops of these saplings onto the outsides of the arched ends. Continue installing each right and left pair. Check spacing and set nails when satisfied. Trim ends flush with the top of the arch.

ARCHES

CROSSBARS

13 Prop up the arches side by side exactly the same distance apart as the width of the end panels. This is the only really important measurement for the whole project—remember, you'll be attaching the top to the sides. Nail the crossbar to the arch base. Cut and attach a doubled ridge and two intermediate purlins to the outsides of the arches.

Design your arbor, build it in the garage and finish assembling it in the garden

Initially we planned to build our arbor on-site, then realized it would be easier to prebuild the two sides and the arched top in the shop, then assemble the components later in the garden. We decided on the dimensions for our arbor by positioning some scrap wood on the ground. We eyeballed the size, scratched our heads and settled on a footprint (base dimension and shape) 5 ft. wide and 4 ft. deep with a height of about 6-1/2 ft. to the bottom of the arch.

Don't pay too much attention to our dimensions. (Our willow bender used his eye and hammer head for most measuring. After all, we are building with sticks.) But several of the measurements really count. The side wall posts must fit inside the outside width of the top panel for fastening. We made both end walls exactly the same width, then made the top arch to fit inside the corners (Photo 13). When you're cutting the corner posts to length, remember that at least 1 ft. will be in the ground (Photo 18), so make sure to cut the posts to accommodate the footing while still leaving plenty of headroom under the arch.

Put it together with nails and screws

We used a combination of 2, 2-1/2, 3 and 3-1/2 in. ring-shank, ungalvanized underlayment nails. Use the longest possible nails that won't split the wood or come out the other side. The ring shanks help hold the fasteners in the wood, especially when it's still green and under the stress of bending. There's no need to use outdoor-grade fasteners, because any fastener will outlive the woodwork, and rusted nailheads will add to the natural, rustic character of the work. If you decide to add decorative twig accents, use twisted light-gauge wire for fastening. For final assembly, use 3-1/2 in. drywall screws (Photos 15 – 17).

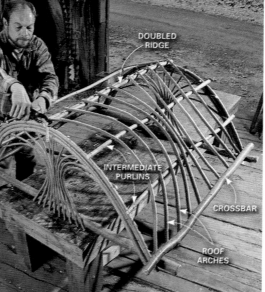

DOUBLED RIDGE

INTERMEDIATE PURLINS

CROSSBAR

ROOF ARCHES

14 Nail roof arches to the inside of the crossbar, to the outside of the intermediate purlins and to one side of the ridge and cut to length.

Crushed rock footings will make it last longer

Although you can simply stick the four legs in the ground, installing some cheap, easy footings made of 4-in. drain tile pipe with some 3/4-in. crushed gravel for drainage will help prevent rot and make the whole structure last longer (Photos 17 and 18). Nearly any gravel will work, but the rough, sharp edges on crushed gravel will lock together to keep the trellis more stable. Using this footing system will provide better drainage around the legs and prolong the life of your arbor. Soaking the legs in wood preservative will further lengthen the life of below-grade wood.

Enhance the beauty with an exterior sealer

A finish that repels water is optional, but it will add to the outdoor life expectancy of your arbor. A clear exterior-grade deck sealer will also enhance the beauty of the natural material. If you apply a finish, do it *before* final assembly to get better coverage and to keep the chemicals away from any plants.

Assembly

15 Screw the side frames to the arch top with 3-1/2 in. drywall screws.

TOP ARCH
SIDE WALLS
3-1/2" DRYWALL SCREWS

8" CORNER BRACE WITH 45-DEGREE ANGLES
SIDE FRAME
HORIZONTAL MEMBER OF TOP ARCH

16 Cut 8-in. long corner braces and screw them to the bottom of the arch and the side framework on all four corners with 3-1/2-in. drywall screws.

4" DRAIN TILE
CRUSHED ROCK

17 Position the arbor exactly in the desired location and draw circles around the legs with spray paint. Set aside the arbor and dig 8-in. wide postholes 18 in. deep.

CRUSHED ROCK
4" DRAIN TILE

18 Cut 18-in. lengths of 4-in. perforated drain tile and lay them in the postholes. Pour in about 6 in. of crushed gravel, set the arbor in the drain tile and level it by adjusting the gravel at the bottom of the hole. When you're satisfied with the placement, fill around the corner posts with more crushed gravel.

Silky-smooth finishes on trim

Follow these four steps (no shortcuts!) and you'll get a perfect finish every time

No matter how skillfully you install your trim work, it won't look good unless it has a fine finish. Uneven color, dust-flecked surfaces and brush marks all distract the eye and ruin the natural beauty of the wood. Yet achieving a smooth, flawless finish doesn't require expensive tools or special knowledge or skills.

Here we'll show you a simple three-day process that'll give you great results every time. We'll show you how and when to sand, using the correct sanding products. (It's not the tedious, mind-numbing job you might think it is!) Then we'll tell you how to apply stain evenly and without blotches on all the surfaces. Finally, we'll show you the best ways to get a smooth satiny surface with a sanding sealer and varnish.

We'll limit our staining techniques to methods that work well on coarse-grained woods, such as oak, ash and walnut. To achieve an even, blotch-free finish on fine-grained woods like cherry, maple, birch, pine and fir you'll need to apply a coat of sanding sealer to the wood before you apply finish. See p. 169 for more details about that.

Wood finishing isn't complicated, but it does require patience and attention to detail. It pays to get each step right the first time. Going back to correct mistakes is time consuming, and it's nearly impossible to achieve blemish-free results.

Choosing stain and finish

We recommend finishing your wood with oil-based stain and varnish (or polyurethane) with a compatible sanding sealer beneath it. These finish types are the easiest to apply.

You'll likely have two sheen choices—gloss (shiny) and satin (flat)—but don't be afraid to mix equal quantities of gloss and satin if semigloss is the look you're after. Few home centers carry alkyd varnishes, so you're better off shopping at a paint or woodworking supply store.

A sanding sealer is the perfect foundation for the varnish topcoat. It's formulated with more solids than conventional clear coats, making it very easy to sand. And varnish adheres better to a well-sanded, sealed surface. Pick a sealer that's designed for the overlying varnish, preferably of the same brand.

Begin by sanding

A good finish starts with sanding the bare wood with a 100-grit sanding sponge and/or paper. This step is crucial for achieving a uniform wood surface that'll absorb stain evenly. It also smooths out surface imperfections, which might show through the clear coat. Your goals are to eliminate the sawmill "burnish" (shiny surface left by the planer), smooth off any standing rough wood fibers and sand out any blemishes. Blemishes can include dirt, fingerprints, machining imperfections and label residue. Don't sand with finer grits at this stage or you're likely to end up with uneven stain.

The sanding tool you select depends on the profile and size of the trim you're finishing. For large areas or deep imperfections like chatter marks (washboard textures) from the mill planers, use a random orbital sander. It's aggressive and cuts and smooths quickly.

For hand-sanding, use a sanding sponge for flat areas (Photo 1), a sanding pad for curves (Photo 2) and a folded piece of sandpaper for tight crevices (Photo 3). Always sand in the direction of the grain and sand every square inch whether you think it needs it or not. Your fingertips and eye will tell you when enough is enough. But look closely with good light before you call the job finished. Otherwise, imperfections like scratches caused by cross-grain sanding or chatter marks will become painfully obvious when you start staining. Another common problem is burn marks. Sometimes extra elbow grease will be needed to eliminate those. This may sound like a lot of work, but if you use fresh paper and sponges, the sanding goes fast.

Clean the room

A clean work area is crucial for a smooth, blemish-free finish. If you have the option, sand the wood outdoors or in a room that's separate from the finishing area.

1 Sand flat surfaces with a 100-grit sanding sponge, in the direction of the grain, until you eliminate imperfections and rough areas.

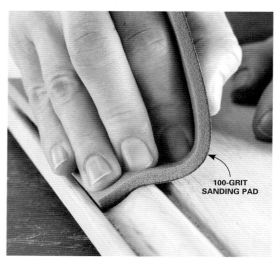

2 Sand curves with a 100-grit pad. You can easily mold it to the contours of the various trim profiles.

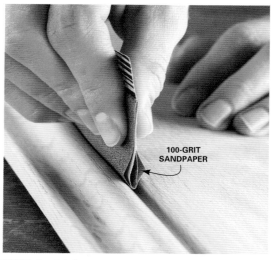

3 Sand tight cracks with folded sandpaper. The edge will wear quickly, so refold the paper often.

If you're forced to sand in the finishing area, wait several hours after sanding before cleaning the room, to give the dust a chance to settle out of the air. Vacuum the floor and any nearby work surfaces. Then damp-mop those surfaces too. Avoid sweeping—it just stirs up more dust. If there are rooms overhead, declare a moratorium on overhead foot traffic during finishing. Otherwise dust on the underside of the floor will rain down on wet finishes. Or do your clear-coat work after everyone's gone to bed. If you're working in a room that's heated or cooled with forced air, warm or cool the area a few hours ahead and then shut off the system until clear finishes are applied and become dry to the touch. That'll keep ventilation fans from stirring up more dust or bringing it in from other rooms.

Brush on the stain and wipe it off fast

The key to getting an evenly stained surface is to saturate the wood thoroughly and then wipe the stain off evenly. Start by stirring the stain. Scrape the stir stick across the bottom and pull up any settled solids, then work them into the solvent until they're all dissolved. (Use the same method to mix the sanding sealer and the varnish later.) The best application method is to simply dip a natural-bristle brush into the stain and brush it right onto the wood (Photo 4). Rags are messy and waste stain. Don't skimp when you're applying stain—more is better.

Wipe off the stain with clean cotton rags in the same order you put it on. The idea is to let it soak into all areas of the wood for about the same amount of time (Photo 5). Wipe with light, even pressure. You'll know if you wipe too lightly because you'll leave streaks. Refold wiping rags frequently so you have

Must-have finishing supplies

High-quality finishing supplies take the pain out of staining. A modest investment in these tools and accessories will greatly speed up the job and increase the quality of your finishing work.

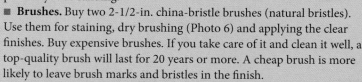

CHINA-BRISTLE BRUSHES

■ **Sanding supplies.** Buy 100-grit (medium) products for sanding the raw wood and either 240- or 280-grit (extra-fine) sanding paper, sponges and pads for sanding between clear coats, depending on the profiles you're sanding.

■ **Brushes.** Buy two 2-1/2-in. china-bristle brushes (natural bristles). Use them for staining, dry brushing (Photo 6) and applying the clear finishes. Buy expensive brushes. If you take care of it and clean it well, a top-quality brush will last for 20 years or more. A cheap brush is more likely to leave brush marks and bristles in the finish.

■ **100-percent cotton painter's rags.** Buy a box at a home center. Don't use old bed sheets or clothes that contain synthetic fibers. They may leave behind dyes and won't absorb stain nearly as well.

■ **Gloves.** A box of disposable gloves will protect your hands from solvents, and you won't have to struggle with putting on reusable ones after coffee breaks.

■ **Mineral spirits.** Buy a 1-gallon can to clean brushes and to thin stain if needed.

■ **Tack cloths.** Find tack cloths in the paint department. Use them to eliminate the last specks of dust after you sand between coats.

4 Saturate the wood with stain by brushing a liberal coat quickly over the entire surface.

WINDOW FAN

2-1/2" CHINA-BRISTLE BRUSH

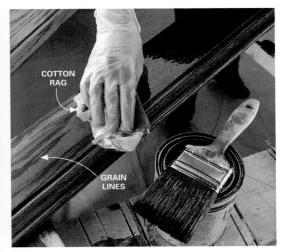

5 Wipe off the stain gently and evenly with clean cotton rags in the same order that the stain was applied. Watch for streaks.

COTTON RAG

GRAIN LINES

6 Clean stain from cracks and crevices with a dry brush. Wipe the brush on a clean rag or brush it on newspaper to clean off the stain between strokes. Let the stain dry overnight.

DRY-BRUSH THE CRACKS

dry cloth for most strokes, and grab a new rag whenever one gets soaked.

Next, "dry-brush" any cracks or crevices that the rag couldn't reach by dragging a dry brush through them (Photo 6). Wipe off the bristles on a rag or newspaper between strokes to keep the bristles dry and to avoid smearing. Don't waste time. It doesn't take long for stain to start drying, and it becomes sticky and hard to remove. If the stain gets tacky before you can wipe it off, simply apply more stain to soften it and then wipe it off again.

Finally, closely examine the surface for smudges, brush marks and blotches. Look for swirls left by rags and wipe them down again. These marks are easy to miss but you will see them after finishing, so examine the surface carefully.

If you spot areas in the finish that seem too light, add more stain. Let it sit for a couple of minutes and then wipe it off again. Work quickly; as the stain dries, it will smudge. Lighten dark areas by rubbing them lightly with a rag dampened with paint thinner. Make these color tune-ups for each piece right after staining. It's easiest to make color corrections while the stain is still damp. Let the stain dry overnight before you start the finish coats. If you're unhappy with grain lines that are too dark compared with the surrounding wood (Photo 5), restain and wipe the whole surface and let it sit overnight again.

CAUTION: Spread out stain-soaked rags and let them dry before disposing of them in a waste container. Piles of damp staining rags are a spontaneous combustion hazard.

Test the stains

Oil stains are the finish of choice among pros because they're forgiving and easy to apply. Avoid "fast-drying" stains. You're better off with ones that require at least overnight drying time. Getting the best color usually requires stain mixing, so buy a few different 4-oz. cans in the color family you're interested in.

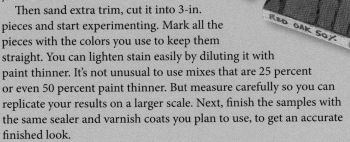

Then sand extra trim, cut it into 3-in. pieces and start experimenting. Mark all the pieces with the colors you use to keep them straight. You can lighten stain easily by diluting it with paint thinner. It's not unusual to use mixes that are 25 percent or even 50 percent paint thinner. But measure carefully so you can replicate your results on a larger scale. Next, finish the samples with the same sealer and varnish coats you plan to use, to get an accurate finished look.

Trying to match a stain that's on existing trim is difficult, especially if the trim is more than a few years old. Even pros rarely attempt it themselves. The best bet is to bring a sample of the finish you want to match, along with raw wood samples, to a paint store that offers a color-matching service.

7 Brush sanding sealer evenly onto the entire length of each board. Take care not to miss any spots.

8 "Tip-off" the surface immediately using long strokes from end to end. Let the sealer dry overnight.

9 Lightly sand the sealer with an extra-fine pad until the finish is smooth to the touch and a uniform flat, frosted color.

LIGHT GRIP

EXTRA-FINE SANDING PAD

TACK CLOTH

10 Vacuum most of the dust from the surface, then wipe off the remainder with a tack cloth. Then brush varnish over the entire surface, tipping it off to minimize brush marks.

Brush on a sanding sealer

Brush on the sanding sealer in the direction of the grain until the whole surface is coated (Photo 7). Shine a strong light on the wet surface to highlight areas you might have missed (they'll be dull). Then add more finish wherever it's needed. Immediately "tip-off" the wet finish by stroking the entire surface from end to end with long, light, overlapping strokes of the wet brush (Photo 8). That'll further even out the coat and help eliminate brush marks. Work quickly; sanding sealers dry fast. If you wait too long before tipping off, you'll leave brush marks. If you see brush marks after tipping off, leave them and sand them out later. Lastly, look carefully at the edges to find any drips and smooth them out with the brush. Leave the wood lying flat during the finish application and while it dries afterward. That'll minimize runs and sags and help finishes to "level out" so brush marks will disappear.

Sand the sealer before varnishing

After the sealer dries, lightly sand the surfaces with 240- or 280-grit (extra fine) sanding pads or paper. You'll know it's smooth enough when you see a fine dust on all the surfaces and they're smooth to the touch (Photo 9). The sanded surface should be uniformly dull. Shiny streaks or spots indicate missed spots.

Sand carefully, especially near sharp corners. It's easy to sand through the sealer and the stain to leave exposed raw wood. If that happens, just retouch with more stain to even up the color. There's no need to reseal small areas. Use a shop vacuum fitted with an upholstery brush to remove most of the dust. Remove the remaining dust by wiping the surfaces with a tack cloth (Photo 10).

Finish up with oil-based varnish

Brush on the varnish and tip it off with the same techniques you used for the sanding sealer (Photo 8). If you're working in a clean room and did a good job of sanding the sealer, one coat will be plenty. Trim doesn't receive much wear or abrasion, so you don't need a tough, thick finish. But if you have dust specks, brush marks or other imperfections, don't try to pick them out of the wet finish. Let the finish dry overnight. If there are only a few specks, pick them out with your fingernail. If there are a lot of specks, resand and add another coat. Either way, specks in the finish mean the room is still dirty. Clean the room more thoroughly or find another, cleaner place to work for the next coat. To add another coat, prepare the surface as you did after the sanding sealer, including sanding the finish with extra-fine sanding grits, dusting the surfaces and wiping everything down with a tack cloth. Then add another topcoat of varnish.

Staining blotch-prone wood

Get a perfect finish on even hard-to-stain woods like cherry and pine

Some types of wood, like pine, cherry, birch and maple, are notoriously difficult to stain. A board that has a nice, attractive grain pattern can end up with dark, splotchy areas after you apply the stain. But there's a simple way you can prevent most stain blotches.

Dark splotches show up when stain pigments become lodged in areas of grain that are more open. Unfortunately, it's not easy to tell which boards this will affect. One test is to wipe your board with mineral spirits. Spots that are prone to blotching show up darker. But the best test is to apply stain to a sample of the wood you're using. If the stain appears uneven or has unsightly dark areas, run the additional tests we show here to determine the best staining process.

Step 1: Seal the wood before applying stain

Most stain manufacturers make prestain conditioners, but you'll get better results with the method shown here. Use a wipe-on oil/polyurethane finish as the sealer. The key is to apply a thin base coat to partially seal the wood before staining. Sanding sealers, dewaxed shellac and wipe-on finishes will all do the trick.

Some types of stain perform better than others on blotch-prone wood. In general, gel or heavy-bodied stains work best. Since these types of stain tend to have a high concentration of pigments, they also work better if you have to add several layers for a darker color (Step 2, p. 171). Just make sure the sealer and stain you're using are compatible. Using products from the same manufacturer is the safest bet.

Photo 1 shows how to make a test board with different concentrations of sealer. The concept is simple. The percentage of solids in the sealer determines how completely the pores in the wood are sealed. If the wood was sealed completely, it would be difficult to get any stain to stick. Diluting the sealer with mineral spirits allows you to experiment with different degrees of sealing. When you apply the stain (Photo 2), you'll see the results. Then you can choose the dilution rate that delivers the best results for your project. (Don't dilute sanding sealers or dewaxed shellac, however.)

Let the sealer dry for a few hours. Then sand the wood lightly with 220-grit paper before applying stain.

An inexpensive turkey baster is a great tool for measuring small amounts of finish and mineral spirits. Mark the baster with a permanent marker. Just draw out equal amounts of sealer and solvent to make a 50 percent solution.

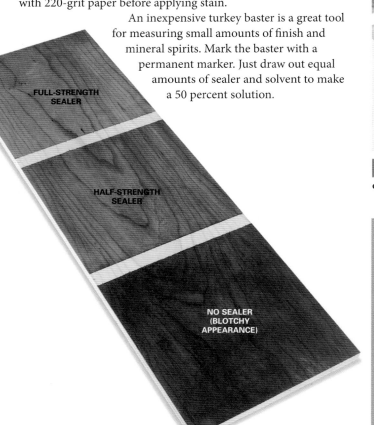

FULL-STRENGTH SEALER

HALF-STRENGTH SEALER

NO SEALER (BLOTCHY APPEARANCE)

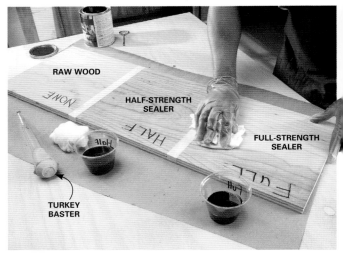

RAW WOOD

HALF-STRENGTH SEALER

FULL-STRENGTH SEALER

TURKEY BASTER

1 Divide a test board into three sections. Leave one section raw, wipe full-strength sealer on one section, and wipe half-strength sealer on the third section. Let it dry for about an hour and sand lightly with 220-grit paper.

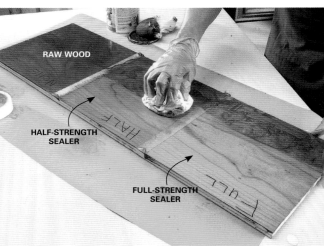

RAW WOOD

HALF-STRENGTH SEALER

FULL-STRENGTH SEALER

2 Rub stain over all three sections with a rag. Wipe it off to leave an even layer. Decide which amount of sealer gives you the desired look.

Seal end grain

End grain can look great and complement the board's surface, but it often ends up too dark. The solution is simple, though. Use the same prestain sealing method shown here to seal the end grain. You can also use this method on woods like oak that don't require a prestain sealer. Just be careful to sand off any sealer that gets on the face of the board before you stain.

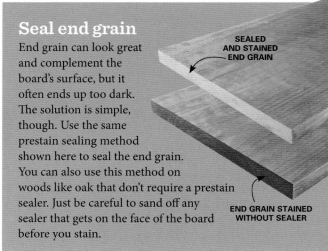

SEALED AND STAINED END GRAIN

END GRAIN STAINED WITHOUT SEALER

Step 2: Apply several coats of stain to get the desired shade

Start by making a test board with your chosen sealer concentration. Then stain the entire board. Let it dry and add a second layer of stain to all but one section. Repeat this process until you get to the desired color depth.

However, applying multiple coats of stain isn't always the best way to achieve a deeper color. For one thing, it'll take a long time to finish the project. You have to wait for each layer of stain to completely dry before adding the next. Otherwise, the new coat will dissolve the previous coat and you'll have a real mess on your hands. In fact, some stains will dissolve the stain below even if it is dry. (That's why testing is critical for a nice finish.) Another problem with multiple coats is that the stain will begin to obscure the natural grain. One solution is to opt for a less concentrated sealer. You'll get a bit more blotchy appearance, but the grain will show up better—a fair compromise.

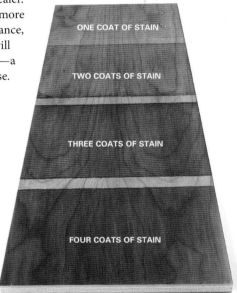

Seal pine before staining

Dark stains on pine can look horrible. In addition to blotchiness, the softer areas between the grain lines soak up stain like a sponge, creating an unnatural look. This photo shows the dramatic difference between the raw and sealed areas of pine using the same stain color. Experiment with sealing the wood on your next pine project. You'll be amazed at the results.

STAINED WITHOUT SEALER

SEALED AND STAINED

Step 3: Finish your test board to get the true effect

Treating your test board just like the finished project will give you a true representation of the final color and depth of the finish. Make sure you sand the test board with the same grit as you intend to use on your project. After you arrive at the desired degree of sealing and number of stain coats, apply the final clear finish to see how it looks (photo, right). This is also a good time to test the effect of different sheens. Most finishes are available in sheens ranging from almost flat to high gloss. You'll be surprised at how much richer the stain looks after a coat of finish.

NATURAL-BRISTLE BRUSH

OIL-BASED FINISH

Edge-gluing boards

Here's how to get great results with minimum hassle!

Gluing boards together to make wider panels is a handy woodworking skill that's easy to learn. Woodworkers with well-equipped shops often buy rough lumber and then rip, plane and joint the lumber to get straight edges for tight-fitting joints. But you can get the same results by carefully choosing boards from a home center or lumberyard. Look for boards with similar color and grain patterns. Then sight down the edge of each board to be sure it's straight. Finally, make sure the boards are flat and not twisted.

Arrange boards for the best appearance

For projects like tabletops where one side of the glued-up boards will be more visible, choose the best-looking side of each board to face up. If the boards vary in shade, arrange them so differences blend as well as possible. Don't put a dark board between two light ones, for example. Finally, flip the boards end for end and shuffle them until the grain patterns look natural and pleasing. When you're happy with the results, draw a "V" (photo below) across the boards with chalk or pencil. If you're assembling several panels, also number them. When it's time to glue the boards together, simply align the marks to make sure the boards are properly arranged.

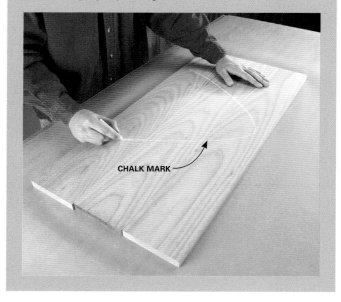

CHALK MARK

FINGER GUIDE

Apply an even bead of glue

Use white or yellow woodworking glue for interior projects. For projects exposed to moisture, use water-resistant glue. Spread a 1/8- to 3/16-in.-diameter bead of glue along the edge of one board. For an even bead that's perfectly centered on the edge, hold the glue bottle with one hand and the spout with the other hand. Move the glue bottle along the board quickly, letting your index finger ride along the board as a gauge to keep the bead of glue centered. Use a spring clamp to hold the board upright while you apply the glue. You only need to apply glue to one of the two boards being joined.

Don't apply too much glue

Using too much glue won't adversely affect the strength of the joint, but it will make a mess that will require extra time to clean up. The goal is to apply just enough glue so that when the boards are clamped there will be an even, 1/16-in.-wide bead of squeezed-out glue along the length of the joint. Also try to avoid getting glue on the face of the boards, where it will cause trouble with finishing later.

Inspect the glue joint before clamping

Separate the boards and inspect the edges. The goal is to have a thin, even layer of glue on each edge. If there are areas where the glue is thin or missing, apply a little more glue to these sections before clamping the boards together.

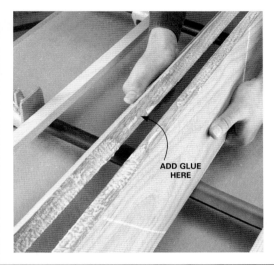

ADD GLUE HERE

Don't skimp on clamps

A good glue joint should have an even bead of squeezed-out glue along its entire length. Add clamps to areas where there is no squeezed-out glue.

NO SQUEEZE-OUT

Slide glued edges together

Press the two boards together and slide them back and forth against each other. This is the best way to spread the glue evenly on the edges of both boards.

TIP

Cover the top of the clamps with masking tape to avoid staining the boards and to make cleanup easier.

FEEL THE JOINT

Align the top surfaces carefully

You'll save yourself tons of sanding by making sure the top surfaces are as close to perfectly flush as you can get them. There are a couple of tricks to make this easier. First, glue and clamp only one joint at a time. It takes a little longer, because you'll have to wait for the glue to set up before removing the clamps and adding the next board. But it's much easier to get good results if you focus on one joint at a time. Second, start clamping at one end and work your way along the boards, making sure the top surfaces are flush as you tighten the clamps. Feel the surface with your finger and adjust the boards up or down until the tops are flush with each other. Then apply enough clamping pressure to close any gaps and squeeze out about a 1/16- to 1/8-in. glue bead.

Scrape glue while it's soft

At room temperature and average humidity, the squeezed-out glue will be ready to scrape in about 20 minutes. Wait until the glue changes from liquid to a jelly-like consistency. Then scrape it off with a chisel or putty knife. If the clamps are in the way, you can safely remove them after about 20 minutes in normal conditions. Handle the glued-up panels carefully, though, since the glue won't reach maximum strength for several more hours.

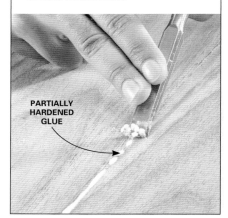

PARTIALLY HARDENED GLUE

Don't walk away from bowed glue-ups

Glue-ups with bows are impossible to flatten after the glue sets. Hold a straight-edge across the glued-up boards to make sure they're flat. Flatten them by driving shims between the boards and the clamps. If the assembly is bowed up, add another clamp on top of the boards.

TIP

Place strips of wood between the clamps and the boards to protect the edges of the boards.

GAP

SHIM

EDGE PROTECTOR

Spray finish on wood

Flawless results with aerosol cans

Brushing on liquid finishes is one way to apply clear coats. But don't discount spray finishes, especially for smaller projects.

Off-the-shelf aerosol cans of shellac, lacquer and polyurethane allow you to quickly apply a finish that's free of brush marks. Spraying is also an efficient way to finish complex shapes. Here are a few simple but important tips and techniques that all but guarantee the best results.

ORGANIC VAPOR RESPIRATOR

Get set up for spraying

Spraying is fast and gives a smooth finish, but it also creates a fine mist of solvent and finish that drifts and settles on everything in sight and is dangerous to breathe. To avoid problems, work outdoors if possible. If you spray indoors, cover everything with plastic sheeting or drop cloths and wear a respirator fitted with organic vapor filters, especially if you're spraying lacquer. Also put an exhaust fan in the window. Read the label on the spray can for additional safety precautions.

Start the spray off the edge

It's hard to get even coverage if you start or stop spraying on the surface you're coating. The spatters that happen when you first push the button can blemish your work, and spray builds up in one spot if you don't move fast enough. An easy and foolproof way to avoid these problems is to start spraying before you reach the edge of the project, move across the project at an even pace, and stop spraying after you've gone past the far edge. This technique guarantees an even, spatter-free coat of finish across the entire surface.

STOP SPRAYING

START SPRAYING

Don't swing the can in an arc

It's natural to swing the spray can in an arc, but this results in uneven coverage. The finish will build up in the center and be light on the edges.

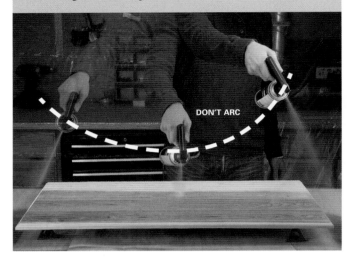

DON'T ARC

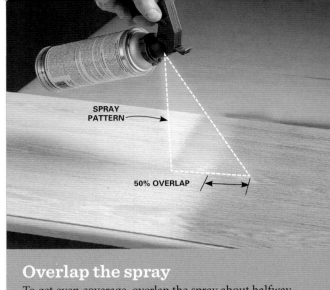

SPRAY PATTERN

50% OVERLAP

Overlap the spray

To get even coverage, overlap the spray about halfway onto the previously sprayed section. If you just overlap the edges, you'll get a narrow band of thicker finish where the two strips meet. Overlapping at least 50 percent solves this problem—you'll apply about the same amount of finish everywhere.

Keep the spray tip parallel to the surface

Focus on keeping the spray tip an equal distance from the surface as you move it along. At the same time, keep the can moving at a steady pace to get an even coat. The goal is to apply just enough finish to wet the surface without creating runs. Prevent runs by applying several thin coats rather than one or two thick coats. The finish may look blotchy after the first coat, but additional coats will produce a uniform finish.

KEEP THE CAN PARALLEL TO THE WORK

Don't dent your finger

If you've ever used spray cans to finish a large project, you know how sore your fingertip can get from pressing down on the spray tip. A spray-can trigger handle saves your finger and gives you better control of the spray. You'll find spray-can trigger handles at home centers and hardware stores.

SORE FINGER

TRIGGER HANDLE

Seal dark stains and exotic wood with a mist coat

Spraying a heavy coat of finish over a dark stain or over some oily exotic woods can ruin your project's appearance. The solvent in the finish can dissolve the stain or the color in the wood and cause it to bleed or get muddy looking. To avoid this, prime these types of projects with several thin mist coats before applying a thicker coat of finish. Apply a mist coat by raising the can higher than normal and moving the can faster than usual. This will reduce the amount of spray hitting the surface. Mist coats dry quicker than a full coat, so you can typically apply several mist coats with less-than-normal waiting time. Wait for the previous coat to dry to the touch before recoating.

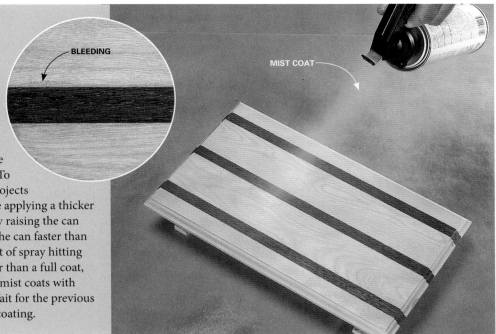

BLEEDING

MIST COAT

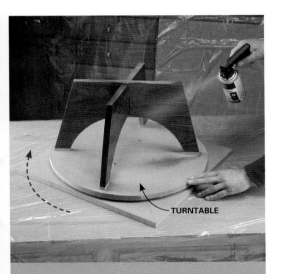

TURNTABLE

Spin your project

When you have a small project with many sides to spray, placing it on a turntable will speed up your job and make it easier to get good results. Instead of trying to move around the project as you spray, just give the turntable a little spin. You can build a turntable like this by mounting lazy Susan hardware to a scrap of particleboard or plywood, and then mounting a plywood or particleboard disc to the hardware. Lazy Susan hardware is available at hardware stores and home centers. Check the instructions before leaving the store so you can pick up any screws you'll need.

Brush, then spray

It gets pretty spendy to build up a heavy, protective layer of finish on a large project just with spray cans. But you can still take advantage of the flawless finish provided by aerosol cans. Start by applying two coats of finish with a brush. Then carefully sand with 220-grit sandpaper and remove all dust before using spray cans for the final coat. If you don't know much about finishes, just make sure your liquid and spray finishes are the same type.

Chapter Six

ROOFING, SIDING & GARAGES

Double the life of exterior paint

Paint rarely fails over broad surfaces. It usually starts small—at a crack in the caulk or a separation in a joint—but these small problems grow and soon become major if you neglect them. Before you know it, you're spending your whole summer scraping and painting your house. Don't let little problems ruin an entire paint job. You'll save a ton of time and money in the long run by giving your exterior paint an annual checkup and spending a day or two each year to keep it in tip-top shape. Follow these seven guidelines to extend the life of your paint and keep it looking like new.

1. Replace cracked and peeling caulk

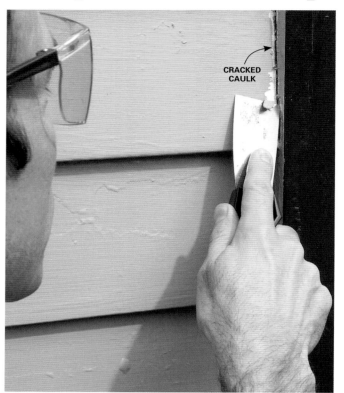

Moisture is the enemy when it comes to your paint job, and joints between siding and trim and around doors and windows are the most vulnerable points of attack. A key weapon in the war against moisture is caulk. Inspect all caulked joints, and clean out any caulk that has cracked or pulled loose (Photo 1). Even a fine crack will absorb water and eventually cause nearby paint to peel. Then spot-prime all bare wood (Photo 2), working the primer back into the gap. The primer improves caulk adhesion as well as seals the wood from moisture. Now apply a urethane or siliconized acrylic caulk (Photo 3). Don't use 100 percent silicone caulks in areas to be painted unless you use the type that says "paintable" (and follow the instructions). Make sure the caulk spans the gap and adheres to both sides. Tool the caulk immediately after applying it. Your caulk job will look neater and it'll adhere better. Allow the fresh caulk to set overnight, then paint.

CRACKED CAULK

1 Scrape or cut away all loose and cracked caulk with a putty knife. Work both sides of the crack until you reach a solid surface.

2 Sand the area with a medium-grit paper or sanding sponge and prime the bare wood. Work the primer back into the crack to seal the wood.

3 Lay on a new bead of caulk to span the crack and smooth it out with your finger. Touch up with two topcoats of paint.

2. Fix loose and peeling paint before it spreads

Peeling, blistering or flaking paint is usually the result of moisture getting under the paint. So once you spot the peeling, get after it quickly before it spreads.

The best tools to remove loose and peeling paint are a heavy-duty paint scraper for broad, flat areas and a flexible 2-in. putty knife for tighter areas. Buy a paint scraper that takes replaceable carbide blades. Carbide blades stay sharp and remove paint faster than regular steel blades. **Tip:** Use a lighter touch on composite (hardboard) siding and trim to avoid gouging it.

Scrape off as much of the loose paint as possible (Photo 1), then sand smooth with a sanding block or power sander (Photo 2). Be sure to sand all bare wood. After sanding, the bare wood should look bright and fresh rather than weathered. Dust off the surface and spot-prime, then paint (Photo 3). To keep the problem from recurring, see "Moisture Causes Paint to Peel," p. 182.

CARBIDE SCRAPER

1 Scrape the area thoroughly with a carbide scraper. Remove all loose paint. Use a flexible putty knife to pop off loose edges.

"MEDIUM" SANDING SPONGE

2 Sand the scraped wood to remove all weathering and to feather painted into unpainted areas. Use a medium sanding sponge or 100-grit sandpaper.

PRIMER

BEHR PREMIUM

3 Prime all sanded areas and repaint. Use two topcoats to ensure longevity.

3. Give horizontal surfaces special attention

1 Scrape and sand peeling horizontal surfaces thoroughly. Remove all loose paint and make sure the surface is completely dry before priming.

2 Apply a special binding primer to the bare wood, making sure to saturate cracks and the edges of the old paint. When it's dry, apply two topcoats.

Windowsills, handrails and other horizontal surfaces are difficult (at best) to keep looking fresh and decently painted. Rain, slush and snow sit on top of them (sometimes all season long), taking advantage of every crack and chip in the paint to soak the wood beneath. To repair, scrape away all loose paint (Photo 1), and smooth the edges of the remaining paint as much as possible by sanding with a medium-grit paper or sanding block. Dust off the surface and brush an anti-peeling, binding agent over the entire board (Photo 2). Binding primer is a clear, thin coating that slides into every crack and crevice, forming a continuous, highly flexible, gluelike seal. Ask for it or a similar product at a paint store. After the binding agent has dried (but within 24 hours), prime with a quality primer and finish with two topcoats. Keep in mind that binding agents are pretty good at gluing down old paint edges, sealing cracks and checks, and sticking to chalky surfaces, but they're no substitute for thorough surface preparation. And even with the best prep work, you'll probably have to touch up horizontal surfaces every few years.

BINDING PRIMER

Moisture causes paint to peel

For best results long term, find the source of the moisture and stop it before you repaint. Most often the problem occurs at joints in the siding or trim, where water can seep into a crack. Joints around windowsills and where wood meets concrete are particularly vulnerable, as are areas that receive a lot of splashing from rain. Maintaining sound caulk at joints and keeping gutters and downspouts clear will reduce many problems.

In some cases, moisture that escapes from your home can cause as much damage as outside elements. When paint peels in sheets down to bare wood or bubbles and blisters (photo at right) on an exterior bathroom or kitchen wall, the cause is usually interior moisture moving outward through the wall. Better ventilation in the room, or applying a moisture barrier primer or paint to the interior wall will often solve this problem.

Another type of paint failure is alligatoring, which is multiple layers of paint that have hardened and cracked. Eventually you'll have to remove all the alligatored paint. **Note:** The older layers may contain lead.

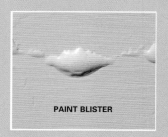

PAINT BLISTER

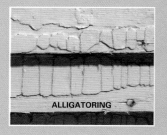

ALLIGATORING

CAUTION: If your home was built before 1979, check the paint for lead. Call your public health department for instructions on how to do it. Don't use the scraping or sanding techniques we show here on lead paint because doing so will release lead dust, the primary cause of lead poisoning. For more information on lead paint, visit epa.gov/lead.

4. Keep your gutters clean and free flowing

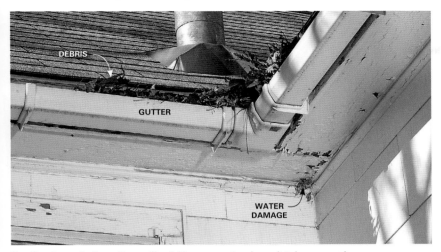

When leaves, pine needles and other debris obstruct gutters and downspouts, water overflows onto the siding and trim. That water usually finds a crack in the paint, quickly soaks the wood underneath and begins lifting paint. A year or two of periodic soaking can cause more damage than a decade's worth of normal weathering (see photo). If the moisture is left unchecked, rot will begin as well. Rot is a major headache and difficult to fix. The best strategy is to cut out and replace all spongy or rotted wood, ideally the entire damaged board. Or if the rotted area is small, you can often dig out all the spongy, loose wood fiber and refill the area with a special two-part epoxy wood filler. Only then can you repaint.

Overflowing or leaky gutters will quickly cause extensive paint damage and encourage rot. Clean gutters in spring and fall.

Keep leftover paint from hardening

Often when you dig out an old gallon of paint to do touch-up work, you discover the old paint has skinned over and hardened. To avoid this problem, keep leftover primers and paints in near-full cans. Paint stores, and many home centers, sell empty quart paint cans and covers. Pour off your partial gallon leftovers into the quart cans to keep them from drying out. Then brush a sample of the color on the side of the can so you can identify it easily. Even better, include the paint color code so you can buy an exact match years later.

5. Rinse off your house once a year

A year's worth of grit and grime can sap the life from any painted surface. When combined with wind and rain, the dirt grinds against the painted surface, dulls it and reduces its life. You need nothing special for an annual washing—just a strong stream from your garden hose. Pay special attention to those areas where dirt and grime gather: under roof overhangs, along eaves, above windows and doors, beneath windowsills, behind shutters, and along the bottom few rows of siding. Take care not to drive water into cracks or open vents, and keep the stream of water away from electrical lines.

Rinse your house annually with a strong stream from the garden hose, paying special attention to those areas where dirt gathers.

6. Seal nailhead stains before they get worse

If left alone, rust stains not only look bad but also allow moisture in and cause the paint to crack and peel. Sand the stain or rust from the area (Photo 1) and drive the nailhead below the surface about 1/16 in. (Photo 2). Prime with a good stain-blocking primer (BIN or Kilz are two examples). When dry, fill with a dab of caulk (Photo 3), smooth with your finger and allow to set before repainting. Caulk shrinks a bit as it dries, leaving a slight dimple. For a perfectly smooth finish, apply an exterior filler with a putty knife. Sand the filler lightly when dry and prime a second time before painting. **Tip:** Treat cedar and redwood staining much the same as nailhead staining. Sand and prime with a stain-blocking primer. Minimize that just-touched-up look by repainting the entire board.

SANDING SPONGES

1 Sand rust and stains away with a medium-grit sandpaper or sanding sponge.

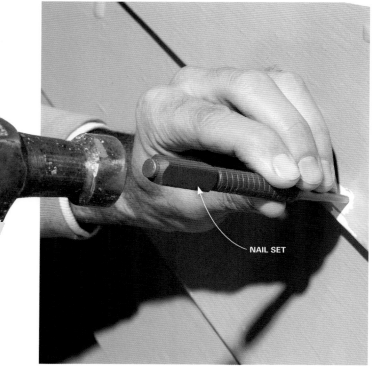

2 Set the nail about 1/16 in. below the surface and prime with a quick-drying, stain-blocking primer.

3 Fill the hole with acrylic latex caulk and smooth it with your finger. After the caulk skins over, repaint.

7. Control mildew

Mildew is a dark, blotchy-looking fungus that'll grow on any moist surface of your home. You'll generally find it in shady areas like under the eaves, on porch ceilings, on north walls and behind shrubbery—any area that stays moist. It may look like dirt or dust, but here's a test to tell if it's mildew: Dab a bit of regular household bleach on the suspect area (Photo 1). Rinse after a minute. If the discoloration disappears, it's probably mildew, because the bleach has killed it.

A simple washing is all that's required to remove most mildew. Scrub the affected areas with a stiff brush, hot water and an all-purpose cleaner (Photo 2). (Wear rubber gloves and eye protection.) Then rinse. If the infestation is particularly bad, you can disinfect the surface as well. It'll keep the mildew from returning as quickly. To disinfect, mix 1/4 cup household bleach per gallon water. Mist the area with a garden sprayer or a smaller spray bottle. Don't rinse off the bleach solution—let it dry on the surface. **Caution:** Handle bleach with care and never mix bleach with ammonia or an ammonia-containing detergent or cleaner—toxic gases may result.

Take steps to prevent mildew. Reduce moisture and promote better airflow around your house by limiting foundation plants and trimming back bushes. Make sure the water from sprinklers doesn't hit the siding. And the next time you paint, check the label on the can to make sure the paint contains a mildewcide. Many exterior paints contain this, especially in regions with high humidity and dampness. If it doesn't, ask the paint dealer (or the paint manufacturer) whether you can add some without harming the paint.

1 Test for mildew by dabbing on a little bleach. Rinse the area after a minute. If the dark stain has disappeared, you have mildew.

2 Scrub the mildewed areas with a stiff brush, hot water and a non-ammonia cleaner. Then rinse with clean water.

Garage door tune-up

Quit fighting it! Tips for a quieter, safer, smoother-operating door.

When you hear the words "tune-up" and "garage" in the same sentence, you probably think of your car, motorcycle or lawn mower. But there's a different type of tune-up, one that's simple to perform and can extend the life of the "equipment" by up to five years: a garage door tune-up.

Squeaking and grinding noises, rough operation and poorly reacting safety mechanisms are sure signs your door needs attention. This article will show you how to maintain and inspect your garage door to ensure it will work smoothly and safely. The garage door in our example is a 16-ft.-wide steel door with an overhead torsion spring and automatic opener. Your door might be slightly different, but most of the maintenance steps described here will be the same.

Safety first

We won't show you how to deal with problems involving a high-tension torsion spring—the type mounted on a rod over your door that acts as a counterbalance and determines how much effort it takes you to raise and lower the door. These springs are dangerous. Some manufacturers now have do-it-yourself–friendly systems that can be adjusted with a power drill, but unless you have this type of system, and the instruction manual, hire a professional. Adjusting or replacing extension springs—the type mounted on each side of your door by the tracks—or the cables connected to them can also be dangerous and should be left to trained professionals.

You can adjust safety systems yourself, particularly the automatic reversal mechanism, but leave repairs to pros. Don't take chances when it comes to safety.

TORSION SPRING

Lubricate the hinges, rollers and tracks

Oiling the moving parts on your door will help it operate more smoothly and more quietly. Make sure to:

■ Apply two drops of regular household oil in each seam of every hinge. Apply the oil on top so it can work its way down and lubricate the entire seam.

■ Apply two drops in each seam of each roller mount bracket on the door, and a drop or two on the ends of each roller pin.

■ Apply six drops of oil on the roller track. To ensure that all the rollers come in contact with the lubricated section, apply the oil about 1 ft. from the curve in the track. **Note:** Do NOT oil the track if your door has nylon

rollers; certain oils can soften, gum up and ruin nylon rollers.

After you've oiled all the parts, use the automatic opener to raise and lower the door a few times to help distribute the oil.

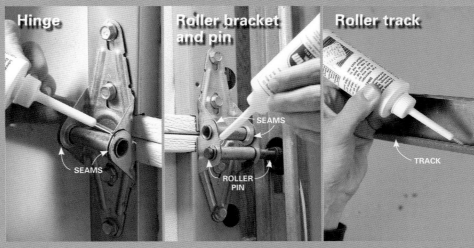

Hinge

SEAMS

Roller bracket and pin

SEAMS

ROLLER PIN

Roller track

TRACK

TIP

Wipe away any grease buildup on the rollers and roller pins before lubricating the door. Grease combines with sand and grit to form a sludge that acts as an abrasive and eats away at the rollers.

Check the door for balance

With the garage door in the closed position, disengage the door from the automatic opener by pulling down on the emergency release handle. Manually open the door halfway and let go. If the door is balanced properly, it should stay in the halfway position or creep down slowly.

If the door closes quickly or if you have to pull it down hard from the halfway position, it isn't properly balanced and will overstress the automatic opener. Hire a garage door professional to adjust the spring tension.

TIP

Manually operated doors have brackets and locking tongues (one on each side) that are operated by cables connected to the exterior handle. If your door has an automatic opener, remove the brackets; if these locks are accidentally engaged while the opener is trying to open the door, you could damage the door or opener.

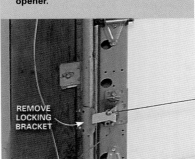

REMOVE LOCKING BRACKET

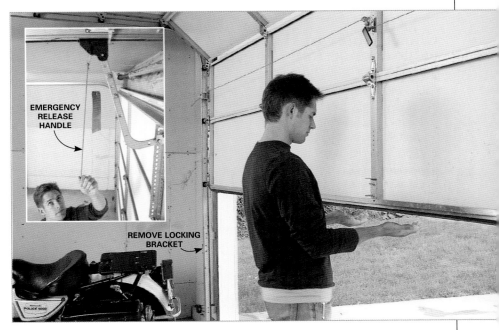

EMERGENCY RELEASE HANDLE

REMOVE LOCKING BRACKET

TORSION SPRING

CABLE

BOTTOM ROLLER BRACKET

Lubricate the cable connections and springs

While you shouldn't attempt to replace or adjust cables or springs, you should lubricate them:

■ Apply one or two drops where the two cables connect to the bottom roller mount brackets. This is also a good time to check the cable for wear (see below).

■ Run a bead of oil along the top of the torsion spring. The oil will eventually work its way down, coating the spring and preventing corrosion.

Check cables and cable connection points for wear

Cables can fray and break in two places: along their length and at the ends where they connect to the roller brackets and spring mechanism. Inspect your cables; hire a professional to replace frayed cables immediately.

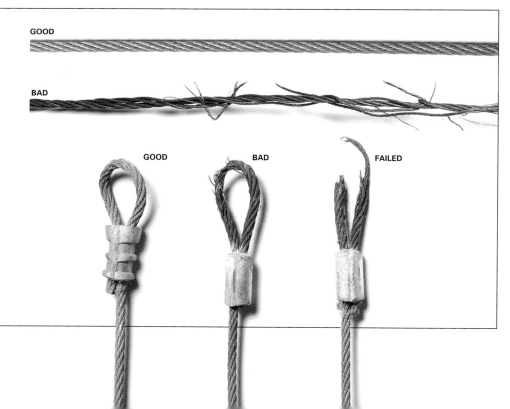

GOOD

BAD

GOOD   BAD   FAILED

SAFETY REVERSING SENSORS

Check the safety reversal features

Today's garage doors and automatic openers include several safety features. To check the safety reversal system, set a 2x4 flat on the ground centered in the opening as shown below. Close the door using the automatic opener. When the door contacts the 2x4, it should reverse itself and open.

To check the safety reversal sensors, start closing the door with the automatic opener, then wave your hand between the safety reversal sensors (photo above). The door should reverse and reopen.

If your door fails either test, read the opener owner's manual for adjustment guidelines. If your adjustments don't fix the problems, consult a trained professional to repair or replace the opener. If your opener lacks these safety features altogether, replace it.

2x4 CENTERED IN OPENING

RIGHT FOR TIGHT

Tighten bolts on garage door and garage track brackets

Tighten the bolts that connect the hinges to the door and those that secure the mounting brackets to the garage framework. Bolts on steel doors (like the one shown) rarely loosen; those on wood doors tend to loosen and should be examined and tightened regularly.

Improve attic ventilation

A well-ventilated attic makes for a healthier house. Here's how to keep the air moving.

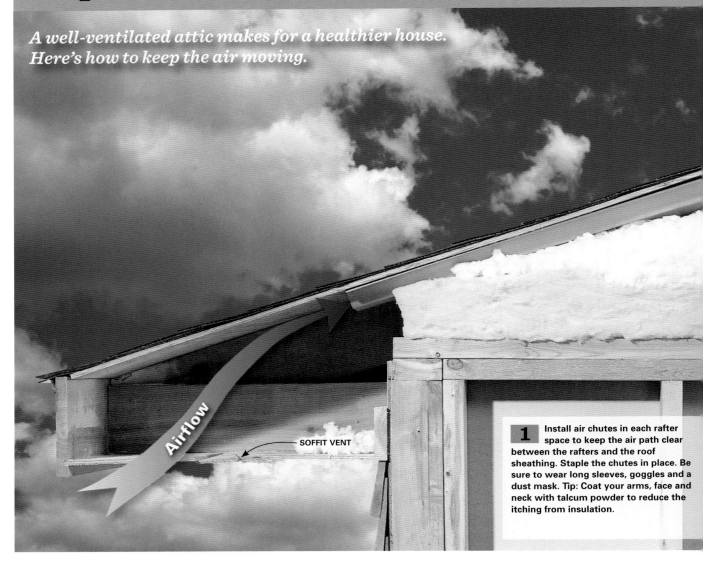

Airflow

SOFFIT VENT

1 Install air chutes in each rafter space to keep the air path clear between the rafters and the roof sheathing. Staple the chutes in place. Be sure to wear long sleeves, goggles and a dust mask. Tip: Coat your arms, face and neck with talcum powder to reduce the itching from insulation.

A well-ventilated attic offers four benefits:

1. It prevents mildew growth and rot on your roof's framing and sheathing by reducing moisture buildup.

2. It helps prevent ice dams in winter by keeping your roof colder.

3. It extends the life of your shingles by keeping the roof cooler in hot weather.

4. It reduces cooling costs in the warm season. The savings will be slight if you have a well-insulated attic space; greater if you have little insulation.

Here we'll tell you when you need additional ventilation, how to install several types of passive roof vents and soffit (eave) vents, and how to keep your ventilation system working.

As you will see, improving attic ventilation isn't expensive, time-consuming or difficult, even for the novice. You only need basic hand and power tools. However, when you climb up on your roof, be sure to follow safety precautions.

Does your house need more vents?

Before you go out and start poking holes in your roof and soffits, check to see if you have the type of problem that attic ventilation can solve.

One common problem is caused by ice buildup along the edges of a roof. These ice dams form when warm attic air melts the snow on the roof and the water refreezes along the colder edge of the roof. The ice traps water behind it, allowing

AIR CHUTE

STAPLER

Airflow

LONG-SLEEVED SHIRT

DUST MASK
AND GOGGLES

AIRFLOW GAP

2 Seal gaps around plumbing drain vent
pipes, ductwork and electrical boxes with
fire-blocking foam or caulk. This helps keep warm,
moist air out of the attic.

SOFFIT
VENT

CLOGGED
SOFFIT VENT

3 Clear your soffit vents every few years with blasts of compressed air. Always do
this after you install air chutes because you'll probably knock insulation down into
the soffit.

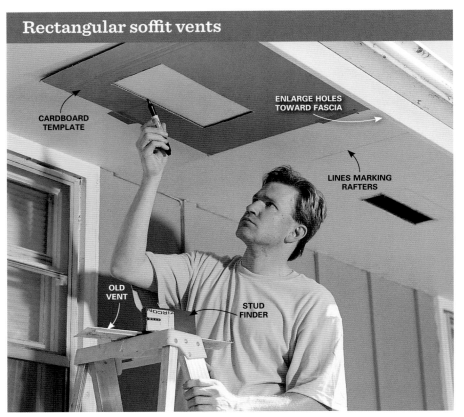

Rectangular soffit vents

CARDBOARD TEMPLATE

ENLARGE HOLES TOWARD FASCIA

LINES MARKING RAFTERS

OLD VENT

STUD FINDER

4 Butt a cardboard template against the fascia and mark your soffit hole locations. Make the vent hole 1/2 in. smaller on each side than the vent you're installing. If you widen existing holes, widen them toward the fascia, but no closer than 3 in. from the fascia to avoid waves and ripples in the soffit plywood. Position the holes between the rafters at equal intervals. You can find the rafters by locating the nailheads or using a stud finder.

5 Drill 3/8-in. starter holes at opposite corners of the vent hole. Then cut out the hole with a jigsaw. If the soffit plywood begins to tear and splinter in the crosscut, use a utility knife to score the cutting line.

6 Install the soffit vent with self-tapping screws. Angle the vent louvers toward the house wall. This prevents blowing snow from entering the vent, and it looks better from the ground.

ANGLE THE LOUVERS TOWARD HOUSE

Five common causes of poor attic venting

■ **Problem 1:** Insulation often clogs the space between the rafters, blocking air from traveling to and from the soffit area.
Solution: Install air chutes or clear them if they're clogged (Photo 1).

■ **Problem 2:** Aluminum or vinyl soffits (eaves) installed over plywood soffits that don't have venting holes.
Solution: Cut holes in plywood soffits as needed.

■ **Problem 3:** Gaps to the attic around plumbing pipes, ducting and electrical boxes. Many experts consider plugging these holes to be more important than ventilation.
Solution: See Photo 2.

■ **Problem 4:** Rectangular roof vents installed on one side of the roof only. Rectangular roof vents work best when the wind blows over the top of them, rather than into them.
Solution: Install rectangular roof vents on both sides of the roof.

■ **Problem 5:** Kitchen and bath fans vented into the attic.
Solution: Vent these fans through the roof or soffit.

FASCIA

2" x 8' CONTINUOUS
SOFFIT STRIP VENT

3" MINIMUM

7 Install a 2-in. continuous strip soffit vent so that it's closer to the fascia than to the house wall. Loosely nail one side of the soffit, then slide the strip vent's flange underneath the plywood.

8 Finish nailing up the strips. The narrowest soffit plywood strip should be at least 3 in. wide.

the water to seep back under the shingles and leak through the roof. Increased ventilation will make the entire roof cold and reduce or eliminate ice dams.

Another common problem is moisture buildup. After cold weather arrives, grab a flashlight and inspect your attic. Cover all your skin to protect it from the itchy insulation, and wear a dust mask. If your attic doesn't have a walkway, take two small (2 x 4 ft.) sheets of 1/2-in. plywood to move around on.

Here are the signs to look for:

1. Frost on the underside of the roof or rafters. Warm, moist air trapped in the attic condenses and freezes on the wood.
2. Water-stained or blackened wood. A sign of mildew or rot. You can also spot this in the summer.

Minimum venting requirements

Most building codes require 1 sq. ft. of venting (technically, "net free vent area," or NFVA) for each 150 sq. ft. of attic. In some circumstances you can have less, so check with your local building inspector. So a house with a 1,500-sq.-ft. attic will need 10 sq. ft. of venting, ideally about half placed high on the roof and half in the soffits. Look for the NFVA of each vent you buy stamped somewhere on the metal or plastic.

3. Heavily rusted nails. A sign that condensation is forming on metal surfaces.
4. Matted-down insulation. A sign of roof leaks from ice damming or other causes.

If you have either ice dams or moisture buildup, improve your attic ventilation. Begin by making sure your existing system works (Photos 1 and 3), plugging major air leaks into the attic (Photo 2) and correcting any other of the "Five Common Causes of Poor Attic Venting," p. 192. If those steps don't solve the problem, add more vents, following the techniques we show in Photos 4 – 17. For help figuring how much venting you need, see "Minimum Venting Requirements," below, left.

Even if you aren't having problems, bring your attic venting up to code when (1) you install new shingles and (2) you add attic insulation.

Add soffit vents first

You can gain the most airflow with the least amount of trouble by installing soffit vents. The two most common are rectangular vents (Photo 6) and continuous strip vents (Photo 7). Continuous strip vents allow perfectly even ventilation along the eaves (Photos 7 and 8), but they're difficult to retrofit in an existing soffit.

Rectangular vents are the easiest to install (Photos 4 – 6). In this project, we replaced all of the 4 x 16-in. vents (28 sq. in.

10 Measure the vent hood size and trim the topmost shingles with a hooked knife blade so they will butt against the vent hood on the top and the sides. You'll have to trim two or three rows of shingles (see Photo 12).

11 Pull nails as necessary so the vent's flange can slide into place. The best time to do this is when the shingles are cool (early morning). Use your flat pry bar to carefully separate the shingles from one another. Apply roofing cement around the perimeter of the hole.

9 Cut a square hole in the roof the same size as the hole in the base of the vent you're installing. Locate the top of the hole about 15 in. below the peak of the roof. Mark the hole with chalk and set your saw depth to cut through the shingles and the roof sheathing only. Don't cut into any rafters. For a roof with a single layer of shingles, start with a depth of 3/4 in. Use an old carbide blade for cutting, and wear safety goggles and hearing protection because you will hit nails.

12 Hold the vent up at an angle and slide it into place. Then set it down into the roofing cement.

13 Nail the flange to the roof on the front edge. Finish sealing the vent by applying cement to the areas where the shingles overlap one another and where they overlap the flange.

RIDGE

OLD RIDGE CAP

BATH FAN HOOD

1-1/2"

14 Remove the old ridge cap with a flat pry bar or square-nose shovel. Pull out any nails left behind. Use a chalk line to mark your cutting line. First, pop a line along the very top of the ridge. Then pop a line 1-1/2 in. down from your ridge line on both sides of it. These will be your cutting lines.

HEARING PROTECTION

GOGGLES

CUT

15 Cut out a slot in the shingles and the sheathing with a circular saw equipped with an old carbide blade. For a single shingle layer, start with a blade depth of 3/4 in. and make sure it doesn't cut into the rafters. If you have an over-hang, stop the slot short so the opening is only over the attic space, not the overhang. If you have a hip roof (no gabled ends), stop the slot 6 in. short of the beginning of the hip. Wear your goggles and hearing protection because you WILL hit nails. Sweep off the sawdust and open the slot with a flat pry bar.

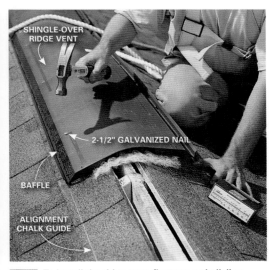

SHINGLE-OVER RIDGE VENT

2-1/2" GALVANIZED NAIL

BAFFLE

ALIGNMENT CHALK GUIDE

16 To install the ridge vent, first pop a chalk line down from your ridge line that's equal to half the width of the ridge vent. Then align the ridge vent pieces. Nail one side of the vent in place with 2-1/2 in. galvanized nails. To keep the line straight, finish nailing the side you aligned with your chalk line before nailing the other side.

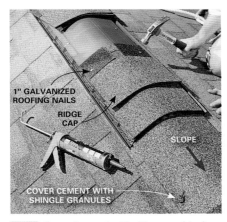

1" GALVANIZED ROOFING NAILS

RIDGE CAP

SLOPE

COVER CEMENT WITH SHINGLE GRANULES

17 Cover the vent with ridge cap shingles using 1-in. galvanized roofing nails. The vent will have a nail line marked on it. You can buy special ridge cap shingles for laminated shingles as shown here, or cut your own ridge cap from three-tab shingles (the shingle packaging will have directions). If you have to stop the ridge vent short of the end of the ridge, install the remaining ridge cap so that it slopes away from the vent.

TIP

Work in cool weather so you don't mar the shingles.

Roof safety tips

Tip 1: Use a safety harness, especially if your roof has a slope steeper than 4:12.

Tip 2: Work only when the roof is dry. Wet shingles can be slippery.

Tip 3: Keep your shoe soles flat on the roof, rather than digging in with the edges.

Tip 4: After making cuts with your circular saw, sweep away the sawdust to avoid slipping.

Tip 5: Don't step on power cords or ropes. They'll roll under your feet and cause a fall.

of net free vent area, or NFVA) with 8 x 16-in. vents (56 sq. in. NFVA) and added more. This increased the soffit ventilation almost five times. An 8 x 16-in. vent is inexpensive and takes less than 10 minutes to install.

How to choose roof vents

We recommend two types of roof vents: heavy-gauge rectangular metal vents (Photo 13) and plastic shingle-over ridge vents with baffles (Photo 16).

Ridge vents with baffles have several advantages: Their low profile and shingle cover make them

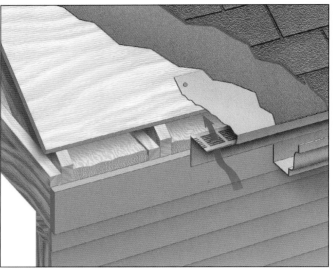

Figure A
Starter vent

If your house doesn't have soffits or overhangs and the roof stops at the wall, you can vent the lower edge of your roof with a "starter" vent (also called "drip edge vent"). To install it, remove the first few rows of shingles and cut away the leading edge of your roof sheathing and the top edge of your fascia. Available from roofing supply stores.

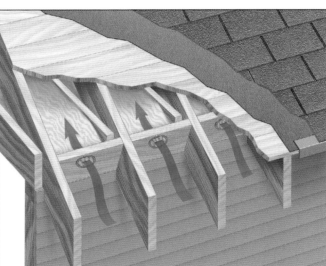

Figure B
Circular vents

These vents, available in 2-, 3- and 4-in. diameters, are ideal if you have eaves but no soffits. Install them by cutting holes into the blocking between the exposed rafter tails and pressing the vents into the holes. Make sure the airflow has a clear pathway through the insulation. Available at roofing supply stores and well-stocked home centers.

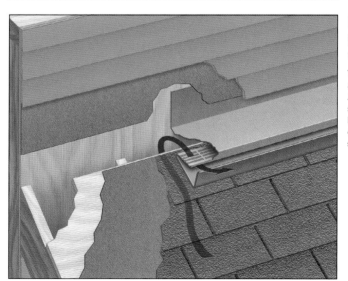

Figure C
Flash filter vent

This vent works where a roof meets a wall. Available from roofing supply stores. (Note: Rectangular roof vents often work in these situations as well.)

blend into the roof, and they distribute ventilation evenly along the ridge. You're also less likely to damage the shingles when you install them.

Ridge vents are available from roofing dealers and many home centers. Follow Photos 14 – 17 for installation tips.

Rectangular metal roof vents work best on hip or pyramid roofs that have a short ridge line. Look for galvanized steel vents. (They are available at roofing supply stores and some home centers.) Follow Photos 9 – 13 for installation tips. Consult a roofing supply store for special installation instructions if you have a metal, slate, cedar or tile roof.

Reader caution

Asbestos has been found in some types of vermiculite insulation. Vermiculite, a lightweight material resembling gravel, was used as attic insulation in perhaps as many as a million homes. If you have vermiculite in your attic, don't disturb it unless you have a sample checked by an accredited laboratory. Disturbing it can release the asbestos fibers, which, once airborne, can enter your lungs and eventually cause lung disease. For a list of accredited testing labs, call your local department of public health. For more vermiculite details, visit epa.gov and search "vermiculite."

Replace damaged vinyl siding

Vinyl siding is tough, but not indestructible. If a falling branch or a well-hit baseball has cracked a piece of your siding, you can make it as good as new in about 15 minutes with a zip tool (available at any home center) and a replacement piece. It's as simple as unzipping the damaged piece and snapping in a new one.

Starting at one end of the damaged piece, push the end of the zip tool up under the siding until you feel it hook the bottom lip (Photo 1). Pull the zip tool downward and out to unhook the bottom lip, then slide it along the edge, pulling the siding out as you go. Then unzip any pieces above the damaged piece. Hold them out of the way with your elbow while you pry out the nails that hold the damaged piece in place (Photo 2).

Slide the replacement piece up into place, pushing up until the lower lip locks into the piece below it. Drive 1-1/4-in. roofing nails through the nailing flange. Space them about every 16 in. (near the old nail holes). Nail in the center of the nailing slot and leave about 1/32 in. of space between the nail head and the siding so the vinyl can move freely. Don't nail the heads tightly or the siding will buckle when it warms up.

With the new piece nailed, use the zip tool to lock the upper piece down over it. Start at one end and pull the lip down, twisting the tool slightly to force the leading edge down (Photo 3). Slide the zip tool along, pushing in on the vinyl just behind the tool with your other hand so it snaps into place.

It's best to repair vinyl in warm weather. In temperatures below freezing it becomes less flexible and may crack.

The downside of replacing older vinyl siding is that it can be hard to match the style and color, and siding rarely has any identifying marks. The best way to get a replacement piece is to take the broken piece to vinyl siding distributors in your area and find the closest match. If the old vinyl has faded or you can't find the right color, take the broken piece to a paint store and have the color matched. Paint the replacement piece with one coat of top-quality acrylic primer followed by acrylic house paint—acrylic paint will flex with the movement of the vinyl.

ZIP TOOL

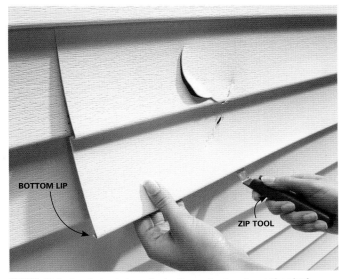

1 Slide the zip tool along the bottom edge to release the vinyl siding from the piece below it.

BOTTOM LIP · ZIP TOOL

UNDAMAGED UPPER PIECE · FLAT BAR · NAILING FLANGE

2 Slip a flat bar behind the vinyl siding and lever out the nails.

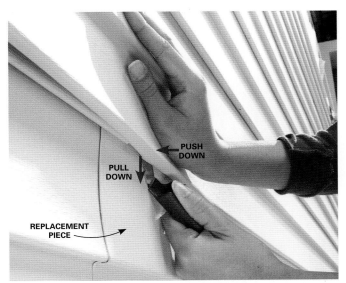

PUSH DOWN · PULL DOWN · REPLACEMENT PIECE

3 Install the replacement piece and hook the lip of the upper siding piece into the slot to lock it into place.

Roof tear-off

Conquer the toughest, dirtiest part of reroofing

Don't be intimidated by the toughest part of reroofing—the tear-off. Here we'll show you how to remove asphalt shingles quickly, so you can move on to the more rewarding part of the job—laying new shingles. We'll also show you how to "button up" the roof by applying new ice and water barrier and felt paper.

Before you take on this big chore, get a bid from a contractor to make sure the savings are worth the strain. The cost of professional roof tear-off varies widely, depending on where you live, the style of the roof and how many layers of shingles it has. In most situations, you can expect to save at least $1,000 by doing it yourself. In some situations, you'll save $3,000 or more.

Planning

Before starting the tear-off, get a building permit and check local building codes. Keep the time between the tear-off and reshingling to a minimum, and wait until clear weather is forecast. Although the underlayment should protect against water infiltration, the felt paper can easily tear or blow loose, making your home vulnerable to rain damage.

If you're having a contractor apply the new shingles, coordinate the tear-off so the new shingles will be installed right away. If you're tackling everything yourself, work in sections. Rip the old shingles off one area, then reshingle before moving on to the next section.

Prep for the tear-off

Doing a little prep work on the ground will keep nails and other debris out of the grass and flower beds, reduce cleanup time and preserve the landscaping. Place plywood over the air conditioner (make sure the power to it is turned off) and over doors or windows near the spot where you'll be tossing the debris off the roof. Then cover plants, shrubs, grass and other areas around the house with inexpensive tarps to vastly simplify cleanup.

Rent a trash container (a 20-cu.-yd. size will handle most roofs). If possible, have it dropped next to the house so you can easily throw old shingles directly into it from the roof.

For safety and better footing, nail the roof jacks below the area you intend to strip first (Photo 1). Buy the adjustable type designed to hold a 2x10 board. Space the jacks no more than 4 ft. apart. Fasten them with at least three 16d nails driven through the roof sheathing into a rafter.

Roof safety

Working on a roof is dangerous, so take precautions.
- Set roof jacks and a 2x10 about 3 ft. up from the roof edge (Photo 1).
- Wear a safety harness, which you can buy at safety equipment stores and some roofing and home centers.
- Wear soft rubber-soled shoes for traction, long pants to protect your legs, work gloves and safety glasses.

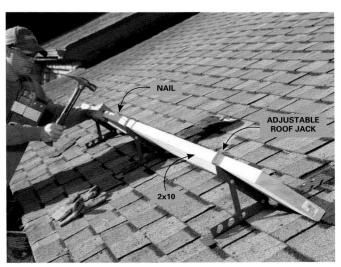

1 Nail roof jacks to the rafters and then nail on a 2x10 to prevent you—and the shingles—from sliding off the roof.

NAIL

ADJUSTABLE ROOF JACK

2x10

SAFETY HARNESS

SAFETY LINE

ANCHOR FASTENED TO ROOF PEAK

2 Use a safety harness system to prevent falls. Wear shoes with soft rubber soles for a good grip and long pants to protect against the skin-scraping shingles.

3 Tear off the ridge caps so you can work the fork under the shingles near the peak.

WORK DOWNWARD

SHINGLE PILE

SCAFFOLDING BOARD

4 Work from the peak down, tearing off shingles in easy-to-carry sections. Tear off a section all the way down to the roof jacks before returning to the peak.

Strip the roof

Start the tear-off at the section farthest from the trash container. Standing at the peak, use a garden fork or a specially notched roofing shovel to tear away the ridge caps and the top courses of shingles (Photo 3). Forks and roofing shovels are available at roofing and home centers. Some roofers prefer forks because they don't get caught on nails, making it easier and faster to remove the shingles. Others like the shovels because they pull out more nails with the shingles.

> **CAUTION:** Watch for soft areas as you walk on the roof. The sheathing may be rotted, and you could break through.

Work the fork under the ridge caps, prying them loose. As they come loose, allow them to slide down to the roof jacks. Or, if they don't slide down the roof, carry them to the edge of the roof and throw them into the trash container.

Once the ridge caps are gone, slide the fork under the shingles and felt paper and pry the shingles up. Some nails will come up with the shingles. Others won't. Ignore them for now.

Remove shingles in a 2- to 3-ft.-wide section as you work down the roof (Photo 4). The shingles will roll up like a ball in front of the fork. Push the shingles down to the roof jacks. Continue tearing off the shingles and underlayment until you reach the roof jacks, then start over at the top of the roof.

Into the trash

As the old roofing material piles up at the roof jacks, carry it to the edge of the roof and toss it into the trash container below (Photo 5). If you couldn't get the trash container close to the house, throw the shingles onto a tarp on the ground. Make the pile on a flat area away from flowers and shrubs.

TRASH CONTAINER

5 Throw old shingles directly into the trash container as they pile up at the roof jacks. Dispose of the shingles before the pile gets too large and they slide off the roof.

SKYLIGHT FLASHING REMOVED

CHIMNEY FLASHING

6 Pull nails carefully around flashings you plan to reuse. Skylight and chimney flashings are often worth saving if they're in good condition.

STEP FLASHING

7 Pull nails from any step flashing you want to save, bend it up slightly and pull out the shingles from underneath.

8 Remove the roof jacks and work the shingles loose along the roof edge with a fork. Then pull them off by hand.

Shingles are heavy. They usually come off in clumps. If you're peeling off two or more layers of shingles, even a small section will be heavy. You may have to pull the shingles apart to make them light enough to carry. Rolling the shingles and felt paper into a ball will also make them easier to handle.

Work with care around roof penetrations

Slow down and work with care when you're next to chimneys, skylights, dormers or an exterior wall. While it's usually best to replace metal flashing, sometimes it's better to preserve and reuse difficult-to-replace types if they're in good shape. But if you see rust and cracks in the metal, replace it. Metal in that condition won't last as long as your new roof.

TIP

Heavily tarred areas usually signal a Band-Aid fix for bad flashing underneath. Replace all this flashing.

If you're keeping the old metal flashing, remove nails and bend it upward off the shingles with a pry bar (Photo 6). Be careful not to damage the flashing. Once it's out of the way, pull any nails and remove any shingles and underlayment that are underneath. Do the same with step flashing (flashing that's interwoven with the shingles) where the roof abuts a wall (Photo 7).

Tear off shingles along the edge

After stripping the shingles down to the roof jacks, remove the jacks. Work the remaining courses loose with a fork or shovel, but don't pry them completely free or they'll slide off the roof (Photo 8).

Loosen the shingles all along the eaves. Then pull off the shingles with your hands, carry them across the roof to the trash

VALLEY FLASHING

9 Pry up the old flashing in the valleys using a fork. Valley flashing is never worth reusing.

10 Pry flashing loose around vent pipes. Use a pry bar rather than a fork to avoid damaging the pipes. Never reuse vent flashing.

RUINED SEAL

PLUMBING FLASHING

11 Sweep the roof clean to avoid slips and falls. Watch for any nails you missed earlier and pull them.

12 Cover the roof right away to protect against rain. Cover the lower end with self-stick ice and water barrier. Then staple down roofing felt to protect the rest of the roof.

ICE AND WATER BARRIER

GUTTER FLASHING

RAKE EDGE

container location and throw them in.

Some roofs have a self-adhering ice and water barrier installed along the roof edge. This asphalt membrane usually pulls up with a fork or shovel, although it may require some scraping. If it refuses to come loose, simply leave it and install your new underlayment over it.

If you don't have time before dark to clean the roof and apply felt, nail down plastic tarps for the night.

Trash old valley and vent flashing

Pry the flashing in valleys and over plumbing vents last. This flashing usually has the same life span as the shingles, so plan to replace it.

Starting at the top of the valley, slip the fork or a flat bar under the flashing and pry the metal edges loose. Continue working down the valley, lifting up the flashing (Photo 9). Pry up and toss out old vent flashing as well (Photo 10).

Clean the deck

Once a section has been completely stripped, go back and pull out protruding nails. Then use a large broom to sweep the roof deck clean (Photo 11). Walk carefully. The shingle granules make the sheathing slippery.

When the roof is clean and bare, inspect the sheathing for damage. Rotted areas and broken boards are the most common problems. Cut out and replace damaged sections as needed. Be sure to use new sheathing that's the same thickness as the old. When removing a damaged section, center the cuts over the rafters so you can nail the new sheathing to the rafters. Also keep an eye out for loose roof sheathing that needs renailing.

"Buttoning up" the roof

Buttoning up the roof is the final prep step before shingling. It consists of installing ice and water barrier and 30-lb. asphalt-saturated felt.

This underlayment acts as a temporary weather barrier to keep rain out. But it won't stop heavy rain and wind, so once you start a section, always try to flash and shingle it by the end of the day.

Ice and water barrier is used at roof edges and other vulnerable areas. To install it, snap a chalk line 36 in. from the edge of the eaves. If you have gutters, you'll want the ice and water barrier to cover all of the gutter flashing that's on the roof (Photo 12).

Starting at the rake edge of the roof, align the ice and water barrier with the chalk line. Tack it at the top with staples every few feet to hold it in place. Once the entire section is tacked along the chalk line, lift up the bottom part, peel off the backing, then let it fall back into place. The ice and water barrier will immediately stick to the roof.

Flip the top part of the ice and water barrier back over the bottom section (the staples will easily pop out), peel off the backing, then set it back into place on the roof. Work carefully to avoid wrinkles. They're a hassle to get out.

Move on to the next section of roof edge, overlapping the vertical seams of the ice and water barrier by 6 in.

Add a second course above the first, if required, overlapping the first by 4 in. Also lay the ice and water barrier in valleys and around chimneys, skylights and other roof penetrations.

Then unroll and staple down 30-lb. felt over the rest of the roof. Use plenty of staples (5/16 in.) to make the felt safer to walk on and keep it from blowing off. This is where a hammer-type stapler pays off. You can drive a dozen staples in seconds.

Clean up the area

Before climbing off the roof, clean any debris out of the gutters. There will be nails and a lot of granules from the shingles that you don't want pouring out of your downspouts the next time it rains.

Run a broom magnet over the yard to pick up stray nails. You can rent the magnet at tool rental stores. Make several passes in different directions. Regardless of how carefully you worked, nails have a way of ending up in the lawn.

When are shingles worn out?

The most obvious sign that your roof needs to be replaced is a leak. Since you don't want to wait until that happens, inspect the shingles every year. Most asphalt shingles have a life span of 20 to 25 years, although they can wear out and need to be replaced in as few as 15 years, especially on the south side of the house.

Signs that shingles are failing include cupping along the edges (the edges curl up) and extensive cracking. In severe cases, the shingles will completely deteriorate. Buckling shingles (the shingles develop a bow and lift up from the roof) are an indication that moisture is getting underneath them. If large sections of shingles are coming loose and falling off, it's time for a new roof.

Shingles typically show signs of wear along the edges first. Rounded or curled corners are early warnings that the roof is ready or nearly ready for new shingles.

Replace the roof when shingles show signs of wear such as curling, buckling, cracking or missing granules.

Prevent black streaks on your roof

Black streaks on a roof are caused by a hardy algae called *Gloeocapsa magma*. As the blue-green algae accumulate, they develop a dark, hardened outer coating, which results in the black stains you see. The algae feed on the limestone in shingles.

The algae will worsen and become more noticeable each year, trapping moisture and causing premature shingle aging and granule loss. If you don't like the streaks, reshingle with algae-resistant shingles. If the streaks don't bother you or you're not ready to invest in a new roof, install zinc or copper strips (available at roofing centers) along the top course of shingles. When rain hits the strips, it produces a solution that runs down the roof and keeps algae, moss and fungus from growing. However, the strips won't eliminate the existing algae.

Chapter Seven

LAWN CARE

Lawn mower maintenance

Keep your walk-behind mower running like new—do these 4 simple fixes now.

Mowing is enough of a chore without having to deal with a rough-running, poor-cutting lawn mower. With just a few bucks' worth of parts and a couple of hours' work, you can get your lawn mower in prime shape to start the mowing season. The following pages show you how to drain the old gas, replace the air filter, put in a new spark plug and change the oil—tasks that will keep your gas-powered mower starting easy, running smooth and cutting clean.

Most engine manufacturers recommend an oil change at least every 25 hours of operation or every three months.

TURKEY BASTER

OLD GAS

1 Using an old turkey baster, suck old gas from your tank. Squirt it into a container approved for gas storage, and dispose of it properly. Refill the tank with fresh fuel.

Add fresh gas at the start of the season

Fuel system problems top the list of lawn mower malfunctions. Many of these, like gunked-up carburetors, are often caused by gasoline that's been left in the mower too long. Although fall is the best time to take preventive measures, you can at least get off to a good start in the spring by replacing the old gas in your tank with fresh gas. Photo 1 shows one method.

Gasoline is highly flammable. Work outdoors or in a well-ventilated area away from sparks and flame. Wipe up spills immediately and store gas in approved sealed containers. To dispose of the old gas, call your local hazardous waste disposal site for instructions.

Most mowers have a mesh screen over the outlet at the bottom of the tank. If you can see the screen through the filler hole, use an old turkey baster to suck up dirt and debris that may be covering it.

Change your oil regularly

Changing the oil in your lawn mower takes about 15 minutes and costs only a few dollars. That's time and money well spent considering that changing oil at the recommended intervals will greatly extend the life of the engine. Most engine manufacturers recommend an oil change at least every 25 hours of operation or every three months.

Older mowers have a fill plug close to the mower deck. Fill this type until oil reaches the threads of the refill hole. Two-cycle

engines that use a gas/oil mix for fuel don't have an oil reservoir on the engine and don't require oil changes.

Before you drain the old oil, run the mower a few minutes to warm the oil and stir up sediment. Then disconnect the spark plug, drain the old oil and add new (Photos 2 – 4). Use SAE 30 W oil (check your owner's manual). There are two ways to drain old oil: through the filler neck (Photo 3) or out the drain plug in the bottom of the engine (Photo 5). It's quicker and easier to drain the oil through the filler neck if your mower has one. If you have an older mower without a filler neck, locate the drain plug on the bottom of the engine and remove it to drain the oil. Pour used oil through a funnel into a plastic milk jug or other container and label it for recycling.

Whenever you tip a lawn mower up on two wheels (Photo 3) to work on the underside, only lift the side with the air cleaner. This prevents oil from running into the carburetor and soaking the air filter. Also, if your lawn mower has a fuel valve, turn it off.

Remember to check the oil level occasionally between oil changes, setting the mower on a level surface. Top it off as needed. Newer mowers have dipsticks with markings that indicate when to add oil. Don't overfill. Check your manual for instructions to see whether the dipstick should be fully screwed in or just set in when you're checking the level. If you accidentally add too much oil, follow the procedure shown in Photos 3 and 5 to drain some out.

2 Seal the gas tank by removing the gas cap and covering the opening with a plastic bag. Screw the cap back on over the plastic bag.

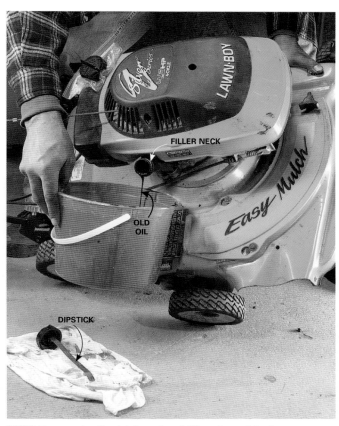

3 Remove the dipstick from the oil filler tube and tip the mower to drain the oil. Pour the used oil into a plastic milk jug or similar container and recycle it.

4 Refill the engine with clean oil. Most engines require about 20 ozs. (5/8 quart). Insert the dipstick and check the oil level. Add oil if needed but don't overfill.

Alternate draining

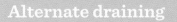

5 Unscrew the plug located on the bottom of the engine and allow the oil to drain into a pan. Lower the mower down on its wheels to make sure all the oil drains. Replace the plug, set the mower on a level surface, and fill the engine with clean oil through the filler hole near the base of the engine.

CAUTION: Always disconnect the spark plug wire from the spark plug (Photo 10, p. 209) before reaching under your mower.

Don't suffocate your mower—change the air filter

Air filters are cheap and easy to replace. Dirty air filters choke the engine, causing it to run poorly and lose power. If your lawn is dry and dusty, check the filter after every few mowings. Otherwise, check it a couple of times during the season. Replace it when it starts to get plugged with dirt and debris. One common test is to shine a flashlight through the filter. If you can't see the light through the filter, replace it with a new one.

Most newer mowers have pleated paper filters that are either flat or cylindrical (Photo 7), while many older mowers have foam filters (Photo 8). Both types of replacement filters are readily available at lawn mower retailers, hardware stores and home centers. Take your old filter along and have your mower manufacturer's name and model number handy.

In a pinch, you can wash foam filters in a solution of laundry detergent and water and allow them to air dry. But since replacements are cheap, it's best to just buy a new one. In either case, saturate the foam filter in motor oil and squeeze out the excess before installing it (Photo 9).

Pleated paper air filters

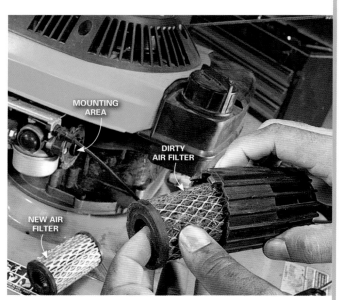

6 Locate the air filter near the carburetor. Unscrew, unsnap or twist off the cover to remove the old filter.

7 Remove the old air filter and replace it if it's dirty. Wipe grass and dirt from the filter cover and the mounting area with a clean cloth before installing the new filter. Be careful not to let dirt fall into the carburetor.

Foam air filters

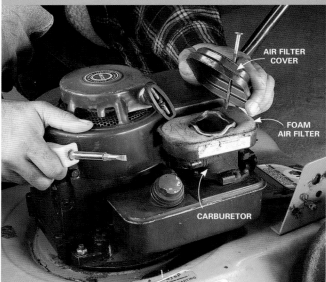

8 Unscrew or unhook the cover and pull out the old filter. Wipe the filter cover parts with a clean rag to remove dirt and grime.

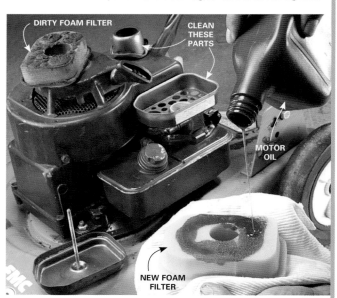

9 Pour about 1/4 cup of clean motor oil over the new foam filter. Wrap the filter in a clean cloth and squeeze it firmly to distribute the oil evenly and remove any excess. Install the filter, making sure the foam lip covers the top of the filter holder. Replace the cover and tighten the screw.

Add pep with a new spark plug

Often a new spark plug will make a big improvement in the way your engine starts and runs. Spark plugs are so cheap and easy to install that it's good insurance just to replace your plug every spring. Check your owner's manual for the correct spark plug, or take the old plug with you to the store to match it up.

10 Remove the spark plug wire by pulling it straight out. If it's stuck, try twisting it slightly as you pull. Wipe off dirt from the area. Use a 3/4-in.- or 13/16-in.-deep socket or spark plug wrench to unscrew the old spark plug. Turn the wrench counterclockwise.

New spark plugs are factory set with a .030-in. gap between the electrodes at the tip of the plug. Inspect the plug when you buy it to make sure there's a gap about the thickness of a matchbook cover. If there's no gap, the plug may have been dropped and damaged. Choose another one.

If you don't own a socket wrench set with a 3/4-in. or 13/16-in.-deep socket for changing the spark plug, pick up an inexpensive spark plug wrench (photo above).

Some maintenance is best left to the pros

The basic maintenance tasks shown here will go a long way toward keeping your mower in good running condition. But there are two more items that would normally be included in a professional tune-up. The first is disassembly and cleaning of the carburetor and linkage. This may be necessary if you've left untreated gas in the tank over the winter and the lawn mower won't start or runs poorly. This repair requires some mechanical experience.

Cleaning grass and debris from the engine's cooling fins (the cooling fins are the metal ridges that cover the engine) is another maintenance task that should be performed periodically. On mowers with exposed cooling fins, this is an easy do-it-yourself job. Use a stiff-bristle brush to clean gunk from between the fins.

On many newer mowers, however, the plastic or metal covering on top of the engine has to be removed first, which may also require disconnecting the fuel tank. Use a flashlight to inspect the cooling fins under these covers. If they look clogged, you'll have to decide if you're up to the challenge or would feel more comfortable letting a pro handle the job.

11 Install the new spark plug by turning it clockwise two or three complete revolutions by hand before switching over to the spark plug wrench to tighten it. Don't overtighten the spark plug. Manufacturers recommend tightening the plug about a half turn after it seats to compress the new washer. Complete the job by pressing the plug wire onto the plug.

First aid for your lawn

5 remedies for your hurting turf

Even the best lawns could use a little therapeutic attention now and again. To help you pull yours out of the rough patches, the following pages offer the best remedies for the most common turf maladies. These remedies will also tell you how to improve your lawn's natural defenses and reduce future maintenance chores.

PROBLEM:
Dog spots on grass

Symptoms: Dog spots are round patches about 4 to 8 in. in diameter with dead grass in the middle, encircled by dark green grass. They're most apparent in the early spring when dormant grass first begins to turn green again.

Cause: Dog urine contains high concentrations of acids, salts and nitrogen, which burn (dry out) the grass roots and kill them. As rain washes the area, the urine is diluted and the nitrogen spreads, causing the grass surrounding the spot to grow faster and turn greener.

> **TIP**
>
> When you're watering new seed, moisten the soil daily and keep it damp—but don't soak it. Over-watering is a common mistake.

Remedy: You have to replant your grass; it won't come back on its own. But first you have to dilute or remove the caustic urine from the soil (Photo 1). Thoroughly soak the area with lots of water. Let the hose run for at least three minutes. Then you can start the replanting process (Photo 2). Add a half inch of new soil to help absorb any remaining urine (Photo 3). Then you can spread new seed, as shown here, or use a commercial yard patch mixture (available at most nurseries or home centers) or even sod. In any case, the secret of good germination is keeping the seed moist. And keep the area moist until the new grass is about 3 in. high.

Recovery time: Four to six weeks

An ounce of prevention

1. Soak your pet's favorite areas in your lawn to get the salts out of the root zone before they kill the grass.
2. Fertilize your lawn in the spring to boost the overall color and mask the darker green dog spots.
3. Train your pet to urinate in a designated area. Replace or repair the grass in this area annually or cover it with mulch.
4. Keep your pet well hydrated to make its urine less concentrated.

1 Soak the patch until the grass is sopping wet to dilute the urine acids and salts and wash them deeper into the soil, beyond the grass roots.

2 Scrape up the dead grass with a hand rake and remove it. Rough up the area to loosen the soil 1/2 in. deep. Seeds germinate better in soft soil.

3 Sprinkle on a 1/2-in.-thick layer of topsoil, then pepper it with grass seed. Cover with a thin layer of new soil. Keep the area moist until the new grass is about 3 in. high.

PROBLEM:
Thatch

THATCH

Symptoms: If your grass feels soft and spongy when you walk on it, your lawn may have a thatch buildup. Thatch is a fibrous mat of dead stalks and roots that settles between the lawn's green leaves and the soil (photo right). When this mat becomes greater than 3/4 in. thick, it can cause your lawn to suffer from heat and drought. Affected lawns will rapidly wilt and turn blue-green, indicating they're hot and dry.

Cause: Cutting off too much at each mowing (letting the grass get too long) and cutting too low. Both will produce more dead grass tissue than microbes and earthworms can recycle. Thatch can develop in any soil but is most often associated with high clay content. Other causes are overfertilization and frequent, light watering, which encourage a shallow root system.

Remedy: Slice open a section of your lawn (Photo 1). If your grass shows 3/4 in. or more of thatch, it's time to rent an aerator. An aerator is a heavy machine

CAUTION: Call your local utility provider or 811 to mark your underground utility lines before you aerate.

that opens the soil by pulling up finger-size soil cores. The lawn will absorb more oxygen and water, which will encourage healthy microbe growth and give worms wiggle room.

Aerate in the spring or fall when the grass is growing but the weather is not too hot to stress the plants (Photo 2). If the machine isn't pulling plugs, your lawn may be too dry. To avoid this problem, water thoroughly the day before you aerate. You can also rake in topsoil (Photo 3) to increase the healthy microorganisms that aid thatch's natural decomposition. Topsoil is available at any garden center.

Recovery time: You can expect the thatch layer to decrease by about 1/4 in. per year, about the same rate at which it forms.

An ounce of prevention

1. Mow often and cut no more than one-third of the grass height.
2. Water your lawn less often but for longer periods to prevent shallow root systems.
3. Reduce the amount of fertilizer you spread at any one time.
4. Reduce the use of pesticides. This will help keep the worm and microorganism populations healthy.
5. Aerate at least once every year if your lawn is prone to thatch.

THATCH

1 Slice the turf grass with a shovel and pry it back. If the thatch depth measures more than 3/4 in., aerate at least 3 in. deep.

CORE PLUGS

2 Make two or three passes with an aerator until you've made 3-in.-deep holes 2 in. apart throughout your yard.

3 Spread 1/4 in. of topsoil on the yard's most thatchy areas and then rake vigorously to fill the holes with loose soil.

PROBLEM:
Fairy ring

Symptoms: Fairy rings are circles approximately 3 to 8 ft. wide that consist of a dark green and fast-growing area of grass surrounding an inner area of partially dead or thin grass. Some rings also produce mushrooms.

Cause: Fairy rings are caused by fungi that live in the soil. As the fungi feed on organic matter, they release nitrogen, causing the grass to turn dark green. As the colony grows, it disturbs the flow of needed water to the turf roots, creating thin or dead spots. Fairy rings often begin with the decomposition of organic matter, such as an old tree stump buried under the lawn.

Remedy: By bringing up the color in the rest of your lawn with a nitrogen fertilizer, you can mask much of the overgreening of the fairy ring (Photo 1). Hand-aerating the ring will break up the fungus and allow the flow of water and other nutrients to the grass roots (Photo 2).

Recovery time: Generally fairy rings can be masked with the application of fertilizer, with results in 10 to 14 days. The grass within the ring will thicken up with aeration in about two to three weeks.

An ounce of prevention

Aeration will help with fairy rings, but maintaining a healthy lawn with a balanced fertilization program is essential. Apply three doses:

1. Apply 1/2 lb. per 1,000 sq. ft. in late April or early May to give the over-wintering grass roots a bit of a boost.
2. Add no more than 1/2 lb. per 1,000 sq. ft. at the end of June or in early July when temperatures are not at their peak. Stimulating growth during a heat wave will stress the plants.
3. Spread 1 lb. per 1,000 sq. ft. at the end of October. The best root growth takes place when the soil temps are between 58 and 65 degrees F. The roots store energy over the winter, making the entire lawn healthier the following spring.

1 Spread 1/2 lb. of nitrogen fertilizer per 1,000 sq. ft. to green up your lawn, but skip the fairy ring zone. This masks the lush green of the fairy ring by blending it into the rest of your yard.

DO NOT FERTILIZE THE RING ITSELF

2 Break up the fungi with a hand aerator (sold at home centers or garden stores). Punch holes every 2 to 4 in. throughout the ring and 2 ft. beyond.

CORE PLUGS

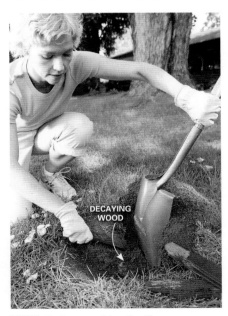

3 Go "treasure" hunting if you see no improvement in three weeks. Dig out rotting stumps, roots, construction debris or other organic materials under your lawn.

DECAYING WOOD

PROBLEM:
Grubs

Symptoms: Grub-chewed turf has patchy areas that wilt and die. You can easily pull up the affected turf if you tug on it. Another indicator of grubs may be increased raccoon, bird or mole activity. They like to dig up and eat the grubs at night. While this may sound good, the moles will kill the grass as they forage for grubs.

Cause: Lawn grubs are the larval stage of moths and beetles. The grubs eat the roots of grass, setting them up to die by dehydration.

Remedy: Be vigilant. Are beetles swarming around your porch light? In the next month, keep an eye out for patches of grass that wilt or are blue-green on hot days. They may be larvae infested. Turn over some turf (Photo 1). If you count six to 10 grubs (white wormlike larvae with black heads) under a 1-ft.-square area of sod, consider using a grub insecticide (available at home centers and nurseries). Or talk to a professional (search online for "grass service") about treating your yard. They will be familiar with the grub problems in your region and the most suitable treatment methods.

If you spot the grubs but your count is lower than six per square foot, baby your lawn to strengthen its natural defenses. Mow on higher blade settings and water thoroughly but infrequently to encourage the grass to grow new, deep roots. Do not cut off more than one-third of the grass height at each mowing, to avoid stressing the plant.

An ounce of prevention

Inspect your turf periodically by pulling on patches that look unhealthy, or have a professional inspect your lawn if you suspect a problem.

1 Pierce the lawn with a shovel in a U-shape. Peel back the lawn (as though rolling up a rug) and count the white grubs in a 1-sq.-ft. area.

2 Treat your lawn with an insecticide if the count is six to 10 grubs in a square foot. Follow the manufacturer's directions carefully. Or consult with a yard service.

PROBLEM:
Shade

Symptoms: Shaded grass will look thin and patchy. Some types of grass actually produce wider blades as the plant attempts to catch more rays. But they also produce far fewer blades, lending a spindly appearance to the lawn. The cold truth is, if your lawn gets less than six to eight hours of sun daily, you are unlikely to sustain lush grass.

Cause: Trees, buildings and bushes.

Remedy: You can increase the sunlight as much as possible by trimming trees and shrubs. Also try starting areas in shade with sod instead of seed. The sod will adjust to the lower level of light. Although all seed varieties have their shade limitations, try overseeding your thin area with a shady grass mix.

Or throw in the towel, grab your trowel and plant a shade-tolerant ground cover. Many will thrive where your turf withered. Lamium (dead nettle) and ajuga (bugleweed) collaborate nicely in providing lovely blooms and an enthusiastic, but not invasive, carpet. This pair fares well, with a hearty tolerance spanning zones 3 to 8, and can be planted right up to your grass. They are fairly low growers and won't get more than a few nicks from a lawn mower.

Also, mulching between the ground cover plants will help retain moisture. This is

especially wise if your new "shade garden" is on a slope; mulch will help prevent your fledging plants from washing out in a hard rain.

Recovery time: The plants and mulch will immediately boost the appearance of an area that was once thin grass. It'll take a couple of seasons for the ground cover to become established and blanket the area.

An ounce of prevention

Avoid the frustration of sun-starved grass by starting a shade garden or ground cover in any area that doesn't receive six to eight hours of good light.

Using a garden hoe, work up the shady area to remove any struggling grass. Plant ground cover or a shade garden.

Fertilizer 101

The more you know, the more you grow!

A trip down the fertilizer aisle at your local garden center can leave you feeling overwhelmed. Colorful bags and bottles line the shelves, each one decorated with flowers, numbers and a loaded claim to improve your yard.

With so many choices and scientific lingo to weed through, how's a person to know which product to pick? This crash course in fertilizers gives you the knowledge you need to walk down that aisle with confidence!

First things first

Before you set foot in the fertilizer aisle, test your soil. Contact your local extension office or look online for a state-certified soil-testing lab. The test results give you an idea of what nutrients your soil may be lacking so you can purchase a fertilizer that will add those nutrients.

On most fertilizer products, you may notice a set of three numbers. That's not a secret code! Those numbers tell you the percentages of nitrogen, phosphorus and potassium (in that order) in the product. Each element is critical for plant health. Nitrogen (N) encourages green, leafy growth. Phosphorus (P), in the form of phosphate, contributes to root development. And potassium (K), in the form of potash, helps to maintain plant and grass vigor. Different plants and soils require different amounts of each element, which is why you'll see variations in the numbers from product to product.

Complete and incomplete

A complete fertilizer contains all three elements (nitrogen, phosphorus and potassium), while an incomplete fertilizer contains just one or two. If a fertilizer is lacking a nutrient, there will be a zero in its place on the label (15-0-0). Incomplete fertilizers are primarily used when only one or two particular elements are missing from the soil.

A soil test is the best way to determine whether you need to compensate with a complete or incomplete fertilizer.

General- and special-purpose

General-purpose fertilizers contain all three nutrients and are intended to meet basic needs of most plants and grasses.

Special-purpose fertilizers are formulated to meet specific gardening needs. For example, some are designed for certain plants, like tomatoes or rhododendrons. Others are blended to encourage lush, green growth with a high percentage of nitrogen. But keep in mind, some companies may label

Drip feeder for containers >

< Bone meal

Fertilizer spikes for perennials >

< Chicken manure

Special-purpose tomato fertilizer >

5-10-5

NET WEIGHT 5 LBS (2.26 kg)

Garden Food
5-10-5
GUARANTEED ANALYSIS

Total Nitrogen (N).....................	5%
Available Phosphate (P_2O_5)............	10%
Soluble Potash (K_2O)...................	5%

Derived from Ammonium Sulfate, Triple
Superphosphate and Potash.   F1381

SINCE 1929

What those numbers mean

These numbers indicate 5 percent nitrogen, 10 percent phosphorus and 5 percent potassium.

Nitrogen (N) encourages green, leafy growth.

Phosphorus (P) contributes to root development.

Potassium (K) helps maintain vigorous growth.

the same product for different plants or grasses. Compare labels to find which fertilizers best fit your lawn needs.

Liquid and solid

Fertilizers are applied in either dry or liquid form. Dry fertilizers are worked into the soil and begin releasing nutrients when they come in contact with water. The nutrients are either delivered to the soil quickly or, if you use a slow-release variety, over a period of several months. Slow-release fertilizers are appealing because they need less-frequent applications and provide a slow, steady diet throughout the growing season with minimal effort.

While you can find ready-to-use liquid fertilizers, they are typically sold as concentrated liquids or granular substances that need to be diluted with water before you use them. Liquid fertilizers are applied to the soil at very diluted solutions. Most deliver nutrients to a plant or grass quickly and need to be applied a few times during the growing season. Liquid fertilizers are ideal for container plants or as a supplement to dry fertilizers when you want to give annuals, vegetables or your lawn an extra boost at the beginning of the season or during periods of active growth.

Organic and synthetic

Organic fertilizers, such as bone meal, fish emulsion and chicken or worm manure, are made of materials from once-living organisms. Unlike synthetics, which immediately release nutrients through water, organics share their bounty as they break down. Although synthetic fertilizers work well for plants or grass that need an instant boost, organics are less likely to

damage a plant or your lawn if accidentally over-applied. Besides their environmentally friendly nature, organics are also known for their ability to deliver nutrients while enhancing soil health.

Sticks, stakes and pellets

These fertilizers bear a resemblance to giant-sized vitamins, and that description actually isn't too far off. The fertilizer has simply been compressed so it can be inserted into the soil around the plant, tree or shrub. The idea is to get the nutrients to the plant's roots as quickly as possible by burying the fertilizer nearby.

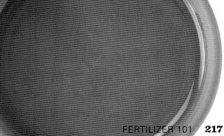

Tree and shrub fertilizer spikes >

All-purpose "shake and feed" >

"Worm Poop" liquid fertilizer >

5-10-5 general-purpose < garden food

How to use a broadcast spreader

This must-have lawn tool spreads everything you need for a healthy, attractive lawn.

Maintaining an attractive lawn takes not only lots of hard work, knowledge, timing and good weather but also the precise (and seemingly endless) application of the proper seed, soil builder and chemicals. Each product you apply requires a different spread rate. Too much is wasteful and could kill your lawn; too little won't do the job.

A good spreader can apply just the right amount of product. The key is to choose a model that has an adjustable spread rate setting to deliver the product uniformly and in accurate amounts to the left, center and right while applying the recommended volume for your lawn size.

Spreaders are widely available from garden and home centers. The following pages show you how to use your spreader more effectively to save time and make your lawn more attractive.

The best operating techniques

The key to operating a broadcaster spreader is to achieve even dispersal at the right concentration. To do this:

■ Dial in the product manufacturer's recommended setting on the spread rate gauge (Photo 2), and test and measure the product's dispersal pattern through the spreader (Photo 3). First, sweep dirt and debris off your driveway and then conduct the dispersal pattern test. With a broadcast spreader, the right side of the dispersal pattern will be a foot or two wider than the left. Use this test information to establish the pattern you'll use to push the spreader across your yard for total coverage with 6 in. to 1 ft. of overlap.

■ Write this "wide side," "narrow side" measurement information on a piece of masking tape and stick it to the back of the hopper so you don't forget the broadcast pattern for each side. Don't

sweep, blow or wash this test material into the street. Sweep it up and dump it back in the hopper.

■ If the product doesn't list a recommended setting for your spreader, consult your owner's manual for generic

IMPELLER BROADCASTING SEED

1 Spread grass seed and other lawn products uniformly, quickly and efficiently using a broadcast spreader.

Two types of spreaders and how they work

Broadcast spreaders (Photo 2) and drop spreaders (photo below) are push-powered workhorses that share many features in common. At the heart of both is a hopper with adjustable holes in the bottom. A gauge mounted on the spreader's handlebar allows you to accurately set the size of these holes (following the recommended setting listed on many bags of lawn products), allowing the proper volume of material to uniformly exit the hopper. Alongside the gauge, a flow lever controls when the material drops onto the lawn by opening and closing a plate

DROP SPREADER

under the hopper holes. But the two machines have their differences, too.

Drop spreaders lay a trail of material the width of their hopper (less than 24 in.). They work best on small lawns and in yards with numerous flowerbeds, sidewalks or patios where you need to carefully control the spread pattern. Unless you're meticulous about lining up adjacent passes, the payload either is laid too thick or misses portions of the grass, resulting in visible striping.

Broadcast spreaders are the choice of the pros and the focus of this story. Broadcasters work best for yards larger than 4,000 sq. ft. They deliver their payload more quickly over a wider area—and without striping the lawn. One of their wheels is geared so that as you push the broadcaster, the drive wheel turns a whirling impeller plate under the hopper that catches and throws the payload. When the shutoff plate is open, the impeller broadcasts the material in a 180-degree arc 7 ft. to 11 ft. wide (depending on the product's granular size and your walking speed).

equivalents of each product. Otherwise you'll have to resort to trial and error. Set the spreader to a light coverage (try a 1/4-in. to 3/16-in. hole in the hopper), apply the product over the recommended square footage, and check how much product you have left in the hopper. Adjust the dial to spread the remaining material over the same area, going perpendicular to the first pattern.

■ Begin your yard pattern by spreading across hills first. This way, you'll have enough lawn product in the hopper to reduce "skipping" over the uneven terrain.

■ Maintain the pace you'd use to take a middle-aged, midsized dog for a walk (about 3 mph). Your walking speed affects how wide and how much product the broadcaster throws. Walking too slow reduces the throw width and increases product density; walking too fast thins out the coverage.

■ Each time you're ready to stop or make a turn, close the flow lever to stop dispersing the product and continue one more stride. This reduces waste and avoids damaging the lawn from saturated product coverage. Avoid pulling the spreader backward when the flow lever is open; you'll release more of the product.

■ Operate the spreader, keeping the impeller plate close to level (Photo 4). Tilting the handlebar up or down from level throws the product too high or low, resulting in uneven coverage on your lawn.

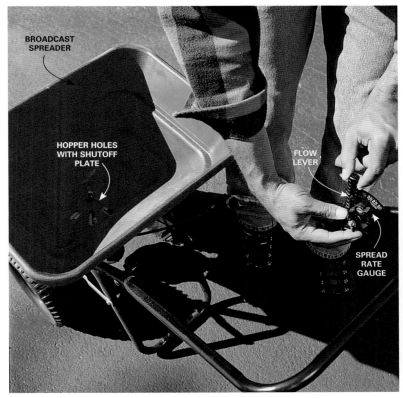

BROADCAST SPREADER

HOPPER HOLES WITH SHUTOFF PLATE

FLOW LEVER

SPREAD RATE GAUGE

2 Close the flow lever and dial in the recommended spread rate for the product you're using before filling the hopper. The higher the gauge setting, the larger the hole size in the hopper—resulting in a faster material flow rate. Whenever you're loading lawn products into the spreader, place the machine on a sidewalk or driveway to avoid having material spills saturate one spot on your lawn and kill it.

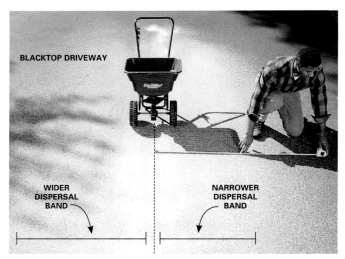

BLACKTOP DRIVEWAY

WIDER DISPERSAL BAND

NARROWER DISPERSAL BAND

SLOPED HILL

DRIVE WHEEL

IMPELLER

COASTING WHEEL

3 Measure the spreader's dispersal pattern for each new lawn product. Place the spreader at the front edge of a 12-ft. wide by 20-ft.-long swept-off section of your driveway. Make sure the flow lever is closed, fill the hopper, then open the flow lever and push the spreader for three paces of your normal walking speed. Close the lever, take one more stride before stopping the spreader and measure both the total width of the resultant dispersal pattern and the total width of each side. Sweep up the test material and put it back in the bag or hopper.

4 Keep the impeller running as parallel to the ground as possible and maintain at least a two-thirds-full load in the hopper when running the spreader across slopes and rough terrain. A level impeller ensures an accurate throwing pattern, while a full hopper acts as ballast to prevent the spreader's drive wheel from lifting or "skipping" across the ground. Skipping makes the impeller throw product in an erratic manner.

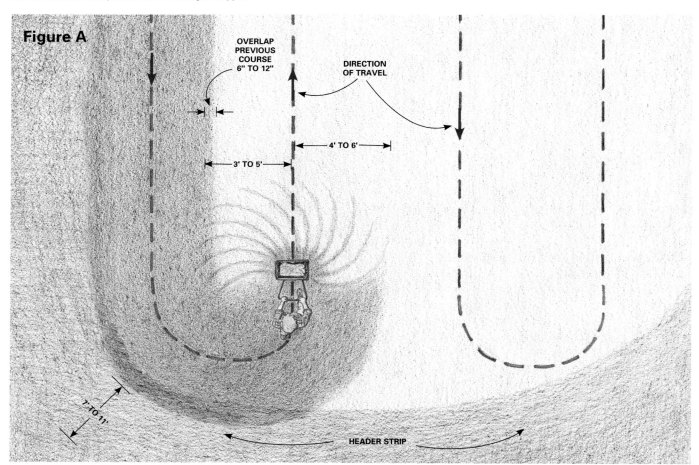

Figure A

OVERLAP PREVIOUS COURSE 6" TO 12"

DIRECTION OF TRAVEL

4' TO 6'

3' TO 5'

7' TO 11'

HEADER STRIP

Follow this optimal pattern for running the broadcaster spreader. Apply a "header strip" by circling the spreader once around the yard's perimeter. Avoid throwing the material payload into adjacent flowerbeds by running the spreader back from those areas the distance your driveway test (Photo 3) showed. Complete the pattern by pushing the spreader on a serpentine route back and forth in the longest direction on the lawn while overlapping the throw patterns about a foot. Shut off the flow lever as you near the end of a row, when the spreader's within 5 ft. of the header strip. Keep the lever off during the turn and open it to begin the new row.

■ Don't overapply fertilizer and weed killer. Follow the recommended coverage rate for each product. Overuse and overapplication can lead to lawn runoff that contaminates lakes and streams. Protect yourself by wearing gloves and a nuisance dust mask when handling chemical lawn products that contain pesticides and herbicides.

Buying and maintenance tips

It's worth the extra money to buy a better-quality broadcast spreader with these features:

■ High-impact polypropylene hopper and tubular steel handles with a baked-on finish for a longer, rust-free life.

■ Hopper capacity of at least 25 to 30 lbs. of product so you'll spend less time refilling the spreader.

■ Large, 8- to 10-in. wheels—preferably high-impact plastic— for easy rolling over bumpy lawns and easier operation.

> **TIP**
>
> **Use your broadcast spreader for grass seed, fertilizers, dethatch mix and weed killer to ensure a healthy lawn.**

Using a garden hose, quickly rinse out the spreader every time you change lawn products. When you're finished using the spreader for the day, invest 15 minutes in maintenance to prolong its life. Lay the spreader on its side and use a forceful blast from a garden hose to thoroughly clean the hopper, wheels and impeller plate. Operate the flow lever back and forth and wash off the shutoff plate inside the hopper. After the broadcaster

is dry, periodically use a light lubricant spray like WD-40 to protect all moving parts, the axle bushings on the wheels and the gear-box. Avoid lubricants that contain Teflon or silicone. They may seal in certain chemicals from the fertilizers and speed up corrosion.

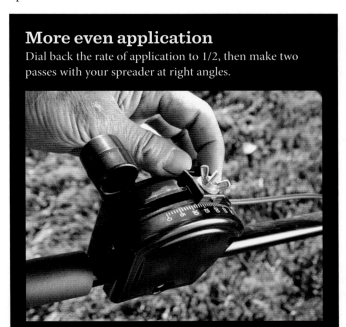

More even application
Dial back the rate of application to 1/2, then make two passes with your spreader at right angles.

Too much fertilizer?

Many retailers promote a four-step fertilizer program for homeowners. Fertilizing more than four times a year is overkill. In fact, most homeowners could get by with two every year. You can cut back on the amount of fertilizer you need by making sure you apply it at the right time of the year—first, around Labor Day; second in mid-October; third in mid to late spring. A midsummer application is optional.

If you apply too much fertilizer, especially in sandy soils, a good share of it will leach through the soil and make its way into our precious groundwater, lakes, streams and wetlands. Lawn grasses only need a certain amount of food. More isn't always better.

Unlike us humans, lawn grasses don't know how to stop eating when they're full! This luxury consumption of nitrogen, phosphorus and potassium actually makes the lawn grasses weak and more susceptible to disease. Excessive fertilizer will create too much thatch, which will ultimately choke out your lawn. Too

much fertilizer also means you'll be mowing far more often than necessary. Too much mowing means excessive soil compaction, exhaust and noise pollution, and excessive wear and tear on your mower.

More than four fertilizer applications a year is a waste. Save time and money by being more judicious in your use of fertilizer.

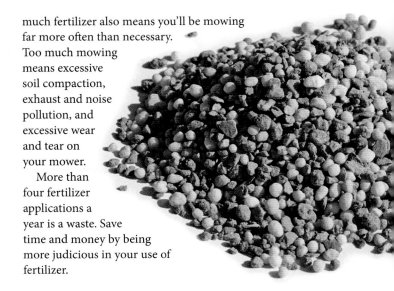

Kill any weed

With the right herbicide at the right time, you can wipe out your weeds in one hour!

Dandelions and ground ivy are common in most yards, as are patches of clover and thistles. Spend an hour spraying a herbicide on your lawn, then within a couple of days, the weeds will be wilting. And they won't grow back after you mow them. Not bad for an hour's worth of weed treatment!

The following pages show you how to kill your weeds in an hour or less. Although there are hundreds of kinds of weeds,

they all fall into one of three categories—broadleaf, annual grassy weeds or perennial grassy weeds—and specific types of herbicides target each weed group.

Whether you want to eliminate weeds before they start growing again (early in the year is the best time to attack weeds) or kill weeds that are already overtaking your lawn, the following pages show you how. Most of the weed treatments you need are available at home centers, and the others at garden centers.

7 tips on weed-killing

1 Don't waste your money or time applying herbicides (except preemergence treatments) when there aren't any weeds. Fertilize instead.

2 Use a pump-up type sprayer to spot-treat weeds that are limited to specific areas. Only mix the amount of liquid herbicides you need that day. They have a very short shelf life once mixed with water.

3 The soil should be moist and the grass growing before you apply any herbicides.

4 Water your lawn thoroughly before applying any weed treatment.

5 Apply liquid herbicides only on calm, windless mornings. When the wind's blowing, you'll not only waste material but also possibly kill nearby shrubs and flowers.

6 Granular herbicides work poorly on viny broadleafs like clover or creeping charlie. Use liquid herbicides on those. Some work better on hard-to-kill broadleaf weeds. Ask for advice at the garden center.

7 Buy concentrated liquid herbicides; they're cheaper than premixed solutions.

Kill annual grassy weeds

Annual grassy weeds sprout from seed each year. The weed dies in the fall, leaving behind seeds that germinate the following spring. Crabgrass is the most notorious grassy weed, but there are others, like yellow foxtail and nutgrass.

CRABGRASS

Early

Use a preemergent herbicide to kill annual grassy weed seeds in the spring before they germinate. Crabgrass preventer is the most common, but you might as well apply a herbicide that also kills broadleaf weed seeds. Crabgrass often thrives along sidewalks and driveways because the ground is warmer there, so be sure to apply herbicide in those areas.

Late

The best way to handle a few scattered annual grassy weeds is to spot-kill them with a postemergence herbicide that's formulated for grassy weeds. Look for Grass Weed Killer or Crabgrass Killer on the label (Crabgrass Killer kills other grassy weeds too).

Mix the concentrated herbicide with water (per manufacturer's directions), then pour the mixture into a handheld sprayer. Spray the individual patches of weeds (Photo 1). To ensure that there's plenty of plant material to absorb the weed killer, don't mow the weeds just before applying the herbicide or for three days after. If you don't kill annual grassy weeds now, you can expect them to seed and produce even more weeds next year.

Too late

There's only one remedy for yards taken over by grassy weeds—spray the entire lawn with a postemergence herbicide (like the ones used in the "Late" stage). Mix the concentrate with water in a pump sprayer (Photo 2).

Spray the yard with the herbicide in the late spring or summer. Apply just enough to get the weeds slightly wet. The weeds should start to die within five to seven days. Spot-kill any weeds that are still growing after seven days.

TIP

Always read the herbicide's label before applying to make sure it will kill the targeted weeds and not harm your lawn.

HANDHELD SPRAYER

CRABGRASS

1 Spray a second dose on weeds that survive the first spraying. Hunt for survivors seven days after spraying.

CONCENTRATED HERBICIDE

2 Save money by mixing concentrated herbicides rather than using premixed versions. Concentrates give you about 60 percent more herbicide for your money.

Kill broadleaf weeds

A broadleaf weed is any undesirable lawn plant that isn't a grass. The plants have actual leaves on stems, and contrary to the name, many have narrow rather than "broad" leaves. Dandelions, plantain, ground ivy (creeping charlie) and ragweed are a few of the most common broadleaf weeds.

CREEPING CHARLIE

Early

Before broadleaf weeds start growing in the spring, apply a preemergent herbicide. It kills weeds before they sprout from seed and even kills some weeds that have just started to grow. Spread the product on the yard between your first and third mowings in the spring. A single application should last a full 120-day season. This is as close to a one-size-fits-all magic bullet as you'll find for eliminating annual weeds. No other product on the market will target both broadleaf and annual grassy weeds and stop them from growing. It's available at lawn and garden centers. A 35-lb. bag treats up to 15,000 sq. ft.

Park your broadcast spreader over a tarp or on the driveway (grains may leak out, and a heavy dose of herbicide on the yard can kill even healthy grass). Fill the spreader (Photo 1) and distribute the herbicide evenly over your lawn.

Late

If a few broadleaves pop up in the yard (you can always count on a few dandelions), spot-kill them with a post-emergence herbicide. Look on the label for "broadleaf killer" then check to see which weeds it targets. Some broadleaf herbicides also kill crabgrass. There's no need to treat the entire lawn, just the weedy areas. Don't let them spread and create a bigger problem.

Premixed herbicides are OK if you have a small lawn and only a few weeds. Otherwise, buy concentrates to mix yourself—they're a better value. Wait until the temperature is between 60 and 85 degrees F. (The herbicide vaporizes too soon in high temps, and weeds don't grow fast enough in low temps to absorb the chemicals.) Mix the herbicide with water (follow the directions) and pour it into a small pump sprayer. Keep the nozzle 6 to 12 in. from the weed and spray until the leaves are slightly wet (Photo 2).

BROADCAST SPREADER

Vigoro 15,000

1 Spills will kill your grass. Park your spreader on a tarp or driveway when filling to avoid herbicide overdoses.

2 Spot-kill broadleaf weeds using a trigger-controlled pump sprayer until a mist forms on the leaves.

Too late

If your lawn has lots of weeds scattered over large areas, don't waste time spot-spraying individual weeds. Killing the weeds is as quick and easy as spraying the weedy area with a hose.

Pour a concentrated postemergence herbicide (the same kind you used for spot-spraying) into a dial sprayer and set the dial on the lid to the manufacturer's recommended mixture (such as 2 tablespoons per gallon of water). Attach the sprayer to a garden hose, turn on the water, and apply an even treatment to the weedy areas in the yard (Photo 3). Apply the herbicide when the weeds are actively growing in the late spring and early summer. You don't need to drench the weeds. A light misting will kill most weeds (if it doesn't, give them a second dose in a week). Spray only on a calm day. Even a slight breeze can carry vapors that can kill plants (anything that kills broadleaf weeds will also kill flowers or decorative plants and could harm trees, so watch for overspray).

TIP

Only spray the weedy areas of the yard—not the entire lawn. You'll introduce less herbicide into the environment.

3 Cover large areas fast with a dial sprayer attached to a garden hose. Avoid spraying on a windy day so the herbicide won't drift onto (and kill) nearby plants.

Kill perennial grassy weeds

Perennial grassy weeds come back every year, just like your lawn grass, and are the toughest weeds to deal with. That's because the herbicides that kill these weeds will also kill your grass. Perennial grassy weeds like Dallis grass and quack grass have deep, expansive root systems that make it impossible to kill them by pulling them out. Quack grass is easy to identify—three or four days after you've mowed your yard, quack grass will be noticeably taller than the surrounding grass.

Early

To spot-kill the weeds, apply a nonselective herbicide. Nonselective herbicides kill plants and weeds alike, so it has to be applied to the individual weeds by hand. Wearing cloth gloves over plastic gloves, wipe the herbicide directly onto the weed (photo, below). Don't worry about covering every single blade. As long as you get most of them, the herbicide will absorb into the weed. It'll take seven to ten days before the weed starts to die. If it's not dead after two weeks, wipe on a second treatment.

Late

The solution is the same later in the year. But the longer you wait, the more work you'll have since these grasses continue to spread all spring and summer. The herbicide is most effective early in the season when grasses grow the fastest. As the weeds take root and become sturdier, they may require more applications to fully kill.

Too late

Once there are too many weeds to spot-treat by hand, it's time for draconian measures. Kill everything and start over. Spray a nonselective herbicide on the weedy area. Wait two weeks. If they're not dead, spray them again.

Once the weeds are dead, mow them as short as possible. After spraying the herbicide, wait 14 days to plant new grass so the herbicide won't kill it.

QUACK GRASS

Apply herbicide to perennial grasses without killing the surrounding grass. Wear a cloth glove over a rubber glove. Dip your gloved hand in the herbicide and wipe it on.

Chapter Eight

CARS & TRUCKS

Safely jack and support a car or truck

Follow these steps—it could save your life!

You can save quite a few bucks by jacking up your car or truck and doing your own repairs and maintenance. But if you want to live long enough to spend all the money you save, you owe it to yourself and your loved ones to bone up on jack safety.

Start by parking your car or truck on a flat concrete surface. Trucks and most SUVs have steel frames that support the entire vehicle. Nearly all cars, on the other hand, are of "unibody" construction; that is, they don't have a frame. So each type of vehicle requires different points of support for jack and jack stand placement.

Consult a repair manual to locate the recommended lift points and support locations for your vehicle. Repair manuals are available at auto parts stores or online. Before jacking, engage the parking brake and chock the rear wheels to prevent car movement. Start jacking from the front of the vehicle. The front end of four-wheel-drive trucks can be raised by placing the jack under the differential. For two-wheel-drive trucks, place the jack beneath the jacking pad under the engine.

Place the jack so the cross member or differential lines up with the recessed area of the jack saddle. Slowly pump the jack handle until the front wheels leave the ground. Then stop jacking and

double-check the jack placement. Look at the front of the vehicle to make sure it's not leaning to one side. If it is, lower and recenter the jack. Otherwise, continue pumping until the vehicle reaches the desired height.

Support the front of a truck by placing the jack stands directly under the frame. Support the rear of the truck with a jack

continued on p. 229

TIP

If you plan to remove your tires, loosen the lug nuts slightly while the car is still on the ground. That'll keep the wheels from spinning while you turn the lug wrench once the car's raised.

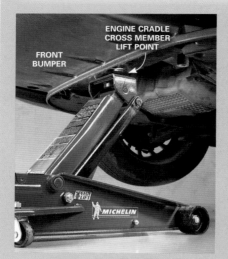

Jack and support a car

For most cars, the recommended front lift point is the engine cradle cross member (Photo 1). Lift and support the front of the car first. (If you start with the rear, the front end may be tilted so far that you can't roll a jack under it.) Place the jack so the cross member lines up with the recessed area of the jack saddle. The jack stand support locations (pinch welds; Photo 2) for cars are usually located behind the front wheels and in front of the rear wheels.

1 Place the recess of the jack saddle directly under the engine cradle cross member.

2 Place the jack stand under the support point. Raise the saddle and make sure it locks into place.

3 Place the floor jack so it contacts the rear lift point and raises the vehicle.

Jack and support a truck

For two-wheel-drive trucks, place the jack beneath the jacking pad under the engine (Photo 1) at the front and under the differential at the back (Photo 3). On four-wheel-drive trucks, place the jack under the front differential. Always place the front jack stands directly under the frame on any type of truck. Support the rear of the truck with jack stands under each axle.

1 Place the jack directly under the truck's front lift point.

2 Place the jack stand directly under the truck's frame.

3 Position the jack saddle directly under the rear differential.

continued from p. 227

stand under each axle. Turn the handle very slowly until the vehicle starts easing down. A quick release will result in a sudden catastrophic drop. Lower the car or truck until it almost touches the saddle of the jack stand. Then make final alignment adjustments before lowering the full weight onto the stand. Remove the floor jack and bring it to the rear of the vehicle.

Locate the recommended rear lift point and repeat the jacking procedure at the rear of the vehicle. Place the two rear jack stands in proper support locations and lower the rear onto those stands.

With the vehicle up on all four jack stands, gently shake the vehicle side to side and up and down. This ensures that the vehicle is sitting squarely on the jack stands and that the jack stand saddles have full contact with the support points. If the vehicle wobbles, stop immediately and reposition the problem jack stand before crawling under the vehicle.

Check your lift cradle!

Most front wheel drive cars have heavy steel engine cradle cross members that can be used with a floor jack. However, some late-model cars have one-piece cast aluminum engine cradles. These vehicles require special jacking procedures. Using the incorrect procedure is not only dangerous, but it can cause extensive damage to your vehicle.

TIP

3/4" PLYWOOD

Place jack stands on plywood support plates when you're working on an asphalt surface.

Check your brakes

You can check the condition of your brakes yourself in two steps. First find a safe area to test your brakes and check for brake pedal pulsation. Brake to a stop from about 30 mph. The pedal should feel smooth with no pulsation at all. Then try braking at highway speeds. If you get pulsation, the rotors are "warped" and must be machined or replaced.

With the engine cold, remove a front wheel. Then use a compass and a tape measure to check the brake pad thickness (Photo 1). A new brake pad is about 1/2 in. thick. Replace the pads when they get down to 1/8 in. Compare the readings top to bottom; they shouldn't vary by more than 1/16 in. If they do, the caliper isn't releasing properly and must be serviced. Finally, check the rotor disc for grooves (Photo 2).

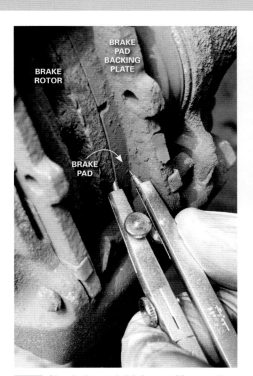

BRAKE ROTOR

BRAKE PAD BACKING PLATE

BRAKE PAD

1 **Check the pad thickness.** Measure the pad thickness by placing the compass points between the backing plate and the rotor. Measure the thickness at both the top and the bottom of the pad.

2 **Check the rotor's condition.** Run your fingernail across the rotor surface. If your nail catches in deep grooves, the rotors should be machined or replaced as a pair.

Change your own fluids

Engine oil

You'll save good money if you change your own oil. Plus, you won't be pressured into buying overpriced add-ons (like wiper blades and PCV valves) every time you go in for a change. Here you'll learn how to change your oil fast and painlessly.

Buy the right oil and filter

Before you head off to the auto parts store, consult your owner's manual for the type and weight of oil specific to your vehicle. It's especially important to follow the carmaker's recommendations for oil viscosity.

In the old days, oil filters were all pretty much the same inside. But not anymore. If your owner's manual recommends extended oil change intervals (every 6,000 miles instead of 3,000 miles), you must buy a filter that's rated to go the distance. In other words, don't fill your engine with expensive synthetic oil and then spin on an economy filter—it won't last. Check the filter box, ask the store clerk, or check the filter manufacturer's website to make sure the filter you buy is rated for extended oil change intervals.

Oil changing tips from the experts

- If the engine is cold, start it and let it run for five minutes to warm the oil. If it's hot, wait at least 30 minutes to avoid getting burned.
- Never use an adjustable wrench or socket on the drain plug. Use the properly sized box-end wrench, usually metric, for the plug.
- Always use jack stands. Never work under a car that's supported by a jack only.
- Use new oil to coat the oil filter gasket before spinning it on.
- Always hand-tighten the filter. Never use a filter wrench.
- Find an oil/oil filter recycling center near you.
- Line up all the oil bottles you'll need for the fill so you don't lose count along the way.

LEFTY-LOOSEY, RIGHTY-TIGHTY

BOX-END WRENCH

POLY DROP CLOTH FOR SPILLS

1 Unscrew the plug and quickly pull it out and away from the oil stream. Clean the drain plug and install a new gasket (if required).

OIL FILTER GASKET

2 Crank off the old oil filter and make sure the rubber gasket comes with it. If not, peel it from the engine.

Changing oil the fast way

If you get all your ducks in a row, you'll be done in about 20 minutes. Start by spreading plastic sheeting on the ground. Then drive your car on top of it. That will eliminate all oil spill cleanup work since you can just toss the entire sheet when you're done, or keep it for the next change if you're lucky enough to go spill-free. Jack up the car, set the jack stands in place, and lower the car. If you're on asphalt, place squares of plywood under the jack stands for support.

Place all your tools on a tray or in a box so everything you need is in one place. That means a box-end wrench for the drain plug, a rubber mallet (Photo 1), a filter wrench, a drain pan and the new filter. Before you slide it all under the car, open a new oil bottle and smear clean oil on the new filter's gasket. Then you're ready to start the job.

Remove the drain plug and get the old oil flowing. Then remove the oil filter and install the new one. Once the old oil is down to a trickle, install a new gasket on the plug (if required)

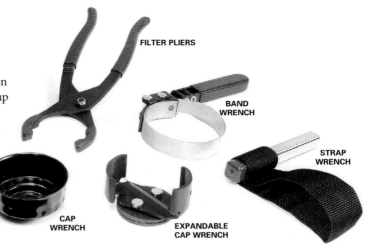

Different oil filter wrenches work best for different cars. Select the one that gives you the most room to maneuver.

and tighten it by tapping the box-end wrench with the rubber mallet. Wipe the drips with a rag and you're done under the car.

3 Refill the engine using a funnel and recap the bottle (to prevent spills) before you toss it into the recycling bin.

4 Pour the used oil into a large jug. Fill the engine and run it until the dashboard oil light goes out. Wait a few minutes. Then check the dipstick and add oil if needed.

TAKE TO RECYCLING CENTER

GLOSSY PAINT

FIBER END CAPS

CELLULOSE FILTER MEDIA

NITRILE ANTI-DRAINBACK VALVE

TEXTURED PAINT FOR GRIPPING

BYPASS VALVE

METAL CONSTRUCTION

SYNTHETIC GLASS/ CELLULOSE FILTER MEDIA

SILICONE ANTI-DRAINBACK VALVE

Don't skimp on a filter

There's a huge difference between an economy filter and a top-of-the-line version. But there's only a small difference in price. If you use conventional oil and diligently change it every 3,000 miles, you can get by with the economy filter. But if you regularly "forget" and go beyond that mileage or use long-mileage synthetic blends or full synthetic, spend the extra bucks on a better filter. Look at these cutaway filters and you can see why the premium filter is a better choice.

Transmission fluid

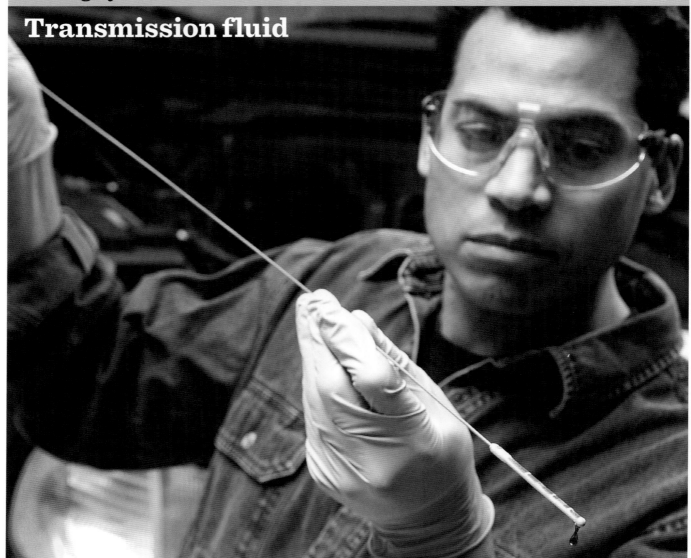

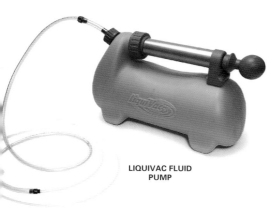

LIQUIVAC FLUID PUMP

This pump is the key to saving you time and money when you change your transmission fluid.

You should change your automatic transmission fluid according to the manufacturer's recommendation—whether that's 30,000 or 100,000 miles. This maintenance task will add tens of thousands of miles—which could be years of service—to a transmission's life expectancy and prevent repairs costing thousands down the road.

A transmission flush-and-fill from a shop will cost you $150 to $200 or more. But you can do it yourself and save about half that. Draining the old fluid has always been a messy, ugly job. That's because it has meant lying under the car, "dropping" the pan—and then getting drenched in fluid. But here's a new way to change your fluid without going under the car and without spilling a drop. The procedure takes less than 30 minutes.

The trick is to work from the top, sucking out the old fluid up through the filler tube. Then refill with fresh fluid. A hand-operated vacuum pump makes the job simple and

New fluid is bright red.

This transmission fluid has been working for 60,000 miles. It turns brown as it degrades—time to change.

VACUUM TUBE

TRANSMISSION FILLER TUBE

1 Remove the dipstick and insert the vacuum tube until you feel it "bottom out" on the bottom of the transmission pan.

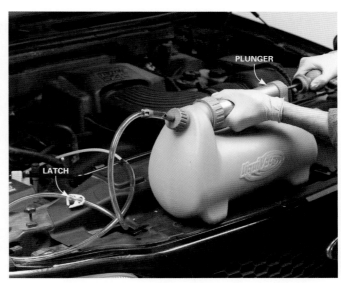

PLUNGER

LATCH

2 Close the latch on the vinyl hose and pump up the vacuum tank with 30 to 50 strokes of the plunger.

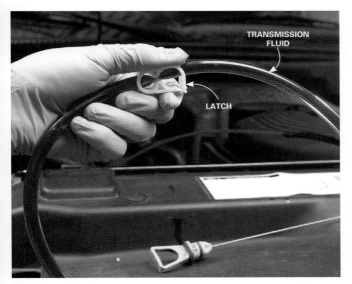

TRANSMISSION FLUID

LATCH

3 Release the latch on the hose and wait while the vacuum draws the old fluid out.

4 Read on the tank the amount of fluid you withdrew and refill the transmission with that amount of new fluid.

clean. You can remove one-third to one-half of the fluid from the transmission at a time. The rest will remain in the torque converter and the transmission cooler. So do the procedure three times at one-week intervals to replace nearly all of the old fluid. The little leftover old fluid will be diluted with plenty of fresh new fluid.

Some manufacturers recommend replacing the filter every time you change the transmission fluid. Go with what your dealership recommends. **Note:** If your transmission pan is leaking, you should either "drop" the pan and replace the gasket, or take it in for service.

Buy the right stuff

Carmakers have made major improvements to transmission fluids. Contact the dealership parts department to see if your car requires a newer fluid. Then call auto parts stores until you find one that stocks it. If you strike out, bite the bullet and buy it from the dealer.

CHRYSLER

GM

HONDA

FORD

Coolant

If you're way past due for a coolant change and your cooling system is corroded, you should take your car in for a professional flush. The same is true if you've mixed different types of coolant in your radiator. But if you're on schedule for a coolant change and your coolant is free of brown, gunky corrosion (extract a little coolant with a baster to examine it), you can skip the flush procedure and perform a simple drain and refill operation yourself and save some money. Here's how.

Start by buying the type of coolant listed in your owner's manual. If your manual calls for an "extended life" coolant that isn't available at the auto parts store, buy it from the dealer. Don't buy a "universal" coolant. Using the wrong coolant can cause premature component failure and void your warranty.

Raise and safely support the front end of your car on jack stands. Place a large drain pan under the radiator and remove the radiator cap. If your radiator doesn't have a cap, remove the pressure cap from the coolant tank. Then open the drain cock and drain the radiator.

1 Open the drain cock by unscrewing, twisting a quarter turn, or twisting and pulling. (The various styles are shown on the top of p. 235.)

DRAIN COCK

QUARTER
TURN

UNSCREW

UNSCREW
AND PULL

QUARTER
TURN
AND PULL

Styles of drain cocks

Drain cocks come in several different styles—screw threads, quarter-turn twist, and quarter turn and pull. Plastic drain cocks become brittle with age and can break easily, especially if you try to unscrew a quarter-turn twist style. So buy a replacement drain cock at the auto parts store before you begin the job (return it if you don't need it).

Then remove the lower radiator hose clamp and hose from the engine to drain the rest of the coolant. Use slip-joint pliers to remove spring-style clamps. If you have trouble accessing or releasing the clamps with pliers, buy hose clamp pliers (photo, right). Reconnect and clamp the radiator hose and reinstall the drain cock after draining.

Follow the coolant manufacturer's directions for diluting concentrated coolant. Mix the coolant and water thoroughly in a clean bucket. To prevent mineral deposits on internal engine and radiator surfaces, always use distilled water—never tap water. Leave the car raised while you refill the radiator to reduce the possibility of air pockets forming in the engine.

Slowly fill the radiator or coolant tank with fresh coolant until the coolant is 1 in. below the neck of the radiator or a few inches below the full mark on the coolant tank. Start the engine and let it run. After the engine warms, you'll see the coolant level quickly drop in the radiator/coolant tank. That means the thermostat has opened and it's time to add more coolant to bring the level to the top of the radiator, or to the "HOT" mark on the coolant tank. Check your owner's manual or service manual to see if your car requires a special air bleeding procedure. Check for leaks, shut off the engine, install the cap, lower the car and go for a spin.

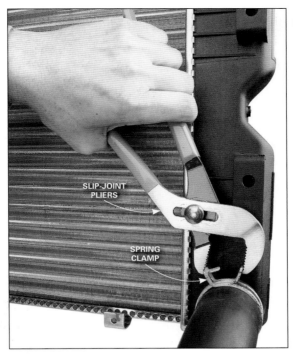

2 Push together the clamp spring with slip-joint pliers and slip the clamp away from the neck. Pull the hose free and drain the remaining coolant. If access is difficult, hose clamp pliers save time and bruised knuckles.

SLIP-JOINT
PLIERS

SPRING
CLAMP

HOSE CLAMP
PLIERS

CAUTION: Used coolant is toxic waste. Pour it into a screw-cap plastic container and drop it off at a recycling center. Sweet-tasting coolant is irresistible to pets—and poisonous. Just a small amount can be deadly. So soak up any spills with paper towels or rags immediately if you have pets wandering around.

3 Stir 1 gallon of full-strength (not premixed) coolant and 1 gallon of distilled water together in a clean bucket before adding the mix to the radiator.

Brake fluid

Some carmakers recommend replacing brake fluid every two years or 24,000 miles. Others don't mention it at all. But it's easy to test your brake fluid. Just dip a test strip into the fluid and compare the color to the chart on the packaging.

You can't do a complete brake fluid flush yourself, but you can do the next best thing—a fluid swap. This procedure won't replace all the old fluid with fresh, but you'll introduce enough new fluid to make a difference.

Use a baster to suck out the dark brown brake fluid (brake and power steering fluids are incompatible, so use a different baster for each). Squirt it into a recycling bottle. Refill the reservoir with fresh brake fluid as shown. Then drive the vehicle for a week to mix the new fluid with the old. Repeat the procedure several times over the next few weeks until the fluid in the reservoir retains its light honey color. **Note:** The brake fluid may damage the baster's rubber bulb, so don't suck the fluid all the way into the bulb.

OLD BRAKE FLUID

Power steering fluid

There aren't any test strips for power steering fluid, so you'll have to rely on the manufacturer's service recommendations or general rule-of-thumb (two years or 24,000 miles). Use the turkey baster method to remove the old power steering fluid. Suck out all the fluid (engine off) as shown. Then refill the reservoir with fresh fluid. Start the engine and let it run for about 15 seconds. Repeat the fluid swap procedure until you've used up the full quart.

Note: Never substitute a "universal" power steering fluid for the recommended type, and never add "miracle" additives or stop-leak products. They can clog the fine mesh filter screens in your steering system and cause expensive failures.

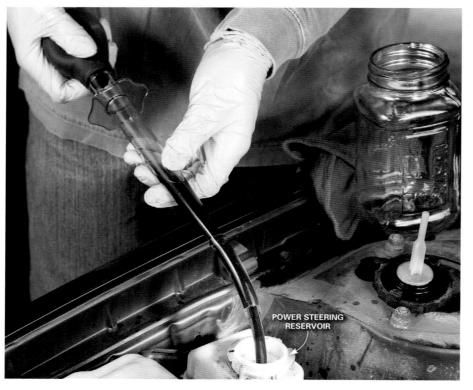

POWER STEERING RESERVOIR

Tips for changing fluids

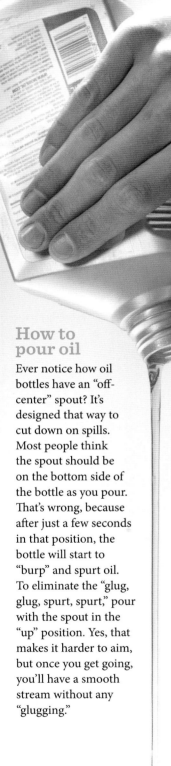

How to pour oil

Ever notice how oil bottles have an "off-center" spout? It's designed that way to cut down on spills. Most people think the spout should be on the bottom side of the bottle as you pour. That's wrong, because after just a few seconds in that position, the bottle will start to "burp" and spurt oil. To eliminate the "glug, glug, spurt, spurt," pour with the spout in the "up" position. Yes, that makes it harder to aim, but once you get going, you'll have a smooth stream without any "glugging."

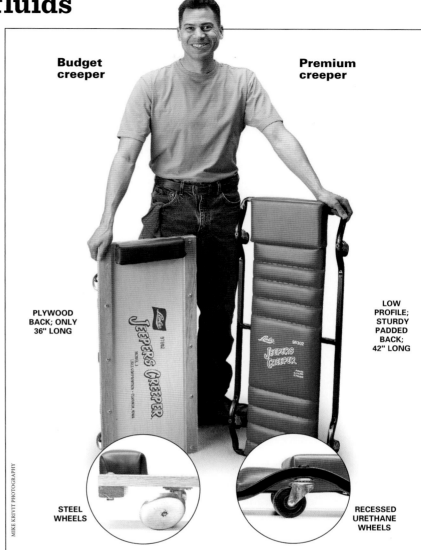

Budget creeper

Premium creeper

PLYWOOD BACK; ONLY 36" LONG

LOW PROFILE; STURDY PADDED BACK; 42" LONG

STEEL WHEELS

RECESSED URETHANE WHEELS

MIKE KRIVIT PHOTOGRAPHY

Buying a creeper

If your idea of changing your own oil is to grab a piece of cardboard and slide under the car, it's time to get with the program: Save your back and invest in a creeper. They range in price from $20 to $200, but you don't need to spend a fortune. You can get a darn good creeper in the middle of that price range (photo above). Here are the four features to look for in a creeper:

1. A sturdy backboard reduces stress on your upper and lower back muscles. Economy models are built with a thin sheet of plywood. Look for a reinforced backboard that will support your back and shoulders.

2. Steel wheels make for rough riding and they get stuck in every crack. Rolling off your creeper to free up a stuck wheel is a real drag. Shop for a creeper that has urethane ball-bearing wheels.

3. Make the best use of limited workspace with a low-profile design. Recessed wheels get you closer to the ground and give you more room to maneuver tools and parts.

4. Wood creepers absorb oil, coolant and fluids, making every spill last a lifetime. Instead, look for a creeper with a heavy-duty chemical- and oil-resistant fabric and firm padding.

Time for a filter change?

Evaluate your own air filter and PCV valve

You take your car in for an oil change. The work is almost done when the technician comes out to talk to you. He's holding your air filter and PCV valve and recommending that you replace both because they "look dirty." Without missing a beat, he explains how critical the air filter is to the efficient operation of your car. He tells you that a clogged air filter, or one that's nearly clogged, can easily cost you 10 percent in gas mileage. With gas prices what they are, he adds, replacement will probably save you more than the cost of the filter. Plus, a dirty PCV valve, well, that's never a good thing. Then he waits for your decision. It's tough to make up your mind about a $25 air filter and an $11.95 PC-whatchamacallit valve when you don't know what to look for.

It's not difficult to check the air filter and PCV valve yourself. Here's what you need to know:

Air filter check

First, ignore the dirt on the leading edge of the air filter pleats. All air filters accumulate dirt on the leading edges in as little as a few thousand miles. Yet most last for about 12,000 miles. You want to know how much dirt has penetrated deep into the pleats. To test the true condition of your filter, hold a shop light behind it. See how much light passes through the inner pleats and compare yours with the three sample photos below. The filter shown on the left is totally clogged and cost the owner a fortune in wasted gas. The filter in the middle shows a clogged area, but the rest of the filter has decent light transmission. It's borderline, and the owner could probably squeeze 2,000 to 3,000 more miles out of it. It should be replaced at the next oil change interval. The filter on the right shows how much light passes through a new filter.

SCREEN

PLEATS

1 Follow the black plastic duct to the air filter box. Unscrew or unsnap the latches. Remove the filter. Note that the screen always faces the engine. The pleats face the incoming air.

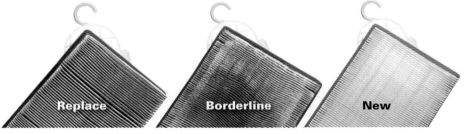

Replace   Borderline   New

2 Hold the filter over a shop light and compare it with the photos above. Reinstall or replace.

The PCV story

The PCV (positive crankcase ventilation) valve is a one-way valve that recycles crankcase gases back into the engine to burn. A plugged PCV valve can result in a rough idle and poor mileage. Worse, it can cause costly oil leaks. Always follow your manufacturer's replacement recommendations. And never replace a PCV valve simply because it "looks dirty." All used PCV valves look dirty. Photos 1 and 2 show two ways to check its real condition.

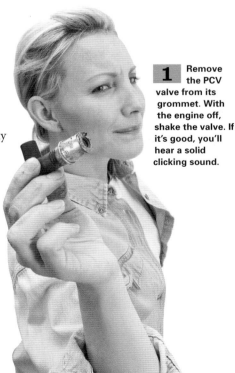

1 Remove the PCV valve from its grommet. With the engine off, shake the valve. If it's good, you'll hear a solid clicking sound.

2 Or, check it in place with the engine running. Pull the PCV valve from its housing and place your thumb over the PCV valve opening. You should feel it click. If the click sounds or feels mushy, replace the valve.

Tire talk

Make your tires last

Most drivers ignore their tires until it's too late. Then they have to spend big bucks to replace them. We'll show you three critical maintenance chores you can do yourself to make your tires last longer. And we'll show you how to diagnose tire problems and correct them early so you can keep driving on the rubber you've got.

Step 1:
Check tire pressure every month

All tires lose air, so check your tires monthly. Always use the same tire pressure gauge and check the air pressure first thing in the morning, not after you've driven on them or they've been sitting in the hot sun. Inflate to the pressures listed on the carmaker's decal (on the driver's door or jamb), NOT the maximum pressure listed on the tire. The recommended tire pressure is based on the weight of your particular vehicle, not the tire brand or tread style.

DIGITAL PRESSURE GAUGE

Step 2:
Use a tread-depth gauge every other month

Forget about the penny-in-the-tread trick. A tread depth gauge only costs a few bucks and is *far* more accurate. Measure the tread depth about 1 in. from each edge and the depth of the center tread. They should all be the same. If they're not, refer to the photos on p. 241 to find the problem and the fix.

Step 3:
Rotate your tires every 6,000 miles

The front tires on front-wheel-drive cars carry a heavier load and perform more work (steering and braking). So they wear faster than the rears. Rotation spreads the wear across all four tires. Skip it and you'll find yourself with two bald tires in the front and two halfway good tires in the rear. You'll lose about 25 percent of the tire set's life.

MEASURE HERE

MEASURE HERE

Never inflate tires to the maximum pressure!

Never assume that the *maximum* air pressure shown on the tire's sidewall is the same as the *recommended* tire pressure. Filling to the maximum pressure always means you're overinflating your tires. The recommended tire pressures for your car are printed on the driver's door or doorpost decal.

It's true that filling tires to the maximum pressure gets you increased gas mileage in the short term. But you'll pay far more in the long run when you replace your tires, suspension parts and shock absorbers, all of which will wear out prematurely. Worse yet, you're risking your life and the lives of your passengers.

Overinflated tires carry the entire weight of the car on the middle portion of the tread. On wet roads, the center tread can't pump the water out to the sides (think of a squeegee with a bulge in the center). So they're more prone to hydroplaning (like water skiing) and also more likely to skid in a stop or in a turn, and blow out on hard bumps. The bottom line: Overinflation is foolish and dangerous. Always follow the inflation pressures shown on the car, not the tires.

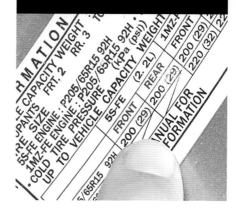

Diagnosing tire problems

WEAR ON ONE SIDE

Bad alignment

This vehicle is out of alignment, and its tires are rolling on their edges. The car most likely pulled to the side, but the driver ignored it. Ignoring the problem was costly. The tires wore out faster, and the vehicle still needed alignment. If your tread is worn on one side, get your vehicle aligned ASAP.

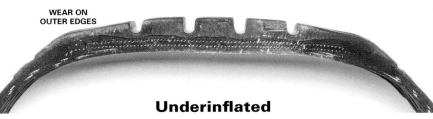

WEAR ON OUTER EDGES

Underinflated

This is classic underinflation and the most common tire wear problem. The center tread puckers toward the rim because there's not enough pressure to keep it in contact with the road. So the full weight of the car rides on the edges. In addition to premature wear, low tire pressure causes excessive heat and possible blowouts. The owner of these tires never bothered to keep the tires inflated.

WEAR ON CENTER

Overinflated

This tire was overinflated. The higher pressure ballooned it into a doughnut shape. Only the center tread was in contact with the road. That's why the center tread wore more than the edges. This owner was diligent (but mistaken) about filling the tire to its maximum inflated pressure. Driving on over-inflated tires is costly—and dangerous.

Fill tires with nitrogen—or not?

It sounds weird, but filling tires with nitrogen is not a scam. Nitrogen leaks less than compressed atmospheric air (because nitrogen molecules are larger than oxygen molecules) and reduces rubber oxidation. But that doesn't mean nitrogen never leaks. The problem is that once you commit to a nitrogen fill, you must stick with it for the life of the tire. The instant you add compressed air, you negate all the benefits.

Since you still need to check and refill your tires, and since nitrogen is hard to find, you'll be married to the dealer forever. That's good if they offer free coffee and doughnuts while you wait, but bad if they're not conveniently located.

Even though nitrogen really is better than regular old air, it's doubtful you'll ever see enough of a benefit to justify paying extra for it. Your tires will probably wear out from normal driving long before the important benefits of nitrogen really kick in. But if you drive less than 5,000 miles per year and plan to keep your tires for 10 years (and don't mind hanging out at the dealer), nitrogen is definitely worth it. By the way, the green caps on tire valve stems indicate the tire is filled with nitrogen.

Chapter Nine

CONCRETE & MASONRY

Installing glass block basement windows

The most practical basement window is also the simplest to install

When it comes to basement windows, there's nothing more practical than glass block. Glass block is weathertight and maintenance-free. It lets in the sun but keeps burglars out.

And installing glass block basement windows is nearly foolproof—if you use preassembled glass block panels. Glass block panels come ready to install, with the blocks mortared together and secured with a metal band. All you have to do is set the panel in place and pack mortar in around it.

SIDE JAMB

SILL

WRECKING
BAR

SAW CUT

CURB

COLD
CHISEL

1 Pry out the old window jamb with a wrecking bar. First cut the wood sill with a reciprocating saw or circular saw. Be careful not to cut all the way through to the concrete or you'll ruin the saw blade. Then rip out the sill, the side jambs and the head jamb. Our sill sat against a sloped mortar "curb," which we had to chip away with a cold chisel before we could cut and pry the sill.

TEMPORARY BLOCK

ROUGH
OPENING

SILL
PLATE

2 Screw a wood block to the underside of the sill plate. This temporary block will keep the glass panel from tipping inward, so make sure it extends down far enough to catch the upper edge of the panel. Many older homes have no sill plate. In that case, just screw the block to a joist.

This isn't exactly easy—large panels might weigh 100 lbs. or more, and filling in alongside the panels (Photo 5) is tedious business—but it is simple. Aside from ordering a panel that won't fit into its opening or dropping the panel, there's not much that can go wrong. Installing panels is fast, too: You shouldn't have any trouble installing two panels in one day.

Here we'll walk you through the process of ripping out old windows and installing glass block panels in a basement made from poured concrete or concrete block. Installing panels in a wood-framed wall or basement is a bit different and not covered here.

The only specialized tools you'll need are the masonry tools shown in our photos: a masonry or cold chisel, a pointing trowel, a margin trowel and a striking tool.

Measuring and ordering

Some home centers carry panels in standard sizes like 14 x 32 in. and 18 x 32 in. You can also have panels custom-made by a fabricator (search "Glass Block" online). With custom-made panels, you can choose from a variety of glass block sizes, colors and surface textures.

Glass block installers and online dealers have dozens of other options that are worth looking into before you order. You can select glass that has more privacy or more clarity, special security glass, hurricane-resistant glass, Low-E glass, brightly colored glass block, glass block with images—you can even order custom glass block with your own designs imprinted on them. You can also order specialty blocks for curves, end walls and angles. Also keep in mind that you can inset vents for dryers or fresh air intakes. You might also want panels with small operable windows built in to allow ventilation. **Note:** Some building codes require that basement windows allow for ventilation. Call your local building inspector.

Fabricators can make panels any size in 1-in. increments. Panels usually can't be returned, so it's vital that you give the fabricators correct measurements. Most fabricators simply ask for the rough opening measurements (see Photo 2), then figure the size of the panel. To determine the size of the panel yourself, just subtract 1/2 in. from both the length and the width of the rough opening. This will allow space to build up a curb under the panel and provide gaps at the sides, which will be packed with mortar (Photo 5). Remember, your measurements must be in whole inches, not fractions of an inch.

Removing the old window

Old sashes often won't come out of their jambs without a fight, so it's a good idea to wear gloves and eye protection in case you break glass as you tug and pry at the sash. If caulk or paint is holding the sash shut, cut through it with a utility knife.

Some jambs are set in mortar or concrete at the sill, so you may have to chisel away part of the curb before you can cut and pry the sill (Photo 1). After that, the side jambs and head (top) jamb will pry off easily. Then finish chiseling away the curb.

Setting the panel

Before you set the panel in place, screw a block to the underside of the sill plate (Photo 2). We placed our block 5 in. from the outer edge of the sill plate so that the 3-in. thick panel would stand 2 in. from the outside of the foundation. But there are no rules here; your panel can stand far inside the rough opening or nearly flush with the outside of the foundation. **Note:** Some older homes have no sill plate; the joists rest directly in the masonry foundation. In that case, screw the block to a joist.

You'll need three wedges to position each panel (Photo 3). Make the wedges thicker and longer than necessary—you'll have more handle to grab on to when you yank them out from under the panel. Our panel had to be raised nearly 2 in. off the bottom of the opening, so we made our wedges 2-1/2 in. thick at the blunt end and about 8 in. long.

Sweep the rough opening clean before you set the panel in place. With a helper, set one end of the panel in the rough opening on top of two wedges and lay the other end on the ground. Then, with your

3 Set the glass panel in place with the bottom resting on two wedges cut from a 2x4. The bottom of the panel will tend to slide inward, so you must have a helper inside to steady the panel as you position it.

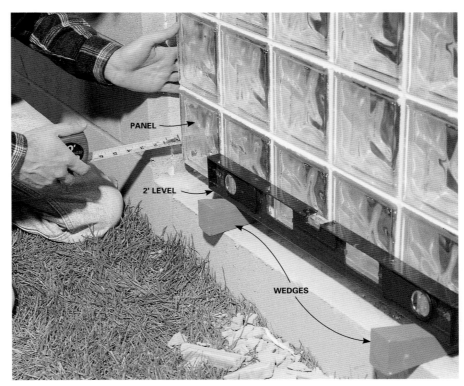

4 Center the panel in the rough opening. Then raise the panel until it's 1/8 to 1/4 in. away from the sill plate by tapping the wedges inward. Level the panel by laying a level across the wedges and adjusting them. Measure at all four corners from the face of the panel to the outer edge of the rough opening. When the panel is positioned, have your helper insert a third wedge near the center of the panel from inside.

POINTING TROWEL

MARGIN TROWEL

STRIKING TOOL

CURB

PLYWOOD SCRAP

MORTAR

CURB

WEDGE REMOVED

5 Pack mortar into the gaps under and alongside the panel. Pack the bottom and smooth the curb first, staying away from the wedges. Give the curb time to harden to the touch before you begin on the sides. That way, crumbs of mortar you drop can be brushed off the curb. Fill the gaps alongside the panel using your margin trowel and a pointing trowel. Then, after the mortar has stiffened a bit, smooth the joints with a striking tool.

6 Remove the wedges and fill in the gaps in the curb after the curb has set for at least two hours. In cool weather you may have to wait up to five hours. Also wait at least two weeks before painting the new mortar.

helper inside the basement, tip the panel up into place (Photo 3) and adjust its position.

Traditionally, glass block units have been mortared on the sides as well as the bottom, but for better insulation (and less mess inside) you can wedge foam caulk backer rods or thin strips of rigid insulation in the sides. Just be sure to leave a space at least an inch deep that you can pack full of mortar on the outside.

Mortaring in the panel

It took about half a 60-lb. bag of mortar mix to install our panel. We mixed small batches—four or five trowel loads at a time—in a small bucket and then dumped the mixed mortar onto a scrap of plywood so that we could easily scoop it up with a trowel.

Spare the water as you mix the mortar. It should be stiff rather than sloppy, about the consistency of wet sand.

Shove mortar under the panel and build up the curb first. Then wait until the surface of the curb has hardened to the touch before you begin to pack the sides. On a hot, dry day, this may

take only 15 minutes. In cool weather it may take more than a half hour. Packing in alongside the panel is slow-going. It took us about 15 minutes per side.

Inside the basement, you'll find clumps of mortar pushed far past the panel, and empty spots under and alongside the panel. Simply slice off the clumps with your trowel and fill the voids. You can build up a sloped curb inside the basement just as you did outside. Or you can cut the curb flush with the panel (as in the photo on p. 247), leaving a flat surface for a trim board or "stool" if you plan to finish the basement.

Glass block without mortar

If you like the look of glass block but don't want to deal with mortar, you can install glass block in a pressure-treated wood frame. Construct it as you would a regular window frame, with a beveled sill at the bottom so that water will run off. Fasten the treated wood to the concrete block with construction adhesive and masonry screws. Set the glass block unit flush on the outside with the 2x wood sides, but leave a 1/4- to 1/2-in. gap on each

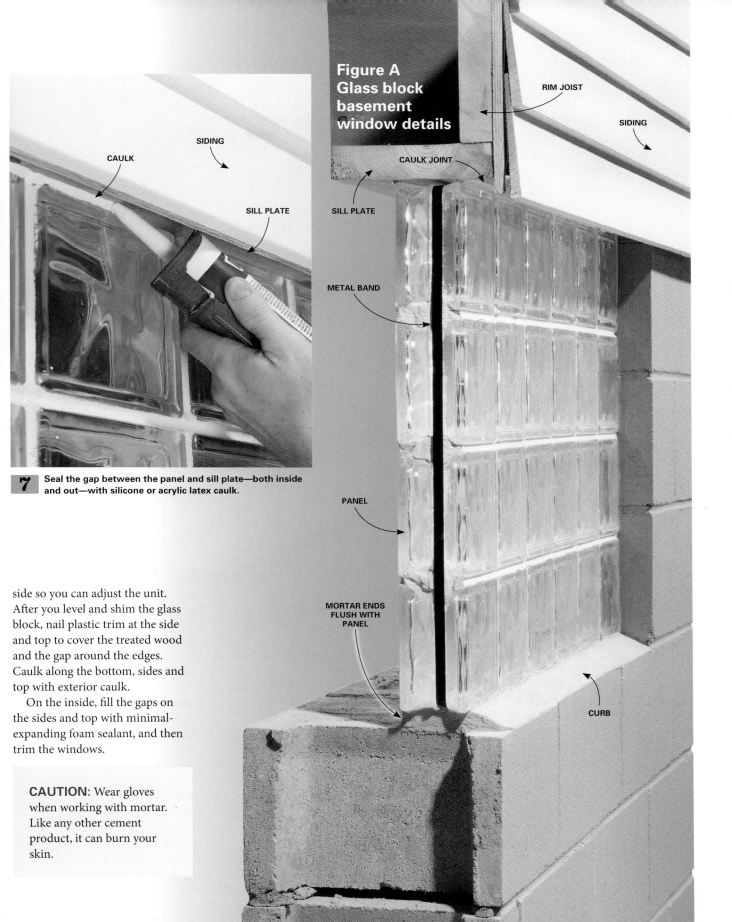

CAULK

SIDING

SILL PLATE

7 Seal the gap between the panel and sill plate—both inside and out—with silicone or acrylic latex caulk.

**Figure A
Glass block
basement
window details**

RIM JOIST

SIDING

CAULK JOINT

SILL PLATE

METAL BAND

PANEL

**MORTAR ENDS
FLUSH WITH
PANEL**

CURB

side so you can adjust the unit. After you level and shim the glass block, nail plastic trim at the side and top to cover the treated wood and the gap around the edges. Caulk along the bottom, sides and top with exterior caulk.

On the inside, fill the gaps on the sides and top with minimal-expanding foam sealant, and then trim the windows.

CAUTION: Wear gloves when working with mortar. Like any other cement product, it can burn your skin.

Finishing concrete

Putting a smooth, durable finish on concrete is a skill you can only master with the proper set of tools and practice. We'll show you the tools and how to use them for each step of the process. And equally important, we'll help you determine when the concrete is ready for the next finishing step.

But you really can't practice these techniques except on real concrete. So it's smart to start with a small project like this garbage can pad. When you get the hang of it, you can move up to a larger slab. But keep in mind that finishing larger slabs (more than about 100 sq. ft.)

is trickier because the concrete may set up too fast.

Here we'll show you how to level the concrete in the forms, round over the edges and make a progressively smoother finish.

Each step in the process requires a different tool. You can make the screed (Photo 1) and darby (Photo 2) from scraps of wood. The rest you'll have to rent or buy. You'll need a magnesium float, an edger, a grooving tool and a steel trowel. Pros buy expensive top-quality tools that will stand up to the rigors of daily use, but less expensive versions are available at home centers and hardware

stores and will work fine for occasional home use.

Concrete is a blend of Portland cement, sand, aggregate (gravel) and water that hardens when mixed. While there are additives that can slow down or speed up the process, and special bagged mixes that set fast, in general, the speed of the process largely depends on the temperature and humidity. Hot, dry weather accelerates the hardening process, sometimes so much that it's nearly impossible to complete all the finishing steps in time. Work while your project is in shade if possible. On cool days, you may spend a lot of time

1 Push or pull the screed board across the forms with a back-and-forth sawing motion. Shove concrete into low spots in front of the screed board. Repeat to remove excess concrete.

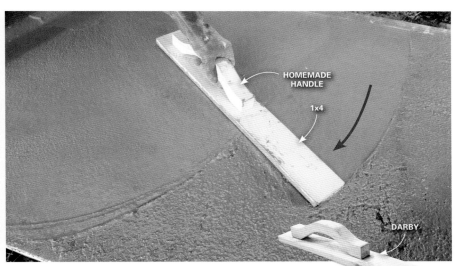

2 Sweep the darby across the concrete in overlapping arcs to flatten the surface, push down lumps and fill voids. Lift the leading edge slightly but keep the darby level with the surface. Make two passes.

3 Wait. Water will appear on the surface. Wait until this "bleed" water and sheen disappear entirely before edging, grooving or floating the concrete.

waiting for the concrete to reach the next stage. That's why we can't give you exact waiting times. But we'll show you how to tell when the concrete is ready for each finishing step.

Screed and darby the concrete right away

Screeding levels the concrete with the top of the forms and begins the process of forcing the larger aggregate below the surface. Use any 2x4 that overlaps the forms by at least 6 in., but make sure it's straight (Photo 1).

Follow screeding immediately with the darby (Photo 2). Your goal is to level out marks and fill small holes left by screeding. In the process, you'll force larger aggregate down, leaving a slurry of cement and sand to fill the surface. The darby should be large enough to reach a little more than halfway across the slab. Make a darby by screwing a handle (we cut a 2x4 with a jigsaw to make a handle) onto a straight piece of 1x4. Longer darbies may require two handles for better control. If you can't reach the entire slab from the edges with a darby, rent a bull float and handle to use instead. Two passes over the surface with the darby are enough. Overworking the concrete will draw too much cement and fine sand to the top and create a weak surface.

CAUTION: It might be hard to believe that concrete can be dangerous. But the strong alkalinity of cement can cause chemical burns just like a strong acid. By the time you realize you're being burned, you may already have skin damage. That's why it's essential to prevent prolonged skin exposure to wet concrete. And why you should be extra careful to keep wet concrete from getting in your eyes. Wear rubber gloves, a long-sleeve shirt, long pants and safety glasses. Wear rubber boots if you'll be wading in concrete. Rinse wet concrete from your skin immediately and remove clothes that have become saturated with concrete.

Edge, groove and float the slab when the sheen is gone

EDGING TOOL

After smoothing the slab with the darby, water will "bleed" out of the concrete and sit on the surface (Photo 3). This is temporary. It'll soon reabsorb into the concrete. However, it's critical to wait until it disappears. Working the concrete before the surface "bleed" water disappears will weaken the surface of the slab when it dries. When all traces of the water are gone and the concrete starts to harden, you can resume finishing activities. Test by pressing your gloved thumb onto the surface near the perimeter. The concrete is ready when pressing hard only leaves a 1/4-in. deep impression.

Start by running the edger around the perimeter to round and compact the corner (Photo 4). Sometimes it's a little tough at first as you push larger aggregate back into the concrete and round over the edge. If the edger is leaving a path deeper than about 1/8 in., wait for the concrete to set a little longer and apply less downward pressure.

Next divide the slab into equal parts with a straightedge and groover (Photo 5). Sidewalks and small slabs need grooves about every 4 ft. Add grooves every 10 or 12 ft. on driveways and garage slabs. Dividing slabs with grooves looks nice, but the real reason is to control cracking. Drying and soil movement cause concrete to crack. The groove creates a weakened spot for the crack to form where it won't be seen. To be effective, the groove must be at least one-fourth the depth of the slab.

Float and trowel the surface to smooth and compact it

Float the concrete when you're done grooving and edging (Photo 6). Floating removes the marks left by edging and brings the surface one step closer to a final finish. You may have to bear down on the float if the concrete is starting to harden. You'll be surprised that with enough scrubbing you'll

FORM

4 Work the edging tool back and forth, using the edge of the form as a guide. Lift the leading edge slightly. Use long strokes, working the aggregate back until you have smooth, round edges.

STRAIGHT BOARD

GROOVER

5 Set a straight board along predetermined marks for control joints. Run the groover back and forth against the straightedge until the bed of the tool is riding on the concrete surface.

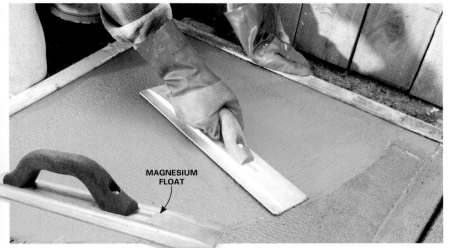

6 Lift the leading edge slightly while you sweep the magnesium float over the concrete in large arcs to compact the surface. Blend in the marks left by the edges of the edger and groover.

MAGNESIUM FLOAT

7 Smooth the surface with a steel trowel after it's partially hardened. Hold the trowel almost flat and swing it in large overlapping arcs while applying pressure.

STEEL TROWEL

8 Drag a broom across the concrete after floating it with the magnesium float to create a non-slip surface. Adjust the downward pressure to create the desired amount of texture.

BROOMED FINISH

be able to bring a slurry to the surface of even a fairly hard slab. If you're happy with the look of your floated slab, you don't need to do any more finishing. Repeat the edging and grooving steps after floating and after troweling to refine the groove and edges. For a decorative border effect similar to what's shown in the inset to Photo 4, run the edger around each section of slab after a final broom finish.

In Photo 7, we show how to put an even, smooth finish on the slab with a steel trowel. Troweling is one of the trickier steps in concrete finishing. You'll have to practice to develop a feel for it. For a really smooth finish, repeat the troweling step two or three times, letting the concrete harden a bit between each pass. At first, hold the trowel almost flat, elevating the leading edge just enough to avoid gouging the surface. On each successive pass, lift the leading edge of the trowel a little more. If you want a rougher, non-slip surface, you can skip this step and do a broom finish (Photo 8). Also, if you order air-entrained concrete delivered, don't trowel the surface.

Broom finish for better footing

Dragging a broom across partially hardened concrete leaves a rough texture that gives better traction in slippery conditions (Photo 8). Special concrete brooms are available, but a regular push broom will work too. Just remember to wash off the bristles as soon as you finish brooming. As with all the other finishing steps, the key to a successful broom finish is to wait until the concrete surface is just right. If concrete starts to pile up in front of the bristles as you drag the broom across, resmooth the broomed area with a float or trowel and then wait a little longer before trying again.

When you're done finishing the concrete, cover it with plastic or keep it moist by sprinkling it several times a day for about a week. This slows the curing process and results in a stronger, more durable slab.

Cutting concrete

Concrete—most of us have a love-hate relationship with it. Love it when we need a permanent, heavy-duty, weather-resistant surface. Hate it when we have to repair, replace or cut the stuff.

The prospect of cutting concrete can be daunting, but it doesn't have to be. Most of the battle can be won by simply selecting the right tools. Following is a rundown of common concrete-cutting tasks—from dinky to monster-sized—and the best tools and techniques for handling them.

Concrete-cutting blades

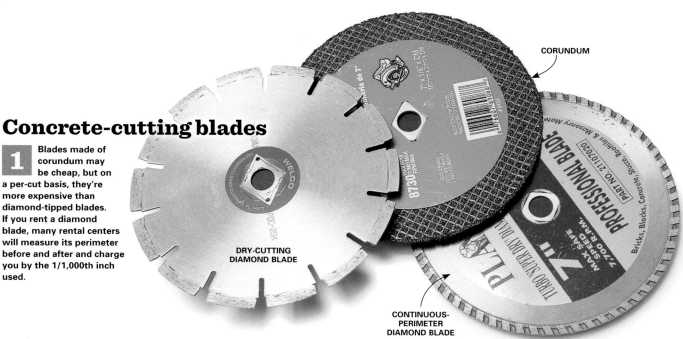

1 Blades made of corundum may be cheap, but on a per-cut basis, they're more expensive than diamond-tipped blades. If you rent a diamond blade, many rental centers will measure its perimeter before and after and charge you by the 1/1,000th inch used.

CORUNDUM

DRY-CUTTING DIAMOND BLADE

CONTINUOUS-PERIMETER DIAMOND BLADE

Diamond blades are a DIYer's best friend

You can make small rough cuts using a cold chisel and sledgehammer (Photos 2 and 3), but the better choice is a circular saw with a special blade. Three basic choices are shown in Photo 1:

Abrasive corundum masonry blades are inexpensive, widely available and capable of cutting through concrete, stucco and asphalt. They're affordable but not fast—in most situations they're capable of cutting only shallow 1/4- to 1/2-in. passes, so any cut is time-consuming. They also wear away quickly. A blade that's 7 inches in diameter at the start of a cut will wear down to 6-1/2

in. after cutting a foot or two along a line—meaning you need to frequently adjust the depth of your saw to expose more blade. Abrasive corundum blades smell, create plumes of fine dust and get so hot they can actually glow. They're an economical choice when you need to make only a few shallow cuts.

Diamond blades consist of a metal blade with a diamond/metal composite bonded to the perimeter. As the blade cuts, the metal composite slowly wears away, revealing fresh, sharp diamond cutting edges. Diamond blades for a standard 7-in. circular saw are more expensive, but since they'll outlast and outcut dozens of abrasive-type blades,

they're worth the cost if you're cutting a lot of concrete. Diamond blades fall into two categories:

Dry-cutting diamond blades most often have a serrated or toothed rim (Photo 1) to help cool the blade and eject waste. They work best when you make a series of gradually deeper cuts to avoid overheating the blade. The downside to dry-cutting masonry is the tornado of fine dust it creates. If you cut concrete indoors, seal off the area with plastic and duct tape. Seal all duct openings as well.

Wet-cutting diamond blades can have either teeth or a smooth, continuous perimeter. Water not only helps cool and lubricate the blade but also keeps the dust

Cutting hollow concrete block

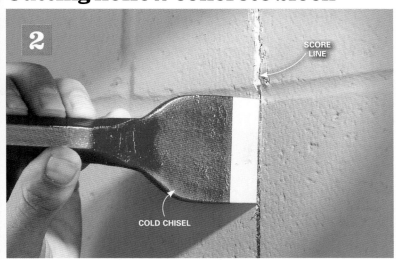

2

SCORE LINE

COLD CHISEL

3

3-LB. SLEDGE

If your cut doesn't need to be exact, use a cold chisel and hand sledge to cut the concrete. Score the length of the cut three or four times with the chisel, then starting at the top or bottom of a block, remove the concrete to one side of the line using increasingly hard whacks of a hand sledge. A circular saw with a masonry blade can also be used to either score or completely cut through the block.

SIGHT, HEARING AND RESPIRATORY PROTECTION

MASONRY CUTTING BLADE

CONTROL JOINT

4

Cutting sidewalks and other slabs

5

Use a standard circular saw, equipped with a diamond blade, for small tasks. For slabs, it's best to cut through the top inch, then use a sledgehammer to break off the rest. The jagged edge left below the cutting line provides a good rough edge for the new concrete to bond to. Gas-powered saws provide both portability and brawn.

WET-CUTTING SAW

6

SLIDING TABLE

Cutting concrete pavers and tile

Rent a wet-cutting masonry saw with a sliding table for accuracy and ease when cutting pavers or tiles. A good saw with a good blade will cut through a typical 4 x 8-in. cement paver in about 10 seconds.

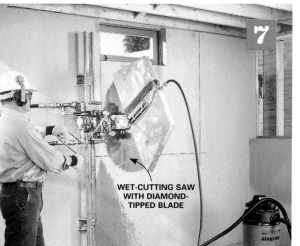

WET-CUTTING SAW WITH DIAMOND-TIPPED BLADE

7

Clean cuts through solid concrete

This wet-cutting, track-guided saw can cut cleanly and completely through 12-in. solid-poured walls. You'll need to hire a pro for a job like cutting an egress window opening, and the job will take three to four hours.

down. These cut the fastest and cleanest, but they require a special saw that can both distribute water and be safely used around it. As a make-do option, you can plug your saw into a GFCI-protected extension cord and have a helper carefully direct a small stream of water just in front of your saw as it cuts.

If you have just one big project, you'll save money and time by renting a wet-cutting saw/saw blade combination. Rental centers carry walk-behind saws for sawing or scoring concrete slabs, as well as a variety of hand-held saws for other tasks.

Note: If a diamond blade stops cutting, it may mean you're cutting a material that's too soft. A hard material is necessary to wear away the metal composite that the diamond cutting edges are embedded in. It may seem contrary, but to sharpen the blade, make a few cuts through a harder material to reveal new, sharp diamond edges.

Concrete-cutting dos and don'ts

■ Don't force a blade into a cut. Let the weight of the saw and the blade do the cutting.

■ When dry-cutting, back the blade off and allow it to run free every 30 to 45 seconds to prevent overheating.

■ You can use a dry-cutting blade with or without water, but a wet blade must always be used with water.

■ Whenever you cut concrete, wear sight, hearing and respiratory protection, especially when dry-cutting.

Masonry tips

BRICK HAMMER

Breaking bricks

The traditional method for cutting a brick is to break it with a masonry hammer. It's not as hard as it looks. Cup the brick in your hand, keeping your fingers below the top edge of the brick. (Our mason doesn't use gloves, but we suggest you do!) Give the brick a solid tap (a very solid tap for firebrick) on the outside edge near the center hole. Avoid hitting your hand.

Cutting chips off stone

Rough-cut stones will often fit together better with a little trimming. The easiest and quickest way to do this is to use a 4-lb. hand maul and masonry chisel to knock "burrs" off the stones so they fit more tightly together.

4-LB. MAUL

CHISEL

Cutting stone slabs without dust

You can cut pieces of field stone that are too big for the tile saw with a regular circular saw equipped with a wet-cutting diamond blade. Find a volunteer to hold a slow-running garden hose right at the cut while you saw your way through. That'll keep the blade cool, speed up the cut and eliminate dust. And don't worry. It's safe as long as you're plugged into a GFCI-protected outlet.

Build a stone wall

Y ou can't beat stone as a building material for a backyard wall. It blends well with any yard and garden, it's always in style and it will last almost maintenance free for generations. We built the walls in this project from blue ledge stone. In this design the stone walls form the perimeter of a curved patio and a stairway, but the techniques are the same for any wall.

Tools and materials

You'll need basic masonry tools—trowel, masonry hammer, 4-ft. level, line level, small whisk broom and jointer. A wheelbarrow will work just fine for mixing mortar by hand. In addition, you'll need three specialty tools—a rubber mallet, a diamond-edged masonry blade for your circular saw and a hand tamper for compacting the gravel under the concrete footings. Other than that, break out your

digging shovels and go to work.

Design to fit your site

These walls are designed as decorative walls, not retaining walls. If you need more than one step or if you have a steeper slope, have an architect or engineer detail the lower part of the wall to handle the extra pressure.

Our wall is made from mortared stone that rests on a reinforced concrete "floating" footing (Figure A). This type of footing works well for walls up to 2 ft. high and less than 20 ft. long built on "average-to-good" soils—that is, sand, gravel and stable clay. But it won't do on soil rich in organic matter or expansive clay. You'll need a deeper footing in those cases. Call in a local structural engineer or architect to review your plans. Also call the local utilities or 811 and have them mark any buried lines before you start digging.

Find stone at a landscape or masonry supplier

A landscape or masonry supplier will carry the best selection of stone. For our wall we selected blue ledge stone. Although technically categorized as a 4-in. veneer stone, it has a random shape that's ideal for our "rubble-style" wall. This stone is sold by the ton, and the supplier will tell you how much wall surface 1 ton covers.

Build the footings

Measure the 12-in. depth for the concrete footings at the lowest spot along the wall layout so they'll be completely out of sight when you're finished. Dig them about 5 in. oversized (2-1/2 in. per side) to leave

Figure A
Wall section details

room for the concrete forms. Then add the gravel base (Photo 1).

Pour the wall footings about 7-1/2 in. thick (Figure A). They don't have to be works of art, just level and flat. Rip 1/4-in. hardboard into 7-1/2 in. strips to form the curved footing (Photo 2). It's a

Materials list

75 sq. ft. wall stone
16 lin. ft. capstone
Twenty 4 x 6 x 16 concrete blocks
1-1/2 yds. concrete
100 ft. of 1/2-in. rebar

Quantities are for the walls shown here. Adjust to fit your design.

1 Spread 4 in. of compactible gravel in the wall trenches, rake it level, then compact it with a hand tamper. Moisten the gravel slightly for better packing.

WALL FOOTING TRENCH
HAND TAMPER

2 For a curved wall like this, form the 2-ft.-wide footing with 7-1/2-in.-wide strips of 1/4-in. hardboard and 1x2 stakes set every 2 ft. Screw the hardboard to the stakes and level the top. Form a straight wall with 2x8s.

1x2 STAKES
1/4" HARD-BOARD

3 Space three rows of 1/2-in. rebar evenly across each footing. Splice pieces by overlapping them 2 ft. and connecting them with two pieces of tie wire. Slip stones under the rebar to hold them 2 in. up and add 20-in. long rebar crosspieces to keep the rows aligned (Figure A).

WIRE TIE

1/2" REBAR

SCRAP STONE

2"

4 Fill the forms with concrete and pull a 2x4 across the tops to flatten and level it. Fill voids, then cover it with plastic and let it set at least two days.

LEAVE ROUGH — NO TROWELING

2x4

5 Drive in pairs of 1x4 batter boards on each end of the straight wall. Angle each board inward to match the wall taper. Tie string lines 10 in. up from the bottom as guides. Dry-fit the stones, starting from the corners. Then spread mortar and set each stone. Move the lines up as you work.

little flimsy for holding concrete, so stake it and pile a little gravel along the outer edges to stiffen it. Don't worry if the form distorts a bit. It'll be completely covered.

To keep the footings from cracking, it's important to place steel rebar correctly, about 2 in. up from the bottom of the footings (Photo 3). Keep everything aligned with crosspieces spaced every 2 ft. Then calculate the volume of concrete you'll need and order it from a ready-mix company. Have wheelbarrows and extra help available on concrete delivery day! When you place the concrete, make sure it flows around the rebar without leaving voids. Leave the top of the concrete pour rough (Photo 4). It'll bond better with the wall mortar.

Build the walls

Selecting and arranging the stones to create a nice-looking design can be challenging. It's something like working a jigsaw puzzle. Relax and allow plenty of time so you won't feel rushed.

To begin, spread out as much stone as you can, separating it into four groups:
- Thin stones, which are great for leveling rows
- Medium-sized stones (3 to 5 in. thick) to use as fillers between the large and thin stones
- Large stones, which you space throughout the wall as dramatic features

1x4 BATTER BOARDS

CORNER STONE

CONCRETE BLOCK FILLER

GUIDELINE ON CONCRETE

- Corner stones, which will have two faces that meet at a 90-degree angle. Corner stones are the most important, because the wall corners are the toughest to fit and build.

Start with the short, straight wall; it'll introduce you to basic wall-building techniques. The key here is to keep the wall straight. You might think you can do this by eye alone, but don't try it. Set up string lines to guide stone placement and to make sure they taper inward toward the top (Figure A and Photo 5). Use your level to set your batter boards accurately. And draw lines on the concrete to help position the first row of stones.

Begin by selecting and dry-fitting the corner stones and a few intermediate stones. Insert concrete blocks where soil will cover the wall (Photo 5). They're much cheaper than the stone. Now set the stones aside (keeping them in order) and mix up a sack of mortar to a thick, but not stiff, consistency. A properly mixed batch of mortar will stick to the stone; test it to get it just right. If you set a stone and all the mortar oozes out, it's too wet. And if it's difficult to push a stone into position, the mortar is too stiff.

Set the corners first, then fill in the zone in between. Lay about an inch-thick bed of mortar under and between stones and squish it down to 3/4 to 1/2 in. by tapping each stone with the trowel handle (Photo 6). Hold each stone in position for

6 Spread a 1-in. bed of mortar over each stone and against adjacent stones. Fill gaps between stones as well. Set each stone so the mortar oozes out but doesn't drip down the wall. Fill open areas inside the wall with mortar and scrap stones.

MORTAR OOZE

7 Set the top row flat and level. When the mortar is stiff, rake it back 1 in. from the face of the stone with a stick. Brush loose mortar away with a whisk broom. If the mortar smears, stop and let it set longer before brushing.

STICK

TOP ROW

RAKED JOINT

WHISK BROOM

8 Draw outside and inside radius lines on the footing with a tape measure hooked over the center stake. Start at one end and dry-set a variety of sizes and shapes around the curve. Then set them in mortar. Use 4- x 8- x 16-in. concrete block in areas that will be hidden.

CONCRETE BLOCK

GUIDELINES

When you're building a stone wall, think of it as a composition rather than as just stacks of rocks held together with mortar. Mix colors and sizes so the wall is pleasing to the eye. Frequently step back and visualize where you'll place the next stone and where you want more color. Always stagger vertical joints and keep the joint sizes equal.

a few seconds to give the mortar a chance to grab. If the stone drops out of position, remove it, scrape out the old mortar and reset it in new mortar. You may have to slip in a stone chip (shim) to keep it in place. Make adjustments right away. Any movement after the mortar stiffens will weaken the bond.

We fit our stones together fairly tightly, but wider gaps will look fine too. The key is to strive for consistently spaced joints throughout the wall. After the mortar stiffens (your thumb should barely leave an imprint when pressed against it), rake it away to leave a shadow line (Photo 7). That will make small variations in

TIP

Mark a bucket to show the amount of water needed to make a perfect batch of mortar. Then use this amount every time you mix a bag.

joint width less noticeable. Remember to completely fill all joints, especially the vertical joints. And let the mortar stiffen under each stone before you set another on top.

Use a variety of stone sizes to create a handsome pattern. Large stones make nice focal points and cover a lot of wall area fast. Set a few of these, then fill in between them with small and medium stones until they're even with the tops of the large stones (photo, above). Stagger the vertical joints. As you work, always think ahead about how the next stone will rest on the one you're setting. If the top of the stone tips slightly inward, following the desired taper, the next stone will be easier to align and set. In general, keep the horizontal joints close to level. And move the guide strings up as you go to keep the taper smooth. Leveling the top of the wall calls for extra care (Photo 11). Plan the last few layers of stones so you

don't have to put extremely thin stones on top to level it off. Frequently check the wall for level; the stones can fool you.

The curved wall is somewhat easier to build than the straight wall, because slightly misaligned stones won't be as noticeable. Since the curved wall is so long, start building from one end (Photo 8). You can't work off string lines. Instead, use a tape measure to check the position of each stone (Photo 9). And check the taper by holding your level plumb along the edges and measuring over to each stone.

Occasionally you'll have to break a stone to get a nice fit. Hold the stone in your hand and strike the edge sharply with a mason's hammer (Photo 10). That'll usually do the trick. If not, set the stone on a soft surface (sand) and hit it harder. Wear goggles to protect your eyes from flying stone chips.

9 Check the radius for each stone with a tape measure. Taper the wall slightly inward by shifting the top edges of the stones in about 1/2 in. per foot of height. Keep the stones roughly level. Rake the joints as the mortar stiffens.

10 Chip away the edge of stones with the glancing blow of a mason's hammer to get a better fit. Stagger the vertical joints by at least 2 in. when possible. Set large stones first and fill in the spaces with smaller ones.

Set the capstones

Check the top of the wall for level and mark the highest spot. Plan to set your first capstone at this spot and squish this mortar joint down tight. Then you'll level the other capstones from it.

Dry-set the capstones on the wall and fit them. Leave a 3/8-in. space between each stone for mortar, or wider if you're using irregular-shaped stone as a cap. You'll probably have to cut a capstone or two with the circular saw and diamond blade to make the overhangs on the ends just right. But avoid small stones. Then remove the stone at the highest point and reset it in a bed of mortar. Gently tap it with a deadblow hammer or rubber mallet to level it in all directions. Set each stone, leveling off the first. On the straight wall, tilt the capstones about 1/8 in. to one side to drain off water. Work quickly. You won't have much time to position and level the stones before

11 Lay the top row perfectly level. Measure down from the top and find or break stones to fit the top course. As before, fill the voids inside the wall with mortar and scrap rock. Then cut the capstones to fit and set them in mortar.

the mortar begins to set. After you set adjacent stones, fill the vertical joint between them with mortar, let it stiffen, then smooth and round the joint with a

jointer (not shown). If you slop mortar on the wall when you set the caps, wait until it dries. Then clean it off with a stiff brush.

Chapter Ten

USING TOOLS

Wire-feed welders

Most rental equipment stores carry these welders, and you'd be surprised how easy and safe they are to operate. You can also find affordable welders at home centers.

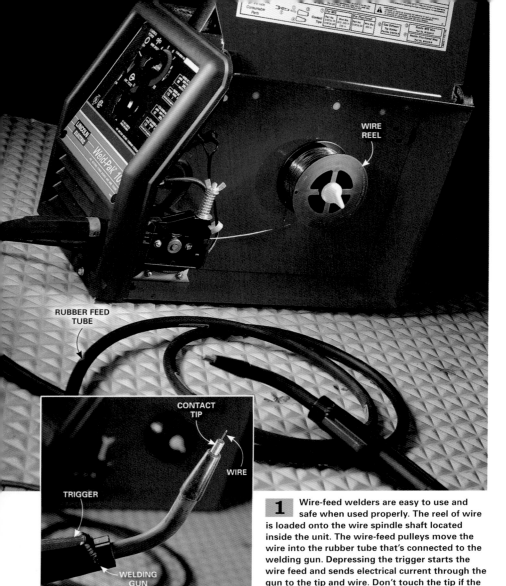

Really user-friendly

Wire-feed welders are self-contained, portable units that are great for repairing metal fences and railings, shop equipment (like the two-wheeled cart in the lead photo), and more. We don't recommend making structural repairs, such as frame work on a car or trailer. Take those jobs to an experienced welder.

Most units are either 115-volt or 240-volt. The 115-volt unit works off standard household electrical current. The 240-volt requires a 240-volt receptacle.

Both are DC arc welders that use an electric arc to melt the wire and the metal to be joined (the "workpiece"). The electrical current that's produced is around 18-volt DC, so it's relatively safe.

Good wire-feed welders can get a little pricey. If you don't plan to use it more than once or twice a year, renting makes sense.

Welding basics

Wire-feed welders use a reel of wire that's loaded onto a spindle located on the side of the unit (Photo 1). The wire is fed through a steel tube that runs to the welding gun (inset, Photo 1). It's then fed through the gun to the weld by depressing the gun's trigger.

Most units have two setting knobs. One controls the wire-feed rate or speed, the other the voltage. The thickness of the metal you're welding determines the wire speed and amperage to use. Thicker metal requires a faster feed and higher heat. Thinner metals require slower speed and lower voltage to avoid burning through the metal.

Welding isn't a skill you'll learn in a few minutes. It can take several hours to feel comfortable and confident, learning how to hold the gun at the correct angle and getting a feel for how fast or slow to move the gun to produce a solid weld.

Read the unit's instruction manual. It has the information you must know about the unit to weld safely and successfully. If you rent the welder, have the rental technician go over how to run the unit.

1 Wire-feed welders are easy to use and safe when used properly. The reel of wire is loaded onto the wire spindle shaft located inside the unit. The wire-feed pulleys move the wire into the rubber tube that's connected to the welding gun. Depressing the trigger starts the wire feed and sends electrical current through the gun to the tip and wire. Don't touch the tip if the trigger is depressed.

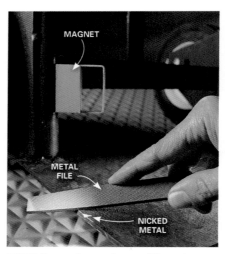

2 To test the metal to see if it can be welded, try attaching a magnet. If the magnet sticks, the metal can probably be welded. You won't be able to weld aluminum unless you buy a separate aluminum welding kit.

3 Clean all paint, dirt, oil or other contaminants from the metal surface. A wire brush usually works best.

Testing your metal

Not all metal can be welded with a wire-feed welder. To see if it can be welded, perform two simple tests. First, try to attach a magnet to it (Photo 2). If the magnet sticks, you can probably weld it. Then, using a metal file, try to nick the metal. If it nicks easily, it'll be easy to weld. Hardened steel is difficult to weld.

There is an exception—cast iron. It will hold a magnet and nick easily, but it can't be welded.

The area to be welded must be free of oil, dirt, paint and rust. If it isn't, the weld won't be sound.

The work clamp (Photo 4) must make solid contact with the metal you'll be welding to complete the electrical circuit. Always try to attach the work clamp as close to the weld joint as possible.

Safety measures

Wire-feed welders are safe if they're operated properly; however, there is the potential for severe injury or death. Be sure to read and follow the manufacturer's instructions. Here are some important points to remember:

■ It's best to weld outdoors. It is safe, however, to work indoors in a well-ventilated area. The fumes and gases can be dangerous. Don't lean over the work as you're welding.

■ Keep all flammable material away from the work area.

■ Keep a fire extinguisher handy!

■ **NEVER** weld on a container that *may* have contained a flammable material, such as gasoline, paint thinner or other solvents. It will explode.

■ **ALWAYS** use the protective face shield. It protects your face from the sparks and has a special glass view-piece to protect your eyes from the intense light of welding.

■ Don't touch the electrode or the metal that you're welding. It will get hot and you may receive a slight tingle from the low-voltage DC going through the object.

■ Don't touch the workpiece with unprotected hands until it has had time to cool, usually 15 to 20 minutes. Even then, use caution.

HEAVY, PROTECTIVE GLOVES

WORK CLAMP

4 Secure the work clamp to the metal surface as close to the weld area as possible without interfering with your ability to work. The clamp must have a good connection to complete the electrical circuit. There should be a fairly loud snapping or crackling sound when you weld. If there isn't, stop and recheck the work clamp's contact with the metal. Be sure to use the face shield!

WELDER'S HAMMER

SLAG

5 Once the weld is complete, you may have some excess weld metal called slag. This can be chipped off with a welder's hammer or with a wire brush.

■ Wear dry, heavy protective gloves (Photo 4). The flying sparks from the arc or the hot workpiece can burn you. Wear a long-sleeve flannel-type shirt. Upper body protectors, like the brushed leather type worn in the opening photo, are also recommended.

■ Always unplug the unit when loading wire or changing a contact tip, or when it's not in use.

Advanced miter saw tips

*8 miter saw tricks
that trim carpenters
use every day*

No doubt about it, the miter saw is one of the most important power tools you can have in your construction arsenal. Whether you have a 30-year-old 10-in. Delta chop saw or a brand new 12-in. sliding-compound saw, we'll show you how to cut more-accurate, cleaner crosscuts than you ever thought possible.

1

Put your mark where the blade falls

When cutting a board to length, most do-it-yourselfers mark near an edge. That makes it hard to align the mark with the blade. Instead, place your mark where the blade touches the wood. After you try it a few times, you can pretty much guess where that spot is. Next, put a light, penciled "X" on the "waste" side of the mark. That'll keep you from cutting on the wrong side of the line and winding up with a board that's 1/8 in. too short.

KEEPER SIDE

BLADE CONTACT POINT

WASTE SIDE

CUTTING MARK

SHIFT TOWARD MARK

2

Sneak up on cuts

It's tough to get the blade to cut exactly at the cutoff mark, especially when you're cutting angles that are marked near an edge. Instead, keep a safe distance away from the mark and dip the spinning blade into the wood. Lift the blade and keep shifting the board slightly until you're right at the mark, and then make the cut.

Cut identical lengths fast

If you're cutting lots of pieces all the same length, use a temporary fence (see p. 268) with a stop. Clamp a stop block to the fence a little bit farther from the blade than the length you're after. Cut the first board, measure or test-fit it, and move the stop slightly toward the blade and try another cut. Repeat until you've reached perfection and then cut the rest of the pieces. But make sure to clamp the stop well so it won't slip. Don't use wimpy spring clamps!

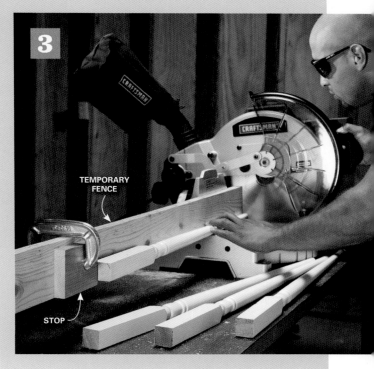

3

TEMPORARY FENCE

STOP

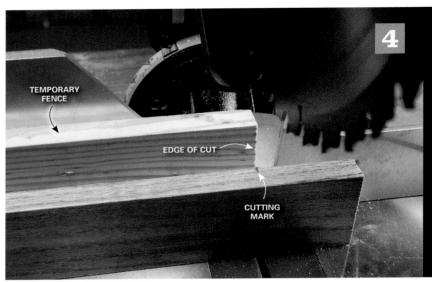

TEMPORARY FENCE

EDGE OF CUT

CUTTING MARK

4 Align cuts instantly

Many woodworkers always have a temporary fence in place, especially with bigger miter or compound sliding saws, because a 3/4-in.-thick fence barely affects the cutting width capacity. And one reason they like the fence is that after the end of the board is cut off, the fence gives them a perfect guide for the blade path. Line up the cutting mark with the end of the fence and you'll have no need to guess or sneak up on marks. Simply mount a fence so the end sticks past the blade a couple of inches and cut off the end. Get your cutting marks aligned with the end, and cut away.

Installing temporary fences

Temporary wood fences have a wide variety of uses, as you see in many of these tips. And as you learn to work with them, you'll think of even more.

Most miter saws have holes drilled through their metal fences for screwing on these wooden fences. If your saw doesn't have these holes or they aren't where you need them, don't be afraid to drill some 1/4-in. holes near the ends of the fences on both sides of the blade. Use any straight board for your temporary fences and choose screws that won't penetrate the other side. If you use softwood fences, you won't even have to drill pilot holes. To install a temporary fence, just clamp it tight against the saw's metal fence while you drive screws into the wood.

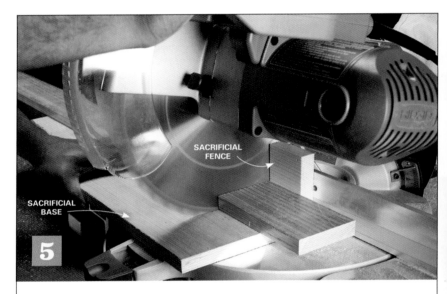

SACRIFICIAL FENCE

SACRIFICIAL BASE

5 Eliminate tear-out

Most of the time, minor tear-out—which can occur on the sides of a board that are against the saw fence and table where the teeth exit the wood—isn't a problem. That's because with most projects, only one edge and one side of the board are on display. But when you need flawless edges on all four sides, you can use this trick: Rest the work on a sacrificial base and against a temporary fence. Both should project past the blade. You don't have to fasten either the base piece or the fence to the saw. Just hold them tight against the saw surfaces.

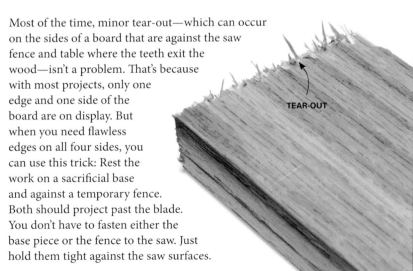

TEAR-OUT

TEMPORARY FENCE

MOUNTING HOLE

6 Back-bevel trim

When fitting miters or butt joints, especially with trim work, you'll often find that the angle is perfect but a tiny gap shows at the front. In trimming windows, a gap occurs when the drywall isn't perfectly flush with window jambs. The solution is to slightly bevel the cut to bring the fronts together. Newer miter saws cut bevels as well as angles; older or less expensive miter saws don't have that capability. With either saw, it's quick and easy to slip a 1/4-in. shim or a carpenter's pencil under the board before you recut the bevel. That'll usually give you just what you need to close up the gap. Really bad gaps may need two stacked shims.

1/4" SHIM

7 Upgrade your blade

Buy a saw blade that's specifically labeled for miter saws, especially if you do fine work. They're not cheap, but they'll give smooth, nearly tear-out–free cuts every time. That's because the teeth are tilted back slightly for smoother crosscutting, which is the type of cutting you'll be doing on your miter saw. You can use this blade to hack the occasional 2x4 to length, but make sure the wood is clean and free of fasteners. (Put in a cheap blade if your brother wants to borrow the saw to frame up his garage.)

Shave off tiny little bits

If you ever need to shave just a little bit off an end, try this. Keep your finger off the trigger and push the blade all the way down and snug the board end against the disc plate (not the teeth). Hold the board tight against the fence while you raise the blade. The teeth will stick out past the disc just a hair, but they'll still slip past the wood. Start the saw and cut through the wood and you'll remove about 1/32 in. with each pass. After you get the hang of this trick, you'll have a good idea of how many times you'll need to repeat the process to cut off the amount you're after.

1/32" REMOVAL

Working safely with powder-actuated tools

HAMMER STRIKES FIRING PIN NUT

PUSH AND HOLD DOWN

These powerful tools are the quickest, most efficient way to fire fasteners into concrete slabs and block walls

2-1/2" FASTENER (DRIVE PIN)

PLASTIC FLUTE

GREEN, LEVEL 3 (MODERATE) POWDER LOAD

YELLOW, LEVEL 4 (HEAVY-DUTY) POWDER LOAD

1 Quickly fasten sill plates to concrete slabs using a powder-actuated tool (PAT). Safety goggles, hearing protection and safe work methods are imperative. Once this hammer-activated PAT is loaded, hold the tool 90 degrees to the work surface. Then, tightly grip it with your arm fully extended, keeping your head in line behind the tool. Firmly push down on the PAT to cock it, maintain that pressure, and strike the firing pin nut with a strong blow from the hammer. Keep your body balanced; as the tool fires, it delivers a recoil.

A ttaching wood to concrete is one of the most basic, time-consuming and iffy tasks in construction. Whether you're anchoring wall sill plates (Photo 1) or attaching furring strips to concrete walls (Photo 3), you'll find yourself engaged in an exacting task, working with seemingly incompatible materials and wondering if everything will stay attached.

If you have a dozen or more permanent connections to make,

2 Simple "stud guns" like this trigger-activated model (far left photo) or our hammer-activated model (left photo) are loaded one shot at a time. Stud guns resemble firearms, and they have much in common. Treat both with respect and NEVER use PAT powder loads in firearms (and vice versa).

DRIVE PIN READY FOR FIRING

BARREL

BARREL

SEATED LOAD IN FIRING CHAMBER

TRIGGER

RECOIL PADDING

GRIP

FIRING PIN NUT

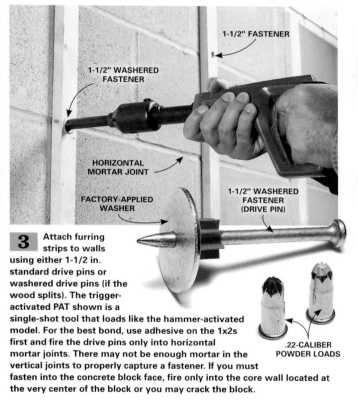

1-1/2" FASTENER

1-1/2" WASHERED FASTENER

HORIZONTAL MORTAR JOINT

FACTORY-APPLIED WASHER

1-1/2" WASHERED FASTENER (DRIVE PIN)

.22-CALIBER POWDER LOADS

3 Attach furring strips to walls using either 1-1/2 in. standard drive pins or washered drive pins (if the wood splits). The trigger-activated PAT shown is a single-shot tool that loads like the hammer-activated model. For the best bond, use adhesive on the 1x2s first and fire the drive pins only into horizontal mortar joints. There may not be enough mortar in the vertical joints to properly capture a fastener. If you must fasten into the concrete block face, fire only into the core wall located at the very center of the block or you may crack the block.

DRIVE PIN WITHOUT PLASTIC FLUTE

4 Conduct a center punch test on poured concrete walls and slabs before you shoot fasteners. Firmly strike a drive pin several times. If the fastener point penetrates the concrete easily, the material is too soft. If the concrete shatters or cracks, it's too brittle. If the fastener point is blunted or bent, the concrete is too hard. When the concrete shows a well-defined impression of the fastener tip, it's the proper hardness. Go ahead and shoot some test fasteners.

save time and money by using powder-actuated tools (PATs); see photo 2. With safety as the highest priority, we'll show you the most popular tasks this tool can do around your house.

Also called stud drivers, stud guns and rem guns, these are heavy-duty tools that fire gunpowder cartridges. This action pushes a piston inside the tool that slams a special heat-treated and hardened steel nail (a "drive pin") through wood and into concrete. It takes only seconds to load and fire a stud gun, so you can drive dozens of fasteners quickly.

Uses and costs

PATs became available in the 1960s and have grown increasingly popular for fastening wood sills to concrete floors (Photo 1) and wood furring strips to poured and block concrete walls (Photo 3).

To finish off a whole basement with scores of wall furring strips and/or floor sill plates, you can use a hammer-activated gun or the more expensive trigger-activated type (shown in Photo 2). For occasional use, rent a heavier-duty tool. Both use the same powder load and standard drive pin.

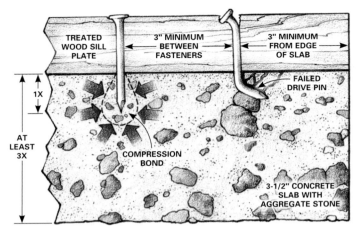

TREATED WOOD SILL PLATE

3" MINIMUM BETWEEN FASTENERS

3" MINIMUM FROM EDGE OF SLAB

FAILED DRIVE PIN

1X

AT LEAST 3X

COMPRESSION BOND

3-1/2" CONCRETE SLAB WITH AGGREGATE STONE

Know the rules for fastening into concrete. The drive pins should penetrate 1 in. to 1-1/4 in. into the concrete, but never protrude through it. Drive pins displace the concrete, which tries to return to its original form, resulting in a compression bond. Follow the spacing rules shown, and only shoot fasteners into concrete that's more than three times as thick as the fastener's intended penetration.

Note: Before you work with stud guns, check with your local building officials. The use of these tools is sometimes restricted with certain construction techniques and situations.

Not suitable for all concrete

PATs have the power to shoot a projectile more than 300 ft. per second and drive a fastener into concrete with such force that it sometimes takes a ton of leverage to extract it. But PATs don't work in every situation. Never attempt to use one to drive fasteners in very hard concrete or stone—or brittle materials like glass, tile or brick. Before using a stud gun, test the hardness of your concrete by conducting a "center punch test" (Photo 4).

Apply these basic rules:
- Follow the spacings shown for placing drive pins and for working near the edges of concrete slabs (Figure A).
- For best results, use these fasteners in concrete aged more than 28 days. "Fresh" concrete fewer than seven days old can't exert a compression bond sufficient to permanently secure a drive pin.
- Follow the results of the center punch test. Concrete that is either too weak or too strong won't hold these fasteners. Instead, use specialty wedge anchors or expansion shield–type concrete anchors. These are also the right choice if you have only a few furring strips to attach to a wall, if the strongest connection is a must, or if someday you may want to take the project apart.
- If you use these fasteners, consider the installation permanent. Extracting drive pins wrecks the wood and damages the concrete base.
- Improve the holding power for permanent installations by using construction adhesives on sill plates and wall framing (Photo 5).
- "Overdriving" these fasteners occurs when too powerful a powder load pushes the gun piston partially out of the muzzle and drives the fastener too deep into the wood. Overdriving is a sure way to damage a PAT (Photo 6). Find the proper powder load by using the weakest powder load first (Level 1, gray) and working toward the most powerful

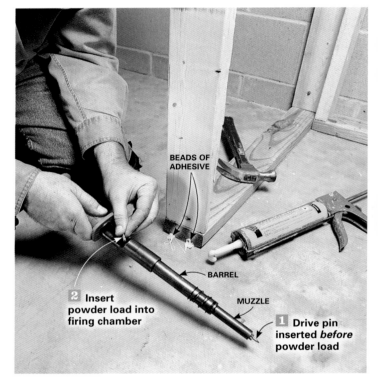

BEADS OF ADHESIVE

2 Insert powder load into firing chamber

BARREL

MUZZLE

1 Drive pin inserted *before* powder load

5 Prepare a shot by first placing one hand on the grip and the other on the muzzle, rapidly pulling the barrel forward. The chamber will open and the piston will be set for firing. For safety, insert the drive pin into the muzzle of the PAT first. Only then, place a powder load into the chamber. Push the load as far as it will go. Hold the tool steady and with the chamber up (so the load doesn't drop out), grab the muzzle and push the barrel backward to the closed position. Once the PAT is fired, the rapid action used to open it for the next shot will eject the spent powder load clear of the tool.

(Level 4, yellow)—until you get the proper drive pin penetration. If drive pin heads consistently go below the top of the board or split your wood, use washered fasteners.

Follow basic safety procedures

Using a PAT has been described as "an intense experience." Learning the proper use of a PAT not only improves your efficiency and speeds up tasks but also directly affects safety. A lot of it is common sense, but follow these additional guidelines:

- Keep the tool and unspent powder loads locked up and away from kids. *Injuries and deaths have occurred when ricocheting projectiles have struck bystanders, or when people have tried to use common nails in stud guns.*
- Use safety goggles (not safety glasses) and hearing protection when working with stud guns.
- If the tool is dropped, check for damage to the barrel and other moving parts and don't use the PAT until it's repaired.

Clean and maintain the tool

Simple maintenance will help you avoid problems like a sticky barrel slide and spent powder load casings that won't eject (which is also caused by using drive pins longer than 2-1/2 in.). Each day, after regular use, inspect the unloaded tool for damage and then take a rag and clean out the chamber and around the barrel. Buy barrel brushes from your PAT tool distributor and clean the gunpowder residue out of the inner working parts. Spray a little WD-40 lubricant on the inside and all over the outside of the tool and then wipe those areas clean and dry.

Don't do this!

BARREL OF HAMMER-ACTIVATED PAT

OVERDRIVEN PISTON

DRIVE-PIN HEAD

6 Avoid overdriving fasteners with too strong a powder load. Repeated overdriving is frustrating, damages the tool, and results in a weaker coupling between the wood and the concrete. Use either a rubber mallet or a block of wood to tap the piston back into the muzzle. Inspect the barrel assembly, and open the tool's chamber to confirm that both the piston and barrel are working smoothly. If the gun is damaged, have it repaired at a service center.

Extract a broken screw

When you twist the head off a bolt, break a screw shank or mangle a screw head, you have a few options: In metal, you can completely drill out a bolt and restore the damaged threads with a tap. Likewise, you can drill out a wood screw and replace it with a larger one. But before you try these tricky methods, try a screw extractor, which usually does the job quickly and cleanly. You'll find extractors at home centers and hardware stores for screw diameters from 3/32 in. to 1/2 in. or larger.

Start by drilling a hole in the center of the screw (Photo 1). If your drill bit won't stay centered on the jagged, broken surface, switch to a smaller bit (1/16 in. or smaller). A smaller bit is easier to control and creates a shallow starter hole for the larger bit. Drill cautiously and apply only light pressure. The worst thing you can do is break off the drill bit inside the broken screw because removing a broken bit is almost impossible.

EXTRACTOR

BROKEN SCREW

1 Drill a hole in the center of the broken screw or bolt using the drill bit size specified by the extractor manufacturer.

Next, insert the extractor and give it a firm tap with a hammer. Then push down on the extractor as you twist it counterclockwise (Photo 2). If the extractor threads won't grab and turn the screw, try these other suggestions:

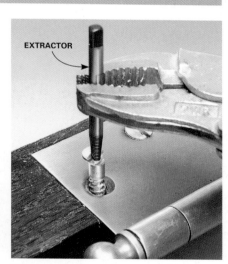

EXTRACTOR

2 Tap the extractor into the hole and turn it counterclockwise with locking pliers or a tap wrench to remove the screw.

- Tap the extractor into the screw with a bit more force. Heat from a heat gun may also loosen stuck threads.
- In metal, apply a penetrating lubricant and let it soak in for 30 minutes.
- Enlarge the hole with a slightly larger drill bit and try again.

Cordless impact drivers

Cordless impact drivers used to be a specialty tool, rare on job sites and scarce on store shelves. Today, you'll see several models at any tool retailer and hear their machine-gun chatter wherever there's construction. When a tool gains popularity that fast, you have to wonder what's going on. And, more important, what you're missing.

Not just for driving screws

Impact drivers make great drills. With small bits (up to 1/4 in. or so), they act like a drill—but at nearly twice the rpm of most cordless drills. With bigger bits, they kick into high-torque impact mode so you can bore a big hole with a small driver.

Prepare for impact

Pick up a set of hex-shaft accessories (drill bits, driver bits, socket adapters). You'll want most of that stuff sooner or later, and buying a kit will save you a few bucks. Check the label and get a set that's tough enough for impact-driver duty.

It's not a hammer drill

An impact driver works kind of like a hammer drill and sounds a lot like one. But it's no substitute for a hammer drill. An impact driver's innards are engineered to generate torque, not powerful forward blows.

One-handed driving

With a standard driver, you have to get your weight behind the screw and push hard. Otherwise, the bit will "cam out" and chew up the screw head. Not so with an impact driver. The hammer mechanism that produces torque also creates some forward pressure. That means you don't have to push so hard to avoid cam-out. Great for one-handed, stretch-and-drive situations.

Hex shafts only

The chuck on an impact driver makes for quick changes; just slide the collar forward and slip in the bit. But you'll have to buy hex-shaft drill bits. Regular bits won't work.

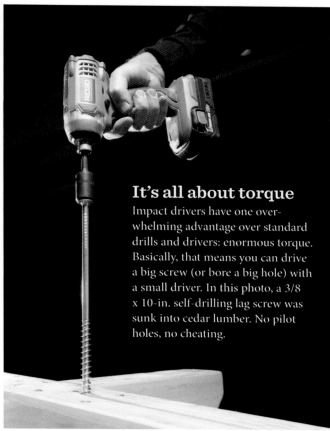

It's all about torque

Impact drivers have one overwhelming advantage over standard drills and drivers: enormous torque. Basically, that means you can drive a big screw (or bore a big hole) with a small driver. In this photo, a 3/8 x 10-in. self-drilling lag screw was sunk into cedar lumber. No pilot holes, no cheating.

Loud. Really loud

An impact driver can bring a heavy-metal drummer to tears. Always wear muffs or earplugs.

They look alike outside, but . . .

The difference is how they transfer torque from the motor to the chuck. On a standard drill or driver, the motor and chuck are locked together through gears; as the workload increases, the motor strains. An impact driver behaves the same under light loads. But when resistance increases, a clutch-like mechanism disengages the motor from the chuck for a split second. The motor continues to turn and builds momentum. Then the clutch re-engages with a slam, transferring momentum to the chuck. All of this happens about 50 times per second, and the result is three or four times as much torque from a similar-size tool.

Impact driver
Torque: 930 in.-lbs.

Standard driver
Torque: 265 in.-lbs.

Paint like a pro with an airless sprayer

An airless sprayer simplifies painting in two ways: First, if you want to speed up a job that requires several gallons of paint, you can apply it twice as fast as with a roller or brush. And second, if you want a glass-smooth finish on woodwork or doors, the airless sprayer can lay the paint on flawlessly.

An airless sprayer works by pumping paint at a very high pressure, up to 3,000 psi, through a hose and out a tiny hole in the spray gun tip. The tip is designed to break up the paint evenly into a fan-shaped spray pattern of tiny droplets. Using different tips, you can spray thin liquids like stain, lacquer and varnish or thicker liquids like latex house paint. With a little practice, you can use an airless sprayer to apply a perfectly smooth finish on doors, cabinets and woodwork. And since an airless sprayer pumps paint directly from a can or 5-gallon bucket, you can apply a lot of material in a short time. This makes an airless sprayer particularly well suited for large paint jobs, like priming bare drywall in a new house or painting a 300-ft.-long privacy fence.

But before you get too excited about the benefits of spray painting, there are a few drawbacks to consider. First, the fine particles of paint don't all stick to the surface. A large percentage of the paint ends up in the air, where it can drift and settle onto everything in sight. This means you'll be wasting 20 to 40 percent of the finish, depending on the application. You'll also have to take extra time to mask off and cover up everything you want to keep unpainted. Outdoor painting is especially risky. Overspray can end up on your shrubs or roof, or drift with the wind onto your neighbor's car.

The other downside is the extra time it takes to flush the paint from the pump and hose and clean up the spray gun. If you're using your own sprayer, rather than a rental unit, you'll also have to clean the filters and install special storage fluid. And if you're spraying oil-based products, you'll have to store or recycle a gallon or two of used solvents left over from the cleaning process. But despite these disadvantages, an airless sprayer can save you a lot of time on big paint jobs and allow you to get a finish that's nearly impossible to get with a brush.

Rent or buy?

Spending more for a sprayer doesn't necessarily get you more features, but it does get you a bigger, better motor and pump, which will deliver longer life and trouble-free operation. Owning a sprayer allows you to spray whenever you want and to ensure that the sprayer is clean and well maintained.

Renting is a good option if you don't expect to use the sprayer very often and want to avoid the extra maintenance. Make sure the hose and pump are clean and that the filters have been cleaned or replaced. Ask for help in choosing the right spray

Figure A
Airless painter parts

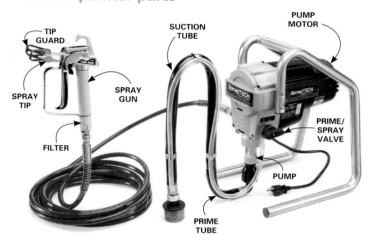

tip for the job. Some rental stores won't allow you to spray solvent-based products like lacquer, oil stain or oil paint, so be sure to ask.

Setting up the sprayer

Whether you rent or buy an airless sprayer, there are a few key setup points. All sprayers have a screen at the intake point. Make sure it's clean. Most sprayers also have a removable filter near the pump and another one in the handle of the gun. Check both to make sure they're clean, and plan to strain your paint through a mesh filter bag to remove lumps so they won't clog the filters.

Prime the pump

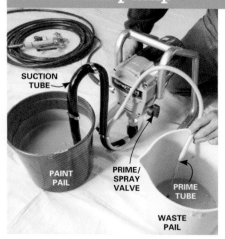

Fill the hose

1 Place the smaller prime tube in a waste pail and the suction tube in the bucket of strained paint. Turn the prime/spray valve to "prime." Switch on the pump. Turn the pressure valve up until the pump starts. When the paint starts flowing from the prime tube, move it into the paint bucket.

2 Clip the prime tube to the suction tube. Let the pump run for about 30 seconds or until no more air bubbles come out of the tube.

3 Hold the gun (guard and spray tip removed) over the waste bucket and pull the trigger. Switch the valve to the "spray" setting. Let go of the trigger when paint is flowing in a steady stream from the gun. Lock the trigger and follow the "Pressure Relief Steps" (see p. 278).

Install the tip

4 Screw the guard assembly loosely onto the gun and align the guard at a 90-degree angle to your desired spray pattern. Insert the spray tip until the tab is engaged. Rotate the tip to face the arrow forward. Snug the guard assembly hand-tight.

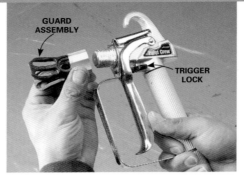

GUARD ASSEMBLY

TRIGGER LOCK

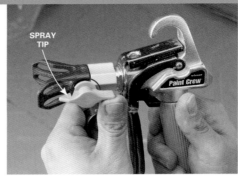

SPRAY TIP

Prime the pump

Before you can start spraying, you have to prime the pump. Photos 1 and 2 (p. 277) show how. You may have to repeat this process if the paint in the bucket runs out while you're spraying.

If paint won't come out of the prime tube, the problem may be a clogged screen or filter, or a stuck ball-check valve in the pump assembly. If the sprayer you're using doesn't have a push-button on the pump to free the stuck ball, try to dislodge it by gently tapping the lowest end of the pump with a hammer. Otherwise follow the suggested troubleshooting procedure in your manual or call the rental store for help.

Fill the hose and set up the gun

Once the pump is primed, you're ready to fill the hose with paint (Photo 3). Then lock the trigger and relieve the pressure before installing the tip guard assembly and inserting the tip (Photo 4).

Pressure relief steps

1. Turn off the power switch.
2. Turn the spray/prime valve to prime.
3. Aim the gun against the side of the waste pail and pull the trigger to release the pressure.
4. Engage the trigger lock.

Choose the right tip

SPRAY TIP

Spray tips slide into a hole in the front of the gun. They're labeled with a three-digit number like 309 or 517 (these may be the last three digits of a longer model number). Doubling the first digit tells you the spray fan width with the gun held 12 in. from the surface. A 415 tip, for example, would have an 8-in.-wide fan, while a 515 would have a 10-in. fan pattern.

The next two digits indicate the size of the hole in thousandths of an inch. Choose a smaller diameter hole (.009 to .013) for thin liquids like stain or varnish and a larger hole (.015 or .017) for thicker liquids like latex paint.

A 411 tip would work well for spraying varnish on woodwork, while a 517 is a good size for spraying large surfaces with latex paint.

Adjust the pressure

Too little pressure will result in an uneven spray pattern. And too much pressure causes excessive overspray and premature tip wear. Photo 5 shows how to dial in just the right amount. If you're still getting "tails" or an uneven spray pattern at maximum pressure, try using a tip with a smaller hole. If the spray pattern is round rather than narrow, the tip is worn and should be replaced.

Spraying technique

Photos 6 and 7 show the correct spray techniques. Here are a few key points:

- Plan your spraying sequence before you start. On doors, for example, spray the edges first. Then spray top to bottom. Then spray at right angles side to side.
- Squeeze the trigger while the gun is off to the side, and then move it onto the work (Photo 6).
- Move the gun parallel to the surface, not in an arc.
- Keep the gun perpendicular to the surface, not tilted (Photo 7).
- Move fast to prevent runs. Several thin coats are better than one thick one.
- Overlap your strokes about 30 to 50 percent.

Troubleshooting

Most spray problems are a result of clogged filters, a clogged tip (below), or a pump that's either leaking or has stuck ball-check valves. Careful cleaning and proper maintenance will prevent most of these troubles.

Other problems, such as runs and uneven coverage, are caused by using the wrong tip size or by a lack of spraying experience. As with most do-it-yourself tasks, practice is the key to success.

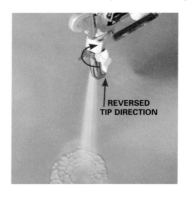

REVERSED TIP DIRECTION

If paint stops flowing or sputters from the gun, the tip may be clogged. Twist the tip 180 degrees. Point the gun at a scrap of paper and squeeze the trigger to clear the clog. Rotate the tip 180 degrees to point it forward again and spray a test strip onto the scrap.

Adjust the pressure

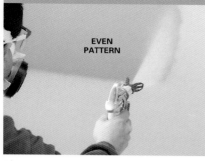

EVEN PATTERN

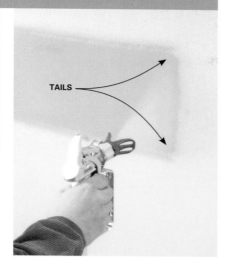

TAILS

5 Turn on the pump and move the prime/spray lever to the "spray" position. Spray a strip of paint across a piece of cardboard to check the spray pattern. If the spray pattern has tails, the pressure is set too low. Turn up the pressure until the paint is evenly distributed across the fan pattern (above).

Spraying techniques

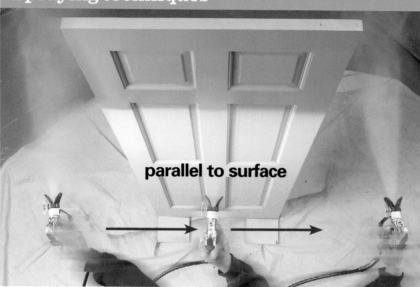

parallel to surface

6 Squeeze the trigger before you reach the edge of the door. Move the sprayer quickly across the door, keeping it parallel to the surface. Release the trigger when the sprayer is past the opposite edge of the door.

7 Overlap about half of the previously painted strip when you make the next pass with the sprayer. Keep the gun perpendicular to the surface.

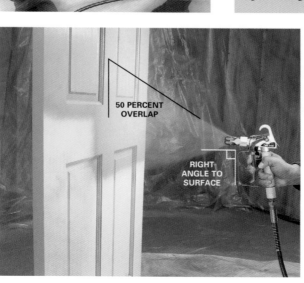

50 PERCENT OVERLAP

RIGHT ANGLE TO SURFACE

Pressure washers

Wash siding, concrete floors, decks and even your car faster and easier

Pressure washers are so much fun to use—and show such dramatic and quick results—that you'll be begging to clean your neighbors' siding, driveways and cars once you've finished your own.

You can rent or buy a pressure washer to clean nearly any outdoor item. By following these tips, you'll learn how to use pressure washers safely and efficiently.

Two types of pressure washers and how they work

Pressure washers, whether they're powered by electric motors or gas engines, run a pump that pressurizes the water from your garden hose to 1,000 lbs. or more, then forces it out through a spray wand. The higher the pressure (measured in pounds per square inch—psi), the tougher the cleaning jobs they can tackle. Both types require a steady, uninterrupted supply of water (in

65-DEGREE "DETERGENT USE" NOZZLE

25-DEGREE "FLUSHING" NOZZLE

ZERO-DEGREE "BLASTING" NOZZLE

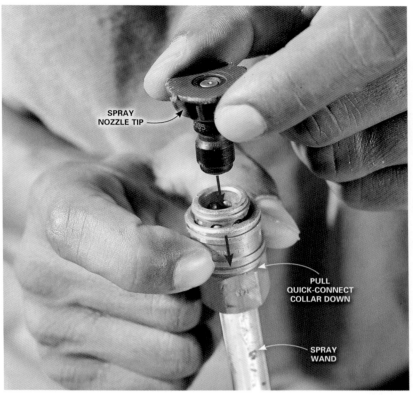

SPRAY NOZZLE TIP

PULL QUICK-CONNECT COLLAR DOWN

SPRAY WAND

Insert individual nozzle tips into the spray wand by retracting the quick-coupling collar, pushing the tip in as far as it will go and releasing the collar. Pull on the tip to confirm that it's firmly locked in position. Point the spray wand away from people and property when starting the pressure washer.

Spray nozzles for different tasks

Pressure washers that deliver less than 2,400 psi generally come with a single adjustable spray nozzle that delivers zero to 60-degree fan patterns. Some brands offer accessory "rotating" or "turbo" nozzles that clean more effectively than standard adjustable nozzles because they spin the water stream.

Heavier-duty units generally come with four or five color-coded, individual nozzle tips (three are shown here). They create specific fan patterns: wider (for using detergents), medium (for general cleaning) and narrower (for blasting deep stains).

gallons per minute—gpm). For occasional use, most home-owners will find that a washer with a pressure range of 1,300 to 2,400 psi works best.

Electric pressure washers deliver 1,300 to 1,400 psi, require about 1-1/2 gpm and are the best choice for light-duty cleaning like washing cars (Photo 3), outdoor grills and garage floors (Photo 4). They are quieter, lighter in weight and more portable than gas-powered washers. Many have built-in tanks for optional detergent use. Always connect electric washers to power outlets

that are protected by a ground fault circuit interrupter (GFCI) and use only 12- or 14-gauge extension cords.

Most pressure washers that you'll find for rent or sale are gas-powered. This type can deliver higher water pressure than the electric kind, some more than 3,000 psi. But gas-powered washers also require more water: 2 to 3 gpm. These washers are the best choice for bigger jobs like preparing siding for painting (Photo 2), removing "aging" stains from wood decks (Photo 5) and deep-cleaning concrete. You can rent one with accessories

SQUEEZE TRIGGER AS ENGINE IS STARTED

NOZZLE TIP REMOVED

SPECIAL DETERGENT FOR PRESSURE WASHERS

WATER INLET FILTER

CHEMICAL INJECTOR

1 To start a gas-powered washer: (1) Clean any debris from the inlet filter. (2) Connect any accessories (like this chemical injector). (3) Run water through the washer for one minute to prime the system and remove any air. (4) Squeeze the spray wand trigger to bleed water pressure, and (5) pull the starter cord to start the engine.

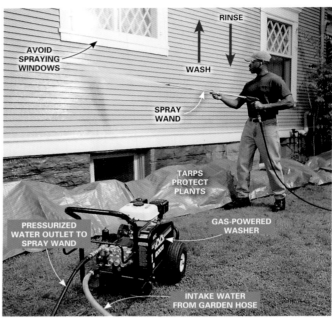

AVOID SPRAYING WINDOWS

RINSE

WASH

SPRAY WAND

TARPS PROTECT PLANTS

GAS-POWERED WASHER

PRESSURIZED WATER OUTLET TO SPRAY WAND

INTAKE WATER FROM GARDEN HOSE

2 Wash siding to prepare it for painting. Begin with the wand's nozzle 4 ft. from the house and slowly move it closer until you achieve the desired cleaning effect. Grip the spray wand with two hands, direct the water stream at a 45-degree angle to the siding and move the water stream constantly.

like chemical injectors (Photo 1) or longer spray wands for reaching high places.

Operating procedures

All pressure washers seem intimidating the first time you use them. Have the rental center or tool retailer instruct you on its use, and follow these guidelines:

Water supply. Make sure your water supply can deliver the gallons per minute specified for your machine. For example, if your pressure washer needs 2-1/2 gpm, time how long it takes your garden hose to fill a 5-gallon pail. The garden hose must be 50 ft. long or less and have a 3/4-in. inside diameter, with standard 3/4-in. hose fittings for connecting to the washer's inlet. To ensure that water circulates unobstructed through the system, check the water inlet filter or screen and clean it of debris. Also make sure the garden and pressure hoses are kink free.

Safety concerns

Pressure washers deliver extreme pressure and can cause serious injuries if misused. For safety, follow these guidelines:

■ Don't point the pressure washer at people or pets or put your hand in front of the nozzle. The pressurized water stream could actually penetrate your skin or cause serious cuts.

■ Wear safety glasses when operating the washer.

■ Don't use pressure washers while working from ladders. Once you squeeze the trigger, the powerful recoil on the spray wand can throw you off balance and off the ladder.

■ Maintain a minimum 6-ft. distance when spraying water around power lines, electrical masts or outlets.

■ Before uncoupling hoses, stop the machine, turn the water faucet off and squeeze the spray wand trigger to release all water pressure in the system.

■ Engage the safety lock on the trigger when you're not actually washing and when changing nozzle tips.

Start-up procedure (Photo 1). Before starting the washer, it's imperative that water be flowing through the washer and out the spray wand. Follow these steps:

- Tighten all hose connections so no air can enter the lines.
- Set the spray wand to a low- or no-pressure setting to prevent recoil, or kickback, when the washer is started. Electric washers and gas washers with variable nozzles should be on low-pressure, wide fan settings. Gas washers with individual nozzle tips (photos, p. 281) should have their nozzle tip removed at this point.
- Completely turn on the water faucet at the house. Squeeze the spray wand trigger to prime the pump and purge air from the system.
- Start the washer (Photo 1). If it's a gas unit, steady it when pulling the starter cord by bracing your foot against a wheel. Let the washer run for a minute to warm up. *To avoid damaging the pump: Never run a washer longer than three to five minutes (depending on the model) while the trigger is off.*
- With the washer running and the trigger locked "off," adjust pressure and spray settings, or insert nozzle tips in the spray wand (right photo, p. 281). Now the washer is ready to use.

Power cleaning techniques

Pressure washing removes dirt and grime, but it isn't designed to strip paint or kill mildew on siding or decks. For the best cleaning results without damaging any surfaces, first test the pressure setting and spray pattern on an inconspicuous place.

When washing house siding, follow these rules:

- Lay tarps around the house perimeter to protect plants and collect paint chips blown off during washing. Houses built before 1977 may have lead paint chips that will have to be collected and properly disposed of at a hazardous waste facility.
- Don't hold the spray wand "head on" to the siding. This drives dirt into the surface rather than washing it away. Hold the wand at a 45-degree angle to the siding and at a distance that yields the best cleaning results without gouging wood or denting metal or vinyl.

SOON-TO-BE-CLEAN BARBECUE

ACCESSORY BRUSH

ACI 822

3 Clean cars and other items with an accessory brush and detergent. First rinse the area with water, then switch to a detergent wash and finish with a rinse.

ELECTRIC WASHER HAS ON-BOARD DETERGENT RESERVOIR

ADJUSTABLE NOZZLE SET FOR LOW-PRESSURE DETERGENT USE

OIL STAINS

4 Scour oil and dirt off a garage floor with a detergent: (1) Rinse surface dirt off the floor at high pressure. (2) Change the nozzle setting to low pressure to dispense detergent. (3) Finish by changing the nozzle back to high pressure and rinsing with water.

15-DEGREE NOZZLE

SPRAY STREAM HELD AT 45-DEGREE ANGLE TO DECKING

FUNNEL ATTACHED TO SCRAP PIECE OF GARDEN HOSE

ENGINE RUNNING

DISCHARGE HOSE ON WATER OUTLET

SPILL BUCKET

"RV" ANTIFREEZE

HOSE COUPLING ATTACHED TO WATER INTAKE

5 Renew deck boards by holding the spray wand at a 45-degree angle 1 to 2 ft. from the decking. Keep the water stream constantly moving. Use a higher-pressure (2,000 psi or greater) gas-powered washer and a concentrated spray nozzle setting (15-degree).

6 Winterize a pressure washer by filling the pump and internal system with undiluted RV-type antifreeze. Insert a funnel into a 3-ft. section of garden hose (one with a male faucet coupling), attach the coupling to the water intake on the washer and slide a 1-ft. section of hose over the water outlet. Start the gas engine and pour antifreeze into the funnel until a steady stream of antifreeze flows from the discharge hose. Stop the engine, pull off the hoses, and seal the intake and outlet with duct tape.

- Work small areas at a time. To prevent streaks, start washing from the bottom and work up. For even cleaning, use long, overlapping strokes. Rinse the siding by working from the top down.
- Avoid driving water up behind the siding by keeping the spray stream level. Use an extension spray wand for reaching higher places. *Be careful when using an extension. The "kickback" can throw it into contact with power lines.*
- Don't spray windows. The high pressure can break them.

Better cleaning with detergents

Detergents and accessory brushes increase cleaning effectiveness while reducing cleaning time. When renting or buying a pressure washer, inquire what accessories and detergents are available for it. To prevent damage to the internal parts, never run bleach in the machine or use detergents not designated for use in pressure washers.

Detergents can only be run through pressure washers using a wide spray pattern. In addition, electric pressure washers require a low-pressure setting on the spray wand. Follow your machine's instructions for using detergents, diluting the detergent and (if necessary) hooking up a chemical injector (Photo 1).

For the best cleaning results, first loosen the dirt with plain water under high pressure using a medium spray pattern. Next, apply the detergent using a wide nozzle setting and let the detergent sit a few minutes to penetrate the dirt. Keep the surface wet to avoid possible discoloration or damage by the detergent. Finish by resetting the nozzle to a medium pattern (or changing the nozzle) and rinsing with plain water. Switch detergents by draining the first detergent from the pressure washer, rinsing the system with plain water and introducing the next detergent.

Maintaining the machine

If possible, store the washer indoors in the off-season to avoid damage to the pump, hoses and spray wand. Otherwise, winterize them using only antifreeze designed for recreational vehicles (RVs); see Photo 6. When a gas-powered washer won't be used for a month or more, prevent damage to the engine by draining the system of gas or adding a gas preservative to the fuel tank.

Angle grinders

Not just for grinding metal, this versatile tool cuts tile, routs out mortar, and sands and polishes

Angle grinders are good for a lot more than just grinding metal. For instance, an angle grinder with a diamond wheel can make intricate cuts in ceramic tile, mortar, stucco and pavers. Wire brush attachments make quick work of rust and loose paint removal. Special abrasive wheels can cut or grind steel. You can even use them for wood carving. We'll show you how to use your angle grinder to accomplish a number of common but difficult cutting, grinding and polishing tasks.

You'll find angle grinders anywhere power tools are sold. Larger grinders are available, but the popular 4-in. and 4-1/2 in. grinders are the right size for most tasks. You can buy an inexpensive angle grinder, but for frequent use or for demanding jobs like cutting stucco or cement, spend more for a grinder with a more powerful motor (look for a motor that draws 5 to 9 amps).

The ability to handle different wheels and accessories is what makes angle grinders so versatile. Your angle grinder includes a spindle washer and spindle nut that you'll install in different configurations to accommodate thicker or thinner wheels or remove altogether when you screw wire wheels and cups onto the threaded spindle. Consult your manual for instructions on mounting wheels and accessories.

You'll find abrasive wheels for angle grinders in any hardware store or home center. Although the wheels all look similar, they're designed for different tasks. Read the labels.

Metal cleaning

Wire wheels remove rust and flaking paint quickly. Wire wheel and brush attachments are designed for different types of stripping, cleaning and deburring tasks. Wire cup brushes work best for stripping paint or rust from broad, flat areas, while wire wheels fit into crevices and corners more easily. Wheel and brush attachments come in a wide variety of styles. Read the packaging to find one that works for your application. Also make sure to match the threads to the spindle threads on your grinder. Most angle grinders have 5/8-in. spindle threads, but there are a few oddballs.

WIRE CUP BRUSH

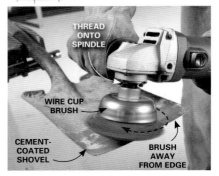
WIRE WHEEL

THREAD ONTO SPINDLE
WIRE CUP BRUSH
CEMENT-COATED SHOVEL
BRUSH AWAY FROM EDGE

Clean rust and caked-on cement and dirt from garden tools with a wire cup. Secure the work with clamps or a vise. Make sure the brush is spinning away from, not into, the edge. Otherwise, the brush can catch on the edge and cause the grinder to kick back at you.

BRUSH AWAY FROM EDGE
CREVICE
WIRE WHEEL

Remove paint with a wire wheel. Again, be careful to work away from, not into, sharp edges. Wire wheels fit into crevices and tight areas.

Cut bars, rods and bolts

If you're patient, you can cut most metal with a hacksaw. But for quick, rough cuts, it's hard to beat a grinder. You can use an angle grinder to cut rebar (left photo), angle iron, rusted bolts (right photo) and welded wire fencing. Use a cutoff wheel for these and other metal-cutting tasks.

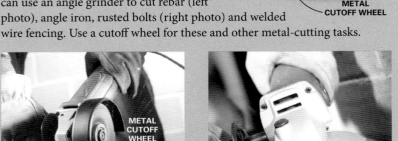
METAL CUTOFF WHEEL

METAL CUTOFF WHEEL
REBAR
END FREE TO DROP

BOLT

Mount a metal cutoff wheel in your angle grinder. Prop up the long side of the rebar and hold it securely. Drop the cutoff wheel through the metal, allowing the weight of the tool to do most of the work. Allow the short end to drop freely to avoid binding the blade.

Grind bolts flush to concrete. You can brush against the concrete, but don't try to cut into it with this wheel.

Cut tile, stone and concrete

Notching and cutting ceramic or stone tile to fit around outlets and other obstructions is difficult if not impossible with standard tile cutters. But an angle grinder fitted with a dry-cut diamond wheel makes short work of these difficult cuts (photos, below).

DRY-CUT DIAMOND WHEEL

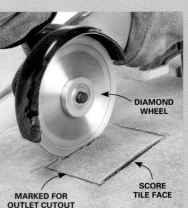
DIAMOND WHEEL
MARKED FOR OUTLET CUTOUT
SCORE TILE FACE

BACK OF TILE
EXTEND CUTS PAST CORNERS

Mark the outline of the cut accurately on both the front and the back of the tile. Clamp the tile to your workbench and score the outline about 1/8 in. deep on the front with the diamond blade.

Flip the tile over and cut through the tile from the back. Extend the cuts slightly past the lines at the corners to make crisp, square corners.

Restore cutting edges

Outfitted with a grinding wheel, an angle grinder is a great tool for restoring edges on rough-and-tumble tools like hoes, shovels and ice scrapers or for the initial grinding of axes, hatchets and lawn mower blades. If you need a sharper edge than the grinder leaves, follow up with a mill bastard file. The photo at right shows how to sharpen a lawn mower blade. Use the same technique to restore the edge on other tools. Orient the grinder so that the wheel spins from the body of the blade toward the edge (refer to the arrow on the body of the grinder to determine which direction the wheel spins). Finally, with the grinder off, rest the grinding wheel against the blade and adjust the angle of the grinder to match the blade's bevel. This is the position you'll want to maintain as you grind the edge. Lift the grinder from the edge, switch it on and let it come to speed before moving it into the blade.

Stroke the grinder across the work in the direction of the handle rather than grinding back and forth. Then lift it off and repeat, concentrating on holding the grinder at a consistent angle throughout the stroke.

It's easy to overheat a

metal blade with a grinder. Overheated metal turns a bluish black or straw color and won't stay sharp for long. To avoid overheating, apply only light pressure and keep the grinder moving. Also keep a bucket of water and sponge or rag handy and drench the metal frequently to keep it cool.

GRINDING WHEEL

SPINNING AWAY FROM EDGE

LAWN MOWER BLADE

Clamp the blade in a vise or to your workbench with hand clamps. Orient the grinder and adjust the blade guard to deflect sparks from your face and body. Align the grinding wheel with the angle on the blade. Start the grinder and move the grinding wheel steadily across the blade while applying light pressure.

Cutting out old mortar

Grinding beats a chisel and hammer for removing old mortar(photo, right). It would be worth buying a grinder just to remove mortar if you had a lot of tuckpointing to do. Thicker diamond tuckpointing wheels remove old mortar quickly without disturbing or damaging the bricks. It's dusty, though, so wear a dust mask and make sure to shut your windows and warn the neighbors.

We've only touched on the jobs you can do with an angle grinder. Browse your local hardware store or home center to get a better idea of the attachments available. They can save you a ton of time.

DIAMOND TUCKPOINTING WHEEL

ANGLE GRINDER

MORTAR JOINT

Grind out old, loose mortar with an angle grinder and diamond tuckpointing wheel. Make two or three 1/2-in. deep passes to completely clear the joint. Stay about 1/8 in. from the brick to avoid damaging it.

Grinder safety

Unlike drill motors that run at about 700 to 1,200 rpm, grinders spin at a breakneck speed of 10,000 to 11,000 rpm. They're fast enough to be scary! Follow these precautions for safe grinder use:

- Wear a face shield and gloves.
- Unplug the grinder when you're changing wheels.
- Attach the handle and maintain a firm grip with both hands.
- Use the guard if possible.
- Run new wheels for one minute in a protected area before using them to make sure the wheel isn't defective.

- Orient the work so debris is directed downward.
- Keep bystanders away. Everyone in the vicinity should wear safety glasses.
- Orient the work so the wheel spins away from, not into, sharp edges. Wheels, especially wire wheels, can catch on an edge and throw the workpiece or cause the grinder to kick back.
- Keep sparks away from flammable materials.
- Clamp or secure the workpiece in some fashion.
- Store angle grinders out of children's reach.

Rental tools that save time and toil

Power trencher

Digging a trench for cable or gas lines means long hours of hard labor. But a power trencher can do all that digging for you in a fraction of the time. This trencher can dig down 24 in. (other models can dig to 36 in.) and is self-propelled.

Stump grinder

There's no need to pay a pro $150 or more to grind out a stump. With a rented stump grinder, you can do it yourself in a few minutes. For a stump that's no more than 18 in. in diameter, rent a light-duty grinder. For bigger stumps, rent a heavy-duty self-propelled monster like the one shown here.

Walk-behind loader

A typical front-end loader makes quick work of moving piles of gravel, sand and dirt. But it won't fit through most fence gates or other tight spots. Instead, rent a walk-behind, track-style machine with a loader or backhoe attachment.

Brush cutter

If you've left "the back 40" unmowed for too long and Mother Nature is taking over, don't waste time—and possibly wreck your lawn mower—by mowing down the brush. Instead, rent a machine designed specifically for clearing tall weeds and saplings.